CELESTIAL FIRE

CELESTIAL FIRE

365 Days with the Holy Spirit

William R. Gibson

ELM HILL

A Division of
HarperCollins Christian Publishing

www.elmhillbooks.com

Celestial Fire
365 Days with the Holy Spirit

Published in Nashville, Tennessee, by Elm Hill, an imprint of Thomas Nelson. Elm Hill and Thomas Nelson are registered trademarks of HarperCollins Christian Publishing, Inc.

Elm Hill titles may be purchased in bulk for educational, business, fund-raising, or sales promotional use. For information, please e-mail SpecialMarkets@ ThomasNelson.com.

All Scripture quotations, unless otherwise indicated, are taken from the Holy Bible, New International Version˚, NIV˚. Copyright © 1973, 1978, 1984, 2011 by Biblica, Inc.˚ Used by permission of Zondervan. All rights reserved worldwide. www.Zondervan. com. The "NIV" and "New International Version" are trademarks registered in the United States Patent and Trademark Office by Biblica, Inc.˚

Cover design based on, *Celestial Fire,* a painting by Kathy Self available at www. colorbrush.com. The artist may be contacted at kathy@colorbrush.com. Used by permission.

Library of Congress Cataloging-in-Publication Data

Library of Congress Control Number: 2018954700

ISBN 978-1-595558367 (Paperback)
ISBN 978-1-595558596 (Hardbound)
ISBN 978-1-595558022 (eBook)

For Elaine, my beloved wife,
partner in life and ministry and prophetess extraordinaire
who has modelled and demonstrated life in the Spirit.

Without the Spirit,
God is far away,
Christ belongs to the past.
The Gospel is a dead letter.
The Church is a mere organization.
Authority takes the form of domination.
Mission is turned into propaganda.
Worship is reduced to bare recollection,
Christian action becomes the morality of a slave.
But in the spirit,
God is near.
The risen Christ is present with US here and now.
The Gospel is the power of life.
The Church signifies Trinitarian communion.
Authority means liberating service.
Mission is an expression of Pentecost,
The Liturgy is a making- present of both past and future.
Human action is divinized.[1]

---

[1] Orthodox Patriarch of Antioch, Ignatios IV, as translated by Metropolitan Kallistos in his 2007 Holy Spirit Lecture, *The Holy Spirit in the Liturgy of St John Chrysostom,* 32. Originally published by Duquesne University, 2011. https://www. duq.edu/assets/Documents/holy-spirit/_pdf/holy-spirit-lecture-2007.pdf.

NOTE TO READER

A question often asked is, "Are there actually 365 references to the Spirit in the Bible?" People want to know, I suspect, because it might seem providential if there were. Allow me to share with you how I came up with my references. First, I followed the lead of the NIV. Wherever the editors capitalized the word "spirit" to signify the divine person, I chose that reference. If a verse mentioned the Spirit more than once, I wrote on each occurrence. A few times, however, I disagreed with their interpretation and treated a lower case "spirit" as the Spirit. A case in point is Pharaoh's question in Genesis 41:38. He asks, "Can we find anyone like this man, one in whom is the spirit of God?" He may not have had the God of the Hebrews in mind, but he recognized someone greater than any Egyptian god helped him. Of course, we know the Spirit of God so filled Joseph with supernatural ability he interpreted dreams no one else could. That is why I wrote a devotional concerning his experience.

On a few other occasions, I broke with my rule of following the capitalization of "spirit" in the NIV in Revelation, a book filled with symbols. I took the descriptor "the seven spirits of God" to refer to the perfect and complete work of the Holy Spirit. In John's gospel with its great pneumatological emphasis I felt it amiss to leave out one of its Spirit passages. I included Jesus' teaching in John 16:7 where the word "Spirit" is not mentioned but he is the unmistakable subject. Our Lord said, "Unless I go away, the Advocate will not come to you." Before leaving this topic, I should point out I followed the NIV even when it translated other words not in the original for "Spirit." This occurs in I Corinthians 14:1 where "spiritual gifts" is rendered "gifts of the Spirit." With just these few variations, I found 365 specific references to the Spirit.

One more thing needs to be said about these references. In no way do I attempt to differentiate between God who is Spirit and the Third Person of the Trinity. To do so would take me far beyond the scope of this daily devotional. I contented myself on writing on every specific mention of the Spirit regardless of how it referred to the Godhead.

Scripture References

I wanted *Celestial Fire: 365 Days with the Holy Spirit* anchored in Scripture. To achieve this goal, I have included a daily Bible reading to give context for the reference under consideration. To get the most out of the daily devotional, I recommend reading these verses first. They provide a broader horizon for viewing the text and my commentary. I have bolded the word "Spirit" to highlight it in the verse. Spirit, in bold, is the reference I am writing about even if it occurs more than once.

I established a way to refer to the Scriptures. Any verse (v) or verses (vv) within the same chapter as the one(s) under consideration are referred to by (v x) and (vv x). A verse in the same book but a different chapter appears as (x:x). A reference in another book includes the book, chapter, and verse in this format (Bk x:x).

Instead of always writing out in full Old Testament and New Testament, I abbreviate these to OT and NT respectively. On occasion, I have used other versions of the Bible. The *New American Standard Bible* is abbreviated NASB and *The Living Bible* as TLB.

Rhema

Each devotional closes with a section called *rhema*. This is where the reader is addressed personally or the readers collectively. The word *rhema* is a Greek term for "word" and often functions as a synonym for *logos;* both are used to refer to God's word. Although the terms overlap in meaning, *rhema* draws attention to a specific word or message, especially to a specific divine revelation. For instance, Jesus said the words (*rhema*) he spoke are spiritual manifestations—something special to indicate his Father was at work in them (Jn 14:10). They are words of eternal life (Jn 6:68). The message Peter preached on the day of Pentecost (Ac 2:14), the word that came to John the Baptist (Lk 3:2), and even the sword of the Spirit, the word of God (Eph 6:17), all employ *rhema*.

In no way do I equate my closing words with the NT usage of *rhema*. However, I want to offer a "prophetic" element to these devotionals. What does the Spirit say to us today about these Scriptures? I try to answer that question with these concluding statements.

Spiritual Preparation

The purpose of these devotionals is to have an enriching time every day with God. The spiritual practice of reading the Scriptures and the devotional need not take long. Reading the commentary takes less than two minutes and the Scripture just a few more. To maximize this experience, I recommend approaching them in an attitude of prayer and an open heart. Whatever God wants to say must be spiritually discerned. Since Scripture was inspired by the Holy Spirit, he is the only one who can open our understanding to grasp it.

May God bless you abundantly!

PREFACE

The book's headwaters began several years ago when I taught a college course entitled, The History of the Pentecostal Movement. Each class commenced by my reading a Scripture that mentioned the Holy Spirit followed up by a few inspirational thoughts. The exercise began with Genesis 1:2, the first instance of the Spirit in the Bible, and continued throughout the semester with successive references. From teaching this course multiple times, a wonderful trove of ideas emerged relating to the Holy Spirit.

These inspirational bits grew when I later served a church as Transition Pastor. Once again, I started the many staff, committee and board meetings the way I did my course. The difference this time was I wrote out my ideas. After a year and a half, I had assembled extensive notes concerning the Holy Spirit.

By this time, a strong sense was bubbling up within me I should write a daily devotional on the Holy Spirit. After checking Christian bookstores and the Internet, I realized how few existed. Francis Chan's, *FORGOTTEN GOD: REVERSING OUR TRAGIC NEGLECT OF THE HOLY SPIRIT* (David C. Cook, 2009) stirred me even more to write. I agreed with him the Church by and large has neglected the Holy Spirit. After reading his book, I was convinced I should help rectify this deficiency.

Excitement grew when I did a computer search and found the word 'Spirit' occurs nearly three hundred and sixty-five times in God's word. I came across enough references for one per day, enough for one year. Hence the subtitle, *365 Days with the Spirit*. Since the word "spirit" can mean wind, attitude, demon or man's inner self, I chose those verses where the context shows it refers to God.

Several components comprise each devotional. Each features a biblical reference to the Spirit. Also included is a Scripture reading to help enhance and anchor the study. Based on these and much research I develop an inspirational thought for the day. I have tried to make each study practical and applicable to life. I am hoping these daily inspirations will increase your knowledge and understanding of the Holy Spirit and enrich your walk with the Lord.

In one year, you will read and study every verse in the Bible about the Holy Spirit. The cumulative effect of studying these references from Genesis to Revelation, I hope, will affect you as they did me. They have energized me and changed my life. I learned so much in my studies on the Third Person of the Godhead I feel we need a new

Reformation. These insights I want to share with you hoping they will impact your life as much as they did mine. My prayer is that the Holy Spirit will bless you as you embark on this extraordinary journey. Keep in mind the Spirit has inspired every mention of himself in the word of God.

DAY 1

JANUARY 1 | GENESIS 1:1–31

THE SPIRIT CREATES A NEW REALITY

*Now the earth was formless and empty, darkness was over the surface of the deep, and the **Spirit** of God was hovering over the waters.*
—GENESIS 1:2

The Bible begins with the dynamic action of the Spirit of God. New realities materialize with his creative bustle. No matter that the earth in its initial stage is chaotic, nor that the world is without form and void, dwelling in darkness. What matters is his powerful and artistic creativity to transform it. His presence provides unlimited promise and possibility. This is how the exciting story of creation (and the Bible) begins.

The Bible says the Spirit was "hovering over the waters." To hover means to move or flutter much like an eagle hatching an egg or stirring up its nest. The Spirit of God was present supervising and overseeing creation as a bird watches its nest. The earth was desolate and barren, but the Holy Spirit was available to transform it. He rescued creation from chaos and made it teem with life.

Are you in need of the hovering movement of God's Spirit? He turns chaos into cosmos. His specialty is to convert waste and uninhabitable darkness into something stunning and bright. Did last year have chaos? Darkness? Bareness? Do you feel wasted, tired, unfruitful or dead? Today begins a new year. If your world is void and without form, filled with darkness, then God has a creative solution for you. Be assured that the Spirit of God has been watching over any chaos in your life, keeping it in check and under control. His resourcefulness is available to bring an exquisite new reality into existence, one filled with wonderful new actualities of fruitfulness and glory.

Rhema: This is a prophetic picture of God's plan for your life. No circumstances are so bad that God cannot make something good and magnificent out of them. As at creation, his Spirit is hovering over you to bring light, life, order, loveliness, and joy into your world. He is ready and waiting to transform your chaos with his dynamic power. Imagine his birthing something new in your life—new actualities pulsating with God's glory. Therefore, do not hesitate to invite God's Spirit to move and act in your life.

JANUARY 2 | GENESIS 6:1–22

GOD'S SPIRIT CONTENDS WITH MANKIND

*Then the LORD said, "My **Spirit** will not contend with humans forever, for they are mortal; their days will be a hundred and twenty years."*
–GENESIS 6:3

Two major themes run through the Bible. First, the Spirit gives life. Second, his departure leads to death. In Genesis 1:2, he brought life. His presence and activity turned chaos into a magnificent creation. Luxurious vegetation covered the land, living creatures swam in the waters, and birds filled the heavens. The third rock from the sun exploded with life.

Wherever God withdraws his Spirit, however, life ceases. Chaos erupts. Noah and the Flood teach us this lesson (Gen 6–9). God says, "My Spirit will not contend with humans forever." Throughout God's word the Spirit (Rom 8:2) always brings life but things always end badly when his presence is resisted or removed. As we will see, tragedy results for anyone fighting his Spirit: lives are cut short.

From the beginning of creation, God desired to dwell with us and guide us into unimaginable blessing. But after Eden's catastrophe, sin and death entered the world (Rom 5:12). Ever since, God sent his Spirit to battle against our fallen human nature and stave off the moral deterioration of society. Without him, we are left to our own devices and, consequently, end up ruining ourselves. His Spirit works not only in us but in society. Because of sin, man's days on earth were shortened to 120 years.

God says his Spirit will not contend with humans forever. The word "contend" has several meanings that appear to apply here. It can mean to stay, dwell, rule or govern. When the Holy Spirit is not governing us or dwelling within, we fall victim to our own ways. Therefore, rejecting him cuts life short.

In the days of Noah men grew tired of the Spirit's pleading and refused to heed his urgings. Although Noah found grace in the eyes of the Lord (v 8), the rest of his generation spurned his preaching and resisted the Spirit's persuasion. When they stopped listening, wickedness and evil increased so much God had no choice but to withdraw his Spirit, destroy them, and shorten life.

Rhema: God gives his Spirit to save us from self-destruction, so let us be sensitive to his voice and discover life!

JANUARY 3 | GENESIS 41:1–40

THE SPIRIT HELPS US MAKE WISE DECISIONS

*So Pharaoh asked them, "Can we find anyone like this man, one in whom is the **spirit** of God?"* –GENESIS 41:38

Someone said, "It takes twenty years to become an instant success." Overnight, Joseph went from a prisoner to a ruler. How was that possible? His wisdom and discernment exceeded everyone else's in the king's court because the Spirit of God was residing in him. Pharaoh recognized this and made Joseph a head of state. His wise, Spirit-inspired decisions would save many lives.

God's Spirit enabled Joseph to interpret the dreams of Pharaoh and offer, life-saving counsel. By divine revelation he knew the next seven years of plenty would be followed by another seven years of severe famine. A suitable response required wisdom from above if they were to avoid devastation. Pharaoh realized he need look no further than Joseph, a man filled with wisdom and the Spirit. Egypt's ruler placed him second in command. That is how Joseph became an instant success. Incidentally, this is the first time the Bible mentions God's Spirit dwells in a person.

Challenging situations need unusual insight. Pharaoh himself perceived that the person he placed in authority needed wisdom and discernment. After hearing Joseph's proposal, he said, "There is no one so discerning and wise as you" (v 39). Staving off the devastating effects of a seven-year famine required drastic action. It would not be easy to enact a twenty percent levy on all the harvests. So, to proceed with such an unpopular decision necessitated great skill and prudence.

Every day we face challenging situations that call for wise decisions. Navigating household rules, financial matters and relationships demand prudent determinations. Because the Spirit knows everything, he can help us understand difficult circumstances and make good choices that do no harm. This way we can avoid undesirable consequences from flawed decisions. God wants us to seek wisdom, so we can help others and escape the follies of life. Joseph received huge rewards for his wisdom as Pharaoh favored and blessed him beyond his wildest dreams (37:5–11).

Rhema: Whenever you are facing a challenging condition, you can ask the indwelling Spirit to supply the insight you need. He will help you make life-enhancing decisions because he loves you. The result of making wise choices is blessing, goodness, and salvation.

JANUARY 4 | EXODUS 31:1–11

ART BEAUTY AND THE SPIRIT

*Then the LORD said to Moses, "See, I have chosen Bezalel son of Uri, the son of Hur, of the tribe of Judah, and I have filled him with the **Spirit** of God, with wisdom, with understanding, with knowledge and with all kinds of skills— to make artistic designs for work in gold, silver and bronze, to cut and set stones, to work in wood, and to engage in all kinds of crafts." –EXODUS 31:1–5*

What a surprise! The first time the Bible states someone is "filled with the Spirit of God" is in connection with the arts. Why? In art, we share something in common with our Creator. He gives us an ability to transform raw material into something creative and beautiful. God himself is the Master Artisan, the great Craftsman of the cosmos. Creation is the work of his hands.

Beauty and worship often go together. God fills Bezalel with his Spirit to help him make the place of worship delightful. He wants his dwelling place stunning and artistic. The entire tabernacle including its articles and furnishings was smashing and a fitting tribute to God. Psalm 27:4 declares, "One thing I ask from the LORD, this only do I seek: that I may dwell in the house of the LORD all the days of my life, to gaze on the beauty of the LORD and to seek him in his temple."

Beauty is a visible form of what is good. Artists are its creators. Their inspired works often mirror and remind us of the mysteries and splendor of creation. Art has a power to elevate our spirit heavenward when contemplating beauty, order, purpose, and design. Since God made us in his image, our spirit recognizes his Spirit at work. When our Creator finished creation with all its artistic touches, he declared it good.

Rhema: Value and appreciate people with artistic gifts, especially in the church. Recognize the power of music, painting, song writing, poetry, pottery or artistic craft to glorify God. Artists have a vital connection with their Creator and, like the Spirit, can convey meaning beyond words. Aesthetic expressions can transcend the rational, finite dimension of words and point to the infinite, just as the tabernacle does. Let every artistic endeavor—whether a tabernacle or a painting—tell God's story.

ART PROPHECY AND THE SPIRIT

*Then Moses said to the Israelites, "See, the Lord has chosen Bezalel son of Uri, the son of Hur, of the tribe of Judah, and he has filled him with the **Spirit** of God, with wisdom, with understanding, with knowledge and with all kinds of skills— to make artistic designs for work in gold, silver and bronze, to cut and set stones, to work in wood and to engage in all kinds of artistic crafts. –EXODUS 35:30–33*

Art belongs to the Spirit. Symbols and images are his tools to convey the truth of God. Artisans like Bezalel are prisms that reflect heaven's light. He is the first person in the Bible said to be filled with the Spirit of God. What God first said to Moses, Moses now echoes to the people, word for word. These words are repeated so the Israelites will know the importance of every facet of the Lord's dwelling place. Every color, every metal, every shape becomes a prophetic picture of the person, plan, and provision of the Lord Almighty.

Bezalel was like the prophets of old: he was anointed and filled with the Spirit so he could communicate God to his people. He transformed ordinary physical things into powerful prophetic proclamations. Beyond the purple, gold, and gems was a deeper reality of God's nature and his salvation. These artistic creations were oracles from above, conveying meaning in ways that words cannot.

Not all art, unfortunately, is of the Spirit. Many art forms today pervert the power and purpose for which the Lord intended them. Instead of revealing the glorious light of eternity, they express the darkness of the human heart.

The purpose of Bezalel's Spirit-inspired art, however, was to capture the hearts and imaginations of God's people. The only two references in Exodus to the Spirit are these. Do they not show the high importance God attaches to the arts? Worship, the arts, and the Spirit work together. The Spirit fills the artists so their creative works reveal God and tell his story. Bezalel uses art for its highest purpose—to proclaim the glory and majesty of God.

Rhema: Creative arts inspired by the Spirit have the power to help us worship. They are prophetic voices that in dramatic representational language drive our emotions, increase our knowledge, and stimulate our sensations.

THE SPIRIT LIGHTENS THE
BURDEN OF LEADERSHIP

*I will come down and speak with you there, and I will take some of the power of the **Spirit** that is on you and put it on them. They will share the burden of the people with you so that you will not have to carry it alone.*
–NUMBERS 11:17

Does God ever ask us to do more than we can handle? Moses was stretched beyond his limit and after a brilliant and distinctive career of leading God's people he could do it no longer. He had run out of gas and was worn out. He flamed out. To hear the man who brought Pharaoh to his knees and liberate an enslaved nation ask to die was not a pretty picture. "I can't do it anymore," he cried out to God. "I can't carry them in my arms anymore—the burden is too heavy for me."

This story reminds us even mighty men and women of God equipped with extraordinary gifts cannot carry the burden of leadership alone. To help lighten the load, God redistributes the power of the Spirit. Moses fell into a common leadership trap of assuming everything depended upon him. That deception led him to believe he was a failure unless he provided everything the people wanted. Similarly, we can become depressed when we focus on ourselves and our problems instead of God and his mighty supply of spiritual resources.

As great as Moses was, he was prone to keep power in his own hands and wear himself out. God's answer was an extravagant proliferation of the Spirit. He would put "some of the power of the Spirit" residing on Moses on seventy elders. Endowing them with the same Spirit that rested on Moses provided him with many qualified helpers. From that day forward, he shared the responsibility of leading God's people. To have seventy more who had his wisdom, understanding, and spiritual ability helped him lead the people.

Rhema: The burden of leadership is real. As a leader, you carry the fears, doubts, sins, and needs of the people. Like Moses, you can become overworked and overburdened. God does not want you to burn out because you carry the weight of his assignments alone. Instead, he wants to multiply his Spirit and anoint others, so they can share the load with you.

THE TRANSFERENCE OF THE SPIRIT

*Then the LORD came down in the cloud and spoke with him, and he took some of the power of the **Spirit** that was on him and put it on the seventy elders.* **–NUMBERS 11:25**

This is the first occurrence of the transference of the Spirit in the Bible. It will not be the last. Moses, for instance, will lay his hands on his successor to empower Joshua to lead the nation. Elisha will receive a double portion of the Spirit that rested on Elijah. Jesus will give his disciples his own power to heal the sick and to cast out demons. In God, the possibility exists for the power and anointing resting on one person to pass to another.

God does transfer his power, anointing, and authority from person to person. Moses needed it to happen because the people were complaining and dissatisfied with his leadership. Their discontent swept through the entire community until he heard every family wailing. They railed against him because they could no longer eat garlic and leeks. Imagine! God's people had tired of "heavenly food." Everyone was angry; it was a mess. Even God himself became "exceedingly angry."

In this case, Yahweh initiated and executed the transmission of the Spirit. In his mercy, he told Moses to select seventy leaders and have them come and stand before the Tent of Meeting. The Almighty came down and met with them to take "of the Spirit that was on [Moses] and put the Spirit on the seventy elders."

God's solution to their bickering was to transfer a portion of the Spirit from Moses to the seventy elders. The anointing on this great leader passed to others to expand the leadership base. In fact, more than enough of the Spirit existed to go around. Moses' anointing was not lessened by sharing it with others.

Rhema: Do not fear losing out if you impart your gifts and empower others. To fear a loss of effectiveness misunderstands the nature of the Spirit and spiritual gifts. Sharing your anointing with others will not diminish your role but like Moses make you even more effective and powerful. Moreover, the transference of the Spirit is a pattern found throughout Scripture, ultimately climaxing in Jesus who pours out his Spirit so you can share in his work.

THE SPIRIT RESTED ON THEM

*When the **Spirit** rested on them, they prophesied—but did not do so again. However, two men, whose names were Eldad and Medad, had remained in the camp. They were listed among the elders, but did not go out to the tent. Yet the **Spirit** also rested on them, and they prophesied in the camp.* **–Numbers 11:25–26**

An amazing thing happened when God heaped his Spirit upon the seventy elders. They prophesied! Some of the Spirit resting on Moses was transferred to them. However, two of the elders for whatever reason did not join the others at the Tent of Meeting. Still the Spirit came on them and they prophesied. The many references to the Spirit in this story tell us how essential he is for leading and governing God's people.

The word "rested" has several interesting meanings. It first occurs in connection with Noah's ark. After the stormed-tossed days in raging seas, the ark came to rest on Mount Ararat. It settled there. In the same way, the Spirit remained on these elders amid their storm. These leaders, empowered by the Spirit, worked to settle the tumult. As oil calms troubled waters, God put his Spirit on the elders to help quell the growing tempest. Moreover, a new order of favor and blessing began after the Spirit came to rest on Israel's leadership.

Having the Spirit is associated with the ability to prophesy. Their newly acquired gift spoke volumes because prophesying signified God had appointed them to leadership with Moses. Now they were equipped to grasp spiritual things, act with wisdom, and resolve difficult matters. Yahweh had given them this special spiritual aptitude so they could help their leader meet the needs of the people. In conclusion, the Spirit equipped them to shoulder with Moses the burden and responsibility of shepherding God's people.

Rhema: God gives you his Spirit to help sustain you in your difficulties. The supernatural power of God equips you with spiritual insights so you can handle crises. When God appoints a person to a ministry, he outfits for the task. He wants to surround his leaders with Spirit-anointed helpers, such as yourself, so his work will not suffer. More important than physical and material needs is an expanded leadership that has the same vision and values as its Spirit-filled leader.

WISHING FOR MORE OF THE SPIRIT

*But Moses replied, "Are you jealous for my sake? I wish that all the LORD's people were prophets and that the LORD would put his **Spirit** on them!"* –**NUMBERS 11:29**

God's unexpected action often blows us away. That happened to Joshua when two disobedient elders received of Moses' Spirit. Although they did not follow Moses' instructions, God nevertheless poured out his power and anointing upon them and they prophesied (v 26).

Joshua was beside himself when he learned of their disobedience so he forthwith urged Moses to stop them. Like many throughout church history, he wanted to curtail the Spirit's movement. He could not handle this "unauthorized" spiritual activity. It did not meet his expectations. Possibly he was jealous for Moses' leadership which he felt was somehow threatened. Joshua may have asked himself, *Why should these two men acquire Moses' anointing? They ignored his command and did not even bother to show up.*

Moses' response was amazing. He has no thought of losing influence or authority because others received of his Spirit. Nor was he jealous. Sharing leadership with seventy-two others was not an issue. The more who operated with God's breath in them the better. He saw no challenge to his leadership, but desired all God's people to receive what he had.

The great prophet wished all the Lord's people were prophets. In that case, everyone would be sensitive to spiritual matters and know the mind and will of the Lord. Think of it for a moment! What if everyone in church were filled with the breath of heaven? If this ever occurred, leaders might not burn out. Many problems would vanish if everyone were unified and minded spiritual things. Where the Spirit abounds, problems about status, reputation, position, prestige or power disappear. The difficulties of the flesh—discord, jealousy, hatred, selfish ambition, envy, and so forth— dissolve.

Moses does not want to limit the Spirit; just the opposite. He wished for the Lord to come with power on all his people. He longed for a new reality full of glory and blessing where every Israelite was filled and became a prophet.

Rhema: We never need to fear too many will receive the Spirit or have too much of God. Our problem is the opposite—too many live without the breath of heaven.

SEEING PROPHETICALLY BY THE SPIRIT

When Balaam looked out and saw Israel encamped tribe by tribe, the **Spirit** *of God came on him.* **–NUMBERS 24:2**

Balaam was a sorcerer for hire. When the king of Moab saw Israel's size and heard of her remarkable victories, he shook in his sandals. To remove the threat and curtail her success, he hired Balaam to use divination to curse the nation. The Lord, however, foiled the enchanter's repeated efforts to utter harm against Israel and made him pronounce blessings instead. The reason: no sorcery or divination will work against God's people (Num 23:23). Instead of employing the tools of darkness, he experienced the provisions of light. When the Spirit came upon him, God opened Balaam's eyes to gaze upon Israel's glorious future. He saw Abraham's descendants prophetically.

With the Spirit's help, Balaam peers upon the nation as God sees her. In the past, he used sorcery and divination to grasp the future. God, however, had prohibited these practices but now shows him the true way to foresee the future. In this visionary state, he beholds Israel's present beauty and her future glory. He "hears the words of God" and "sees a vision from the Almighty" (v 4). Falling prostrate his "eyes are opened" so he can receive God's revelation. By God's Spirit Balaam prophesies his vision and pronounces powerful blessings on the nation.

The Spirit enabled the enchanter to observe what the nation would become under God's blessing. Prophetically he pictured Israel in the land of promise, a place as lovely as the Garden of Eden oozing with abundance and fertility. He saw the blessed nation victorious over her enemies. Israel was like a lion crushing and crunching her attackers. His prediction concluded with these words: "May those who bless you be blessed and those who curse you be cursed" (v 9).

Rhema: People with the prophetic gift have eyes to see what God sees and ears to hear what God speaks. They must not resort to fortune tellers, horoscopes, or occult practices. The Lord directs their attention to things we often miss or ignore. Prophets are to the church what eyes and ears are to the body. Every church needs its prophets. Through their prophetic gifts, God speaks to us with timely revelations. Where no one sees prophetically, the people run wild (Prov 28:19).

The Spirit of Leadership

*So the LORD said to Moses, "Take Joshua son of Nun, a man in whom is the **spirit** of leadership, and lay your hand on him."*
–Numbers 27:18

Who will ever replace Moses? A huge leadership question surfaced when it came time to find his successor. Choosing the right person is never easy and if not done well, a crisis of leadership results. Someone must finish what Moses started. Knowing these things better than anyone, he pleads with God for a suitable replacement.

The Lord responds to Moses' request by selecting Joshua, "a man in whom is the Spirit," ("of leadership" does not occur in the original but is an addition supplied by NIV). Essential for such an extraordinary task was possession of the Spirit (Deut 34:9). A new leader with the Spirit will be able to lead the nation into blessing and fullness. When God chose Joshua, he directed Moses to lay his hands on him. Then the Holy Spirit will endow him with superlative abilities to watch over, lead, and care for Israel. With divine enabling, he will "lead them out and bring them in" so they would not be like sheep without a shepherd (v 17).

Moses asked for the "God of the spirits of all mankind" to choose his successor. Instead of trying to put forward his own flesh and blood to succeed him, Israel's leader leaves the selection up to God. He understood the Lord who knows men's hearts and sees their inner qualities would make the correct choice. In the Lord's work, succession is never a popularity contest. Moses has the good of the people as his primary concern rather than any personal or family benefit. His example encourages us to seek God for leaders who are full of the Spirit.

Rhema: God calls some of us to be leaders. Good overseers bring great blessing to others and will place their well-being before self-interest. We are fortunate and blessed when we have them as our supervisors. Families, schools, organizations, companies, governments, and churches benefit when Joshua-like leaders are in charge. They will not only move his work forward but also provide needed protection and care. Every sphere of life requires competent leaders. Our heavenly Father wants to gift leaders with his Spirit to provide what is best for his children.

FILLED WITH THE SPIRIT OF WISDOM

*Now Joshua son of Nun was filled with the **spirit** of wisdom because Moses had laid his hands on him. So the Israelites listened to him and did what the LORD had commanded Moses.* –**DEUTERONOMY 34:9**

No one needed wisdom more than Joshua. Moses had just died, ending a brilliant life of unsurpassable greatness and achievement. No prophet ever arose in all Israel like him whom the Lord knew face to face. Who could ever duplicate his many miracles, signs, and wonders? He brought Pharaoh to his knees and led God's people out of Egypt. No one ever showed such mighty power or performed such awesome deeds as he did. His successor will need all the help and wisdom heaven can offer him (Jas 3:17).

Joshua faced challenging assignments that tested every facet of his being. Trying to lead a million freed slaves into the Promised Land was no easy task as his predecessor discovered. Seven nations greater and more powerful than his needed defeating. The Israelites could not outnumber or outpower their enemies, so they would have to deploy shrewd God-given strategies. To divide the conquered land and allot it to the twelve tribes demanded prudence. Joshua needed much discernment to keep sibling rivalries and jealousies at bay. Besides these things, he still needed to win the loyalties and trust of the people.

The people were willing to follow and obey Joshua because they realized he handled crises well. They did not rebel or murmur but were eager to follow him into battle and risk their lives. Because God endowed him with the Spirit who made him wise, they shadowed him wholeheartedly.

Rhema: Do you find yourself in a challenging situation? If so, you can ask the Lord for more of the Spirit who gives wisdom. He will supply you with this spiritual gift so you can see and understand what matters in every circumstance. With it you will avoid the unintended consequences of poor decisions. Wisdom will allow you to see and choose the highest aspects of life—the superior and best things. That is why the pursuit of wisdom brings wealth and blessing. It helps you make decisions with the best outcomes. If you lack wisdom, you can ask God to supply it generously without hesitation (Jas 1:5).

JANUARY 13 | JUDGES 3:1–11

THE SPIRIT MAKES THE DIFFERENCE

*The **Spirit** of the LORD came on him, so that he became Israel's judge and went to war. The LORD gave Cushan-Rishathaim king of Aram into the hands of Othniel, who overpowered him.* –JUDGES 3:10

Othniel was Israel's first judge. When the people found themselves in trouble and oppressed by an enemy, they cried out to God for help. The Lord answered by raising up a judge or a deliverer like Othniel to free them. These judges were passionate for the Lord and led their nation to renew its walk with him. They removed idolatry from the land and taught God's people his word. Their primary function, however, was to go to war and defeat Israel's oppressors. Then the nation enjoyed a prolonged period of peace.

Othniel means "the lion of God; powerful one." The Holy Spirit empowered him to serve the nation as a deliverer. The powerful king of Mesopotamia had subjected Israel for eight years because Yahweh had withdrawn his protection. "The Israelites did evil in the eyes of the Lord; they forgot the Lord their God" (Judg 3:1). Consequently, spiritual decay made them vulnerable. Soon after Joshua's death a new generation grew up without having an experience with God. Nor did they know what the Lord had done for them. During this national crisis in response to their cries for help, the Spirit came upon Othniel. He delivered Israel and led them back to spiritual vitality. The supernatural power of the Spirit was the difference between domination and deliverance.

Even though the foreign oppressor possessed far more resources, the Lord helped Othniel deliver his people. Years of bondage and slavery ended because one man empowered by the Spirit was willing to do battle for God. The Spirit filled him with extraordinary zeal and courage. Someone said, "With the appointing comes the anointing." After Othniel's stunning victory, the land enjoyed peace for forty years.

Rhema: With the Spirit's help, you can make an impact on your world. With so many overwhelming problems around, you might wonder what one life can do to effect change. Even if you feel outnumbered or have few resources, the Spirit can come to your aid. Like Othniel, the Holy Spirit can help an ordinary person do extraordinary things. One person with the Spirit can make a world of difference.

JANUARY 14 | JUDGES 6:1–35

CLOTHED WITH THE SPIRIT

Then the Spirit of the LORD came on Gideon, and he blew a trumpet, summoning the Abiezrites to follow him. –JUDGES 6:34

God wrapped his Spirit around Gideon like we would put on a coat. What an amazing picture of empowerment. The word translated "came on" means to clothe. All his fears and weaknesses were covered with a coat of supernatural power. When the Holy Spirit outfitted him, boldness replaced paralysis. This helps explain how the cautious, careful, and cowardly man rose up and became a mighty warrior. Because of this anointing, Gideon accomplished the impossible.

What God asked Gideon to do was beyond human expectations. He faced an army as "thick as locusts." The enemy came against him with "camels as numerous as the grains of sand on the seashore" (Judg 7:12). It was suicidal! Yahweh wanted him to lead a small group of 300 volunteers to destroy an army of 120,000. When the Spirit clothed him with power and courage, he took charge and blew a trumpet to round up warriors. He exuded a new decisiveness and sprang to life. This Israelite went from hiding in a winepress to becoming a fearless commander. After the Spirit descended on Gideon, he gained a new confidence. Attired with spiritual strength, he was equipped to take on whatever the foe might bring against him.

Rhema: When you are facing difficulties that are far greater than you can handle, remember Gideon. Realize your Lord wants to bundle you up with his Spirit. When he does, he covers all your fears, anxieties, and weakness. He dresses you in his strength and power. It is as if you were putting on an invisible shield capable of warding off every weapon of the enemy. He is always faithful to see you through whatever battles you face in life. The Spirit equips so you can come against your adversary. You can say, "I can do everything through him who gives me strength" (Phil 4:13). No matter how great the odds against you, your God wants to cover you with his Spirit. Jesus told his disciples to wait in Jerusalem until they were "clothed with power from on high" (Lk 24:49). When you are "clothed with the Spirit of God," you are empowered to do more than you ever imagined possible.

DAY 15

THE SUFFICIENCY OF THE SPIRIT

*Then the **Spirit** of the LORD came on Jephthah. He crossed Gilead and Manasseh, passed through Mizpah of Gilead, and from there he advanced against the Ammonites.* –JUDGES **11:29**

Jephthah was one of four Judges upon whom "the Spirit of the Lord came." Like Gideon, the Spirit empowered him to lead God's people against their enemy. When the Spirit came on Jephthah, he sprang into action—he crossed, he passed through, and he advanced against. In no time he devastated Israel's enemy. He had to learn, however, victory comes from the Spirit.

Jephthah learned at great cost he must trust in the sufficiency of the Holy Spirit. At first, he was prone to achieve his desired results by diplomacy and deals. Because he had a way with words, he was in the habit of trying to persuade others to agree with his demands. He attempted this with the enemy but failed. Then he tried his negotiating skills with God. Jephthah felt he needed something more than the Holy Spirit's power to ensure victory. Rather than relying on the Spirit, he tried to make a deal with God. As a bargaining chip, he made a foolish vow he later lived to regret. All he needed to do was have complete trust in the capability of the Holy Spirit.

He vowed to the Lord, "If you give the Ammonites into my hands, whatever comes out of the door of my house to meet me when I return in triumph from the Ammonites will be the Lord's, and I will sacrifice it as a burnt offering." (vv 30–31). God gave him an amazing victory, but not because he bargained for it. Jephthah's name means "he opens his mouth" but he need not have put his foot in it.

To his horror, the first thing that came out of his house was his virgin daughter. She met him with dancing and singing as she celebrated her father's victory. At once he realized he must keep his vow and sacrifice her. In fact, his rash and foolish vow interrupted the Spirit's flow and blessing in his life.

Rhema: You need not make deals with the Lord for him to help you. To bargain with God to manipulate a victory is unnecessary. The empowering of the Spirit is enough to secure stunning victories.

JANUARY 16 | JUDGES 13:1–25

THE STIRRING OF THE SPIRIT

*The woman gave birth to a boy and named him Samson. He grew and the LORD blessed him, and the **Spirit** of the LORD began to stir him while he was in Mahaneh Dan, between Zorah and Eshtaol.*
–JUDGES 13:24–25

Samson is an enigma. He is the strongest man in the Bible, but many see his heroic efforts offset by human weakness. No matter what one thinks, one thing is for sure: Samson is a man of destiny. The Lord selects him and empowers him by his Spirit to do his will. Of Israel's twelve judges, no one is moved on by the Spirit more than he is.

Early in his life, "the Spirit of the Lord began to stir him." The Hebrew word for stir is a strong term that means to trouble, drive, push or impel. This is key to understanding Samson's life with its many unusual events. While he was still young and living an exemplary life, the Holy Spirit began to trouble him and push him to do something regarding their enemy.

When God's Spirit begins to move is always a wonderful day. Great things happen! New and creative realities come into existence. Let us covet such occasions! With Samson God is up to something new and great. The stirring of the Spirit indicates the status quo is about to change. The days ahead will be better than the days past. A new chapter of God's deliverance begins with him.

When God's Spirit is not stirring, we should be troubled. In Samson's day, no one was crying out to heaven because the enemy oppressed them. No one appeared especially concerned they had to coexist with the Philistines. Samson, on the other hand, rose to change these disastrous conditions because he was impelled by the Holy Spirit.

Rhema: Are there situations that trouble you? Who needs deliverance? Help? Victory? God is looking for someone through whom his Spirit can work. When his Spirit is stirring, it means he is getting ready to do a new thing or bring about change. He does not want his people oppressed and harassed by the enemy. He desires them to live in freedom and victory. Pray, "Lord, allow your Spirit to move in me, to stir me and use me."

DAY 17

PROTECTED BY THE SPIRIT

*The **Spirit** of the LORD came powerfully upon him so that he tore the lion apart with his bare hands as he might have torn a young goat. But he told neither his father nor his mother what he had done.* **–JUDGES 14:6**

Samson, the strongest man who ever lived, displayed spectacular physical acts whenever the Spirit would come upon him. He was one of Israel's heroic judges. The Rambo of the OT. The nation of Israel had its real superstrong man whose unusual strength came from the Spirit. Three times "the Spirit of the LORD came powerfully upon him." This happened whenever his life was in danger.

The power of the Spirit is manifest to protect Samson from imminent danger. God's Spirit works to safeguard his people in many ways. In Samson's case, the Spirit engulfs him with might so he can defend himself. A case in point is when a ferocious lion sprang out of nowhere and attacked him. Supercharged with the Spirit, he tears the lion apart with his own hands as if it were Styrofoam.

This remarkable feat takes place as Samson was on his way to a small Philistine town of his oppressors. There a young foreign woman had caught his attention. This budding love affair seems to be of the Lord. "His parents did not know that this was from the Lord, who was seeking an occasion to confront the Philistines; for at that time they were ruling over Israel" (Judg 14:4). Many have failed to understand this about Samson including his parents and have criticized him in error.

The first skirmish with the enemy occurred because God "stirred" Samson. Behind the scenes, the Spirit brought about "an occasion to confront the Philistines." He is not the carnal, sensual man falling for a woman he should not, but he is the servant of the Lord raised up to bring about great victories over the enemy. The Spirit of the Lord came upon him with power to enable him to fulfill the purposes of God. Throughout these God-arranged conflicts, the Spirit saved him from harm.

Rhema: The Spirit of the Lord is also with you when you face difficulties and danger. Even in those strange and hard-to-understand places of your life, the Spirit is present to lead and protect.

JANUARY 18 | JUDGES 14:8–20

DISTURBED BY THE SPIRIT

*Then the **Spirit** of the LORD came powerfully upon him. He went down to Ashkelon, struck down thirty of their men, stripped them of everything and gave their clothes to those who had explained the riddle. Burning with anger, he returned to his father's home.* –JUDGES **14:19**

During his wedding festivities, Samson gave a riddle. The brain-teaser centered around the lion he had killed with his bare hands whose corpse had become a beehive. The riddle went like this: "Out of the eater, something to eat; out of the strong, something sweet." He gave the word puzzle to his thirty Philistine attendants. If they could explain it by the end of the seven-day feast, he would give each one a complete outfit of clothes. If they failed, they must give him thirty sets.

Unable to answer his riddle they realized they must pay up, something they were loath to do. So they pressured Samson's new bride into wresting the solution from him. Without delay she threw herself upon him, saying he would prove his love to her if he told her the answer. His wife cried and sobbed the entire honeymoon trying to extract it. Incidentally, the Philistines had threatened to kill her and her family if she did not get them what they wanted. After seven days of blubbering, Samson acquiesced.

Samson's wife told his groomsmen the answer. When he realized their duplicity, the Spirit of the Lord came on him like a spiraling tornado. He went to another town and slayed thirty Philistines, took their clothes, and paid off his obligation.

In Israel, Samson was a hero because he inflicted losses upon the enemy. In the power of the Spirit he became a one-man military machine. He wreaked havoc on their strongholds. The nation's strongman was not content to coexist with the enemy who was oppressing and subjugating God's people. Disturbed by the Spirit, he sprang into action rather than slump along defeated and cower in the face of evil.

Rhema: God gives the Holy Spirit to help you achieve unpopular and unpleasant tasks. You need his strength, for instance, whenever you must take a stand against evil or witness before a hostile crowd. Expect his divine presence to stir and empower you so you can act against injustice and oppression and establish truth and freedom.

STANDING ALONE IN THE
POWER OF THE SPIRIT

As he approached Lehi, the Philistines came toward him shouting. The **Spirit** *of the LORD came powerfully upon him. The ropes on his arms became like charred flax, and the bindings dropped from his hands.*
–JUDGES 15:14

Samson felt he has "a right to get even with the Philistines." After all, they had coerced and threatened his new wife, ruined his wedding, and gave her to his best friend. In the end, they killed her and burnt her father to death. Such atrocities demand redress.

In retaliation Samson caught three hundred foxes and tied their tails together in pairs. Then he fastened a torch to their tails and released them into their ripened crops. Their grain fields, vineyards, and olive groves went up in smoke. So did the Philistines.

God allows the conflict between Samson and the Philistines to heat up. When he learns what they did to his wife and her father, he says, "I won't stop until I get my revenge on you." His attack is vicious. The battle becomes an international concern when the Philistines threaten Judah with war unless they surrender Samson. He allows his own countrymen to bind him up with ropes and turn him over to their foe.

The Philistines gloated, sensing a great victory when Samson was bound and delivered to them. As they were shouting their battle cries, "the Spirit of the Lord came powerfully upon him." The ropes on his arms became like charred flax, and the bindings dropped from his hands. The Spirit came upon Samson with such a mighty force he can slay a thousand Philistines with a jawbone of a donkey. Once again, the Spirit of the Lord gave Samson a decisive victory and saved his life.

What is the matter with his backstabbing, double-crossing, cowering compatriots? Why are they not pursuing their enemy and throwing off the yoke of oppression? Without any backup, Samson just gave them a stunning victory at Jawbone Hill. He had to stand alone for God because Israel was complacent and willing to coexist with a cruel enemy.

Rhema: In times like these, God's Spirit gives us courage to face the enemy. When others are making deals with the devil, God is looking for someone to stand up for him in the power of the Spirit.

January 20 | I Samuel 10:1–8

The Spirit Can Change One's Personality

*The **Spirit** of the LORD will come powerfully upon you, and you will prophesy with them; and you will be changed into a different person.*
–I Samuel 10:6

Amazing things happen when the Spirit begins to work in our life. He can improve our personality and turn us into another person. When the Spirit gets a hold of us, our character and behavior undergo a major overhaul. Then those who knew us before will realize our nature has changed.

To change our temperament is difficult. Few succeed in transforming their interior design and inner makeup, but what is hard for man is easy for God. Just one touch of the Spirit and Saul became another man. Right away, the Spirit turned his inner world upside down and gave him a change of heart. He became a new person with a new personality.

Saul experienced this radical transformation after Samuel anointed him with oil. The Holy Spirit came upon him and turned him into an extraordinary person. Immediately, he became a man of the Spirit and began to prophesy like the prophets (v 9). Family and friends wondered what had taken place. The powerful endowment from above equipped Saul to lead Israel as their first king.

Personal transformation preceded ministry. The Holy Spirit anointed Saul to equip him to be king, a task he did not expect. He needed divine help if he were to meet the responsibilities and daily challenges of leading and protecting God's people. One of his first tasks, for example, was to free the Israelites from the Ammonites (11:11). Becoming a ruler and leader was a huge life change. In one moment, his transformation was complete. He had a new understanding, a new will, and new behaviors. As long as he operated under the guidance of the Holy Spirit, his success and stunning victories continued.

Rhema: You should not be afraid to allow God's Spirit to transform you. His power will help you become what he wants you to be, a person with a new interior and new capabilities. God can change and transform you by a single touch. Pray and ask the Lord to send his Spirit to give you a complete makeover. He wants to change you into a person who is sensitive to spiritual things and healed from personality defects.

DAY 21

THRONES, DOMINIONS, KINGDOMS, AND THE SPIRIT

When he and his servant arrived at Gibeah, a procession of prophets met him; the **Spirit** *of God came powerfully upon him, and he joined in their prophesying.* –I SAMUEL **10:10**

Israel's monarchy began in a most surprising way. To differentiate it from other kingdoms, the Spirit came with great power upon her first king. Right away Saul joined a school of prophets and began to dance, sing, and twirl around to their music as he prophesied. After Samuel had anointed him with oil, the Spirit changed his timid heart to a heart of a lion. Signs and wonders happened in his life to show God had chosen and enabled him to do whatever his hand found to do. Uniquely, a new government structure began with a king who had the Spirit upon him.

People had asked for a king so they could resemble the surrounding nations. Instead, God gave them one who was unique. Israel's sovereign was endued with his Spirit—one who could prophesy. This meant her king could hear from above. In prophetlike fashion, Saul began to flow and move in spiritual things. Right from the beginning he understood what God wanted. His early achievements were miraculous because he relied on the Spirit.

God wanted Israel's monarchy characterized by values different from the surrounding kingdoms. Earthly thrones and dominions are too often tainted by political ambition and self-interest with little concern, if any, for heaven's throne. From the outset, Israel's throne exhibited a spiritual nature. To rule is far more than a mere human enterprise preoccupied with worldly interests. Rather, governing is a gift from God. For this reason, earthly dominions should concern themselves first with the heavenly. People always benefit when their rulers are in tune with God's will.

Rhema: In this world, we must not permit material values to take precedence over the spiritual. The heavenly is more important than the earthly. In short, we must seek first the kingdom of God so his blessings will follow. As long as Saul put the Lord first he was blessed with mighty victories. God desired to establish his kingdom and set him high above the thrones and dominions of this earth. Similarly, he has anointed us with his Spirit so we will walk in his ways and be successful in all our exploits.

JANUARY 22 | I SAMUEL 11:1–15

ANGER AND THE SPIRIT OF GOD

*When Saul heard their words, the **Spirit** of God came upon him in power, and he burned with anger.* –I SAMUEL **11:6**

After the Spirit descended on him and he changed into a new man, Saul "burned with anger." We rarely associate rage with the Holy Spirit but sometimes it is the right emotion. This was such an occasion. For a second time, God's Spirit came upon him in power.

Saul's own people, possibly members of his own family and tribe, were under attack. To be of the tribe of Benjamin meant they belonged to Israel's smallest and weakest clan. Their savage foe proposed cruel and unusual terms of coexistence. "Let us gouge out your right eye" they taunted, "or face war and enslavement."

The men of Jabesh sent word throughout Israel asking for help. When Saul heard their adversary's proposal he became furious, and the Spirit filled him with power to retaliate. Like Gideon, Jephthah, and Samson years before, the Spirit empowered the new king to contend with the enemy. First, he called together an army of 30,000 and then attacked the Ammonites numbering 300,000. He experienced phenomenal results. They so smashed their tormentors that no two warriors were left standing together. This stunning victory led to Saul's public coronation.

As strange as it may sound, the Holy Spirit helped stoke Saul's fury. Anger, on occasion, is appropriate and needs expression. "Be angry but sin not," Paul said (Eph 4:26). And zeal drove Jesus to cleanse the temple (Jn 2:17). This rage was not of the flesh; it was not the carnal, sinful wrath of man. Saul flamed with anger because a cruel oppressor threatened to bring shame and ruin to God's people. That is why his nostrils flared and his countenance changed. Although he glowed white hot his vehemence was not personal. The Spirit inflamed him to deliver his clan.

Rhema: Anger is a great motivator. Without it, individuals and nations would cower in fear and let the enemy run all over them. Our adversary only comes to steal, kill, and destroy. The Spirit incites godly anger to motivate us to come against the oppressive and cruel spiritual forces of darkness. God wants his people free, and this was Saul's first opportunity to liberate them from the cruel clutches of the oppressor.

JANUARY 23 | I SAMUEL 16:1–13

LIVING EVERY DAY IN THE POWER OF THE SPIRIT

*So Samuel took the horn of oil and anointed him in the presence of his brothers, and from that day on the **Spirit** of the LORD came powerfully upon David. Samuel then went to Ramah.* **–I SAMUEL 16:13**

The Spirit began something new with David. From the day Samuel took the horn of oil and anointed him king of Israel, God's Spirit came upon him and continued to work in his life. Up to now he came on others for specific assignments, but this shepherd boy enjoyed the Spirit's availability every day.

David's daily connection with the Spirit must count as one reason for his many successes. Only his family saw his initial anointing, but Israel saw its results. He became a man of destiny with amazing accomplishments. When the Spirit came powerfully upon Jesse's son, he stayed with him "from that day on" even to the end of his days. David had a more sustained supply of heaven's helper than those before him.

Realizing God's Spirit was with him daily affected his outlook and expectations. David enjoyed a wonderful consciousness of the abiding Spirit as evidenced in his question, "Where can I go from your Spirit?" (Ps 139:7). Such confidence allowed him to achieve many outstanding accomplishments. No matter what difficulties he experienced or perils he faced, he knew God's Spirit was with him. The key to understanding David's rise to prominence was his charismatic anointing.

Rhema: *You too have access to the Spirit's expanded and continuous ministry. His constant indwelling means he is always present to work in your life. You never need to live a day without his influence. Every day you can live in his power. He will always supply the comfort, understanding, and wisdom you need. He creates a hunger for God and gives you an inner power to live in victory.*

Think of it! What might you attempt knowing you have the Spirit with you? His might and power empower you every single moment. The Spirit stayed with David throughout his life. In his day he was the exception, but his experience pointed to an era when the Spirit will remain in us every day. What God made available to only a few he now gives to everyone who believes on Jesus Christ.

THE WITHDRAWAL OF THE SPIRIT

*Now the **Spirit** of the LORD had departed from Saul, and an evil spirit from the LORD tormented him.* –I SAMUEL **16:14**

The Spirit's withdrawal helps explains Saul's tragic end. Although he still wore the crown, the anointing had left him. Israel's first king once walked among the prophets; now a demon torments him. With the Spirit he experienced greatness; without the Spirit he became a disaster. Nothing accounts for his downward descent more than the departure of God's presence.

The Holy Spirit came upon Saul as a special anointing to help him serve God as Israel's king. His disobedience, however, led God to transfer the kingdom to David. The anointing could only rest on one king at a time. Although it took many years for Saul's kingship to end and for David to wear the crown, changes began immediately when the Spirit withdrew from him. From the moment the anointing came to rest mightily on David, he experienced a meteoric rise to national recognition. Saul's demise was marked with many missteps.

To begin well is not enough; we need to walk every day relying on the Spirit. Success accompanied Saul at every turn, but when he acted on his own initiative and didn't rely upon the power from above he stumbled. He disobeyed God and rebelled against his word. As long as he relied upon divine guidance he did well, but without it he became fearful, jealous, and haunted by an evil spirit.

Rhema: Saul's demise teaches us a great lesson: the Holy Spirit makes a difference in our lives. Having the Spirit of God operating in our lives is something we must treasure and guard. When we have God's Spirit, we have his wisdom, guidance, and help. In fact, we have a kingly anointing, so we can reach our destiny and be victorious over our enemies. Without his anointing, we flounder, struggle, and have trouble hearing God. We will suffer defeat at the hands of our enemies without his protective covering. The Holy Spirit is an amazing gift. Should he depart, we can lose his blessings. Therefore, let us do nothing to grieve him or to diminish his work in our lives. To his regret, Saul discovered without the Spirit he did not hear the Lord's voice again or have God's blessing and favor.

THE SPIRIT CHANGES THE ATMOSPHERE

Word came to Saul: "David is in Naioth at Ramah"; so he sent men to capture him. But when they saw a group of prophets prophesying, with Samuel standing there as their leader, the **Spirit** *of God came upon Saul's men and they also prophesied* –I SAMUEL 19:19–20

This is an amazing account of the power of the Spirit to change the atmosphere. David had fled the country because King Saul tried to pin him to a wall with his spear. He escaped to the safest place he knew, to Naioth where Samuel was instructing a school of prophets. When Saul found out where David was, he sent a detachment of tough soldiers to capture him. As soon as these warriors stepped into the prophetic ether, they melted. The presence of the Spirit was so strong the soldiers became powerless pussycats.

While Samuel and the prophets prophesied, the Spirit came upon Saul's men and they prophesied. The spiritually charged atmosphere transformed and immobilized these rock-hard men. They found themselves in an epicenter of spiritual power. When Saul heard what happened to his posse, he sent another detachment and the same thing happened. He did this three times. The Spirit's power apprehended each cohort. Because the spiritual air was so overpowering, none of them could carry out their evil orders. In that wonderful environment of prophetic exuberance, even the most hostile antagonist burst out praising God.

Have you ever wondered what to do when you find yourself in an environment filled with hate? Toxic places chock-full of anger, rage, or poisonous thoughts are hazardous to your wellbeing. David fled the lethal jungle of Saul's court and sought a place with God's presence. Wherever the Spirit of the Lord is there is peace.

Rhema: Whenever you find yourself in a poisonous environment, you can follow David's example. He removed himself and found friends who knew how to worship the Lord "in the Spirit." Together with other like-minded folk, he enjoyed an outpost of heaven. Even if you are alone, you can still enter God's glorious presence. Remember, the Spirit works to overcome contaminated situations, negative emotions, and hostile enemies. Therefore, create opportunities for him to saturate toxic wastelands and invigorate your soul. The Lord inhabits the praises of his people.

JANUARY 26 | PSALM 91:1–16

SAFE IN THE SPIRIT'S PRESENCE

*So Saul went to Naioth at Ramah. But the **Spirit** of God came even on him, and he walked along prophesying until he came to Naioth. He stripped off his garments, and he too prophesied in Samuel's presence.*
–I SAMUEL 19:23–24

Whom do you turn to when in trouble? When life is a mess, what do you do? When David was fighting for his life, he ran to God; he sought out a place where he knew the Spirit dwelt. He was trying to escape the evil intentions of the most powerful man in the nation. King Saul deployed vast resources at his disposal to capture and kill David and even positioned spies everywhere to watch his every move. Jesse's son realized he would be safe with Samuel who lived in God's presence.

After three failed attempts to capture David, Saul finally came himself. When he arrived the Spirit tasered him, rendering him powerless, unable to touch David. Like his soldiers before him, he too began to prophesy. The Spirit so captivated him he stripped off his clothes, lay down naked, and prophesied all day and night. As long as God's Spirit overpowered Saul, no harm came upon David. He was untouchable.

Stopped in their relentless pursuit Saul, and his men beheld Samuel and his student prophets worshiping God. As they played their musical instruments and sang praises, heaven came down. Naioth means dwelling place; Samuel and the Spirit of the Lord dwelt there. Upon entering that realm, David found himself protected by an invisible, forceful shield. When Saul entered, however, he was incapacitated and rendered helpless. Most likely he took off his royal robes to show God was in control.

Rhema: Many important lessons can be gleaned from this remarkable account. First, our enemies have no power over us when the Spirit is present. More powerful than any of our adversaries is God's power from on high. Second, to retain a tremendous spiritual experience, an individual must fully surrender to God. Third, the most important tutorial is to follow David's example and make God's presence our dwelling place. Although many may seek to harm us, the Spirit protects us when we are in God's presence. "He who dwells in the shelter of the Most High will rest in the shadow of the Almighty" (Ps 91:1).

DAY 27

TURNING LIFE'S EXPERIENCES INTO SONGS OF THE SPIRIT

The **Spirit** *of the LORD spoke through me; his word was on my tongue.* –II SAMUEL 23:2

We sometimes wonder why we go through adversities. It would be great if we could Photoshop our lives touching them up here or there to crop out certain unpleasant experiences. Might not our lives be better if we edited out the disappointments and discouragements? As desirable as that might seem, we know it will not happen. David, however, found another way to handle these dark and difficult times.

As his departure drew near, he uttered these words, "The Spirit of the LORD spoke through me; his word was on my tongue." His psalms mostly result from processing life's events by faith. This is why many refer to him as the sweet psalmist of Israel, "Israel's singer of songs." As God's Spirit moved upon him, he looked at his experiences a new way. Israel's songwriter reframes the good and the bad, his victories and failures with a spiritual perspective. These struggles became the basis of his songs. Someone said, "When life dishes you a bowl of lemons, turn it into lemonade."

As the Spirit came upon him, he found strength to turn his misadventures into songs. Given that, more is known about David than anyone else in the Bible. Through his psalms, we become acquainted with his feelings, fears, strengths, victories, and weaknesses. Approximately half the Psalms were written by him and in thirty of them, he expresses how the Lord was his refuge and strength. Many of his lyrics are based on his deliverances and trials. They became a songbook for a nation and eventually the world because God's Spirit breathed new life into his experiences.

David's songs became an outlet for the Spirit. He was God's mouthpiece offering the nation a living word from the Most High. By the Spirit he spoke of God's love, comfort, protection, counsel, and promises. The Spirit helped him resolve life's perplexities and convert them into bold declarations of faith. Once, life was so unbearable he pretended to be insane. Rising from the depths of despair he began his song with, "I will extol the Lord at all times" (Ps 34:1).

Rhema: Likewise, let God help you turn your defeats, struggles, and unpleasant experiences into songs of the Spirit.

KEPT SAFE BY THE SPIRIT

*I don't know where the **Spirit** of the LORD may carry you when I leave you. If I go and tell Ahab and he doesn't find you, he will kill me. Yet I your servant have worshiped the LORD since my youth.*
–I KINGS 18:12

Elijah had gained quite a reputation for eluding King Ahab. For three and a half years, the prophet was nowhere to be found because God hid him. Many people believed the Holy Spirit carried him off to safe undisclosed places. Ahab desperately wanted to get his hands on him because he blamed him for the prolonged drought.

Ahab threatened officials like Obadiah with their lives if they knew Elijah's whereabouts but managed not to report it. A warrant existed for his arrest. The king even went so far as to pressure other nations to return him if they found him hiding within their borders. He had become invisible. Elusive. Mysterious. God orchestrated his disappearance. That is why many thought the Spirit had removed him from the face of the earth.

During the worst of times, God knows how to protect those who love him. Unusual times often call for unusual provisions. During the severe famine, for instance, God took care of Elijah by first commanding the ravens to feed him and then a poor widow. Although she was a foreigner, God restocked her meager resources daily. By replenishing her olive oil and handful of flour, this recurring miracle provided food for the widow, her family, and Elijah.

In the end, a whirlwind carried the prophet of fire up to heaven. During his life, however, he had an unshakeable confidence in the Lord's preservation and protection. While on earth, God looked after his faithful servant and supported him in miraculous ways, so he lived undetected for years.

Rhema: Never limit God by thinking there are things he cannot do. This was Obadiah's problem. He had no trouble believing God can take care of Elijah but questioned whether God could take care of him. God, however, goes to great lengths to provide and protect his own. The Lord Almighty may hide you by the brook Kerith or command his ravens to feed you (17:4). But know he is able to do immeasurably more than you are able to ask or even imagine (Eph 3:20).

JANUARY 29 | II KINGS 2:1–10

A DOUBLE PORTION OF THE SPIRIT

When they had crossed, Elijah said to Elisha, "Tell me, what can I do for you before I am taken from you?" "Let me inherit a double portion of your **spirit***," Elisha replied.* **–II KINGS 2:9**

If you could ask for anything you want, what would it be? The day Elijah is whisked away in a chariot of fire, he offers Elisha this opportunity. "Ask whatever you want! Tell me what I can do for you before the Lord takes me away." Without hesitation, Elisha asks for a double portion of the Spirit that rested on his mentor.

His request for a double portion was extraordinary. He was asking for the inheritance provision of the firstborn be applied to him, but with a twist. Instead of applying this custom to the material realm, he harnessed it to the spiritual. The prophet of fire was one of a kind, empowered with an abundant supply of the Spirit. So, to ask for a double portion of the Spirit was a difficult request.

A double portion meant that the firstborn son received twice as much inheritance as any other son. Elisha requested twice as much of the Spirit's power and anointing to rest on him than on the other prophets. Further, he asked for the privilege of succeeding Elijah. As his successor, he relished the responsibility for continuing his ministry. While he served Elijah as his apprentice, he saw what the Spirit accomplished and wanted more. A greater anointing would empower him to obtain even greater things for the kingdom of God.

Elisha refused to settle for the status quo—he craved an increase of the Spirit's power. Not content to let Elijah and his amazing ministry pass, he asked to carry it on. Hungry for the things of God, he would settle for nothing less than a fuller, richer blessing of the Spirit. Elisha knew to meet the challenges and opportunities ahead he needed an intensification in anointing. Although such a spiritual upgrade was hard to secure, it was granted.

Rhema: You too can ask for more of the Spirit in your life. A greater impartation. An increase in anointing. You might not be an Elijah or Elisha, but you can hunger and thirst after God for all he has to offer.

January 30 | II Kings 2:11–15

Stepping Out in the Spirit's Anointing

The company of the prophets from Jericho, who were watching, said, "The spirit *of Elijah is resting on Elisha." And they went to meet him and bowed to the ground before him.* –II Kings 2:15

Elisha received the double portion of the Spirit that rested on Elijah. Now what? God gave him what he wanted but what difference would it make? Sometimes when the Lord grants people things they asked for, they do nothing with it. When Elisha received this powerful blessing, he began to use it. As the Spirit came to rest on his shoulders, he took his first steps and moved in his greater anointing.

To receive more anointing is not enough: one must start moving in the Spirit and show he is at work in one's life. The first thing Elisha did was pick up the mantle that fell from Elijah's shoulders. This same mantle touched his own shoulders when God first called him. Taking it in his hand, he smacked the Jordan River and asked, "Where is the Lord God of Elijah?" Where is the God who answers prayer, raises the dead, and sends fire from heaven? As he struck the river, the waters parted here, there, and everywhere. The Spirit of God who made Elijah so powerful now settled upon Elisha. By duplicating his master's last miracle, he demonstrated he had inherited his empowerment.

As the waters split open, Elisha returned to the other side. A company of the prophets from Jericho observed him part the Jordan. This miracle convinced them the Spirit of Elijah now rested on him and the transfer of authority had taken place. So, these men presented themselves to Elisha to show their willingness to submit to his prophetic authority.

Rhema: When God gives you a grace, a spiritual gift, or a new anointing, begin to move in it and use it right away. Elisha did not sit idly back and wait until he could grow and perfect his newfound anointing. Instead, without hesitation he began to move out under the power of God. Then he discovered the destiny that awaited him. You too can step out in faith, use what the Spirit has given you, and enter the wonderful future God has in store for you.

DAY 31

PARTICIPANTS OR SPECTATORS OF THE SPIRIT?

*"Look," they said, "we your servants have fifty able men. Let them go and look for your master. Perhaps the **Spirit** of the LORD has picked him up and set him down on some mountain or in some valley." "No," Elisha replied, "do not send them." –II KINGS 2:16*

A great distinction separates participants from spectators. Elijah and Elisha are participants taking part in one of the most dramatic transfers of spiritual power in history. The "sons of the prophets" are spectators who only observe it. How sad they remain passive while the dynamic duo is fully engaged.

The spectators appear as mere boys among men, beginners among the masters. Thinking they could find Elijah after his momentous departure reveals their lack of spiritual astuteness. Elijah's ministry concludes with his dramatic ascension as Elisha's begins with a stunning miracle. Granted these events are outstanding, spiritual spectacles never to be repeated. Their students content themselves, however, with climbing up to the nosebleed seats to observe.

Even in spiritual matters, believers are segregated into participators or spectators. Why were they not all participants? Did not the Spirit tell them of Elijah's departure? Knowing the Lord was going to take Elijah, they "went and stood at a distance." Why did they not take part in this spectacular event? Meanwhile, Elisha hangs on to Elijah like a dog with a pork chop. He determined to allow nothing on earth that day to separate him from the illustrious prophet. No way was he going to be a mere spectator.

Too bad the company of prophets were only bystanders. Look at what they missed! They did not cross the Jordan on dry ground, nor did they feel the heat of the chariot and horses of fire. As spectators, they missed the heavenly tug of the whirlwind that caught Elijah up to heaven. None received any increase of the Spirit on their lives. It was terrific stuff to check out, but Elisha experienced it firsthand.

Rhema: When God is moving, do you want to be spectators or participants? Look at what Elisha received for all his effort and zeal! He was given a double portion of the Spirit. He found his destiny. Therefore, do not be afraid to embrace what God is doing. Join him! Seize the opportunity and participate in it!

LOYALTIES FORMED BY THE SPIRIT

Then the **Spirit** *came on Amasai, chief of the Thirty, and he said: "We are yours, David! We are with you, son of Jesse! Success, success to you, and success to those who help you, for your God will help you." So David received them and made them leaders of his raiding bands.*
–I CHRONICLES 12:18

When the Holy Spirit brings people together, great things can happen. These were difficult days for the king in waiting, a fugitive running from Saul. Many had deceived and betrayed him, so anyone wanting to join him was treated with extreme caution. Amasai approached David to join forces with him because the Spirit prompted him. Their divine encounter resulted in a powerful relationship between them.

When the Spirit touched Amasai, he pledged his loyalty to David. It marked a major turning point in his life, possibly the tipping point in the future king's rise to power. He might not have been as successful if the Spirit did not join them together in a bond of loyalty. David needed a military leader to assure him of more victories, so the Spirit caused and created their strategic and unique partnership.

Amasai's exploits were already legendary. He led the Thirty, the name given to the thirty most powerful warriors in the land. They had distinguished themselves for their military prowess. Prudently, David made them the core of his army and appointed them his personal bodyguard. It was as if the Spirit foresaw his need, so drew them together.

Amasai was not only valiant but also a man of the Spirit. Because of his prophetic ability, he spoke revelation into David's life and told him of amazing victories awaiting him. The Spirit gave him spiritual insights and a much-needed supernatural word of encouragement. David needed men like him who walked with God and heard from heaven. Because of his spiritual sensitivity, he committed himself and his fighters to the son of Jesse. By accepting them, David was provided a fierce, courageous, and intensely loyal cohort to whom he could entrust his life.

Rhema: Partnerships created by the Spirit are special. By working together, David and Amasai experienced incredible victories. With their unique talents, they furthered God's noble mission. Perhaps the Spirit will nudge you to come alongside and support someone in ministry.

DAY 33

BLUEPRINTS FROM THE SPIRIT

*Then David gave his son Solomon the plans for the portico of the temple, its buildings, its storerooms, its upper parts, its inner rooms and the place of atonement. He gave him the plans of all that the **Spirit** had put in his mind for the courts of the temple of the LORD and all the surrounding rooms, for the treasuries of the temple of God and for the treasuries for the dedicated things.* –I CHRONICLES 28:11–12

No one in the Bible had such a strong heart for worshiping the Almighty as does David. Before he died, he wanted to turn Jerusalem into a great worship center. Gripped by passion for the Lord's dwelling, he devoted the last part of his life to this noble project. Israel's great king collected the building materials, organized the workers, and drafted the plans according to what the Spirit had shown him. He did everything possible to ensure Solomon would build the temple in accordance with the divine design.

Just as God gave Moses the specific details for constructing the tabernacle, so the Spirit gave the temple's schematics to David. Down to the last detail everything was according to a celestial plan deposited into his heart. Of these blueprints, David said, "I have in writing from the hand of the Lord upon me, and he gave me understanding in all the details of the plan" (v 19). God insisted on these details because this was to be his house, the place where he would dwell and manifest his wonderful presence. Every aspect was a type and shadow reflecting the spiritual realities of heaven and the great doctrinal truths of salvation.

Rhema: God has a wonderful blueprint for your life. Since you too are his dwelling place, let his Spirit influence and determine its grandeur. Even its smallest detail will be by divine decree. His Spirit will give you the details; the one who inhabits eternity will guide you each step of the way. He loves to write heaven's plans upon the tablet of your heart and show you things beyond the veil. Let him show you the glories of God's throne, the bounty of his treasuries, and the unexplored storerooms of his purposes for you. Therefore, build your life according to his plans.

FOLLOWING THE SPIRIT LEADS TO SUCCESS

*The **Spirit** of God came on Azariah son of Oded. He went out to meet Asa and said to him, "Listen to me, Asa and all Judah and Benjamin. The LORD is with you when you are with him. If you seek him, he will be found by you, but if you forsake him, he will forsake you.*
–II CHRONICLES 15:1–2

D o we understand the reasons for success and failure? Without prophetic insight, we have little way of knowing. The Holy Spirit, however, gave King Asa the reason for his stunning victory. He moved the prophet, Azariah, to tell the king the explanation for his recent triumph.

Asa's victory is noteworthy for several reasons. Not only outnumbered two to one, but the king had been on a spiritual crusade. He was cleaning up the nation and implementing powerful reforms to end the flagrant sins in the land. The king purposed to bring the nation back to God. "Asa did what was good and right in the eyes of the Lord his God" (14:2). The Holy Spirit revealed their recent victory resulted from the king's spiritual zeal.

Through the prophet, the Spirit said to King Asa, "The LORD is with you when you are with him. If you seek him, he will be found by you." In other words, the prophet was saying, "Your remarkable success proves Yahweh is with you and his blessing is on your life. Your victory stems from your zeal for the Lord. If you continue to adhere to his cause, you may expect his presence and blessing to continue." Through this prophetic word, the Spirit declared to king and country victory, blessing, and peace result from a faithful walk with God. Asa sought the Lord wholeheartedly and for that God rewarded him with great success.

Azariah, in addition, delivered a warning through the Spirit. If they were careless and forsook God, he would forsake them but if they adhered to the prophetic word, they would continue to succeed.

Rhema: *The Spirit's message to the king and his army is a lesson that runs throughout Scripture. Dire consequences result from abandoning God, but wonderful blessings—success and victory— arise from living for him. Following the Spirit's guidance is always the key to God's best but ignoring it, failure.*

THE SPIRIT'S PROMISE OF VICTORY

*Then the **Spirit** of the LORD came on Jahaziel son of Zechariah … as he stood in the assembly. He said: "Listen, King Jehoshaphat and all who live in Judah and Jerusalem! This is what the LORD says to you: 'Do not be afraid or discouraged because of this vast army. For the battle is not yours, but God's.'"* –II CHRONICLES 20:14–15

In spiritual warfare, the Spirit is a master tactician. He knows the precise way to defeat the enemy. His tactics will protect us from our adversaries even when they launch a surprise attack. Jehoshaphat, king of Judah, called on God for help when several nations swarmed against him like a locust plague. Salivating with envy, they swooped upon the nation to plunder its God-given wealth. In himself the king realized he was powerless and had no game plan other than turning to God. What were they to do? Jehoshaphat inquired of the Lord and proclaimed a fast and his people rallied together to seek the Lord. As these hostile forces crossed the Jordan and were nearing the gates, the Spirit sprang into action with an unusual strategy.

The Spirit came upon Jahaziel, inspiring him to declare an awesome prophecy. The battle is not theirs but the Lord's. No need to shake in their boots or become discouraged because God will intervene. They will not have to fight this battle, only trust the Lord. If they stood firm, they will see his deliverance.

Armed with this prophetic word, King Jehoshaphat appointed singers to go in front of Israel's army. "As they began to sing and praise, the Lord set ambushes against" the enemy. The members of the coalition became so confused they attacked and destroyed each other. It took the king and his men three days just to collect the spoils from this dramatic victory. He returned to Jerusalem praising God with musical instruments.

Rhema: Praise and worship are powerful weapons against your adversary. The devil hates it when you celebrate God's glory and demons are thrown into confusion. Whenever the enemy attacks, you can follow Jehoshaphat's example: fast and pray but also magnify the Lord with singing and praise. The battle is not yours but God's. If you have faith in him and believe the Spirit's promise, you will be victorious (v 20).

FEBRUARY 5 | II CHRONICLES 24:17–25

REBUKED BY THE SPIRIT

*Then the **Spirit** of God came on Zechariah son of Jehoiada the priest. He stood before the people and said, "This is what God says: 'Why do you disobey the LORD's commands? You will not prosper. Because you have forsaken the LORD, he has forsaken you.'"*
–II CHRONICLES 24:20

The Holy Spirit rebukes people for their wicked deeds. When they turn away from the Lord, the Spirit rises up to stop them. This takes place in the current story. The Spirit spoke a word of rebuke through Zechariah because the king and the nation abandoned the Lord. All Joash's good works done in the beginning of his reign were undone by forsaking God at the end. Because he reversed his earlier reforms, the Spirit censured him.

King Joash lost his spiritual mentor when the priest Jehoiada died. Throughout his long life, the priest had advised him many times and provided beneficial oversight and exceptional spiritual influence. He "did what was right in the eyes of the Lord all the years of Jehoiada the priest" (v 2). As soon as his tutor died, however, the king and the people forsook God. "The Lord sent prophets to the people to bring them back to him" (v 19) but they would not listen. The king even had the prophet, Zechariah, killed for his prophetic ministry. This dastardly deed precipitated king Joash's demise.

Serious consequences resulted from executing his mentor's son and the nation's prophet. From that time forward, victories and prosperity evaporated. For such treachery, God forsook them. The king soon discovered how hard it was to live without the Lord's help. To avert destruction, he resorted to bribing the enemy with the temple treasures. Giving away the sacred things dedicated to God was reprehensible. Therefore, he did not prosper; rather, he was wounded in battle. Before recovering, several of his own officials assassinated him for his misdeeds. His subjects refused to bury him with their kings but the godly priest he murdered received a royal burial.

Rhema: No one likes reproof or correction. A rebuke is like taking a hammer to chisel away the undesirable parts of our lives. God does that in his love whenever he sends his Spirit to censure us. He wants to ensure we continue to enjoy heaven's blessings by remaining faithful to our God.

THE SPIRIT OF GOD IS GOOD

*You gave your good **Spirit** to instruct them. You did not withhold your manna from their mouths, and you gave them water for their thirst.*
–NEHEMIAH 9:20

The Holy Spirit is good. The word "good" signifies a pleasant, joyful, and an agreeable experience. It first occurs in Genesis 1:4: "God saw that the light was good." Immediately, darkness was dispelled to make life possible. The Holy Spirit's work and presence gratifies and benefits like bright beams in the morning. Light makes us feel alive and alert.

Many helpful and valuable results materialize whenever the Spirit is at work. Someone is going to be blessed. Something good is going to happen. Whatever he does brings an intense level of satisfaction. He satiates us with good things. He is the author and creator of true joy, peace, and beauty. The fruit of the Spirit, after all, is goodness (Gal 5:22).

In Nehemiah's day, something good was happening. A national revival broke out. People spent their days with God. They listened to his word, confessed their sins, and sang his praises. Heaven invaded earth! For eight days straight, they praised God for his goodness. They realized he had kept his promises and lavished them with his "abounding love."

During this powerful move of God, leaders reviewed their history and realized how much God had blessed them. They recounted blessing after blessing. During their wilderness wanderings, for instance, they experienced the Spirit's presence as the pillar of fire by night and the cloud by day. They had supernatural shelter and guidance. Every morning the Israelites were greeted with a miracle supply of manna. They realized the Spirit's presence and activity supported and sustained them. God's "good Spirit" instructed them with teachings surpassing the wisdom and knowledge of Egypt. The Spirit taught Moses and inspired him to write of the excellencies of the Almighty, the mysteries of creation, and the ways of God.

Rhema: The Holy Spirit is good! He leads into all truth. With understanding and illumination he feeds your soul. Whenever you open the Bible you can ask him to make it real, to make it come alive, and to instruct you in God's ways. In fact, every manifestation of the Spirit is none other than the glory of God's presence blessing and benefitting you in some way.

FEBRUARY 7 | NEHEMIAH 9:26–38

WARNED BY THE SPIRIT

*For many years you were patient with them. By your **Spirit** you warned them through your prophets.* –NEHEMIAH 9:30

God's Spirit is always looking out for us, always having our best interests at heart. He is more concerned with our well-being than we are ourselves. He wants God's absolute best for our lives. To ensure we continue to enjoy God's greatest blessings, he warns us. As an alarmed GPS, he guides us on a path that leads to abundance and blessing. For this reason, his Spirit beeps whenever we get off track.

One way he guides to God's best is to alert us when our trajectory is at variance with his. To express his disapproval he will admonish, chastise, or warn. The alarm rings, yellow lights flash so we will avoid shipwreck. In Nehemiah's time, he warned of the dangers of going astray by cautioning them in a gentle, loving way through their prophets.

The Spirit's admonishments were to persuade Yahweh's people to alter their course and change their direction. If they made midcourse corrections, their future will be bright. Had they heeded his warnings in the first place, the exiles would have avoided deportation.

God's Spirit warned Israel and Judah throughout their entire history. From their first ruler until they went into exile, he admonished, alerted, and reproved them. "Yet they paid no attention." Arrogance, disobedience, and rebellion flowed from their hardened hearts. They even killed the prophets to silence his warnings. When they disarmed the alarm system, they found themselves in a mess. How sad and unnecessary to suffer slavery, hardship, and distress. Through all this, however, God who is merciful and gracious continued to show kindness and speak gently. Because they confessed these sins during Ezra's revival, God offered them a new beginning.

Rhema: Since God's Spirit knows all things, his warnings are more than conjectures. Because he sees upcoming events, he can witness to those imminent realities. There is no guessing what might happen. He actually "sees" where our actions will take us. Parents admonish their children about the consequences of their behavior. What is different with the Spirit, however, is he knows the actual results because the future is permanently present to him. Given that he is timeless and inhabits eternity, he lovingly alerts us to actual future danger.

THE SPIRIT GIVES LIFE

*The **Spirit** of God has made me; the breath of the Almighty gives me life.* –JOB 33:4

Job languishes under the shadow of death. He squats on a garbage dump sick and surrounded by sullen critics insinuating his sin caused his terrible plight. Have you ever found yourself in similar circumstances wondering if you can make it one more day? When adversity strikes, we can feel isolated, hopeless, and defenseless. In such times, we can draw upon God's Spirit to renew and sustain us.

Elihu reminds Job that the Spirit, the breath of the Almighty, gives and sustains life. Both believe man is more than mere dust. What distinguishes human life from the material universe is the Spirit, the one who made us and sustains us. He is the animating power of man's life, endowing him with the ability to communicate with God and each other. To utter words and understand their meaning separates mankind from matter. Consciousness is possible because divinity bestows man with intelligence and infuses him with life. This capacity to know and to speak truth comes from our Maker (Gen 2:7). The grand explanation why man, taken from the dust, can think, speak, and understand is the breath of God.

That our existence depends upon God's Spirit is an awesome, practical revelation. His breath sustains and preserves us. He is the one who keeps us alive, helping us to continue another day. Divine breath restores our life, renews it, and causes it to flourish. Not only does his creative power generate life but also carries it to completion. Life is a mystery best explained by the Spirit whose invisible power is the cause of every living thing.

Rhema: Learn to live every day in the Spirit's creative and renewing power. He can cause you to overflow with a vitality that comes only from above. The origin, maintenance, and development of your life is a result of his work. As the source of your renewal and ongoing freshness, let his breath keep you going. Wherever you find yourself today, whatever the circumstances, draw in his breath and let it infuse your being with life— the life of the Almighty! Relearn how to breathe for by his breath you live and have your being. O, breath of heaven, renew me today!

GOD WILL NOT WITHDRAW
HIS SPIRIT

If it were his intention and he withdrew his **spirit** *and breath, all humanity would perish together and mankind would return to the dust.*
–JOB 34:14–15

Job developed negative thoughts about his Maker. No wonder. For no apparent reason, he lost his health, possessions, and children. We might curry negative thoughts too should we find ourselves tormented with no explanation. One of the great mysteries of life is why do the righteous suffer? Job is "blameless and upright," a man "who feared God and shunned evil." Why is he going through hell?

What further muddies Job's judgement is the seeming trouble-free life of sinners. Perhaps like Job you have asked yourself why you are going through fiery trials. You have only tried to live for the Lord. Many around you have not, yet they are not experiencing tribulation. This broken man saw his grievous affliction as an unfair incongruity that led him to entertain an unthinkable notion: the Almighty is not just.

Elihu tries to correct Job's destructive thinking with this argument: "If it were God's intention to withdraw his Spirit and breath, all humanity would perish and return to the dust." Yahweh created us in love and he will not go against his purpose by withdrawing his Spirit. He has no plan to take back his Spirit and terminate life on earth. This will never happen. The Creator cares for his creation and has no intention of returning the universe back to nothingness.

Have no doubt our Maker does what is right because he is God. His loving preservation of life proves it. He cannot be wrong or unjust. Elihu said to Job, "It is unthinkable that God would do wrong, that the Almighty would pervert justice" (v 12). In effect he is saying, *If you really knew God you would not insinuate he is doing wrong by you for he is perfect and pure. Besides, no one else has the entire responsibility for the human race. By the way, my friend, who appointed you to look after this world?*

Rhema: God has no desire to crush you; he is not willing that any perish. His eternal loving purpose is to give you his Spirit, not take him away, to fashion you in his image so you can live with him forever.

FEBRUARY 10 | PSALM 51:1–19

DO NOT TAKE YOUR HOLY SPIRIT FROM ME

*Do not cast me from your presence or take your **Holy Spirit** from me.*
—PSALM 51:11

After David's terrible sin, he prayed for God not to reject him or remove his Holy Spirit. Adultery with Bathsheba and murdering her husband had grieved the Spirit. David knew he would be nothing if it were not for God's Spirit kissing his life. No doubt he remembered what happened when King Saul displeased God. The Spirit was taken from him and placed on David. That gracious gift made him successful in all his ways. No way does he want what happened to Saul to transpire in his life.

David could not stand the faintest prospect of living one day without God's presence. That would mean the Holy Spirit was eradicated from him. For David, life without constant friendship and fellowship with his Maker is abhorrent. Reveling in his presence with face-to-face encounters was one irreplaceable essential in his life. He spent long periods soaking in his presence.

David understands what constitutes a Spiritless life. There is no favor, no blessing, no anointing, no helper, no guide, no renewal, no joy, and no peace. One factor distinguishing his life from Saul's was not his talent or ability but the Spirit's activity. Having the Holy Spirit gave David a personal, immediate relationship with God. Nothing was more wonderful than enjoying these intimate divine encounters.

The errant king prays, "Do not take your Holy Spirit from me." He can put up with the loss of many things but losing God's Spirit is detestable to him. Sometimes individuals conceive of the Holy Spirit as an impersonal power or influence in their lives, but not David. Others may judge having the Spirit is no big deal, but they err. For him, nothing is more important!

Rhema: What should we do if we experience a terrible failure like David's or even one much less? He prayed, "Create in me a pure heart, oh God, and renew a steadfast spirit within me" (v 10). We should ask God to forgive us and to furnish us his Spirit. The blessed Holy Spirit is a powerful friend who will supply the needed resources to begin again. Above everything else, we need God's Spirit to empower us and work in our lives.

LORD, SEND YOUR SPIRIT TO RENEW THE EARTH

*When you send your **Spirit**, they are created, and you renew the face of the ground.* —PSALM 104:30

Life on this planet needs constant renewal. To prevent this world from becoming desolate, the Spirit must mitigate the effects of sin and the fall. Without constant divine intervention, the destructive powers of disease and decay would reign supreme. Creation groans, nature wears out, the curse ravages. That is why God sends his Spirit to restore the earth. Our existence and every other glorious expression of life is predicated on his constant renewal of creation.

Ever since man fell in Eden, God's Spirit has been busy creating new life to replace the old and dying. He dispatches his Spirit to renew a curse-tarnished creation. Every manifestation of life depends on him. Divine renewal extends to all the birds of the air, all the beasts of the field, and the vast number of creatures of the sea. Every living thing needs the restorative breath of God. We exist by a special act of our Creator—he breathes into us his life-giving Spirit. Above all else, he wants us to flourish by renewing us every day with his breath. By his Spirit, God continues to create living things and replenish the work of his hands. When one generation ends, his Spirit creates a new generation.

We need to remind ourselves to praise our Creator. The self-admonition, "Praise the Lord, O my soul" begins and ends this Psalm. Intentionally, purposefully, take the initiative and bless the Lord for creation and its renewal. So let us wonder at his greatness, for he clothes himself in light and is brighter than the sun. Marvel at his mighty power to turn nature's elemental forces to our benefit. Thank him for making this world a fit place in which to live. Praise his Majesty because he provides for us and sustains all his creatures. In addition, bless the Lord for sending forth his Spirit to make the earth new again.

Rhema: Honor your Maker by filling your innermost being with awe and appreciation for his wondrous works. Invite his Spirit to renew, restore, and recreate whatever is deteriorating in your life. Do not forget to delight yourself in the Lord who day after day replenishes, rejuvenates, and refreshes you.

FEBRUARY 12 | NUMBERS 20:1–13

REBELLING AGAINST THE SPIRIT

*By the waters of Meribah they angered the Lord, and trouble came to Moses because of them; for they rebelled against the **Spirit** of God, and rash words came from Moses' lips —*PSALM **106:32–33**

This Psalm refers to Israel's serious sin of rebelling against the Spirit. Their sins included unbelief, discontent, jealousy, idolatry, and apostasy. By the waters of Meribah, an unthinkable tragedy happened: they caused Moses to sin. Ever since they left Egypt, the Israelites committed a multitude of moral mistakes because they refused to hearken to the Spirit's voice. So the writer sums up their many offenses as an insurrection against God's Spirit.

What does it mean to rebel against the Spirit of God? It means to ignore or resist him. Throughout their journey the Spirit spoke to them, but they did not listen. Many times people do not recognize his voice or understand his language. One way he speaks is through miracles. In experiencing many amazing wonders, the Israelites didn't recognize him at work. Instead of allowing his message to fill them with faith, they recoiled in unbelief.

The plagues of Egypt, the daily manna, the pillar of fire, and the cloud by day were the ways the Spirit spoke to them. He was in these miraculous works declaring God's love. In these supernatural signs the Spirit shouted, *God loves you. He is in your midst. He is looking out for you. He is leading you to a land of blessing. You are special.*

Meribah developed into a bitter experience where Israel contended with the Spirit. They "quarreled with the Lord" (v 13). The Spirit spoke one thing but they said another. He said, "God is good." The people said, "We have been brought here to die." The Spirit said, "God will provide," but they said, "We have no water." The consequences of their unbelief were severe. They not only angered the Lord, but they moved Moses to sin.

Rhema: The Spirit works to create faith. His miracles speak of God's powerful provisions. Unbelief, on the other hand, disguised as grumbling and complaining, openly flaunts him. Instead of overflowing with faith they moaned bitterly. Despite the divine dialogue they still did not believe. How could they fight against this much evidence? Their unbelief was a serious sin because it constituted rebellion against God's Spirit.

WHERE CAN I GO FROM YOUR SPIRIT?

*Where can I go from your **Spirit**? Where can I flee from your presence?*
—PSALM 139:7

There is no escaping the Spirit. This realization gave David great comfort. Israel's ancient songwriter has just described the pleasure and wonder of God's intimate and personal knowledge of him. The Lord knows everything about him, where he is, what he is thinking, what he will say. Such thoughts are too wonderful to take in. The ubiquitous presence of the Spirit mesmerizes him.

To face difficulties, knowing the Spirit is present, is always reassuring. No one protects, guides, and teaches as he does. Even when we find ourselves opposed and in hostile circumstances, the Spirit is present. David finds hope in this awareness especially as he faces many challenges.

God's Spirit is with you, behind you, ahead of you, and all around you. In every imaginable and unimaginable place, he is ever present. Of course he is in heaven above, but also in the depths of the earth. Should you picture yourself as far away as the rising morning sun he is there; likewise, he is on the far side of the sea. You cannot escape his presence by hiding in the darkness for "the darkness will not be dark" to him.

This one certainty can help you live every day with courage and gratitude. Everything you do, say, or think is open to his scrutiny. God's Spirit keeps a close, watchful eye over you. Wherever you go or whatever the circumstances, he is there. His hand steers and holds you steady. He knows you inside and out. Your entire interior as well as your exterior is before him. To know and to be known by someone so important and powerful satisfies the deepest longings of the soul.

Rhema: There is no place in heaven overhead or on earth below where you are without the Spirit. He is nearby at every turn of the way. Nothing can separate you from his attendance. Even amidst frightful forces you are in his company. Were your enemy to find you, he would first have to overtake the Spirit who surrounds you. He is ever present to hear your cry and answer your prayer. Because of him you are never alone in this world!

FEBRUARY 14 | PSALM 143

THE GOOD SPIRIT GUIDES IN TIMES OF TROUBLE

*Teach me to do your will, for you are my God; may your good **Spirit** lead me on level ground.* —PSALM 143:10

David's enemies brought him low and wore him out. He faced one scrape after another. Exhausted, he cried out, "The enemy pursues me, he crushes me to the ground; he makes me dwell in darkness like those long dead" (v 3). God's servant was desperate. He was in danger and does not have the strength to continue. If God does not hurry and come to his rescue, his life is finished.

Putting words to his feelings he laments, "So my spirit grows faint within me; my heart within me is dismayed" (v 4). The enemy has been pursuing him, hounding him as a hunter's prey, heaving and hiding. Trembling and trapped, David knows without the Spirit's guidance he is dead.

In times of desperation, we need to not only know God's will but also do it. David makes two requests of God. To do God's will requires both instruction and direction. His first prayer beseeches the Lord to teach him to do God's will. Certainly, this is not a time to do something rash or foolish. A misstep would be fatal. Because he is backed into a corner with few options, he focuses on doing God's perfect will. Likewise, the question on our minds when in a similar circumstance should be: what does the Lord want me to do?

The second petition requests God's good Spirit to lead him on level ground. David has had enough rough patches in his life and now seeks divine directions to flat pasturelands. There his tired and exhausted soul can lie down and find rest. He urgently calls for the Spirit to give him insight. Illumination. Direction. To get out of his present mess, he needs a divine solution.

Rhema: The sweet psalmist of Israel describes the Holy Spirit as good. From a musician's perspective, good means to play a song or instrument well. With all life's dissonance, David realizes the good Holy Spirit will orchestrate a pleasing and delightful outcome. Only God's good Spirit can skillfully guide him into pleasant harmonies charted for him. Likewise, you too can ask the Spirit to make your paths straight and help you accomplish God's perfect will.

FEBRUARY 15 | ISAIAH 4:1–6

THE SPIRIT OF JUDGMENT AND FIRE

*The Lord will wash away the filth of the women of Zion; he will cleanse the bloodstains from Jerusalem by a **spirit*** of judgment and a **spirit*** of fire. (*NIV footnote, the Spirit).* —ISAIAH 4:4

God's Spirit can clean up a moral mess and restore a person. The prophet Isaiah tells of a future era when the Messiah will clean up the land through the Spirit. "In that day the Branch of the Lord will be beautiful and glorious, and the fruit of the land will be the pride and glory of the survivors in Israel" (v 2). What sin destroyed he will restore. Bloody wars reduced the population to only one man for every seven women. Filth and bloodshed scarred Israel, but a glorious era is coming when fruitfulness will abound. When David's offshoot comes, he will return the land to its former glory.

Isaiah paints a prophetic picture of our full and glorious restoration. The Branch, the Messiah, will send the Holy Spirit as a blast of wind and fire to bring us back to God. His kingdom comes with fire. John the Baptist said of Jesus, "He will baptize you with the Holy Spirit and fire. His winnowing fork is in his hand, and he will clear his threshing floor, gathering his wheat into the barn and burning up the chaff with unquenchable fire" (Mt 3:11–12). The Spirit goes after sin like fire. He burns the dross and impurities from our hearts; he consumes the moral filth and makes us holy.

Rhema: The Spirit's work in our lives is described in terms of judgment fire. Like Isaiah (6:6–7), we need cleansing before we can enjoy the presence of the Lord. After a thorough purging, he comes to dwell in us. This remarkable spiritual transformation is a supernatural work that can only occur through a process of cleansing and refining. Our spiritual renewal and restoration is so amazing the prophet compares it to the glory of God during the Exodus. He covers us with "a cloud of smoke by day and a glow of flaming fire by night" (v 5). Heaven is open. The disgrace is removed. Our lives become beautiful and glorious. We are fruitful once again. The Spirit of fire restores in us the glorious image of God.

PERFECT ENDOWMENT OF THE SPIRIT

*The **Spirit** of the LORD will rest on him—the Spirit of wisdom and of understanding, the Spirit of counsel and of might, the Spirit of the knowledge and fear of the LORD.* **–ISAIAH 11:2**

Centuries before Jesus the Messiah was born, Isaiah described his endowment of the Spirit. Seven attributes describe his special equipping to bring justice to the nations. Because he has the Spirit of the Lord resting on him, he will have wisdom, understanding, counsel, might, knowledge, and reverence for God. Seven is the number of perfection—he will receive a complete anointing. No world ruler will ever compare to him or be his equal because his extraordinary abilities will come from above. Therefore, a world wrecked by insurmountable challenges, confusion, and discrimination is offered glorious hope.

The prophet Isaiah writes of a time when sin reduced the royal family to a mere stump. The line of kings like a concealed root had little visible promise. Years will pass without their having power or glory, only ignominy. Then a promise of new life emerges when a shoot will come up from the stump of Jesse, King David's father (v 1). Exaltation follows this state of humiliation. The Branch refers to the Messiah, the one upon whom God's Spirit will rest with perfect endowment. Once the Spirit comes upon him, Jesus will be equipped to rule and handle every world problem.

He is first characterized by having "the Spirit of the Lord." Jesus will enjoy God's own Spirit to anoint and equip him as the Messiah. In fact, his mighty ministry will be defined by the Spirit. In his humanity, Jesus was full of the Spirit and did everything in that power and fullness. Moreover, the primary purpose of the Spirit in his life was to help him bring justice to the poor, needy, and marginalized (v 4). He will intervene powerfully in human affairs to bring justice and deliverance to the disenfranchised.

Rhema: What is your problem today? From what injustice do you suffer? Is chaos or confusion suffocating your life? The superabundance of Jesus' spiritual anointing explains his successful ministry. The Spirit qualified him for all his God-given tasks. Therefore, his complete and full endowment enables him to help you in every situation.

THE SPIRIT OF WISDOM AND UNDERSTANDING

The Spirit of the LORD will rest on him—the **Spirit** *of wisdom and of understanding.* –ISAIAH **11:2**

Living in an age of confusion requires the Holy Spirit's help. Turmoil and uncertainty cloud every day. Pills, depression, global warming, and ordered disorder baffle and perplex. We need wisdom and understanding to navigate our personal problems. "By wisdom a house is built, and through understanding it is established" (Prov 24:3). God wants to help us with our complex difficulties.

God's answer to our perplexities is Jesus who has an unlimited supply of the Spirit of wisdom. This is the second attribute of the Spirit on him. As the Messiah, God equips him with extraordinary wisdom. The Spirit gives him heightened executive abilities, allowing him to rule with brilliance. As King of Kings he will not judge by what he sees or hears but by a magnified sense of righteousness and justice. Because he has the Spirit he avoids making wrong decisions.

Rhema: With this skillful ability, Jesus can guide and advise you. What a privilege and blessing to come under his gracious rule and know the way he leads is best. As your guide, he will direct with wisdom through all the hazards of life. He knows the way out of your difficulties and how to resolve impossible circumstances.

Besides wisdom, the Spirit equips Jesus with supernatural understanding. He can comprehend our complex conditions and relationships. This is the third of these seven attributes of God's Spirit given to him. The one who is of the house and lineage of David always exercises understanding. The shoot from Jesse far outshines human insight and challenges the absurdities of our existential confusion. Through the Spirit he has a total grasp of issues so no negative fallout results from his directives. The Spirit gives him understanding in all things.

Rhema: The Spirit enables Jesus to provide superb answers to your most difficult questions. No one comprehends your needs and the deep issues in your life like he does. The Spirit of the Lord rests on him. The wisdom and understanding your circumstances demand are more than met in him. All the intelligence and discernment of the Godhead dwells in him (Col 1:19). Therefore, understand no complexity or confusion exists in your life he cannot resolve.

FEBRUARY 18 | ISAIAH 11:6–12; EPHESIANS 1:15–23

THE SPIRIT OF COUNSEL AND MIGHT

*The Spirit of the LORD will rest on him—the **Spirit** of counsel and of might.* –ISAIAH 11:2

Everyone needs advice. "Plans fail for lack of counsel, but with many advisers they succeed," said the wisest man (Prov 11:22). None is wise enough to avoid making mistakes because one is too embarrassed to seek counsel.

Unlike our need, Jesus asked no one for advice for he always knew what to do. Never was he in need of human consultation. Instead, people came asking him what they should do. The reason he did not consult with others was the Spirit of counsel rested on him. Therefore, his advice was perfect. After all, he was the Wonderful Counselor spoken of in Isaiah 9:6.

Rhema: "The Spirit of counsel" who came upon Jesus is the same Spirit he gives you. The Lord called him, "another counselor"—someone to direct you with life's issues. He is greater than your problems. His inspired insights can help you crack complex cases, deal with problematic people, and take the right course of action. He is a "helper" extraordinaire whose assistance is not limited to your walk with God but extends to practical matters pertaining to home, family, work, or schooling.

"The Spirit of might" is the fifth spiritual attribute the Messiah will possess. It means he will have the strength to implement his will because his power will surpass all others in heaven and earth. That is why the "wolf will lie with the lamb and the leopard will lie down with the goat" (v 6). There will be no uprisings; neither nation nor individual will no longer harm or destroy. His ultimate achievement will be to restore the earth to its pristine state before man fell. All nature will be at peace. The reign of the Messiah will usher in a comprehensive concord, so people will dwell in security. When he removes the curse, the earth will be full of the knowledge of the Lord (v 7).

Rhema: Remember, the Holy Spirit who empowered Jesus makes his power available to you. Our Lord was greater than any problem or foe because the Spirit of might was upon him. Just as he triumphed over demons, the devil and death, so he clothes you with the power of his might.

FEBRUARY 19 | JOHN 17:1–26

THE SPIRIT OF KNOWLEDGE
AND FEAR OF THE LORD

The Spirit of the LORD will rest on him...the **Spirit** *of the knowledge and fear of the LORD.* –ISAIAH 11:1–2

Have you ever wanted an authentic, life-changing encounter with God? To get so close to him you tremble before his divine transcendence? Only in the Spirit is access to the Holy One possible. The Messiah was given that special ability because he was perfectly endowed with the Spirit. He received the "Spirit of the knowledge of the Lord." Consequently, he would know God in the most intimate and comprehensible way imaginable.

No one ever experienced the Father like Jesus. He revealed him and gave us his words. The author of Hebrews says he was "the radiance of God's glory the exact representation of his being" (Heb 1:3). To see, hear, and know the Son is to see, hear, and know the Father.

Rhema: The Son gives you his Spirit so you will have a heightened spiritual apprehension of God. Being able to encounter him is such a marvelous blessing. When you have his Spirit, you can know your heavenly Father and enter an intimate relationship with him. With the Spirit of knowledge, you gain an understanding of him impossible any other way. The veil between flesh and spirit is removed so you can behold his glory (II Cor 3:16–18).

The seventh and final characterization of the Spirit promised the Messiah is "the Spirit of the fear of the Lord." Jesus, the promised Messiah, always had the correct response to his Father. He always recognized God's authority and submitted to it. The Spirit enabled him to obey heaven without hesitation or reservation. His motivation had nothing to do with self-interest but everything to do with the divine agenda. The breath of the Almighty so permeated him he carried out God's will entirely. "My food," he said, "is to do the will of him who sent me and to finish his work" (Jn 4:34).

Rhema: God gives you his Spirit to help you in every area of life but especially in your relationship with him. Follow Christ's example and seek the Spirit who teaches you the fear of the Lord. Then you can say as Jesus did, "I seek not to please myself but him who sent me" (Jn 5:30).

THE SPIRIT OF JUSTICE

*He will be a **spirit** of justice to the one who sits in judgment, a source of strength to those who turn back the battle at the gate.* —ISAIAH 28:6

Driving while intoxicated is both dangerous and illegal. Dangerous because alcohol affects the driver's judgment. Illegal because an impaired motorist is a menace. This chapter opens with a prophetic warning against drunken leaders intoxicated not with wine but pride. How can they "drive" the nation with blurry eyes and distorted judgment? Wealth has made them giddy partygoers unable to see the inequity they created. To steer the country towards justice, they need the Spirit's help.

The ruling classes bowed over in drunken stupor endangered the nation. Instead of putting their trust in the Lord and treating people with fairness, they allowed self-indulgence to distort their judgements. Unless they changed, the prophet warned, an enemy would come and consume them as hastily as one eats a summer fig. Then their prosperity will fade like a trampled flower.

The prophet Isaiah denounced the prevailing cultural conditions. Against their sinful societal structures he cried, "Woe to those who make unjust laws, to those who issue oppressive decrees, to deprive the poor of their rights and withhold justice from the oppressed of my people, making widows their prey and robbing the fatherless" (Isa 10:1–2). Despite these injustices, God promised them a leader with the Spirit of justice who will reshape their moral and social consciousness. He will not only challenge their inequitable rule and culture of death but also create a new society of life. No longer will he allow rulers to bend the law to their own advantage.

The Spirit is indispensable in bringing justice to the poor, oppressed, and marginalized. His power is key to social transformation if the disenfranchised are to be treated with fairness and equality. In a just society everyone is safe, secure, and equal before God. Rights are not based on race, gender, or social standing.

Rhema: Through the Spirit, the Messiah will create just communities (Acts 4:32–35) where everyone is equal despite societal distinctions. Divisive walls will tumble. Injustices healed. Social outcasts welcomed. The exploited liberated. The voiceless heard. The Spirit of justice shapes community life so everyone's conditions improve, everyone is loved, and everyone is treated with dignity.

FEBRUARY 21 | ISAIAH 30:1–32

FORMING AN ALLIANCE
BIRTHED OF THE SPIRIT

"Woe to the obstinate children," declares the LORD, *"to those who carry out plans that are not mine, forming an alliance, but not by my* **Spirit**, *heaping sin upon sin; who go down to Egypt without consulting me; who look for help to Pharaoh's protection, to Egypt's shade for refuge."*
–ISAIAH 30:1

Where do you go for help when the enemy comes in like a flood? Repeatedly, the nation of Judah relied on political alliances with pagan nations. Instead of trusting the Spirit, they relied upon the arm of flesh. Their leaders made associations with ungodly nations to secure a sense of protection. It's a terrible mistake to lean on man instead of the Spirit. God wants us to make partnerships he creates.

The prophet Isaiah warned them to avoid turning to "Do-Nothing" Egypt for help. Any treaty with them for protection will not turn out well because plans without God are doomed to failure and lead to humiliation. It is a huge mistake to go our own way and trust men rather than consult the Lord. Security based on Egypt is worthless; it is like shade that offers little help. Someone said, "The horses of Egypt can never take the place of the chariots of God."

You will be blessed when you make plans directed by the Spirit. Several wonderful blessings are described in this chapter. God will be gracious and arise to show you compassion (v 18). The Lord not only hears and answers your cry (v 19) but he guides, saying, "This is the way, walk in it" (v 21). God promises you a fruitful and productive life (v 23). And victory. You will sing again and celebrate the good things he does for you (v 29). The final blessing of aligning yourself with God is he himself will take care of your adversary (vv 31–32).

Rhema: Rather than a frenzied flight to the world when trouble and threats arise, you should trust in the Lord. He says, "In repentance and rest is your salvation, in quietness and trust is your strength" (v 15). If you want help and protection against your foe, you need to rely upon the Spirit for direction. That will do you far more good than any worldly support. He is your shield, your very great reward (Gen 15:1).

FEBRUARY 22 | ISAIAH 32:1–20

THE SPIRIT TRANSFORMS THE DESERT INTO A FRUITFUL FIELD

*The fortress will be abandoned, the noisy city deserted; citadel and watchtower will become a wasteland forever, the delight of donkeys, a pasture for flocks, till the **Spirit** is poured on us from on high, and the desert becomes a fertile field, and the fertile field seems like a forest.* **–ISAIAH 32:14–15**

Do you ever feel like your life is a wasteland haunted by bad memories? Perhaps you feel abandoned and deserted. If so, God wants to pour out his Spirit upon you and transform your desert into a beautiful garden.

Jerusalem's transformation from a desert to a gorgeous garden is a prophetic picture of what God's Spirit can do for you. A fierce enemy devastated the once happy and prosperous city that now sits in ruins. Instead of choirs and commerce, the city of God is a wilderness for the flocks. Donkeys make their home in the abandoned city. The king's palace silent and deserted sobs with despair and desolation. These wretched conditions persist until the Almighty pours out his Spirit from on high.

God promises to pour out his Spirit to turn the wasted city into a fruitful field. Then the desolate becomes fertile, the barren, fruitful. The fragrance of new blooms fills the air. Birds chirp. Leaves rustle. Grass sashays. Buzzing bees surf from flower to flower. Prosperity and blessing dance on the streets. Safety and security join together in song. This is what God desires to do with you. He wants to transform your abandonment and desertion into a glorious garden of delight.

The outpouring of the Spirit is our hope. Tremendous blessings follow. Justice. Righteousness. Peace. Security. Our lives are like lush fields overflowing with the abundance of God's grace. "The trees are bearing their fruit; the fig tree and the vine yield their riches" (Joel 2:22). Joy and festivities replace mourning and lament. Fear and dread are exchanged for quietness and confidence. Instead of death and destruction, peace and life abound.

Rhema: The fruits of the Spirit's outpouring are glorious. Because he empowers and indwells us, our fortunes are reversed. Our lives are restored to their fullest. What the enemy destroyed he renews. Bountiful blessings abound—"Vats will overflow with new wine and oil" (Joel 2:24). Enter the garden and let him walk and talk with you.

FEBRUARY 23 | ISAIAH 34:1–17

THE SPIRIT AND THE END OF ALL THINGS

*Look in the scroll of the LORD and read: None of these will be missing, not one will lack her mate. For it is his mouth that has given the order, and his **Spirit** will gather them together. He allots their portions; his hand distributes them by measure.* –ISAIAH **34:16**

This awesome prophecy refers to the end. The Spirit is involved in the ultimate climax of history and creation. He is in absolute control of both. Everything God foretold in his word in relation to creation's grand conclusion culminates with the Third Person of the Trinity. Even to the tiniest detail—everything in "the scroll of the Lord" will come to pass (Mt 5:18). God's amazing Spirit brings everything in his word to its completion.

The Spirit's role is significant in the final day. Few realize he is moving history along in accordance with God's word. From creation to consummation, he nudges nature and the nations toward their final destiny. The Lord is angry with the nations because they have not taken him into consideration. His wrath even extends to the heavens: "All the stars in the sky will be dissolved and the heavens rolled up like a scroll; all the starry host will fall" (v 4). The invincible Spirit governs creation, judgment, and the end.

History concludes with a huge apocalyptic slaughter. The Lord singles out Edom as an example of his judgment and vengeance. It applies, however, to every nation that holds him in contempt and hates his people. She is reduced to a state of perpetual desolation, the haunt of desert animals, such as owls and ravens (v 11). The Spirit controls these creatures (nature, if you like). In the end he will herd them together as in a Hitchcock movie for the great end-time supper. "His Spirit will gather them together." Anyone wanting confirmation need look no further than the Scriptures. Eschatological events will unfold as written—even Jesus foretold the gathering of the birds in the final struggle against God (Mt 24:28, 35).

Rhema: The Holy Spirit not only works in our lives and the church but also in creation and history. How fitting that he who was so active in the beginning has an essential role in the end. He rounds up everything for the final rendezvous with God.

NO ONE CAN ADVISE THE SPIRIT

*Who can fathom the **Spirit** of the LORD, or instruct the LORD as his counselor?* —ISAIAH **40:13**

We may be tempted to "instruct" the Lord when experiencing unresolved issues. Perhaps, we have an urge to give him a piece of our mind. We may think we have better ways or solutions. To imagine we know more than the one who created this universe is ridiculous. God is not looking for our advice but seeking to direct us by his Spirit.

Nobody can fathom the Spirit of the Lord or act as his counselor. We cannot direct him or tell him what to do. Who is wise enough to advise him? Everything he has ever done he has accomplished without our input. At creation, not a single person existed to provide him with the blueprints, building codes, or measurements for his magnificent work. Indeed, he was the master of all facts, scientific constants, and necessary ratios to make everything work harmoniously. No one was present when he brooded over the waters to transform their chaotic condition into a life-supporting cosmos.

When he created the universe, there was no sentient being qualified to tell him how. God's Spirit does not consult the best and brightest on earth when he has a task to do. He is sufficient in himself. The brightest minds any nation might offer him are unworthy of comparison—they are like a drop in a bucket, mere dust on the scales.

The all-knowing Spirit knows the deep things of God and is the giver of wisdom and knowledge. He is the teacher of all truth, the illuminator of our minds, and the revealer of divine mysteries. His infinite knowledge far exceeds ours. No one has anything whatever to offer him by way of knowledge, insight, or advice but he has much to offer us.

Rhema: How heartening to have God's wise Spirit available to help. When you are facing difficult and impossible tasks, he can advise you. Since he is creation's architect he can well solve your most difficult challenges. No problem ever overwhelms him; he is never without a superb solution. If you ask, God will breathe wisdom and understanding into your soul. The Spirit is more than able to counsel and direct you in all your affairs.

GOD BLESSES HIS SERVANTS WITH THE SPIRIT

Here is my servant, whom I uphold, my chosen one in whom I delight; I will put my Spirit on him, and he will bring justice to the nations.
—ISAIAH 42:1

God is always searching for individuals who happily subject themselves to do his will. In particular, he chose Adam and the nation of Israel for this task. Adam he placed in the garden to carry out his desires and purposes on earth (Gen 2:5). Israel was his chosen servant to bring his blessing to the Gentiles (41:8–10). Instead Adam disobeyed, and Israel was blind and deaf to what he wanted (vv 18–22). Therefore, the Lord continued to look for someone else to work for him out of love and obedience.

Isaiah prophesies of a servant who honors, loves, and obeys God as he deserves. Upon that person the Lord puts his Spirit. This anointing sharpens his understanding of God's will and creates a willingness to do it. Consequently, he succeeds in doing what no one else has ever done. He perfectly obeys God and brings justice to the nations. As an intimate friend and ambassador, he works to fix humanity's problems. His divine assignment is to transform society and bring the social order into harmony with his will. Hence, the Spirit anoints him to set a broken world in order and establish it as God intended.

Who is this amazing servant? He is none other than Jesus (Mt 12:18–21). By application, everyone who receives the Spirit and serves the Lord will experience the same honor and benefits. The first benefit is God upholds his servants so they will succeed and not fail. Second, he chooses them and showers them with his favor and affection. Third, the Lord delights in them by making them the apple of his eye. Last, the Almighty blesses his laborers with his Spirit and empowers them to do his will.

Rhema: The Lord delights in us when we yield ourselves to him as obedient servants. Whereupon, he puts his Spirit on us to help us labor for him. By giving us his Spirit, we join in his mission and receive the grace and spiritual abilities to bless others as Jesus did. Ultimately he empowers us, so we can serve him and finish his assignment.

FEBRUARY 26 | ISAIAH 44:1–28

GOD POURS OUT HIS SPIRIT
ON OUR OFFSPRING

*For I will pour water on the thirsty land, and streams on the dry ground; I will pour out my **Spirit** on your offspring, and my blessing on your descendants.* —ISAIAH 44:3

Going through a dry and thirsty spell? God promises to pour water on the longing land and streams on the gasping ground. Pouring out his Spirit is like a deluge that can turn a desert into a well-watered grove. Dying and withering twigs are metamorphosed into blossoming orchards. Similarly he promises torrents of living water to flow over our dry and barren souls and restore the vigor of our youth.

In relaying the prophesy, Isaiah introduces a new Scriptural promise. God vows to pour out his Spirit upon our offspring and bless our descendants. This prophecy looks to a future time of spiritual renewal. A season is coming when he will refresh his people with rivers of water and they will enjoy renewal and new growth. This outpouring causes their bareness to end; they will flourish as "trees by flowing streams" (v 4).

Heathen hire blacksmiths to pour molten metal into molds to produce dumb idols (vv 9–20) which do not hear or speak. God, in contrast, pours his Spirit into individuals so they can hear him and proclaim his revelation. The living Spirit animates his people. Consequently, they spring to life with newfound energy to do his will. No longer do they dishonor him by rebellious deeds. Because of their spiritual transformation they will proudly say, "I belong to the Lord" (v 5). Formerly they were a laughingstock among the nations but now they are a glorious people. In this way, God's people become a community of living witnesses enlivened by the Spirit.

Rhema: This wonderful pledge applies to you. God commits to rain his Spirit upon your dry and thirsty soul. If your life is arid and unfruitful, he assures you his Spirit will restore your youthful vitality. Picture green fields luxuriating beside babbling brooks. Streams of fresh, clear water flooding the dried-up recesses of your heart. This prophecy extends to your offspring, for he promises to release his Spirit upon your children. The blessing is for you, your children, and those who are far off. Let him guide you to the place where his river flows (Gen 2:10).

FEBRUARY 27 | ISAIAH 48:1–22

GOD, PROPHETS, AND THE SPIRIT

Come near me and listen to this: "From the first announcement I have not spoken in secret; at the time it happens, I am there." And now the Sovereign LORD has sent me, endowed with his Spirit. –ISAIAH 48:16

Can we have a supernatural, inspired, and trustworthy word from God? Absolutely. Because a close relationship existed among God, his prophets, and the Spirit, we can have an unshakeable confidence in it. Throughout the OT, Yahweh spoke absolute truth through his prophets. Since they acted under the Spirit's influence, they never corrupted or contaminated his word, nor did they add to or take away from it. As a result they delivered the pure, unadulterated, trustworthy word of God.

When Isaiah brought a divine message, he wanted the people to realize God was speaking through him by the Spirit. He was sent invested with a power from on high, so he could speak for the Lord and tell the nation Babylon will fall (vv 14–15). When he spoke for the Almighty, he was not voicing his own thoughts but conveying a living, divine message.

This verse contains two important truths: God speaks so we can understand him and what he says comes to pass. He says, "I have not spoken in secret." The Almighty is not so secretive, mystical, or ambiguous no one understands him, otherwise he could not communicate. Adam, Eve, Noah, Abraham, Moses, and the prophets understood God's message spoken to them. Isaiah not only comprehends the Lord's message, but he is sent "endowed with his Spirit."

Secondly, what God says happens. The Sovereign Lord declares, "At the time it happens, I am there." Every fulfilled prophecy is amazing proof his predictions are true. He adds, "I foretold the former things long ago, my mouth announced them and I made them known; then suddenly I acted, and they came to pass" (v 3). We do well to listen to his prophets because they delivered God's life-giving message which always comes to pass.

Rhema: God who is the first and the last (v 12), the Creator (v. 13) speaks the truth. Wise is the person who puts their trust in his word. After all, he is the living God and although he declares (through his prophets) the most outlandish things, they will take place. Guaranteed!

THE GLORY OF ISRAEL AND THE SPIRIT

*"As for me, this is my covenant with them," says the LORD. "My **Spirit**, who is on you, will not depart from you, and my words that I have put in your mouth will always be on your lips, on the lips of your children and on the lips of their descendants—from this time on and forever," says the LORD. –ISAIAH 59:21*

Have you ever wondered what is in store for the nation of Israel? Abraham's descendants have endured terrible atrocities and yet they continue. Enslaved by ancient Egypt. Exiled by the Babylonians. Destroyed by the Romans. Practically exterminated in the Holocaust. Do things ever improve? Isaiah offers a glorious end time vision involving their restoration by the Spirit.

God promises his Spirit will not depart from them and his word will always remain in their mouth. The Lord comes to Zion with a wonderful end-time restoration. His covenant with them ensures the fulfillment of his promises and the continual possession of the Spirit. His Spirit enables everyone to know God's revelation, and he preserves it from generation to generation. In addition, he is going to make God real among them and make his word come alive. No longer is his word external, for the Spirit internalizes it to create intimacy with the Almighty. He promises them his Spirit forever. Their end-time spiritual transformation is so perfect Israel becomes the envy of the world.

The apostle Paul cites verses 20–21 as he explains the "mystery" when "all Israel will be saved" (Rom 11:25–27). At the end of the church age when "the full number of the Gentiles has come in," God saves Israel. At that time, he will turn "godlessness away from Jacob." His Holy Spirit comes upon them so they can finally fulfill their mission in the world. So glorious is her restoration nations will come for her light and blessing.

Rhema: Just as the Spirit brings to pass this great spiritual renewal and national transformation, so also will he renew you. By his Spirit God will enable you to fulfill his plan and reach your full spiritual potential. Like Israel, he will restore, renew, and transform you. In fact, when his Spirit comes upon you in power his word will be on your lips.

MARCH 1 | ISAIAH 61:1–11; LUKE 4:14–21

THE SPIRIT ANOINTS THE MESSIAH

The Spirit of the Sovereign Lord is on me, because the Lord has anointed me to proclaim good news to the poor. He has sent me to bind up the brokenhearted, to proclaim freedom for the captives and release from darkness for the prisoners, to proclaim the year of the Lord's favor and the day of vengeance of our God, to comfort all who mourn, and provide for those who grieve in Zion—to bestow on them a crown of beauty instead of ashes, the oil of joy instead of mourning, and a garment of praise instead of a spirit of despair. —Isaiah 61:1–3

This is one of the most beautiful passages in the Bible. It foretells the powerful effects the Messiah accomplishes through the Spirit. Jesus applied this prophecy to himself (Lk 4:18–19. Therefore, we can expect wonderful things to happen because of his anointing. The possessor of the Spirit received an amazing ability to shower our lives with one blessing after another.

Rhema: His primary task is to proclaim the good news to the poor. If you are afflicted, defenseless, and oppressed, he gives you something to sing about. When bowled over by circumstances and beat up by life, he offers comfort and joy. Has tragedy or misfortune shattered your life? He will gladden your heart. What is his joyful word of hope and encouragement for you? He has come in the Spirit's power to bind up your broken heart.

What a time of joyous celebration! The Spirit makes his message and ministry brighten your countenance. A new era of unprecedented fortune and blessing is yours—he sets you free and releases you from dark prisons. You are in the year of the Lord's favor, the age of Jubilee! He makes his promises personal to you. When you are troubled and afflicted, he encourages. He comes with a vengeance to dispense with your oppressors. The Lord comforts you when grieving and throws his arms around you when attacked by the enemy. If your dreams go up in smoke, he gives you a crown of beauty. If you are crying, he wipes away the tears and pours upon you the oil of joy. So put on the garment of praise and let go of the spirit of despair.

MARCH 2 | ISAIAH 63:7–10; PSALM 78:11–22

GRIEVING THE HOLY SPIRIT

*Yet they rebelled and grieved his **Holy Spirit**. So he turned and became their enemy and he himself fought against them.* —ISAIAH 63:10

Grieving the Holy Spirit is a grave mistake. Things do not go well when people wound him, and if they are hostile towards him, he turns against them. Instead of wooing, he revokes his blessing. For the Holy Spirit to turn against an individual, city, or nation only to fight against them is dreadful.

Some believe how they treat the Spirit does not matter. Since he is invisible they think he can be overlooked. They feel justified in minimizing his influence in their lives. However, to defy and distress any member of the Godhead is a monstrous mistake. For instance, the nation of Israel discovered this to their ruin when they rebelled and grieved the Holy Spirit. After he stopped working among them and withdrew his defensive shield, they lost their spiritual covering and became prey to the enemy. To their horror and disbelief, their adversary not only dragged them out of the Promised Land and hauled them into exile but also destroyed both Jerusalem and the temple.

Just so no one misunderstands, God is good. The prophet recounts his faithfulness even in the face of Israel's sinful past. Though their rebellion pained the Spirit, the Lord showed them kindness. With amazing displays of love, he showered them with goodness and compassion (v 7). He took part in their troubles and saved them by the angel of his presence. With a fatherlike tenderness he lifted them up and carried them (v 9) over the rough patches.

Despite showering them with goodness and love, Israel still defied and disobeyed the Spirit. When his loving ways were met with hostility, he was upset and offended. He was their friend and helper. How could they mistreat him with bitterness and disdain? In time, the Holy Spirit reversed course and acted against them. Consequently, four centuries passed before God sent them another prophet empowered by the Spirit.

Rhema: The most important thing we can do is welcome the Holy Spirit into our lives by embracing his full operation and activity. Do not grieve him (Eph 4:30). Instead, let us love, honor, and respect him. Seek him! Cry, "Come Holy Spirit you are welcome in me."

MARCH 3 | ISAIAH 63:11–13; 64:1–5

YEARNING FOR THE HOLY SPIRIT
OF YESTERDAY

Then his people recalled the days of old, the days of Moses and his people—where is he who brought them through the sea, with the shepherd of his flock? Where is he who set his **Holy Spirit** *among them?*
—ISAIAH 63:11

Have you ever longed for the good old days when the Holy Spirit seemed to move more than today? When little appears to be happening in God's Kingdom, our hearts yearn for the former days. As a natural tendency, we tend to look back with nostalgia to more glorious times. This is the situation in Isaiah's time. "Then his people recalled the days of old, the days of Moses and his people."

When they remembered the time of Moses and the Exodus, they thought of God's Holy Spirit. Back then they experienced wonderful things because God had set his Spirit among them. Moses accomplished amazing miracles by "the glorious arm of power" as God assigned or attached his very presence, the Spirit, to them. The Spirit made God's presence recognizable. No miracle, however, was so great as their deliverance from Egyptian slavery. He was in the wind that divided the waters. Throughout their wilderness wanderings, they experienced the Spirit's goodness and mighty deeds. Those miraculous manifestations of his power are hard to duplicate. The spiritual condition in Isaiah's day caused them to yearn for God's intervention once again.

The prophet prays, "Oh, that you would rend the heavens and come down, that the mountains would tremble before you!" (64:1). They wanted a new display of God's power just as in Moses' time. If the Spirit returned and moved once more, they could experience a new Exodus and be restored to their former glory.

Rhema: God answered Isaiah's prayer. The heavens were rent, and the Holy Spirit was poured out at Christ's baptism (Mk 1:19). If your heart yearns for a fresh move of God, realize a new dispensation of the Spirit has commenced. How can you take part in it? You can ask God to lead you out of bondage and oppression. To part the seas. To keep you from stumbling. You are living in the age of the Spirit. The heavens have been rent. The Spirit has been poured out. Let the mountains tremble! God has made his Spirit available to you.

THE SPIRIT GIVES REST

*Like a horse in open country, they did not stumble; like cattle that go down to the plain, they were given rest by the **Spirit** of the LORD. This is how you guided your people to make for yourself a glorious name.*
–ISAIAH 63:13–14

God provided his people a deep, satisfying, and restorative rest. To give them rest was the work and ministry of the Holy Spirit. The prophet reminded Israel of the time when the Spirit of the Lord gave the people respite. He freed them from their troubles and turmoil, their wanderings and wars, and gave them peace so they could settle down.

The Israelites found the Spirit's rest a wonderful blessing. Their hard life of slavery in Egypt was behind them and the wilderness wanderings were over. Now they could cross the Jordan and enjoy their inheritance. They occupied cities they did not build and harvested crops they did not plant. The Spirit guided them to a land flowing with milk and honey.

Isaiah pictures them as a herd led down the mountain to a watered, fertile valley. There they found restoration, a chance to catch their breath. The Spirit made them lie down in luxuriant pastures and satisfied their souls. He brought them beside quiet waters and quenched their thirst.

Rest offers many benefits. People who can quiet themselves live longer and healthier lives. They are more creative and successful. To show its importance, even God ceased from his labors on the seventh day. When Moses was weary of carrying the people and burdened down with a load of concerns, God promised him rest. The Lord said, "My Presence will go with you, and I will give you rest" (Ex 33:14). God relieved him of his stress and helped him find courage and strength to go on.

Rhema: If you find yourself going crazy trying to keep all the balls in the air, think about a breather. Are you battle-fatigued? A weary wanderer? Remember, the Spirit of the Lord led his people into a blessed reprieve. God does not want you running around feeling as if the wheels are coming off your wagon. Why not invite the Spirit to come now and replenish you? He can recharge, renew, restore, replenish, and regenerate you. Let him guide you into that rest!

MARCH 5 | EZEKIEL 1:1–18

THE SPIRIT HELPS US IN CHAOS

*Each one went straight ahead. Wherever the **spirit** would go, they would go, without turning as they went.* **–EZEKIEL 1:12**

D rastic times demand drastic answers. How could God allow the destruction of Jerusalem? Also, a fierce enemy had taken Ezekiel and his countrymen into captivity. Like an earthquake rattling the foundations, many wondered how the Exile was permitted to happen. Consequently, they needed a revelation of God's glorious sovereignty. They needed to know in their deepest chaos God was still in control. To this end, the prophet was given an unusual apocalyptic vision.

The vision begins amidst a portending storm when the heavens open to reveal God sitting on his throne. The hand of the Lord comes upon Ezekiel to enable him to understand their confused condition, so he can explain it to his compatriots. The lesson is simple: the one seated on the throne can handle the chaos on earth. This tragic judgment was no accident because God is the ruler controlling earth's events.

In this unusual revelation, Ezekiel sees God enthroned between four marvelous angelic beings. They are cherubim also called living creatures (see 10:14–15) who enact God's will throughout his entire creation. Each one has the face of a man, an ox, a lion, and an eagle to symbolize their authority over the created order. The four are his agents who move straight ahead as directed by the Spirit. God's throne is like a warrior's chariot that moves at lightning speed.

To know God was governing the universe and moving the affairs of men forward should give them reassurance. Many had difficulty understanding God's severe judgment, even though it served his purpose. Heaven does not pause; it waits for no man. Everything proceeds according to the divine will. God exercised just as much authority over the Holy City as he does over creation. The Sovereign Lord is in full control. He is the all-present, all-powerful, all-knowing, and all-wise God.

Rhema: If you are rattled to the foundations like Ezekiel, realize God is governing. Any trauma or chaos in your life must be set alongside his sovereignty. He will use it for good. The Spirit moves heaven's throne so the Lord is always on top of every situation. When you are experiencing pandemonium, understand in the final analysis he is in charge.

MARCH 6 | EZEKIEL 1:19–28; REVELATION 4:6–11

THE SPIRIT MOVES HEAVEN AND EARTH

*When the living creatures moved, the wheels beside them moved; and when the living creatures rose from the ground, the wheels also rose. Wherever the **spirit** would go, they would go, and the wheels would rise along with them, because the **spirit** of the living creatures was in the wheels.*
–EZEKIEL 1:19–20

Are you feeling bewildered today? Are you troubled by a darkening future? Are storm clouds gathering? Dealing with the imponderable? Driven away from home by unfortunate circumstances? Ezekiel and his fellow exiles were asking themselves these and similar questions. Things could not get worse. They were in exile, uprooted from home, and their place of worship destroyed. Desperate for hope and meaning, they needed reassurance God can move heaven and earth.

An enormous storm was breaking out of the north. No fear: God was in it. Ezekiel lived during a troublesome time when circumstances appeared out of control. It looked as if Babylon called the shots and evil was in charge. God wanted to remind his people he is the one controlling things on earth, not earthly kings and kingdoms. His majestic sapphire throne rose above the thunderous clouds. In the vision, his chariot throne touched the earth with its wheels. The rims were full of eyes to show he had perfect insight into their situation.

Ezekiel saw the secret and ultimate reason why things happen on earth. The Spirit determines everything. The cherubim bearing God's throne act on earth in response to "wherever the Spirit would go." Throughout Scripture, cherubim or the living creatures are associated with God's presence. Both in the tabernacle and temple, the Lord manifested himself between these golden angels (Ex 25:17–22; II Chr 5:7). By this language, Isaiah is saying God is present even though the enemy removed the golden cherubim from the temple. Contrary to their belief, God dwells with them even in "unclean" Babylon.

Rhema: Whatever you are facing no matter the circumstances, he is with you and in charge. In fact, through his Spirit he is still in control of everything in heaven and on earth. Know this today, the awesome radiance of God's glory covers you. Furthermore, the sovereign Lord knows and understands your predicament. His Spirit is the all-powerful driving force that moves heaven and earth on your behalf.

MARCH 7 | EZEKIEL 2:1–10

THE SPIRIT STRENGTHENS US
FOR DIFFICULT ASSIGNMENTS

He said to me, "Son of man, stand up on your feet and I will speak to you." As he spoke, the Spirit came into me and raised me to my feet, and I heard him speaking to me. –Ezekiel 2:1–2

Standing on your own two feet is difficult. To be self-sufficient and never ask for help is near impossible. Although independence might seem a worthwhile goal, it is hard to achieve. Many things, for instance, can knock us down. People can make our life miserable. Besides, God can give us a grueling assignment as he did Ezekiel, a task so tough it is humanly impossible.

After Ezekiel experienced God's glory, he fell facedown. The one sitting on the throne gave him the title, Son of man, which occurs over ninety times in the book. Why? It indicates his weakness, humility, and frailty. Like us, Ezekiel cannot stand in his own strength and is incapable of doing God's will without his help. To obey and serve the Lord requires the power of the Spirit. Empowered from on high he rises up to stand on his feet. Total dependence on God's power distinguished him as "the prophet of the Spirit."

The prophet had a remarkable relationship with the Holy Spirit throughout his ministry. After God's Spirit entered him, he was supernaturally strengthened. Without divine enablement, he could not stand up to leaders and carry out his difficult job. After all, God was sending him to a rebellious and obstinate nation aptly described as briers and thorns. God said, "You live among scorpions" (v 6). In the end, however, "they will know that a prophet has been among them" (v 5). The Spirit would validate his ministry and remove any doubt he was a man sent from God.

Rhema: The Spirit can also help you should God give you a tough job. Like Ezekiel, your work may occur in challenging conditions. People will not always be accepting especially when you must give them an unpopular message. Their faces may frighten you. Times of suffering, doing without, and enduring misunderstanding can stretch you. What people say might sting like a scorpion. Through it all, however, the Holy Spirit will raise you up in his power, so you can stand tall for God.

MARCH 8 | EZEKIEL 3:1–15

THE SPIRIT OFFERS A
NEW PERSPECTIVE

*Then the **Spirit** lifted me up, and I heard behind me a loud rumbling sound as the glory of the LORD rose from the place where it was standing. It was the sound of the wings of the living creatures brushing against each other and the sound of the wheels beside them, a loud rumbling sound.*
–Ezekiel 3:12–13

Imagine having a divine perspective and being able to hear what God hears and see what God sees. That ability can give us a superior, far-reaching heavenly vantage point. With a celestial view, we will see life's events in a new way not bound by terrestrial limitations but open to endless possibilities.

The Spirit gave Ezekiel a heavenly perspective. Considering things from the Spirit's viewpoint recurs often in Ezekiel's life, permitting him to see what others do not. While they only saw trees, he saw the forest. Many obstructions limit our human observation, but the Spirit's is boundless. The view from the top of the mountain far exceeds the one from the valley. When the Spirit lifted Ezekiel up into the presence of God, he gained a valuable new vista.

At times life becomes so complicated the way forward is obscure and the dangers unknown. This happened to the nation of Israel. They had lost their way. Not only had they thrown away their compass, they tore up the chart. Consequently, many missteps made their life miserable. Now they faced their greatest national crisis since entering the Promised Land but could not see their way out of their tangled mess.

The Spirit came upon Ezekiel and raised him up so he could give the nation spiritual guidance. What he saw and heard in God's presence he shared with them. He beheld the glory of the Lord rising from its resting place because massive changes were soon to occur. With a divine outlook, he gazed beyond their struggles, mistakes, and failures to God's solution.

Rhema: When you experience a life-changing event, you need heaven's perspective. Events such as personal breakdowns, midlife crises, family tragedies, or major setbacks may mess you up. Lest you lose your way, like Israel, God's Spirit can provide a much-needed perspective. He can lift you up above the perplexities below and help you live in the powerful reality of the eternal.

GRIPPED BY THE SPIRIT

*The **Spirit** then lifted me up and took me away, and I went in bitterness and in the anger of my spirit, with the strong hand of the LORD on me. I came to the exiles who lived at Tel Aviv near the Kebar River. And there, where they were living, I sat among them for seven days—deeply distressed.* –**Ezekiel 3:14–15**

Have you ever struggled with God's will? Did you ever push back against it? Ezekiel was like Jonah who wanted to run from the heavy task laid on him. Instead, the Spirit lifted him up, tore him away from his comforts, and deposited him among the dejected exiles. Gripped by "the strong hand of the Lord" meant the Spirit got a hold of him.

What God asks us to do is not always easy. Ezekiel's difficult job required he tell the nation extremely disturbing news: the temple's destruction and their deportation happened in accordance with God's will. He did not need to be a rocket scientist to realize he would face stiff opposition. At least Ezekiel was honest when he says, "I went in bitterness and in the anger of my spirit." He is boiling mad. When the Spirit plunked him before the exiles living in Tel Aviv, he sat in their midst for seven days in complete silence. He was blown away.

Amazing things happened, however, when the Holy Spirit wrapped his hands around Ezekiel. The reluctant and reticent prophet was transformed into a willing and dynamic spokesperson for God. When God's Spirit seized him, he became powerful in the hands of the Lord. He was gripped and raised up to do God's will. Like Stephen, "They could not stand up against his wisdom or the Spirit by whom he spoke" (Acts 6:10 NIV 1984). This phenomenal experience explains how Ezekiel was able to accomplish everything asked of him.

Rhema: When the Spirit grips us, we can expect profound changes in our lives. The weak become strong, the wayward straight, the shy bold. The Holy Spirit made Ezekiel a match for the people. They were hard; he became harder. They were stubborn; he became more stubborn. Gripped by the Spirit, he could outlast, outwait, and outwit them. Imagine what his grip can do to you!

MARCH 10 | EZEKIEL 3:22–4:17

A FRESH TOUCH OF THE SPIRIT

Then the Spirit came into me and raised me to my feet. He spoke to me and said: "Go, shut yourself inside your house." –EZEKIEL 3:24

There are many reasons for needing a fresh touch of the Spirit. We can be spiritually stuck or drained from working in overdrive. Physical, emotional, and spiritual exhaustion can sap our strength. Then devotion flags. Intimacy wanes. Monotony dulls. God never intended for us to have only one spiritual encounter no matter how wonderful. Instead, he desires to take us from one blessing to another in an ongoing, continuous relationship with us.

Ezekiel needed spiritual revitalization. He was exhausted. So much had happened to him in such a short time after he agreed to minister among the exiles. His life changed forever. To equip him for the unusual task, God made him "as unyielding and hardened as they are." He had to ingest "words of lament and mourning and woe" (2:10). Even the thought of his new assignment precipitated an emotional meltdown. Remember, he sat among the exiles for seven days completely overwhelmed. All these things necessitated an additional visitation of the Spirit.

The prophet needed a brand-new touch of the Spirit for another reason: his next assignment. Although his draining ministry was unique, it was also complicated and contradictory. God commissioned him to speak to the exiles by becoming speechless. He must act out God's messages and endure seven years of pantomime, his dumbness being a sign to them God was done speaking. By observing Ezekiel, moreover, they could see what was happening in Jerusalem. He must be bound with ropes and confined to his house to depict the siege of Jerusalem. For as long as the enemy attacked the city, Ezekiel had to act out these harsh realities. No wonder he needed a fresh anointing.

Rhema: Do you find yourself stressed? Drained by difficult demands? Like Ezekiel you too can experience a renaissance of the Spirit by inviting him to rejuvenate you. This was the second time the Spirit entered Ezekiel and raised him to his feet. One more time the hand of the Lord came upon him (v 22) and he experienced "the glory of the Lord" as before by the Kebar River (v 23). If you need renewing, ask him for a fresh touch of the Spirit.

MARCH 11 | EZEKIEL 8:1–18

A FRESH VISION OF THE SPIRIT

*He stretched out what looked like a hand and took me by the hair of my head. The **Spirit** lifted me up between earth and heaven and in visions of God he took me to Jerusalem, to the entrance of the north gate of the inner court, where the idol that provokes to jealousy stood. And there before me was the glory of the God of Israel, as in the vision I had seen in the plain. –Ezekiel 8:3–4*

Do you need a fresh vision for your life? A new perspective to help you understand God's ways? Do you desire to view your situation from above rather than from below? Perhaps, like Ezekiel, you feel stuck, bound by four walls and limited by meager resources. If you answered yes to these questions, then you know how he felt.

The prophet needed a new vision. Who wouldn't? He had spent hundreds of days confined to his house staring at four walls. Daily he lay on his side speechless subsisting on a starvation diet. Jewish leaders sat before him waiting anxiously for a fresh word from the Lord. But he was stuck in repetitious monotony.

Fourteen months after his first vision, he saw the glory of God again. Lifted by the hair he is taken in spiritual ecstasy to Jerusalem and deposited at the entrance to the northern door of the temple. While suspended between heaven and earth, the Spirit gave him a visionary tour of the terrible things occurring in the place of worship.

This lengthy revelation comprising four chapters (8–11) began a new phase in Ezekiel's ministry to the exiles. As a prophet, he saw their terrible behavior so troubling to God. They thought God did not see their secret idolatry (v 12). To them it did not matter what they did, but it mattered to God who observed their wicked ways. With fresh prophetic insight, Ezekiel gained a new assessment of the events taking place. It put everything in perspective. Now he could help these leaders understand the reasons for their exile.

Rhema: Visions are spiritual X-rays to assist us make sense of what is transpiring in our lives. Without them, people perish (Prov 29:18). The Spirit can lift us above our limited earthly view and bless us with fresh vision for our lives.

MARCH 12 | EZEKIEL 11:1–4

THE SPIRIT REVEALS ROOT CAUSES
OF OUR PROBLEMS

Then the **Spirit** *lifted me up and brought me to the gate of the house of the LORD that faces east. There at the entrance of the gate were twenty-five men, and I saw among them Jaazaniah son of Azzur and Pelatiah son of Benaiah, leaders of the people. The LORD said to me, "Son of man, these are the men who are plotting evil and giving wicked advice in this city."* –EZEKIEL 11:1–2

Thank God for a prophet like Ezekiel who sees what others miss. With X-ray vison, his eyes penetrated walls to dig out the root cause of the nation's troubles. While others sat in darkness, he detected the spiritual perverseness being promulgated by Judah's political leadership. The Spirit turned on a great searchlight to illuminate the secrets of darkness responsible for ruining the land.

Once again the Spirit lifted Ezekiel up to conclude his vision begun in chapter 8:3. He was transported from the temple's inner court to its outer entrance. Because he was present "in the Spirit," he observed several leaders giving people bad advice contrary to God's word. These shapers of public opinion blatantly deceived the citizens of Jerusalem by offering them false promises. They lied about the city's safety and security while "plotting evil and giving wicked advice."

Past prophets had warned of Jerusalem's imminent destruction, but these promoters of iniquity claimed the opposite. Ezekiel heard them misleading the people, saying, "There is no impending danger. Just go on as you are. Jerusalem is secure. The walled city is an iron pot that will protect you from the enemy's fire and fury." The prophet nevertheless challenges these false claims. Without the Spirit, they were blind to their looming obliteration. Ultimately, the underlying reason for Jerusalem's destruction was traced back to one thing: the glory of the Lord had departed from the temple. In contrast to the leaders, Ezekiel saw behind the scenes.

Rhema: Similarly, the Spirit can reveal to us the underlying root of our problems. This is true for individuals seeking counselling or for churches and institutions facing difficulties. God's Spirit is an archaeologist who can dig down to the basic reasons. We can pray, "Holy Spirit will you show us what is at the bottom of this problem." Then wait for the answer.

MARCH 13 | EZEKIEL 11:5–21

THE SPIRIT KNOWS WHAT WE ARE THINKING

*Then the **Spirit** of the LORD came on me, and he told me to say: "This is what the LORD says: That is what you are saying, you leaders in Israel, but I know what is going through your mind." –EZEKIEL 11:5*

Knowing for sure what another thinks is impossible (I Cor 2:11). For instance, someone may say one thing but mean something else even though their body language might offer insights into what is going on in their mind. But only God truly knows what they are thinking. He knows their every thought, feeling, imagination, memory, and idea.

God instructs Ezekiel to tell the leaders he knows what is going through their minds. He sees their wicked schemes and rebellious counsel. The Bible says the Lord searches our hearts and understands our plans and intentions. To hide from his scrutiny is impossible; his understanding is unsearchable.

The Spirit falls afresh on the prophet and gives him a word of knowledge. Especially troubling was telling the people about their judgment (v 13). God says to him, "Therefore, prophesy against them; prophesy, son of man" (v 4).

To fulfill his assignment, the Spirit of the Lord must continue empowering him. Not only was God aware of what was on the leaders' minds, but he also knew what was on Ezekiel's. If he were anything like us, he needed to be kept on track. Our minds tend to drift, lose focus, and jump to conclusions. The Spirit knows our thoughts and feelings. This revelation is a double-edged sword. If we are plotting evil, it is frightening to realize God knows all our thoughts. On the other hand, if we love him and seek to do his will, his knowledge comforts us.

Rhema: May the Spirit give you understanding of the Lord's knowledge of you. "You have searched me, Lord, and you know me. You know when I sit and when I rise; you perceive my thoughts from afar. You discern my going out and my lying down; you are familiar with all my ways. Before a word is on my tongue you, Lord, know it completely. You hem me in behind and before, and you lay your hand upon me. Such knowledge is too wonderful for me, too lofty for me to attain" (Ps 139:1–6).

PROPHETIC MINISTRY BY THE SPIRIT

The glory of the LORD *went up from within the city and stopped above the mountain east of it. The* **Spirit** *lifted me up and brought me to the exiles in Babylonia in the vision given by the* **Spirit** *of God. Then the vision I had seen went up from me, and I told the exiles everything the* LORD *had shown me.* **–EZEKIEL 11:23–25**

One of the most amazing things about God is he speaks to us. He delights in revealing the future as well as reminding us of the past. He converses with us by various means. In fact, he is always speaking.

OT prophets were faithful to relay whatever God said to them. They were his anointed messengers with a living word from him. The Lord spoke to them by dreams, visions, impressions, and by an audible voice. In Ezekiel's case, the Spirit was so prevalent in his life he showed him visions of God. The Spirit fell upon him, lifted him up, and transported him. He also suspended him between heaven and earth for spiritual insight. In the power of the Spirit he voiced "everything the Lord had shown" him. By exerting divine control over him, God ensured Ezekiel would without error or distortion convey to his people what he saw and heard.

In the vision's final scene, Ezekiel witnessed the dramatic departure of the glory of the Lord. The Shekinah leaves (see Day 298 for definition) Jerusalem and stops on the Mount of Olives, outside the city. God wanted the exiles to know no hope remained for the city because his presence had left. The leaders, however, failed to understand the things that belonged to their peace. The prophet, on the other hand, pictured for them the cosmic realities behind the city's fall. Because their sinful abominations caused God to withdraw his presence first from the Holy of Holies and finally the city itself, they were doomed.

When the vision ended, the Spirit returned the prophet to the exiles in Babylon. God told him to share everything he had seen and heard. Like a TV camera, he recorded the events hundreds of miles away in Jerusalem and broadcasted them to those sitting before him.

Rhema: God speaks and as he spoke to Ezekiel by the Spirit, so he wants to speak to you.

MARCH 15 | EZEKIEL 36:22–38

A COMPLETE TRANSFORMATION
BY THE SPIRIT

I will give you a new heart and put a new spirit in you; I will remove from you your heart of stone and give you a heart of flesh. And I will put my **Spirit** *in you and move you to follow my decrees and be careful to keep my laws.* –EZEKIEL 36:26–27

To have a change of heart is difficult especially if it is as hard and unresponsive as stone. The natural inclination of the heart tends to rebellion. That is why God supplies a new heart that is warm and responsive to him. A radical change of human nature leads to a radical change of behavior.

God promised Israel a complete spiritual transformation, one in which they would have a new disposition and become more sensitive to the ways of the Lord. He vows to give them a new heart and put a new spirit in them. Then their thoughts, feelings, and moral center will yearn to follow his directives and please him in every way. When he puts his Spirit in them, they will receive the inner power and motivation to follow the Lord.

These marvelous promises refer to a future time when God will save his people from their sins (v 29 c.f. Mt 1:21). For his name's sake, God sprinkles them with clean water and removes all their impurities. To replace their old rebellious granite hearts requires the power of the Holy Spirit. No program, philosophy, or ethic have the power to change human nature. Only God can perform a spiritual transplant. The amazing thing is his Spirit who withdrew from the temple will return once again to dwell among his people, but in a far different way.

Rhema: What wonderful promises! For anyone who has been living in exile suffering the bitter disgrace of life apart from God, rejoice. Your future is bright. Welcome the Holy Spirit. Welcome his fresh activity in your life. No longer need you be weary of the desolation, defilement, and disgrace of wayward ways. The Spirit provides the dynamic to turn your heart's desires to God. He transforms from the inside out and fits you for God's service and presence. God replaces any unresponsiveness with his Spirit, so you can walk in his ways and love him with all your heart.

THE LIFE-GIVING SPIRIT AND
THE VALLEY OF DRY BONES

*The hand of the LORD was on me, and he brought me out by the **Spirit** of the LORD and set me in the middle of a valley; it was full of bones. He led me back and forth among them, and I saw a great many bones on the floor of the valley, bones that were very dry. He asked me, "Son of man, can these bones live?"* –EZEKIEL 37:1–3

The Spirit of the Lord takes Ezekiel to a valley full of dry bones and asks, "Can these bones live?" They represent the scattered nation of Israel that had no king, no temple, and no land. The nation is dead. A long time has passed as the bones "were very dry." The enemy destroyed everything and dispersed God's people among the nations. These bones represent a terrible national tragedy. They are a graveyard! Is it possible for them to rise again?

Do you feel dry and your situation hopeless? Has your parched condition persisted forever? This is how the exiles were feeling (v 11). Some problems are too big for us to solve. But with God all things are possible. Amazing things happen when God's word and his life-giving Spirit unite in our valley of broken dreams.

God said to Ezekiel, "Prophesy to these bones and say to them, 'Dry bones, hear the word of the Lord.'" The Lord declared, "I will make breath [Heb *ruah*] enter you, and you will come to life" (vv 5–6). As soon as Ezekiel prophesied, something astounding happened. "There was a noise, a rattling sound, and the bones came together, bone to bone" (v 7). His prophetic words created a new reality and transformed their pathetic condition as sinews and flesh covered these skeletons.

Then the Lord told Ezekiel to prophesy to the "breath" and command it to come from the four corners of the earth. "Come, O breath, and breathe into these slain, that they may live." As he did that, breath entered them and they came to life. The nation sprang to life and rose up as a great army.

Rhema: This is prophetic picture of the Spirit's power to make you alive in response to God's rhema word. Therefore, pray, "Come Holy Spirit and breathe into me so I may live!"

MARCH 17 | EZEKIEL 37:11–28

THE SPIRIT AND THE REBIRTH
OF THE NATION OF ISRAEL

*"I will put my **Spirit** in you and you will live, and I will settle you in your own land. Then you will know that I the LORD have spoken, and I have done it," declares the LORD.* **–EZEKIEL 37:14**

Sometimes believing God is hard. He promises things so outlandish they seem impossible. Have you ever found yourself in that situation? Some of his promises sound improbable. Take these exiles, for instance. They were saying, "Our bones are dried up and our hope is gone; we are cut off" (v 11). In their minds, the possibility of the rebirth of their nation was pure fantasy. To gather them out of the nations and bring them back to their land was not feasible.

For some Israelites, their condition appears so hopeless they cannot even pray. God addresses their incredulity head on. He says, "My people, I am going to open your graves and bring you up from them; I will bring you back to the land of Israel" (v 12). God promises to restore the nation regardless of their desperate condition. It matters not they have no ruler and no place to call their own. Even if they think of themselves as a bunch of dry bones scattered over the valley of death, they will rise again. To repeat: even if they consider themselves dead, the Spirit will enter them and they will live. Israel's restoration is possible because of the amazing role of the Holy Spirit.

Rhema: What God promised Israel he can do for you. If you feel dead and disconnected, invite his Spirit to breathe divine life into you. Are you open to the possibility of a new life? God says, "I will put my Spirit in you and you will live." Are you living in a boneyard of dried-up expectations? God desires to breathe his Spirit into you. Do you find yourself in a valley of bleached bones? No matter, you will rise again. Let him connect you to a living community. He wants to revive and restore you. Through his Spirit he desires to give you a new beginning. This is God's word for you: "You will live." There is no limit to your future in God. With him, all things are possible (Mk 9:23).

THE SPIRIT AND THE FACE OF GOD

*I will no longer hide my face from them, for I will pour out my **Spirit** on the people of Israel, declares the Sovereign* LORD. *–*EZEKIEL **39:29**

The Holy Spirit is God's agent responsible for the full, glorious restoration of Israel. He will no longer hide his face from them. Instead, he pours out his Spirit. The spiritual deluge upon Israel in the last days is a sign of the restoration of her fortunes. The Spirit's dynamic ministry ushers in her magnificent destiny. Reborn, restored, and made righteous. Israel's splendid future is brought about in the end times by the power of the Holy Spirit.

The Holy Spirit will seize the nation and enable her finally to achieve God's purposes. She will become the head instead of the tail. In her, all the nations of the earth will be blessed. The Lord even destroys all her enemies (38–39) and restores her kingdom (Acts 1:6). The nation's fullness (Rom 11:15–16) coincides with earth's greatest blessings. The Spirit marshals in a new era for Israel and the world.

A direct connection exists between the "face of God" and the promise of the Spirit. God says, "I will no longer hide my face from them." He then adds, "I will pour out my Spirit on the people of Israel." The reference to the face of God (mentioned three times in these verses) is a special term. It goes back to the blessing of Aaron and his sons with which they blessed people. They were to say, "The Lord bless you and keep you; the Lord make his face shine on you and be gracious to you; the Lord turn his face toward you and give you peace" (Num 6:22–26).

Rhema: God associates the ultimate fulfillment of Aaron's blessing with the outpouring of the Spirit. When you believe on Jesus Christ God makes his face shine on you. He gives you his Spirit, so you can always behold his face and enjoy his grace and peace. Having his Spirit means God will never hide his face from you. To have his face shine on you means you are a recipient of God's greatest blessing. Your unparalleled and ultimate state of blessedness is to live face to face with him now and forever (II Cor 3:18).

MARCH 19 | EZEKIEL 43:1–12

THE SPIRIT REVEALS GOD'S GLORY

*The vision I saw was like the vision I had seen when he came to destroy the city and like the visions I had seen by the Kebar River, and I fell face-down. The glory of the LORD entered the temple through the gate facing east. Then the **Spirit** lifted me up and brought me into the inner court, and the glory of the LORD filled the temple.* –EZEKIEL **43:5**

The Holy Spirit wants to show us the glory of the Lord. He glories in revealing the manifested presence of God. To make us aware of God's invisible but awesome presence is his role. The brighter, clearer, and stronger we see his glory the better. He lifts us so we can realize God's dwelling among us.

In a vision, the Holy Spirit brings Ezekiel into the inner court of the new temple where he sees it filled with the glory of the Lord. The reappearance of his glorious presence is the climax of the book. Nothing is more important than this. The return of the manifested presence of God completes his dealing with Israel. It happens after Israel reoccupies the Promised Land and their Messiah is ruling the nations of the world. With every enemy defeated, God sets up his throne in the new temple. The book closes with these words: "THE LORD IS THERE" (48:35).

God has always wanted to dwell among us, but sin prevented it. Ezekiel speaks of a day when the great tragedy is reversed and defilement is undone. To be in his presence means we are face to face with the Almighty, cleansed and made holy. No cloud hides him, no barriers push us away. Just pure presence of God. He says, "This is the place of my throne and the place for the soles of my feet. This is where I will live among the Israelites forever" (v 7).

Rhema: In Christ, we become a holy temple, a "dwelling in which God lives by his Spirit" (Eph 2:21–22). The Holy Spirit brings us into the presence of God. As he did with Ezekiel, he takes us by the hand into the inner court (Heb 12:22–24). There, in the Spirit, away from the problems and disappointments of life we can "see the glory of God filling the place."

MARCH 20 | DANIEL 4:1–8

THE MAN WHO HAD THE
SPIRIT OF THE GODS

*When the magicians, enchanters, astrologers and diviners came, I told them
the dream, but they could not interpret it for me. Finally, Daniel came
into my presence and I told him the dream. (He is called Belteshazzar,
after the name of my god, and the* **spirit** *of the holy gods is in him.)*
–Daniel 4:7–8

To live up to the light we have received is important. Nebuchadnezzar,
the ancient master of Babylon, didn't. Many disturbing incidents
in the account indicate not all is well with his soul. He slights Daniel,
for instance, and renames him Belteshazzar after his heathen god.
Moreover, he lumps the Holy Spirit who gave Daniel remarkable spiritual gifts with the other pagan gods. Make no mistake, these insults
were deliberate.

Nebuchadnezzar knew Daniel's unusual prophetic gifts came from
God (2:47). Many years earlier he had elevated Daniel and "placed him
in charge of all [his] wise men" (2:48). Daniel was promoted because
he interpreted one of his dreams when no one else could. It seems
odd when the king has another troubling dream he does not first call
in Daniel. Instead, he summons his magicians, enchanters, astrologers,
and diviners to interpret the dream, but none were able. Although the
emperor had seen the one true God at work, he remained uncommit-
ted to him.

God wants us to live authentic lives. King Nebuchadnezzar failed
to act according to his spiritual understanding. That is when he received
this mysterious dream about a large tree. A messenger from heaven
ordered it cut down. Daniel interpreted the dream and said the king
was the tree visible to the ends of the earth. He would become insane
for seven years and be reduced to a mere stump. Twelve months later
the king began behaving like an animal and had to give up his empire.
His madness would end only when he admitted, "The Most High is
sovereign over the kingdoms of men" (v 25). His mental breakdown
continued until he "could acknowledge that Heaven rules" (v 26).

*Rhema: What was the outcome of Nebuchadnezzar's strange spiritual jour-
ney? He had a remarkable change of heart and testified to God's miraculous
signs and wonders (vv 2–3). In his last recorded words, he praised, exalted, and
glorified the king of heaven (v 37).*

MARCH 21 | DANIEL 4:9–17

UNDERSTANDING MYSTERIES BY THE SPIRIT

*I said, "Belteshazzar, chief of the magicians, I know that the **spirit** of the holy gods is in you, and no mystery is too difficult for you. Here is my dream; interpret it for me." –DANIEL 4:9*

For many people, their lives are a mystery. Shrouded in enigma they hunt for a satisfactory explanation. They wish they could resolve the inexplicable stuff and discover a reason or root cause for it. Daniel believed if he asked God to reveal a mystery he would.

So did Nebuchadnezzar. He believed no mystery was too difficult for Daniel to unravel. The Spirit gave him an extraordinary ability to understand the baffling and inexplicable. The king knew he had "the spirit of the holy gods" in him. This odd descriptor was his "politically correct" way of referring to God's prophet without offending all his magicians, astrologers, enchanters, and diviners. Unlike Daniel, they did not have the Holy Spirit. The king was confident in him because he did.

The Spirit gave this exiled Hebrew divine power to understand secrets so baffling and enigmatic only God can make them understandable. He foretold amazing future events, such as the great mystery of the Times of the Gentiles (Lk 21:24). He attributed this prophetic gift to the Lord "who reveals deep and hidden things" (2:22). The cryptic, obscure, and secret things of darkness were brought to light through the Spirit. Daniel said to the king, "There is a God in heaven who reveals mysteries."

Dreams and visions are the language of the Holy Spirit. Nebuchadnezzar's baffling dream required a spiritual gift to make it understandable. The king realized that no mysterious dream was too difficult for the prophet to interpret. On another occasion when the king had a weird dream, Daniel asked God for the explanation. When he answered, Daniel praised and thanked him. He extolled, "You have made known to me what we asked of you, you have made known to us the dream of the king" (2:23).

Rhema: Daniel had a heightened sense of the gift of prophecy that few have. Still, let's not limit God. We can ask the Spirit to help us when we encounter mysteries in our lives. He knows the answer to every puzzle and if he knows it, he can reveal it (I Cor 13:2).

THE SPIRIT IMPARTS A WORD OF KNOWLEDGE

There is a man in your kingdom who has the **spirit** *of the holy gods in him. In the time of your father he was found to have insight and intelligence and wisdom like that of the gods.* –DANIEL 5:11

No one in the OT had a greater spiritual ability to "interpret dreams, explain riddles and solve difficult problems" (v 12) than Daniel. When fingers of a man's hand emerged and wrote on the palace wall, "Mene, Mene, Tekel, Parsin" King Belshazzar shook in his boots. His face turned pale and his legs gave way. Immediately he called for his wise men to decipher these strange words. None could. As a last resort he called Daniel because he had God's Spirit in him.

Like his father before him, Belshazzar failed to acknowledge the one true God. Instead, he mocked him. In an act of defiance and irreverence, he brought out and drank from the sacred gold and silver goblets taken from the temple in Jerusalem. When he toasted his false gods, the mysterious writing appeared.

Daniel reprimanded the king before interpreting the handwriting. He said, "You did not honor the God who holds in his hand your life and all your ways" (v 23). In addition, he charged, "Instead of walking in humility before the Almighty you set yourself up against heaven." Then the Spirit imparted to Daniel a "word of knowledge" so he can solve the mystery and explain the words. Numbered. Weighed. Divided. He told him, "God has numbered your days, weighed you on the balances and found you wanting. Your magnificent kingdom will be divided and given to the Medes and Persians." That night Belshazzar was slain, and Darius the Mede seized the empire.

Besides this stunning miracle, the Spirit enabled Daniel to unravel mysteries, solve puzzles, and foretell future events. No enchanter, astrologer, or diviner came close to matching his spiritual acumen. Consequently, the ancient world's most powerful rulers requested he interpret their dreams. In addition, the Spirit gave him visions of the end times and empowered him to figure out the length of the captivity (9:2).

Rhema: Developing your spiritual gifts does not depend solely on God. In Daniel's case, he purposed to maximize them by watching his diet, praying three times a day, and studying God's word.

MARCH 23 | JOEL 2:23–28

GOD WILL POUR OUT HIS SPIRIT

And afterward, I will pour out my Spirit on all people. Your sons and daughters will prophesy, your old men will dream dreams, your young men will see visions. –JOEL 2:28

Joel is best known for declaring an end time outpouring of the Spirit. The prophet announces the Spirit will usher in an era of spiritual renewal, a time of great blessing and fruitfulness. The people of God can be glad and rejoice because the Lord will send them abundant showers of blessing (v 23) and heal their land.

What makes this prophecy so remarkable is its inclusive spectrum and the Spirit's enlarged role. In the last days, all believers will experience his amazing indwelling. This promise contrasts with the OT provision where God gave his personal anointing to special people to help them do his work. Joseph received a spiritual ability to interpret dreams. Bezalel was filled with the Spirit to make the tabernacle esthetically appealing. Moses, Joshua, various judges, the prophets, and the kings received God's Spirit to help them perform extraordinary tasks. Now Joel prophesies God will pour out his Spirit upon everyone who calls on the name of the Lord (v 32).

This astounding prophecy follows a terrible locust plague that destroyed everything. God promised to repay his people for all the years the locust devoured their crops. What the enemy destroyed, God pledges to restore. His answer to the enemy's destructive work is the Holy Spirit's blessing.

The promise is also for us. The Lord declares he will pour out his Spirit in such copious amounts that even our offspring will take part. Men and women, young and old will become prophetic. Old men will dream dreams and young men will see visions. Our sons and daughters will prophesy. When the enemy beats us up, God deluges us with his Spirit. When we feel dry in our soul, God promises streams of blessing from on high. Joel describes this end-time wonder in agricultural terms. Our fruit trees bear their fruit, our threshing floors spill over with grain, and the vats overflow with new wine and oil.

Rhema: What a select group of elites enjoyed in the past is now available for you. By believing in Christ, you are a beneficiary of the Spirit's abundant blessings.

MARCH 24 | JOEL 2:28–32; ACTS 2:14–21

THE SPIRIT BREAKS DOWN BARRIERS

*Even on my servants, both men and women, I will pour out my **Spirit** in those days.* –JOEL 2:29

Societal and cultural divisions dissolve when God pours out his Spirit. He counteracts fallen humanity's practice of partitioning people into factious classes. Age, sex, race, wealth, clothing, education, color of skin, and even neighborhoods subjugate and divide. People suffer discrimination when cruel conventions exclude them. Moreover, social hierarchies and structures prevent unity and foster inequality, grief, and despair. Joel laments such societal carnage and sobs, "Surely the people's joy is withered away" (1:12). In contrast, God has him announce an answer. God will pour out his Spirit on all people to overcome man-made customs and replace them with a new equality.

Joel foretells a mighty spiritual outpouring that results in the formation of a new prophetic society. In that day, the constant and continuous flow from heaven will overpower pride and prejudice, privilege and prerogatives. Power structures established to pillage and impoverish are exploded. When people live in the power of the Spirit, they love and bless instead of hate and envy.

This prophecy anticipates charismatic communities that do not restrict communication by gender. God says, "Your sons and your daughters will prophesy." In Spirit-filled movements, women gain prominence and have a voice rather than be sidelined by oppressive structures. In the OT few women prophesied but in the age of the Spirit, there are no second-class citizens. Everyone has a voice, regardless of gender.

Age discrimination, moreover, is eradicated by the Spirit. His mighty outpouring includes both youths and elderly. Old men will dream dreams and young men will see visions. Age is no impediment to receiving divine revelation. All ages take part in the new prophetic movement. Another barrier to be surmounted is the socioeconomic. God says, "Even on my servants…I will pour out my Spirit in those days." The Spirit transforms class obstructions and caste systems to create a new egalitarianism.

Rhema: Following the day of Pentecost, the new Spirit-filled believers gave evidence of this prophecy. The prophetic proclamations of mere fishermen made rulers tremble. Women became apostles, leaders, deaconesses, and pastors. All material goods were held in common. The poor were blessed, the sick healed, the captives freed. The release of the floodgates of heaven began to transform society. It continues today.

MARCH 25 | MICAH 3:1–12

THE SPIRIT GIVES THE
TRUE PROPHET AUTHORITY

But as for me, I am filled with power, with the Spirit of the Lord, and with justice and might, to declare to Jacob his transgression, to Israel his sin. –MICAH 3:8

One of the most unpopular tasks God ever assigns anyone is to confront those in authority. What makes it difficult is when leaders abuse their power and harm people. Micah's message to the rulers of his day (vv 1, 9) concerns their moral depravity. "Her leaders judge for a bribe, her priests teach for a price, and her prophets tell fortunes for money" (v 11). For him to challenge the entire power structure of Jerusalem demands power from above.

The heads of the house of Jacob abused their position and were guilty of prostituting justice. People who needed impartiality were rendered powerless and suffered injustice. Not only were these power brokers covetous, but they also inverted morality, calling the good evil and the evil good. They extorted the defenseless and built their cities through dishonesty and treachery. "To declare to Jacob his transgression, to Israel his sin" was a difficult mission. That is why the Spirit filled Micah with power.

His thorniest task, however, was to oppose religious leaders (vv 5–7) who no longer received revelations from God. They were men pleasers afraid to speak the truth, but instead only told people what they wanted to hear. Their message tickled the ears. Everything they said was misleading. To fear man more than God was their horrible mistake. They had no word from the Lord because he hid his face from them. Without revelation they became powerless false prophets.

Micah filled with the Spirit's power differentiates himself from these false prophets. In contrast to them, he does not speak his own words but only those God puts in his mouth. What a difference! Revelation. Light. Truth. Might. Justice. When he speaks he has a sure word from the Lord, a word filled with divine energy. He knows not only the responsibility but also the thrill and pleasure that comes from declaring God's word.

Rhema: Micah is an example of how to have a credible ministry. People of the Spirit know when someone has a word from God. They have divine authority because they hear from heaven, receive revelation, and have prophetic insight.

STRENGTHENED BY THE SPIRIT'S PRESENCE

"But now be strong, Zerubbabel," declares the Lord. "Be strong, Joshua son of Jozadak, the high priest. Be strong, all you people of the land," declares the Lord, "and work. For I am with you," declares the Lord Almighty. "This is what I covenanted with you when you came out of Egypt. And my Spirit remains among you. Do not fear."
—HAGGAI 2:4–5

Have you ever given up or been derailed by discouragement? Ever wondered how to get going when you are as low as a snake's belly? God's people faced this situation when they returned from the exile. Surrounded by enemies, hindered by scant resources, and dejected by unrealized expectations they gave up.

So many problems confronted them they stopped working on the temple. Their initial enthusiasm and zeal evaporated as fear and discouragement seeped into their souls. When they began rebuilding God's house, shouts of joy gave way to tears of sorrow. As soon as they laid the foundation, the workers realized it paled in comparison to Solomon's. Their hands drooped and they wept, immobilized by despair.

God sent Haggai the prophet to hearten them. Zerubbabel, the governor, Joshua, the high priest, and the people needed cheer. The Lord's prophet came to them with a specific word of encouragement designed to steel their resolve and get them back to work. Like a coach calling his team together after their first setback, Haggai inspired them to resume building.

Although daunted by the task and discouraged by circumstances, the power of his prophetic word was effective. He said to the despairing workers, "Be strong and work." Three times he exhorted them to be tough and carry on. Just as God was with their forefathers when they came out of Egypt, he is with them now. He is Immanuel! The returning exiles needed reassurance. "Suck it up; you will make it. I am with you," declares the Lord. Furthermore, they had the Holy Spirit. God said, "My Spirit remains among you."

Rhema: Here's God's word of encouragement for you. The Spirit's power and presence will give you stability and establish you and your work. He is not lying down on the job, but he is present to prop you up and support you. He is immovable, indestructible, and unchangeable—as he was with the Israelites, so he is with you.

MARCH 27 | ZECHARIAH 4:1–14

NOT BY MIGHT NOR BY POWER
BUT BY MY SPIRIT

So he said to me, "This is the word of the LORD to Zerubbabel: 'Not by might nor by power, but by my Spirit,' says the LORD Almighty. "What are you, mighty mountain? Before Zerubbabel you will become level ground." –ZECHARIAH 4:6–7

Is a huge mountain facing you square in the face? Are there insurmountable challenges strewn across your path? Do enemies surround you hoping you will fail? Do you lack energy to carry on? Well, there is good news.

Zerubbabel was facing a massive mountain when he agreed to rebuild the temple. Impossible obstacles stared him in the face: apathy, enemies, and limited resources. Overwhelmed by the assignment, he wondered how he could tackle it. Perhaps he said to himself, *We do not have an army to defend us. We do not have enough labor for the job. Nor do we have sufficient resources to complete the task.* Faced with such challenges, he was distraught and discouraged.

Although he lacked the means, God gave him a powerful prophetic word. The Lord sent the prophet, Zechariah, to hearten him with a vision of a golden lampstand with a bowl on top. Beside the lampstand were two olive trees connecting the bowl with pipes. Therefore, a continuous and abundant supply of olive oil poured into it. This was a prophetic picture of the Spirit supplying everything they needed.

Zechariah promised the governor success. Not by more human help but by an abundant supply of the Spirit. "It is not by might nor by power, but by my Spirit," says the Lord. The Spirit's power will help him accomplish this huge and formidable undertaking, not their abilities, strengths, or brilliance.

Rhema: When you are facing a mountain, you can latch onto this wonderful promise by faith. You also may struggle with your limitations and weaknesses and wonder how you will make it. Like Zerubbabel, your true source of strength is not found in human resources but in the divine. The continuous and abundant supply of God's Spirit can help you succeed when your strength is inadequate. The mountains you think are so insurmountable become level ground. So, do not focus on the mountain. Instead, challenge it by allowing God to work through you by the Spirit's power.

MARCH 28 | ZECHARIAH 6:1–8

THE SPIRIT INFLUENCES
MAJOR WORLD EVENTS

*Then he called to me, "Look, those going toward the north country have given my **Spirit** rest in the land of the north." –*ZECHARIAH **6:8**

Has your spirit ever been troubled? Have you felt agitated by events? Well, the Holy Spirit is a person who likewise experiences these emotions. Whenever people or incidents distress him, he acts. He works, contends, and stirs until a favorable outcome occurs. Just as we experience inner peace and rest when we resolve disturbing matters, so also does the Spirit.

What troubled the Spirit was the Babylonian treatment of Israel, one of the most desperate situations in human history. The way they defiled Jerusalem, destroyed the temple, and deported the people disturbed him. Think of how the "north country" treated Daniel! What kind of people throw their captives to a den of lions or into a fiery furnace for not bowing to the king? Their cruel mistreatment of God's people so agitated the Spirit he does not rest until these perpetrators are removed and pay for their brutality.

This story takes us backstage to see world events from a divine perspective. The prophet, Zechariah, sees "four spirits of heaven, going out from standing in the presence of the Lord" (v 5). Their activity reveals God's control of nations. These high-level spiritual beings (angels) patrol the whole earth doing his will. Likened to war horses pulling royal chariots, they influence and intervene in major happenings in the world. The four spirits ensure justice among the nations. Angelic chariots of war are on their way to respond to whatever troubles God's Spirit.

In fact, these angels helped the Persians inflict punishment and destroy the north country (Babylon). The victorious Persians, in contrast, treated God's people well. They released these captives and allowed them to return to their land. With generous financial and military aid, they helped them resettle. Even the treasures and articles of the temple were returned. It was miraculous. God's Spirit was responsible for these favorable events. Now he can rest.

Rhema: We need to realize God directs world events not only through emperors but more importantly through his angels and the Holy Spirit. When nations do things pleasing to the Spirit, things go well for them. If they disturb and agitate him, he will not rest until justice prevails.

MARCH 29 | ZECHARIAH 7:1–14

THE PERILS OF IGNORING OF THE SPIRIT

But they refused to pay attention; stubbornly they turned their backs and covered their ears. They made their hearts as hard as flint and would not listen to the law or to the words that the Lord Almighty had sent by his **Spirit** *through the earlier prophets. So the Lord Almighty was very angry.* –ZECHARIAH 7:11–12

Failure to listen to God's Spirit comes with a huge price. Refusing to heed his voice led to unnecessary trouble and woe for his people. They rejected his message through the law and prophets. He spoke to them while they prospered and enjoyed peace (v 7), but paying him no attention now will have dire consequences not unlike the exile from which they returned. God was furious with their obstinate refusal to open their ears to his Spirit.

The OT prophets were God's agents empowered by the Spirit to declare his words. "In the past God spoke to our forefathers through the prophets at many times and in various ways" (Heb 1:1). His revelation came in bits and pieces, in dreams and visions, in signs and symbols. Marvelous messages of life, promises of future blessing, reminders of mighty deeds, and dire warnings came from the Lord Almighty through his Spirit-anointed spokespersons.

God in his great mercy continued to speak even though they rejected his words. Through the prophet Zechariah, God said they refused to pay him attention. They were rude. Even though God was speaking, there was no way they were coming under his authority. Like an ox, they refused the yoke. Instead of listening, they stuck their fingers in their ears and made their hearts as hard as flint.

At what cost did they reject the Spirit? Seventy years of captivity is the clearest answer. Now every year on the anniversary of Jerusalem's fall they fasted to mourn their loss. Should they continue this exilic practice (v 3)? If they had listened to him, they would have avoided this tragedy altogether. Their cities and homes would still be standing. Prosperity and peace would have continued. Instead of heeding the Spirit, they experienced the fury of God's wrath and lost everything.

Rhema: The lesson is unmistakable. Listening to the Spirit leads to life, prosperity, and blessing. Refusal leads to destruction and desolation (v 14).

MARCH 30 | ZECHARIAH 12:10–14; JOHN 19:28–37

THE SPIRIT OF GRACE AND SUPPLICATION

*And I will pour out on the house of David and the inhabitants of Jerusalem a **spirit** of grace and supplication. They will look on me, the one they have pierced, and they will mourn for him as one mourns for an only child, and grieve bitterly for him as one grieves for a firstborn son.*

–ZECHARIAH 12:10

At the end of the age, a mighty outpouring of the Holy Spirit causes Israel to repent and turn to God. The Spirit (NIV footnote) of grace and supplication falls upon them. Never has such a spiritual transformation of this magnitude occurred. Recipients will seek the Lord and call upon him. National blindness gives way to recognizing the Messiah's true identity. Shock at this discovery causes remorse to fill their hearts as they realize they pierced him (Jn 19:34). With spiritual eyes opened, they understand whom they crucified. "They will look on me," God says, "the one they have pierced."

The outpouring of the Spirit produces epic remorse and repentance. Only then do they accept their tragic rejection of God. The one they pierced is the Lord "who stretches out the heavens, who lays the foundation of the earth" (v 1). How could they be so blind to kill their Creator? Sorrowful remorse intensifies as if one is grieving for the death of an only child. This climatic deluge of the Spirit is the only power that overcomes millennia of obdurate hardness. The Spirit will induce nationwide mourning and lead them to cry out to God. From the least to the greatest, every clan and family will seek God with their whole hearts. In one day, a nation is saved! (Rom 11:25–26).

This is the last OT reference to the Holy Spirit. Like other prophets, Zechariah forecasts the Spirit's massive outpouring in the last days and connects it with Israel's glorious restoration. A mighty spiritual deluge will rain upon the nation. How fitting to see the Spirit's vital role from creation (v 1, c.f. Gen 1:2) to consummation.

Rhema: As with Israel, no heart is too hard for the Holy Spirit to melt and turn to God. In fact, none of us would ever seek God or enjoy his favor without the Spirit of grace and supplication.

MARCH 31 | MATTHEW 1:18–25

WITH CHILD THROUGH
THE HOLY SPIRIT

*This is how the birth of Jesus Christ came about. His mother Mary was pledged to be married to Joseph, but before they came together, she was found to be with child through the **Holy Spirit** –MATTHEW 1:18*

The first mention of "the Holy Spirit" in the NT is associated with Christ's birth. As in the OT, so the NT begins with the Spirit's creative work. Christ's birth, initiated and facilitated by the Spirit, is the beginning or "genesis" of something new in creation. Indeed, his birth is the beginning of a new creation! In fact, an entirely different genus of man enters human history with his birth. Therefore, God's amazing story of creation and redemption takes a huge step forward when Jesus was conceived by the Spirit. His birth is an event so significant it will affect the entire creation.

How exciting to realize God is doing something unique? The birth of Jesus Christ is like no other. According to his human lineage he is the offspring of Abraham and David (v 1). According to the Spirit, however, his origins are of God. His mother Mary became pregnant through a miracle. Before she and Joseph consummated their marriage, "she was found to be with child through the Holy Spirit."

This is awesome! Without the Holy Spirit, the man Jesus would not exist. It is true the Son of God is eternal and has always existed, yet he would never have taken on human flesh and been born of a woman without the direct involvement of the Spirit. The Spirit unites for eternity in one person the human and divine natures of Christ.

Rhema: This close connection between Jesus and the Holy Spirit will continue through his life. Not a day, not a moment will he live or minister without the Spirit. He is the "Christ" mentioned four times in the first eighteen verses (vv 1, 16–18), and 535 times in the NT. What does this mean? Jesus is the long awaited promised Messiah, the one who exists by the Spirit. We call him "Immanuel," that is, "God with us" (v 23) because he was conceived by the Spirit. In exalting Christ, we must be careful we do not overlook the fact that the origin and significance of his amazing life begins with the Spirit.

APRIL 1 | MATTHEW 1:18–25

BEGOTTEN OF THE SPIRIT

But after he had considered this, an angel of the Lord appeared to him in a dream and said, "Joseph son of David, do not be afraid to take Mary home as your wife, because what is conceived in her is from the **Holy Spirit**.*"* –MATTHEW 1:20

He wanted out of his marriage because his wife was pregnant and he was not the father. Joseph thought he had made the biggest mistake in his life when Mary told him she was with child. If he followed through on his thoughts, he would make an even greater error. In his "dark night of the soul," he contemplated ending their relationship with as little disruption as possible. With no word from the Lord, Joseph almost tripped and missed God's best for his life. Just then, the angel of the Lord appeared to him in a dream and gave him divine directions.

In mercy, God spoke to Joseph informing him of Mary's innocence. The heavenly messenger revealed she had not committed adultery, so he should take her home as his wife. Then the angel added, "What was conceived in her was from the Holy Spirit." The word used in the genealogy for "begetting" occurs here. Her pregnancy results from the Spirit—the Spirit "fathered" or begat Jesus. The one who will "save his people from their sins" has a human mother but a divine father.

Who fathered Jesus Christ matters. Thirty-eight times in the genealogical record, Matthew tells us who fathered (begat) whom. Starting with Abraham who "was the father of Isaac," Matthew proceeds to the end of the family tree. His pattern changes, however, when he declares that Jesus was born of Mary and not Joseph (v 17). The author wants to make sure his readers understand Jesus had no human father in the biological sense.

Rhema: Jesus, born of a woman, but conceived by the Holy Spirit is one of the most amazing revelations in the Bible. He is fully man and fully God. Being born of a woman means he can represent us and stand before God in our place. Fathered by the Spirit ensures he is sinless and qualified to save us from our sins (v 21). Therefore, Jesus is a "man of the Spirit" who did not inherit Adam's fallen nature.

APRIL 2 | MATTHEW 3:1–12

BAPTIZED WITH THE HOLY SPIRIT
AND FIRE

I baptize you with water for repentance. But after me comes one who is more powerful than I, whose sandals I am not worthy to carry. He will baptize you with the **Holy Spirit** *and fire.* –MATTHEW 3:11

This was the first time in four hundred years anyone saw or heard a real prophet. The divine silence ended; something new had burst onto the scene with the arrival of John the Baptist.

John stunned the crowds when he told them someone more important and powerful than he was coming. The Baptist said, "I baptize you with water but he will baptize you with the Holy Spirit and fire." John was a mere voice in the wilderness (v 3), but the one coming after him would display fiery power and change lives. When people repented, he baptized them in water. His successor, however, would baptize in the Holy Spirit. John felt he was not worthy to carry his sandals. Imagine someone so mighty in God he could immerse people in the Holy Spirit.

The word *baptize* describes this new Spirit experience. It means to drench, immerse, plunge, or submerge. John submerged people in water; his successor will immerse them in the Holy Spirit. The prophet was announcing the greatest release of the Spirit the world has ever seen. He baptizes them when they changed their lives. The coming one will do something far more important: he will baptize them with the Spirit's power and set them ablaze for God.

Rhema: We must never minimize the importance of the Holy Spirit in relation to the gospel. From the outset, the gospel message includes the great experience of being baptized in the Spirit. It is inseparable from the good news. The first thing John the Baptist said about Jesus defining his coming concerns the baptism in the Holy Spirit. The new era of the Spirit inaugurated by Jesus is linked to the "kingdom of heaven" (v 2). Prophets such as Ezekiel and Joel foretold of a day when God would pour out his Spirit upon people. No one in the OT ever experienced it because the baptism in the Spirit belongs to the end-times kingdom of God. Like fire, the promised deluge of the Spirit will transform and purify our lives and usher us into God's abiding presence.

THE SPIRIT DESCENDS LIKE A DOVE

*As soon as Jesus was baptized, he went up out of the water. At that moment heaven was opened, and he saw the **Spirit** of God descending like a dove and alighting on him.* **–MATTHEW 3:16**

Why did the Holy Spirit descend on Jesus like a dove? The dove is an emblem of purity, gentleness, and inoffensiveness. Its voice is soft and sweet, its shape comely. The dove is beautiful—its wings "are sheathed with silver, its feathers with shining gold" (Ps 68:13). The poor offered it upon God's altar. When Jesus sent out his disciples, he told them to be "as innocent as doves" (10:16).

The Spirit descended upon Jesus as a dove to show we never need to be afraid of him. If the Spirit came in the form of an eagle, it might terrify us and signify we are its prey. A dove is not like a cocky crow but inoffensive. It coos and woos. In gentleness and meekness, the Spirit of Christ settles upon us as on the wings of a dove. The Holy Spirit is not going to harm us in any way even though many fear him. When he descends upon us, it will be as if the wings of an angel touch us. When we are needy and feel weak and oppressed, Jesus will come to us with his dovelike Spirit.

Since the time of Noah and the flood, the dove has been a symbol of God's peace. When the gentle bird returned to the ark with an olive branch in its beak, Noah knew that God's judgment was past. The descent of the Holy Spirit as a dove upon Jesus presents a clear message: in Jesus, we have peace with God—heaven is open. Jesus offers peace to those beaten up by the storms of life, for all who find themselves at odds with God.

Rhema: Jesus says to you, "My Spirit is like a dove. So, I will not hurt or harm you. I will speak soft soothing words to you. If you are weak and heavy-laden, I will give you rest. I will come to you meek and lowly. If you are a bruised reed, I will not break you. If you are discouraged I come along side of you in the Spirit of gentleness."

APRIL 4 | MATTHEW 4:1–11

OVERCOMING TEMPTATION
BY THE POWER OF THE SPIRIT

*Then Jesus was led by the **Spirit** into the wilderness to be tempted by the devil. –MATTHEW 4:1*

Why did the Holy Spirit lead Jesus into the wilderness to be tempted by the devil? One reason: to show Jesus lived in victory by the Spirit's power. Although tempted in all points as we are, he overcame every ferocious inducement. He was victorious because he relied upon the Spirit and wielded the rapier of God's word. As a man, he was dependent on the indwelling power from on high. Instead of succumbing to the sinful solicitations, Jesus powered through them.

Temptation is not necessarily bad. After all, he was in God's will and led by the Spirit. Yielding to Satan's enticement, however, is the problem. Overcoming temptation produces growth and spiritual development. Notice when these temptations transpired! They followed immediately after his baptism, his first public step towards the cross. Consequently, his heavenly Father declared his pleasure with his Son. Similarly, the enemy often challenges us after we achieve a spiritual milestone. Any time we take a step forward in God, we can expect conflict with our adversary.

The temptation of Jesus is important because it shows he succeeded where everyone else failed. After the Spirit came upon him, he was led into the desert where Satan baited him. Every inducement was overcome with the Spirit's help. The deceiver was trounced. Therefore, this great victory qualified the Lord to destroy the works of the enemy.

Jesus shows us how we can overcome temptation. In divine strength he stood against his fiendish foe. When he fought him with God's word, the slithering serpent fled. For every spiritual attack our Lord said, "Look, devil, God has spoken and what he said in the past is still true today." With each of these Spirit-inspired declarations, he thwacked the tempter.

Rhema: Whenever you are tempted, you can do as Jesus did. You must never try to stand up to your archenemy in your own strength: like Jesus, your power must come from above. The Spirit led him and remained with him, so he did not have to battle the devil alone. God's Spirit will also help guide and empower you. Moreover, he will bring to your consciousness God's word, so you can withstand the enemy's attack.

APRIL 5 | MATTHEW 10:1–23

THE SPIRIT OF YOUR FATHER
SPEAKS THROUGH YOU

*But when they arrest you, do not worry about what to say or how to say it.
At that time you will be given what to say, for it will not be you speaking,
but the **Spirit** of your Father speaking through you.*
–MATTHEW 10:19–20

Every day many real-life situations make living for Jesus difficult. Whether at work, school, play, or with family, we may experience open hostility. Once people know we are his followers, we can expect opposition. They might give us an icy reception or even make things uncomfortably hot. Nevertheless, when persecution comes, the Spirit of our Father will give us the precise words to speak.

Jesus promises the wonderful help of the Holy Spirit when persecuted. Should we be arrested for witnessing for him, we need not fear. In the hour of hostility, the Spirit will tell us what to say. Just as the Twelve were sent to witness for him and promised supernatural assistance, so are we. If called upon to answer our adversaries, the Spirit will speak through us.

Many examples of divine help occur in the Bible when believers have faced antagonists. The Jewish court, for instance, arrested and imprisoned Peter and John because they healed a cripple (Acts 4:1–22). These authorities did not approve of their message. To tell people Jesus rose from the dead made those who crucified him look bad. When the apostles were called upon to give an account of themselves, the Holy Spirit came on Peter. Replying with dynamic incisiveness, he told them the healing was "an act of kindness" done in the name of Jesus. Astonished by his words, the Jewish rulers dismissed the apostles immediately but forbade them to speak in his name.

Rhema: You never need to worry what to say when you are in scary situations. Sometimes you will be like a sheep among wolves. In the hour of crisis, the Spirit of your heavenly Father will help. He is the all-wise, all-knowing, and all-powerful helper from above. As the Father's gift to his children, he will assure you of his love and care. Not only that, he will flood your consciousness with his words and wisdom. Should you find yourself under fire for your faith, you can trust him to give you the appropriate words.

THE SPIRIT'S ANSWER FOR HOSTILITY

Here is my servant whom I have chosen, the one I love, in whom I delight;
*I will put my **Spirit** on him, and he will proclaim justice to the nations.*
–Matthew 12:18

Even though he encountered intense opposition, the Lord did not quarrel with his adversaries. Nor did he raise his voice on the streets. To incite the masses with inflammatory rhetoric was not his *modus operandi*. Instead, his ministry was so gentle and meek "a bruised reed he will not break, and a smoldering wick he will not snuff out" (v 20). In contrast to the hatred and venom of the Pharisees, Jesus expressed gentleness, a fruit of the Spirit.

Matthew connected Jesus' gentle behavior with his reception of the Spirit. At his baptism the heavens opened, and the Spirit descended on him as a dove. The Father said, "This is my Son whom I love; with him I am well pleased" (3:17). The author cites Isaiah 42:1–4 to explain why Jesus, in the face of conflict, behaves without malice. He is God's chosen and beloved servant who has the Spirit of heaven resting on him. He used his God-given power to serve and bless, not dominate or retaliate.

When Jesus confronted human misery, he met it with mercy because his heart and attitude were not inflamed by hell but by the Spirit. Mercy seeks to relieve suffering. For this reason, Jesus healed a man on the Sabbath. To rescue one of his precious sheep who had fallen into a pit (v 11) was an act of kindness. On the other hand, the Pharisees who protested his compassion did not have the Spirit of God working in them. Instead, they condemned Jesus and wanted to kill him for "working" on the day of rest and relieving a man of his misery.

How should we who have the Spirit respond to antagonism? Jesus provides an excellent example. What was his reaction when his critics sought to slaughter him (v 14)? Without nastiness or vengefulness, bitterness or resentment, he withdrew from conflict and went elsewhere. God's servant continued to do good by healing the sick. In fact, he healed all their sick (v 15).

Rhema: The Father gives us the Spirit of Christ so we can be gentle when we face hostility.

APRIL 7 | MATTHEW 12:22–29

CASTING OUT DEMONS
BY THE SPIRIT OF GOD

*But if it is by the **Spirit** of God that I drive out demons, then the kingdom of God has come upon you.* –MATTHEW 12:28

It always astonishes me to discover how many opposed Jesus. In this chapter, opposition reached a feverish pitch. The Pharisees accused him of doing miracles by the power of the devil. When he healed a blind and mute, demon-possessed man, his opponents exploded with venom. His critics sneered, "It is only by Beelzebul, the prince of demons, that this fellow drives out demons" (v 24).

The Pharisees' contempt for Jesus was vicious. They accused him of performing mighty deeds by Beelzebul, a dunghill god, the god of the flies. How could those who prided themselves in knowing God's law fail to recognize the Messiah? Our Lord came in the Spirit's power to bind up and destroy Satan, not partner with him.

Jesus did not let their accusations go. In effect he said, *Guys just think about what you are saying. If Satan is behind my miracles, then he is fighting himself and his kingdom will not stand. Don't you realize I must be stronger than Satan because I am shutting him down and spoiling his goods. You guys should know I am the new boss in town and I am setting up my kingdom. To drive out demons by God's Spirit is proof.*

Casting out demons by the mighty Holy Spirit showed the glorious kingdom of God had arrived. For him to be in league with Satan was impossible—he was warring against him! Every time he performed a miracle, cast out a demon, or healed the sick, he was inflicting huge losses on Satan. Jesus came in the Spirit's power to defeat the devil and to free people from his grasp.

Rhema: Jesus came to demonstrate his dominion over darkness and invade enemy strongholds. Therefore, realize he is Lord over the demonic realm. He said, "The kingdom of God has come upon you." Take part in God's kingdom now! Enjoy it! Experience it! Of course, you will luxuriate in its fullness when Christ returns. In the meantime, you can experience God's kingdom at work in your midst. Right now, by the Spirit of God he wants to nullify the devil's work in its many manifestations.

APRIL 8 | MATTHEW 12:30–37

BLASPHEMY AGAINST THE SPIRIT

*And so I tell you, every kind of sin and slander can be forgiven, but blasphemy against the **Spirit** will not be forgiven.* **–Matthew 12:31**

Blasphemy against the Spirit is attributing the works of the Holy Spirit to Satan. The Pharisees did this when they rejected Jesus' miracles and put him in league with the devil. How blasphemous to accuse him of doing miracles by Satan's power! He did them in the power of the Holy Spirit. They knew full well God, not evil, was at work in our Lord's mighty deeds.

At issue is the question: how do we know spiritual truth and discern between a supernatural work of the devil and one of the Spirit? A mighty manifestation, in itself, is insufficient because the arch deceiver can perform them too. We must, therefore, listen to the Sprit's unmistakable voice.

The Spirit's testimony is on two levels: he speaks to individuals both by an outer witness and an inner witness. The outer concerns the miracle itself which is his own dynamic manifestation. As such he invests it with a wow factor, making it a wonder. A miracle is also a sign pointing to something beyond itself. A case in point is when Nicodemus came to Jesus and realized no one could do such amazing works unless God was with him (Jn 3:2). The Spirit was, in fact, working in and through our Lord's mighty deeds, and in effect saying, *This is God at work.*

In addition to his outer witness, he gave a much more powerful inner witness to the viewers of Christ's miracles. The Holy Spirit spoke directly to their hearts, certifying God's activity. Through his inner and outer voice, he endowed each supernatural deed with ultimate truth which they must either accept or reject.

Rhema: Attributing his works to the devil is unforgivable because it goes against the Spirit's testimony on both an objective and subjective level. No greater testimony exists than this for he is God. Blasphemy against the Spirit is a rebellious rejection of God's revelation in Christ. Behind Jesus' every word and deed stands the Holy Spirit. To harden one's heart against such knowledge is spiritual suicide. No one can come to faith or become convinced of spiritual truth without his witness. He is, after all, the Spirit of truth.

APRIL 9 | MATTHEW 12:38–50

DO NOT SPEAK AGAINST THE SPIRIT

*Anyone who speaks a word against the Son of Man will be forgiven, but anyone who speaks against the **Holy Spirit** will not be forgiven, either in this age or in the age to come.* –MATTHEW 12:32

To rail against the Holy Spirit is fraught with eternal danger. The Pharisees accused Jesus of operating with an evil spirit. Their malicious claim of colluding with the devil was unforgiveable. They knew better. Every day he performed many Messianic signs foretold by their prophets. Having people turn to Christ, however, was not on their agenda. In response to his powerful signs and wonders, they tried to discredit the Son of God because of their own unbelieving wicked hearts. In doing so, they aligned themselves with the powers of darkness determined to prevent people from coming to Christ for life and salvation.

Jesus had harsh words for these Spirit-slanderers. When they attributed his deeds to the devil, they revealed the turpitude of their hearts. To accuse him of casting out demons by the power of Satan was evil. Pure wickedness. He exposed their true nature with a proverb. "Make a tree good and its fruit will be good, or make a tree bad and its fruit will be bad, for a tree is recognized by its fruit" (v 33). He continued his denunciation by calling them a brood of vipers. Then he asks, "Being evil how can they say anything good?" The Pharisees' hatred of Jesus climaxed with a complete rejection of him. Afterwards they went out to conspire how they might kill him.

To speak disparagingly of the Third Member of the Trinity is inexcusable. "Anyone who speaks against the Holy Spirit will not be forgiven, either in this age or in the age to come." Because they rejected God's grace and the Spirit's witness, they could not come to faith.

Rhema: Be careful how you speak about the Holy Spirit. An open attitude and a tender sensitivity to his work and witness pleases the Lord. The Spirit's role is to always bear testimony to Jesus. His miracles bore a divine seal of approval and attested he was the Son of God because the Spirit bore him witness. To close one's minds to his testimony is to spurn God's self-vindication and imperil one's soul.

SPEAKING BY THE SPIRIT

*He said to them, "How is it then that David, speaking by the **Spirit**, calls him 'Lord'?"* –MATTHEW 22:43

Sometimes Jesus asked tough questions that baffled the mind. People peppered him with difficult queries all the time. Many were hostile and designed to trip him up, but he answered each one. On this occasion, however, he asks his own tough question. A question so deep and profound none ever dared to ask him another (v 46).

Why would David, the greatest historical figure in the Bible, call his own son, "Lord"? Psalm 110:1 states, "The LORD says to my Lord: 'Sit at my right hand until I make your enemies a footstool for your feet.'" Who could be superior to David? He spoke by the Spirit, so this was not a misstatement. Although he wrote the Psalm its true author was the Holy Spirit. David's words are correct and authoritative because the Spirit inspired them.

Jesus asks, "How is it then that David, speaking by the Spirit, calls him 'Lord'?" The query posed a puzzle: how was it possible for one individual to be both David's descendant and yet divine? The crowd believed the Messiah would be an heir of their famous king. This belief was true as far as it went. Never for one moment, however, did they entertain the thought of David's offspring being eternal and seated in heaven with God. How was it feasible to be David's son and Lord? They struggled to get their minds around that paradox of being son of David and Son of God.

His son will have greater honor and authority than David because he will sit at the right hand of God. How is that possible? No one could answer his question. By inspiration of the Spirit, David points beyond his genealogical son to the incarnation. "If then David calls him 'Lord,' how can he be his son?" The answer requires more than biology; it calls for the miraculous. The resolution does not come from logic but revelation.

Rhema: Our natural minds are incapable of understanding the things of God, even Scripture. To get beyond this limitation requires a revelation of the Spirit. Therefore, we must always pray for him to give us wisdom, understanding, and revelation so the eyes of heart may be enlightened (Eph 1:17–19).

APRIL 11 | MATTHEW 28:16–20

BAPTIZE IN THE NAME OF THE SPIRIT

*Therefore go and make disciples of all nations, baptizing them in the name of the Father and of the Son and of the **Holy Spirit**.*
–MATTHEW 28:19

Why does Jesus include the Holy Spirit in the baptismal formula? In the Great Commission, he instructed his apostles to baptize in the name of the Father, the Son, and the Holy Spirit. He wants us to enter into and enjoy the new era brought into existence by his resurrection. As believers, we have a new relationship with the Father, Son, and Holy Spirit.

As he himself had his Father and the Spirit at his baptism, so he ensures their involvement at ours. He wants us to recognize the participation of all three persons of the Godhead in our salvation. The role and importance of each, including the Holy Spirit's, is not to be minimized or overlooked.

By including the Holy Spirit in the baptism of new believers, Jesus was saying the Holy Spirit is very important in their lives. They are to esteem him as much as they do the Father and the Son. He is a person as much as they. Each member of the Trinity welcomes them into a wonderful relationship with them. So, to elevate the Father or the Son to the exclusion of the Spirit is not only wrong but it distorts our knowledge of God.

The Holy Spirit is essential for carrying out the Great Commission. Without his help, we will fail to make disciples. His role is to convict, illumine, and bring those who are dead in sins to new life in Christ. Moreover, the many glorious benefits of our Lord's redeeming work become ours only through the Holy Spirit. Therefore, we must never ignore or exclude him in our confession of faith.

Rhema: The Holy Spirit has a distinct and personal ministry to you. He is the one who brought you to faith in Christ and involved himself in your conversion. When you were a sinner and turned to Jesus, he was involved. Your entire spiritual life exists because of him. The Third Person of the Trinity is the one who continues to open your understanding to the truth of God. He works in you every day to make you more like Jesus and give you access to the Father.

APRIL 12 | MARK 1:1–8

HE WILL BAPTIZE YOU
WITH THE HOLY SPIRIT

I baptize you with water, but he will baptize you with the **Holy Spirit.**
–MARK 1:8

Feel the electricity and excitement in the opening of Mark's gospel! "The beginning of the good news of Jesus Christ, the Son of God" (v 1) explodes with divine action. A voice crying in the wilderness. An ancient prophecy comes to pass. Swarms of people scramble to listen to an eccentric prophet. Revival breaks out. The heavens rip open. The Holy Spirit descends as a dove. A divine voice thunders from above. All this in the first eleven verses! Like a shining sunrise, a new era dispels the night.

John's audience sensed God was up to something momentous. They showed up in droves to listen to the sensational preaching of the Baptist as he prepared "the way for the Lord." By diverting people's attention from himself, he riveted it on someone far greater. Look at the spiritual momentum! The anticipation! From the banks of the Jordan he shouted, "After me comes the one more powerful than I, the straps of whose sandals I am not worthy to stoop down and untie. I baptize you with water, but he will baptize you with the Holy Spirit."

The one who will baptize in the Holy Spirit supersedes John. This is the climax of his preaching, an integral part of the gospel. Not only does he connect the good news with the Spirit but states the new baptism is the reason Jesus came. Spirit baptism is of ultimate significance. The forerunner immerses in water but the coming one immerses in the Holy Spirit. John's prophetic sign, water baptism, is upstaged, his own role diminished. The primary reason Jesus came, John announced, was to baptize believers in the Holy Spirit.

Rhema: The good news concerning the Son of God begins with a promise of receiving the fullness of his Spirit. This unique experience characterizes Jesus' coming. To stress its importance, each of the four gospels records this amazing pronouncement: he will baptize you with the Holy Spirit. This wonderful moment of fulfillment empowers you to live free from oppression. It drenches you with the dew of heaven. It bathes you in the immediate presence of God. Jesus came to immerse you into the kingdom of God. Heaven is open.

APRIL 13 | MARK 1:9–11; ISAIAH 64:1–7

HEAVENS RIPPED OPEN AND
THE DESCENT OF THE SPIRIT

*At that time Jesus came from Nazareth in Galilee and was baptized by
John in the Jordan. Just as Jesus was coming up out of the water, he saw
heaven being torn open and the **Spirit** descending on him like a dove.
And a voice came from heaven: "You are my Son, whom I love; with you
I am well pleased." –MARK 1:10*

Have you ever wished for God to show up, rip the heavens open,
and intervene in your affairs? Many of God's people have longed
for such a manifestation of his presence. The prophet Isaiah lamented,
"Oh, that you would rend the heavens and come down, that the mountains would tremble before you!" (Isa 64:1). He wanted Yahweh to
show up in a powerful way and help. If you are going through a rough
patch and wondering where God is, you may have wanted to cry out
as Isaiah did. Mark, however, tells us the good news: the Almighty has
already opened heaven and come down to help. He is present! And he
is not silent!

God ripped the heavens open and came down at the baptism of
Jesus. Unseen hands tore heaven apart like a piece of cloth. The Spirit
descended on him as a dove and God spoke. This observable historic event was the beginning of Christ's public ministry. Because he
received the Spirit's fullness in the waters of Jordan, he can baptize
people with the Spirit.

Splitting the heavens shows the awesome power Jesus received
from the Spirit. God's strength now comes to rest upon his Son who
will use that power throughout his ministry. This makes him much
stronger than John. Let no one fear his awesome might—omnipotence descended on him as a dove.

God removed any uncertainty about who received this mighty
endowment of the Spirit. He declared Jesus was his Son whom he
loved and with whom he was well pleased. The Father's acknowledg-
ment of his only beloved Son helps us understand who Jesus is.

*Rhema: You can invite the Lord into any situation with his earthshaking,
heaven-ripping power. Let the mountains tremble before him! He has come down
to do "awesome things that we did not expect" (Isa 64:3). He "acts on behalf of
those who wait for him."*

COMPELLED BY THE SPIRIT

*At once the **Spirit** sent him out into the wilderness, and he was in the wilderness forty days, being tempted by Satan. He was with the wild animals, and angels attended him.* **–MARK 1:12–13**

Make no mistake, the wilderness to which the Spirit drove God's Son was no Garden of Eden. Throughout the Bible the wilderness is a cursed place. It is desolation's domicile, abandonment's abode fit only for ferocious beasts, the haunt of demons. The Spirit who descended upon Jesus at his baptism now thrusts him into this wasteland. There Satan will tempt him for forty days.

Why does the Spirit drive our Lord into a wild desert? The term "sent out" often refers to a forceful, violent expulsion. The same word occurs when Jesus casts out demons. Mark may have in mind Adam and Eve's unfortunate expulsion. They were kicked out of paradise for disobeying God. The wilderness is the result of their sin. At his baptism, the Son of Man identified himself with sinful man in need of repentance; here he faced sin's consequence.

The wilderness typifies testing. To take our place and represent us before God, he must prove obedient. This is the reason Jesus retraces the steps of Adam, the first son of God, who failed in a garden. Jesus, the "second Adam," must overcome and succeed where the first failed. During this entire ordeal, our Lord is under the direct guidance and help of the Holy Spirit. He succeeds where everyone else failed, proving himself worthy to represent us.

In the strength of the Holy Spirit, he went head to head with our arch foe. If Jesus is going to kick Satan out of people, he must first triumph over him. The expression "Satan" means adversary or opponent. For forty days empowered by the Spirit Jesus faced our adversary and did not yield to temptation. Proven victorious, he is ready to begin public ministry.

Rhema: You are in the cosmic conflict just like Jesus. It is encouraging, however, to know the same Spirit that helped him overcome the adversary is available to help you. Although cruel forces of evil attack, his Spirit is present to strengthen you daily. You do not have to fight temptation in your strength but in the Spirit's mighty power.

APRIL 15 | MARK 3:20–30

SLANDERING THE SPIRIT

*"Truly I tell you, people can be forgiven all their sins and every slander they utter, but whoever blasphemes against the **Holy Spirit** will never be forgiven; they are guilty of an eternal sin." He said this because they were saying, "He has an impure spirit." –MARK 3:28–30*

Do you ever sense you are the enemy's target? It is like you have a bull's eye painted on your back. People say nasty falsehoods about you. Society's movers and shakers oppose you. Even family members do not try to understand you. You feel hurt and under attack. If you do you are in good company, for that is how many treated Jesus.

Trials and testing did not end with his forty-day temptation in the wilderness. His adversary continued to attack him every which way he turned. Jewish teachers from Jerusalem misled the people by repeatedly saying Jesus "had an impure spirit." We can surmise Satan was behind these false accusations. His mother and brothers misunderstood the conflagration and turned against him. When they witnessed his uncharacteristic reaction to these falsehoods, they thought he was crazy.

Jesus came as the strong man to bind Satan, so how can he be in league with him? That is the question he put to his audience. He was not an ally of the adversary but his fierce foe who came to bind him and plunder his house. Our Lord came to free every person Satan has tied up and imprisoned.

Nothing disturbs God more than attributing the work of the Spirit to the devil. To accuse Jesus of driving out demons by the prince of demons pains the Father, Son, and Holy Spirit. Anyone asserting God's Son is possessed by Beelzebul provokes divine outrage because everything our Lord did was in the power of the Spirit. To claim otherwise is to slander the Holy Spirit. Such damnable blasphemy is an eternal sin heaven will never forgive.

Rhema: Make no mistake. The Holy Spirit was at work in the life and ministry of Jesus. His miracles were manifestations of the Spirit; his mercy, the fruit. Therefore, to claim he is working by the power of Satan is a lie from the pit of hell and unpardonable. This accursed unbelief closes the heart to God's saving grace revealed in his Son.

APRIL 16 | MARK 12:35–40

SPEAKING BY THE SPIRIT

While Jesus was teaching in the temple courts, he asked, "Why do the teachers of the law say that the Messiah is the son of David? David himself, speaking by the **Holy Spirit***, declared: 'The Lord said to my Lord: "Sit at my right hand until I put your enemies under your feet." ' "David himself calls him 'Lord.' How then can he be his son?"*
–MARK 12:35–37

To properly understand and interpret what the Spirit says in Scripture without the Holy Spirit is impossible. On a purely intellectual level, Israel's religious experts showed they could not. Although they studied God's word and thought they knew it, they failed to grasp its most important message. To fathom what the Spirit revealed to David about the Messiah required spiritual illumination.

When a huge crowd gathered around Jesus in the temple, he asks them a question. "Why do the teachers of the law say that the Messiah is the son of David?" He wanted them to understand their teachers were not wrong to claim the Messiah will descend from David, but their teaching did not go far enough. Israel's greatest king under the Spirit's influence spoke of the Messiah not only as his son but also as his Lord. They missed this essential truth.

Mark wrote his gospel to help people realize the identity of the Messiah. Because many did not have the Spirit, they failed to grasp Jesus was the Messiah, the Anointed One, the Son of God. Jesus' close connection with the Spirit is reflected in his name, Christ which means anointed. Jesus is the promised Messiah. This is important because eternal life depends upon knowing who he is.

To study Scripture without spiritual illumination prevented these scribes from understanding God's word. The Spirit must illumine what he spoke through David. "Speaking by the Spirit" meant the Spirit revealed prophetically an infallible truth to David. How can a son of his sit at God's right hand and be his exalted Lord? We cannot understand this unless the Spirit shows us the Messiah preexisted with God and became man.

Rhema: Invite the Holy Spirit to help you read God's word. Without divine illumination, you will not grasp its spiritual meaning nor be able to interpret it correctly. Only the one who inspired its earthly authors can help you apprehend his intention.

APRIL 17 | MARK 13:9–13; EXODUS 4:10–17

THE SPIRIT GIVES US THE RIGHT WORDS

*Whenever you are arrested and brought to trial, do not worry beforehand about what to say. Just say whatever is given you at the time, for it is not you speaking, but the **Holy Spirit**.* –MARK 13:11

We derive great comfort knowing the Holy Spirit is present whenever we are facing a crisis. If asked to defend our faith, we need not worry over the words to speak. Jesus said, "It is not you speaking, but the Holy Spirit." He is our best friend who gives wonderful counsel and helps us communicate in ways far above our own ability. Even in difficult situations he will give the right words to declare.

During these end times, many who share the good news about Christ are hated and handed over to authorities for punishment. Sharing the gospel in cultures or countries hostile to Christianity often produces abhorrence of the messenger. Family members may even turn and betray their own. For many the cost of following God's Son is persecution. For this reason, he urges us to be on our guard and yet not be anxious. Right on the spot, the Holy Spirit will tell us the keywords we need to utter.

God cares about us when hostile or harsh predicaments threaten. He wants to make sure we have the needed wisdom and words to get us through rough circumstances. Just think of how God was with Moses when he had to go up against Pharaoh. At first Moses complained he lacked eloquence and was "slow of speech and tongue." God, however, said to him, "Moses, I made man's mouth now go, I will help you speak and will teach you what to say." With God's help, Moses confronted Pharaoh and emancipated the Israelites.

Rhema: What God promised Moses Jesus promises you. Your Lord knew from firsthand experience how the Spirit helped him. When he faced antagonistic audiences crying for his blood, the Holy Spirit gave him amazing answers. Time and again he had an appropriate answer for a hostile audience armed with loaded questions. Likewise, you need not face enemies of the gospel alone. In the Holy Spirit you have confidence, boldness, insight, and authority. He gives all this and more to help you share the grand news concerning Jesus Christ.

APRIL 18 | MARK 14:32–42

THE SPIRIT IS WILLING BUT THE FLESH IS WEAK

*Then he returned to his disciples and found them sleeping. "Simon," he said to Peter, "are you asleep? Couldn't you keep watch for one hour? Watch and pray so that you will not fall into temptation. The **spirit** is willing, but the flesh is weak." –*MARK 14:37–38

How can we explain the disciples' lack of concern for Jesus in his hour of need? In the Garden of Gethsemane, their friend experienced great anguish of soul. Distressed and troubled he is overwhelmed with sorrow even to the point of death. In this horrific ordeal, he takes them along looking for support. Instead of praying with him one hour, what do they do? They sleep.

Jesus explains their emotional indifference in terms of flesh and Spirit. It matters not his death is imminent. He comes to them and finds Peter, James, and John fast asleep. Waking them, he chides asking, "Could you not keep watch for one hour?" The reason, he explains, is the weakness of the flesh. Our Lord said to them, "The Spirit is willing, but the flesh is weak."

What are we to do when the flesh, our weak human nature, seeks to escape responsibility? We have a choice. We can allow human feebleness to dominate our decisions and behavior or God's Spirit. Either one will rise up and override the other. Jesus let the Spirit move him to willingly offer himself up to God. When we allow the power of his Spirit to control us, he will torpedo our self-interest and empower us to do God's will.

During his own bout of temptation, our Lord resorted to spiritual resources. He was victorious in Gethsemane because of prayer and dependency upon the Spirit. Resolve and determination to "drink the cup" came from above. His disciples, by contrast, fell into temptation because they did not draw upon the available divine resources. Peter ended up denying the Lord three times. Judas betrayed him for thirty pieces of silver. In the end, all his disciples fled and forsook him. The difference between our Lord and the Twelve was he relied upon the Spirit.

Rhema: Jesus walked in the Spirit. Although he was the Son of God, he depended upon the Holy Spirit to counter the weakness of human flesh. So can we!

APRIL 19 | LUKE 1:1–17

FILLED WITH THE SPIRIT
EVEN FROM BIRTH

*He will be a joy and delight to you, and many will rejoice because of his birth, for he will be great in the sight of the Lord. He is never to take wine or other fermented drink, and he will be filled with the **Holy Spirit** even before he is born.* **–LUKE 1:14–15**

What an amazing prophecy! What a special child! "He will be filled with the Holy Spirit even before he is born." No wonder "he will be great in the sight of the Lord." He is a joy and a delight. Receiving the Spirit so early in life equipped and qualified him for a spectacular ministry. After six months in his mother's womb, John was filled with the Spirit.

Luke begins his gospel with the births of John the Baptist and Jesus. Their remarkable nativities show a new era has begun. John is filled before he is born. Jesus is conceived supernaturally. Such an increase in the Spirit's activity characterizes the new Messianic Age. This was just the beginning. The OT prophesied a universal outpouring of the Spirit and with John and Jesus' births it was just getting underway.

The prophetic gift began as soon as he was filled. While still in the womb, John recognized the mother of the Messiah who was pregnant with Jesus. When he heard Mary's voice, John the Baptist leapt for joy. Before either was born he bore witness to Jesus. He gained prominence by becoming his forerunner and pointing men and women to Jesus. According to Jesus, John was the greatest person ever born. Incidentally, in the gospels only John and his parents are said to be filled with the Spirit before Pentecost. Since he received this fullness at the start of his life, he could begin immediately to carry out God's great plan for him.

Rhema: Notice how important the Spirit is in Luke's gospel. Young and old, men and women can access his presence and power. It is never too early to be filled with the Spirit. Whether you are a tender foot or timeworn to have the living God enter your life is never too soon. If you are going to fulfill your destiny and life's purpose, you will need the Holy Spirit. The sooner, the better.

April 20 | Luke 1:16–25; Malachi 4:5–6

Ministering in the Spirit and Power of Elijah

And he will go on before the Lord, in the **spirit** *and power of Elijah, to turn the hearts of the parents to their children and the disobedient to the wisdom of the righteous—to make ready a people prepared for the Lord.* –Luke 1:17

It takes the power of the Holy Spirit to turn people to God. Elijah did it in his day and John the Baptist will do it in his. There is no substitute for the Spirit of God. If things are going to happen in the kingdom of God, it will be because of his mighty work. Human reasoning, eloquence, programs, and resources will fail because people resist coming to God. To counter sin, rebellion, unbelief, apathy, hostility, and hardness of hearts, the power from above is essential.

John comes endowed with divine strength like a new Elijah challenging rulers and people to examine themselves and see if they are ready for God. Elijah is the greatest biblical example of calling a people back to God. Standing alone atop Mount Carmel he confronted a degenerate nation that had turned from their Maker. He dared the prophets of Baal to let the God who answers by fire be God. Israel's God answered by fire and Elijah slew the false prophets. Like Elijah, John's Spirit-inflamed preaching will call a nation to repentance and bring it back to God.

The same Spirit and power Elijah enjoyed is promised John. Because he is clothed with power from on high, he will awaken in the people a sense of sin and a desire for God. Only the "violent wind from heaven" can accomplish these spiritual results. The prophet of the Highest will have great success in carrying out his spectacular assignment and many will turn to God. The Almighty will unveil his might in John's preaching as he proclaims the long-awaited Lord's coming. His spiritual assignment is to prepare and equip people through powerful preaching swilling with divine energy.

Rhema: John the Baptist illustrates the importance of associating power with the Spirit. He inflames preaching, causes prophetic activity, and produces stunning results. To turn hearts to God and prepare them for a revival requires an invasion of power from on high. Ask the Lord to send you forth in the Spirit and power of Elijah.

April 21 | Luke 1:26–38; Exodus 40:34–38

Overshadowed by the Spirit of God

*The angel answered, "The **Holy Spirit** will come on you, and the power of the Most High will overshadow you. So the holy one to be born will be called the Son of God." –LUKE 1:35*

Overshadowed. What a beautiful delicate word, pregnant with meaning. God in all his exaltedness and authority will envelop you like a cloud and you will be surrounded with a brilliant swirl of glory. Such a juxtaposition of concepts—omnipotence casting a mere shadow. It is like Peter's shadow (Acts 5:15) falling across the sick bringing new life and health to the infirm that lay in his path. The power of a billion suns throws a gentle haze over the young virgin and the holy one is conceived. What an amazing way to describe the creative power of the Holy Spirit!

Mary wants to know how she will conceive the Son of the Most High. Angel Gabriel told her she will be with child and give birth to a son whom she must name Jesus. "How will this be," Mary asked him, "since I am a virgin?" He replied, "The Holy Spirit will come on you and the power of the Most High will overshadow you. God's holy, powerful presence will descend on you like the OT cloud that settled upon the tabernacle. You will be filled with the glory of God."

The power of the Highest overshadows Mary to bring forth a child who is the holy Son of God. This infant owes his existence to the Spirit. Jesus is unique and different from every other person because he does not have a human father. Instead, he is the Almighty clothed with human flesh. Immanuel. God with us. Divine life manifests itself in him. Therefore, Jesus can declare, "I am the life of the world."

Rhema: As you go throughout the day, think of the Holy Spirit overshadowing you. "Whoever dwells in the shelter of the Most High will rest in the shadow of the Almighty" (Ps 91:1). Our Lord wants you to enjoy the security of his protection and the shelter of his love. With his Spirit, he wants to put you in the shade of his Shekinah presence and fill you with the glory of God.

APRIL 22 | LUKE 1:39–56

ELIZABETH IS FILLED WITH THE HOLY SPIRIT

*When Elizabeth heard Mary's greeting, the baby leaped in her womb, and Elizabeth was filled with the **Holy Spirit**.* –LUKE 1:41

What an amazing moment. The expectant mothers of two of history's most famous people meet. Mary is pregnant with Jesus and Elizabeth is expecting John the Baptist. The Holy Spirit is present and operating in their remarkable encounter. Things happen. As soon as Mary greets her relative, a force from on high erupts. Elizabeth is filled and little John still in his mother's womb leaps for joy.

The Spirit's presence and participation has everyone in this story prophesying— John, Elizabeth, and Mary. Even before the Baptist is born, he discerns the importance of Mary's child. Through the Spirit he recognizes who Jesus is and at once is overcome with joy. The Spirit makes Jesus real to John before either of them is born. His remarkable spiritual sensitivity and prophetic acuity are an early sign of his life's direction.

We can see the Spirit's renowned role in Elizabeth's life. She is filled with the Spirit and breaks forth into prophetic utterance. Possessed with a heightened spiritual understanding, she knows the significance of the moment. By revelation, she proclaims Mary is "the mother of my Lord." Incredible. In addition, the Spirit enables her to discern her child's response to Mary's baby. Both Elizabeth and her infant are ready to come under the Lordship of the little one in Mary's womb. Aged Elizabeth comes alive in God.

The Holy Spirit bursts upon the scene to signify a new age has begun. In narrative form Luke displays its marvelous characteristics as he begins his gospel. He describes an age where women prophesy. Where leaping for joy, loads of revelation, and a profusion of prophecy take place. God is bringing salvation to the world, and the Spirit is present to help celebrate it. The Holy Spirit gives Elizabeth a profound spiritual understanding of God's redemptive provision. She prophesies with a loud voice his dramatic action in bringing a Savior to the world. Revelation gushes out of her like champagne bursting from a bottle.

Rhema: Extraordinary things happen when the Holy Spirit comes on the scene. There is a powerful demonstration of God's presence. People respond with joy. Excitement fills the air. Prophecy breaks out and individuals are blessed.

APRIL 23 | LUKE 1:57–79

ZECHARIAH IS FILLED WITH THE HOLY SPIRIT

*His father Zechariah was filled with the **Holy Spirit** and prophesied*
–Luke 1:67

The question on everyone's mind was, "What then is this child going to be?" Several unusual events surrounding the birth of John the Baptist prompted their query. Everyone realized God's hand was on him. His birth to aged parents was extraordinary enough, but what stunned everyone was Zachariah's recovery of speech. For nine months he had not spoken a word. He was struck dumb for not believing the angel who told him his wife would conceive a son (v 20). These events caused mouths to wag all over the country.

Zechariah recovered his speech when he named his son John. The child was to be named and circumcised eight days after his birth, according to Jewish custom. Everyone present expected his parents to call him after his father. Elizabeth, however, protested and said, "No! He is to be called John." Astonished by her insistence, they asked Zechariah what he wanted his son named. Motioning for a tablet he wrote, "His name is John." "Immediately his mouth was opened and his tongue set free, and he began to speak, praising God" (v 64).

Not only did Zechariah get his voice back, but he was filled with the Spirit and began prophesying. With loosened tongue, he broke out in prophetic song praising and extolling God. He gave a magnificent prophecy exalting the Lord who kept his promises of salvation. Then he prophesied about his newborn son. By the Spirit, Zechariah proclaimed John's historic role. "And you, my child, will be called a prophet of the Most High; for you will go on before the Lord to prepare the way for him, to give his people the knowledge of salvation through the forgiveness of their sins" (vv 76–77).

Rhema: Luke values the Spirit's work by highlighting his actions. Members of Jesus' family, for instance, are people of the Spirit—his mother, uncle, aunt, and cousin. Incidentally, they are the only ones said to be filled with the Spirit in the gospels. By relaying these remarkable events, the author tries to show what it is like to act with the Spirit's fullness. To anticipate Pentecost, he discloses that Spirit-filled people prophesy, praise God, have a deeper understanding of Scripture, recognize God at work, and exalt Jesus.

APRIL 24 | LUKE 1:80; 3:1–14

GROWING IN THE HOLY SPIRIT

And the child grew and became strong in **spirit***; and he lived in the wilderness until he appeared publicly to Israel.* –LUKE 1:80

How do we grow in the Spirit? Before John the Baptist began his prophetic ministry, he was developing spiritually. Filled with the Holy Spirit before he was born did not keep him from cultivating a spiritual life. He did not sit back and wait to be used of God, but he determined to grow in God. Every day he became stronger as he prepared for the work to which he was called.

The wilderness became his home. Away from life's hustle and bustle and with few inroads into his time, John developed a walk with God. In solitude and quietness, he learned to hear the still small voice. Spiritual sensitivity requires extended times of being alone with God. To become powerful in God is a process not a onetime event. If he was going to turn the hearts of the fathers to their children, he needed more of the Spirit.

To dwell in the wilderness meant he lived a simple uncluttered life. Few things robbing him of time and energy allowed him to live solely for God. Molded by a power from above his life took on a heavenward focus. He became a student of the word, for Luke says the word of God came to him in the desert (3:2). God gave him a living word for the nation, a specific message that gripped hearts and changed lives.

God appointed him to call a sinful and broken people to repentance. To minister with the effectiveness of an Elijah necessitated waiting on the Lord and hearing from heaven. Because he grew in spiritual things, John shook the nation and brought it to its knees. His Spirit-formed ministry marked a turning point in God's economy; the gospel era began.

Rhema: You can learn much from John about how to grow strong in the Spirit. Time alone with God and a detachment from the things of this world will hone your spiritual sensitivities, enabling you to hear God's unmistakable voice. John became more powerful as the years went by. Jesus said of him, "Truly I tell you, among those born of women there has not risen anyone greater than John the Baptist" (Mt 11:11).

APRIL 25 | LUKE 2:21–25

THE HOLY SPIRIT KEPT HOPE ALIVE

*Now there was a man in Jerusalem called Simeon, who was righteous and devout. He was waiting for the consolation of Israel, and the **Holy Spirit** was on him.* –LUKE 2:25

Do you enjoy pleasant surprises? One fascinating feature about the Holy Spirit is he keeps things interesting. He authors many unexpected blessings, such as when Mary and Joseph brought baby Jesus to the temple. As obedient and devout parents, they dedicated their firstborn to God. No one expected the Spirit to move an old man at that precise moment to come and bless them with a prophetic word.

All his life he had been waiting for this moment. Luke describes him as a person who got a hold of God and walked carefully with him. The Spirit told him he would see Israel's Messiah in his lifetime. Simeon treasured this hope in his heart and nothing could dissuade him. Neither the silence of the years nor the delay of heaven deterred his expectation. It was not easy to keep looking for the "consolation of Israel" and stay faithful to God to the end of life. Throughout his days, however, the Spirit kept his hope constant and strong.

Desmond Tutu said, "Hope is being able to see that there is light despite all the darkness." The Holy Spirit's work is to convince us our hope is valid. Difficult days and long delays can cripple it. But he assures us our hope in God's promises will not disappoint (Rms 5:5). He wants us to live out our days full of anticipation expecting he will show up and make a way even if none exists. Like Simeon, let us face every new day with confidence the Lord has everything under control. It does not matter what is going on in the world or in our lives because the Spirit fills our souls with comfort and expectation. He gives us a deep settled peace and buoys us with courage and confidence. Let the Spirit keep our hope alive as we wait for the Lord to return, restore, and renew.

Rhema: The Holy Spirit offers us comfort during difficult and depressing times. He soothes our hearts with anticipation of God's glorious salvation as we await the Lord's coming. In the meantime, he comes alongside to offer encouragement, comfort, and hope.

APRIL 26 | LUKE 2:21–25; MATTHEW 2:9–23

PERSONAL REVELATIONS
FROM THE HOLY SPIRIT

*It had been revealed to him by the **Holy Spirit** that he would not die before he had seen the Lord's Messiah.* –LUKE 2:26

Have you ever needed some advice? Perhaps, a heavenly directive or a warning? Whenever we require direction or seek clarity on a matter, we can ask God. Revealing those divine tips and alerts is one of the Holy Spirit's tasks.

Simeon apparently had asked God if he would see the Messiah before he died. In response, the Holy Spirit answered his prayer by telling him he would. As a devout and righteous man, he lived in communion with God and kept his soul open for a divine word. The Spirit leaked to him this wonderful secret that came to pass when the parents of Jesus presented their newborn in the temple.

Several times throughout the Bible, God gives personal revelations to individuals. Through the Spirit he offers them helpful and crucial information. The word "revealed" in this text is the same word that occurs when Joseph was "warned" in a dream to flee Bethlehem (Mt 2:12). If Joseph did not heed this advice, King Herod would have killed baby Jesus.

The word rendered "revealed" comes from the ancient business world and means to give advice to enquirers. Here are a few more NT examples. The wise men who came to Bethlehem to worship infant Jesus, the newborn king, were likewise "warned" in a dream not to go back to Herod (Mt 2:13). Minding the revelation, they returned home by another route. God spoke to Cornelius through an angel and "instructed" him to fetch Peter and listen to his words (Acts 10:22). Likewise, Noah received a revelation "instructing" him to build an ark (Heb 11:17). Moses was "warned" to follow the heavenly pattern when he built the tabernacle (Heb 8:5).

Simeon received this personal revelation because he had been asking the Lord. That he was "righteous and devout" means he had a conscientious and cautious walk with God. In this respect, he resembled Noah, Moses, Joseph, and Cornelius. These particular individuals, the Bible informs us, were careful to obey the Lord. After they obeyed, God gave them even more precious and valuable revelations.

Rhema: From Simeon's experience we learn the Holy Spirit gives personal, life-saving revelations.

APRIL 27 | LUKE 2:25–35

MOVED BY THE HOLY SPIRIT

*Moved by the **Spirit**, he went into the temple courts. When the parents brought in the child Jesus to do for him what the custom of the Law required, Simeon took him in his arms and praised God.* –LUKE 2:27

Simeon must have been an exceptional man of the Spirit. Within three verses, the Holy Spirit is mentioned three times. The breath of God fills his sails. See how the Spirit rests on him, reveals a secret to him, and moves him to take up baby Jesus in his arms. How easily he prophesies and praises God. Simeon's auspicious meeting with baby Jesus and his parents was choreographed by the Spirit. Without a doubt, he was a man moved by the Spirit.

Simeon represents the finest in the Jewish faith. He is devout, expectant, righteous, and sensitive to the Spirit's leading. By the Spirit, he understands God's ultimate purpose in sending Jesus. Holding the child, he prophesies, "For my eyes have seen your salvation, which you have prepared in the sight of all nations: a light for revelation to the Gentiles, and the glory of your people Israel" (vv 30–32). In an instant, he recognizes that the infant is the Savior of the world.

The Spirit led him to the right place at the right time so he could bless the parents and speak into their lives. Inspired by the Spirit, he tells Mary what to expect. "This child is destined to cause the falling and rising of many in Israel" (v 34). "Those who encounter her son," he adds, "will experience ruin or renewal, a stumbling or a soaring. In the end, however, an awful tragedy would befall her son and will pierce her soul" (v 35). Simeon departs this world satisfied. He says, "Sovereign Lord, as you have promised, you may now dismiss your servant in peace" (v 29). With peace and joy he completes his days.

Rhema: Amazing things happen when we allow God's Spirit to move us. The wind of heaven directed Simeon's coming and going. By obeying his gentle leading, he never experienced loss or unhappiness. He enjoyed the once-in-a-lifetime opportunity to speak prophetically into Mary and Joseph's lives and hold the Savior in his arms. Because he followed the Spirit's prompting, he finished life a happy man.

APRIL 28 | LUKE 3:1–20

THE MINISTRY OF THE HOLY SPIRIT

*John answered them all, "I baptize you with water. But one who is more powerful than I will come, the straps of whose sandals I am not worthy to untie. He will baptize you with the **Holy Spirit** and fire." –*LUKE **3:16**

What does it mean to be baptized with fire? To answer, John distinguishes his work from the Messiah's. He baptized with water; his successor will baptize with fire. Spirit baptism will be a new, greater manifestation of God's presence and power.

To show the superiority of Spirit baptism, Luke contrasts John and Jesus. Both have miraculous births and early encounters with the Holy Spirit. Angels announce their nativities. In each comparison, however, Jesus is always superior. John is filled with the Spirit before he is born but Jesus is conceived by the Holy Spirit; later he receives the Spirit without measure. In saying, "I baptize with water but he will baptize you with the Holy Spirit and fire" John admits his baptism does not hold a candle to Jesus' fire.

Jesus has an incomparable relationship with the Holy Spirit. Only he can baptize with the Spirit. To baptize with water is one thing but far greater is the power and authority to baptize with the Spirit. The Holy Spirit accomplishes more than water ever can. Jesus' baptism, for instance, empowers, enlightens, and ignites. In addition, it purifies stuff in our lives water cannot affect. Like a refiner's fire, Spirit baptism is transformative, purging out the dross of the world. It is an immersion in God himself. How wonderful! How marvelous! We are brought into a living and dynamic encounter with Elijah's God who answered by fire. And with Moses' God who appeared to him in a burning bush and spoke from the fire on Mt. Sinai.

Rhema: John testifies to Christ's unsurpassed and unique work which he refers to as a baptism of the Spirit. His baptism in distinction from John's is a baptism of fire. Fire purifies, illuminates, and indicates God's presence. Such is the Holy Spirit's work in our lives. We might think John's baptism unto repentance was wonderful. As great as it was, it pales compared to what Jesus offers us. The baptism of the Holy Spirit and fire is an immersion into a full and wonderful encounter with Christ himself.

THE HOLY SPIRIT DESCENDS IN A BODILY FORM

*When all the people were being baptized, Jesus was baptized too. And as he was praying, heaven was opened and the **Holy Spirit** descended on him in bodily form like a dove.* –LUKE 3:21–22

Only Luke mentioned the Holy Spirit descended upon Jesus in a bodily form. Why? Always the historian, he anchored the descent of the Spirit as a factual event in history. He wanted people to realize the Holy Spirit is real and his presence known. Likewise, as a physician he has an interest in the physical body and yet he knows the Spirit is invisible to the human eye. God is spirit, and no one has ever seen him. When we experience the Holy Spirit, we encounter something more than our own subjectivity. We experience objective and perceptible indicators of his presence (see Ex 13:21–22).

The Spirit resembles wind or breath. In fact, Hebrew uses the same word for all three terms. Although wind is invisible, we are aware of its movement. We can feel, hear, and see it rustle trees or blow in our faces. Wind is unseen but real. In a similar way, the invisible Third Person of the Trinity makes his presence and activity known to us.

On the day of Pentecost, for example, no one saw the Holy Spirit. Believers did experience, however, his presence. They saw something like "tongues of fire" and heard the roar of a rushing mighty wind. His awesome arrival affected their senses. When they were filled with the Spirit, they knew it for they all began to speak in other tongues. John experienced the Spirit's coming on Jesus similar to what would happen at Pentecost. He observed the manifestation, the eternal breaking into time and space.

Rhema: Luke wants to show the Spirit's reality and importance in Jesus' life. If our Lord needed the Holy Spirit to live out his life with a power from above, how much more do we? Holy Spirit experiences are real and what John witnessed was more than a figment of his imagination. The same is true of our Holy Spirit experiences. One or more of our five senses detect his presence and activity. Seek to be aware of his movement and manifestation. He is not to be feared but welcomed and embraced.

WE CAN NEVER HAVE TOO MUCH
OF THE HOLY SPIRIT

*Jesus, full of the **Holy Spirit**, left the Jordan and was led by the Spirit into the wilderness, where for forty days he was tempted by the devil. He ate nothing during those days, and at the end of them he was hungry.*
–Luke 4:1

How instructive to realize Jesus was full of the Spirit. Some people are full of themselves. Others are full of anger, rage, or jealousy; and sad to say, some are even full of evil. Jesus is full of God. He is under the Spirit's control. This is how he lives. Neither world, flesh, nor devil controls him, only the power from on high. The devil tempts him to no avail because he has heavenly strength. Divine fullness is to the soul what a sumptuous meal is to the body. He does not need to turn stones into bread because God's Spirit satisfies and energizes him.

What does it mean to be full of the Holy Spirit? This question is important to Luke because he is the only gospel writer to note this about Jesus. When our Lord leaves Jordon where he was baptized, he returns with the full measure of the Holy Spirit. His rich, abundant endowment from heaven is like a river overflowing its banks. It means he is miraculously guided, enabled, and anointed to overcome the devil and begin his public ministry.

The Spirit descends on Jesus before his temptation and before he commences ministry. Luke shows how important this is in his life. He is not only "full of the Holy Spirit" (v 1) but also "led by the Spirit" (v 1) and returns to Galilee "in the power of the Spirit" (v 14). His victorious life and powerful ministry is an outflow of his spiritual anointing (v 18).

Rhema: We can never have too much of the Holy Spirit. Living in spiritual fullness takes precedence over satisfying the needs of our flesh. God wants his children to live above the low plane subsistence of carnality. After the Holy Spirit descended upon Jesus, his Father declared, "You are my Son, whom I love; with you I am well pleased" (3:22). He lived his life on earth as a person saturated with the Spirit. God wants us to do the same.

MAY 1 | LUKE 4:1–13; DEUTERONOMY 8:1–20

LED BY THE SPIRIT

*Jesus, full of the Holy Spirit, left the Jordan and was led by the **Spirit** into the wilderness, where for forty days he was tempted by the devil. He ate nothing during those days, and at the end of them he was hungry.*
–Luke 4:1

Occasionally the Spirit leads us into strange situations. If it were up to us, we would not choose them. Who in their right mind wants to meet the devil? Go hungry? Be alone? Any of these conditions will stress us. How we respond, however, proves our character and tests our faith. God permits these challenges not so we will sin but so we will grow.

As soon as the Spirit came upon him, Jesus submitted to him. To live as the Son of God who pleases his Father meant he completely followed the Spirit's leading. As strange as it may sound, he led him into the wilderness to be tempted by the devil. This trying ordeal was pivotal in proving he was indeed God's Son who delighted his Father (3:22).

The devil shows up to challenge his Sonship. He says, "If you are the Son of God." By this he says, *Let's assume for the sake of argument you are God's Son, then why are you going hungry? A loving Father would not let his child starve. Use your power, therefore, to make bread and relieve your hunger.* See what the tempter does—he distorts God's word, adds "if" to it and then turns it against our Lord. What does Jesus do? He answers the devil with the sword of the Spirit, a *rhema* word of God (Eph 6:17). He replies, "Living as God's Son is far more than having bread. Man lives by every word (*rhema*) that proceeds out of the mouth of God" (v 4, Deut 8:3).

Rhema: Although the Spirit will lead you into perplexing circumstances, he always does it for your good. God will never tempt you to sin but allows testing to see what is in your heart. Since he is good, he will always provide. So rely upon the Holy Spirit to lead you, to give you a rhema word, and help you overcome temptation. After all, everyone who is led by the Spirit is a child of God (Rms 8:14).

MAY 2 | LUKE 4:14–15, 31–44

THE POWER OF THE SPIRIT

*Jesus returned to Galilee in the power of the **Spirit**, and news about him spread through the whole countryside. –LUKE 4:14*

Do you feel weak, overwhelmed, and under attack? Jesus should have after forty days of fasting and fighting the foe. Instead, he returned to Galilee in the power of the Spirit, the same power he received when the Holy Spirit came on him at his baptism. Now he comes equipped to wreak havoc on his enemy.

God's work requires the Spirit's mighty power. Several English words such as "dynamic," "dynamo," and "dynamite" are derived from *dunamis*, the Greek term for "power." We need *dunamis* to change things, to move obstacles, to bring the nonexistent into existence and especially to come against the enemy. That is how Jesus released the oppressed, healed the sick, cast out demons, and proclaimed the year of the Lord's favor. He gave his disciples power and said, "I saw Satan fall like lightning from heaven. I have given you authority to trample on snakes and scorpions and to overcome all the power of the enemy; nothing will harm you" (10:18–19).

The success of his Galilean ministry is attributed to the Spirit. Understand the Holy Spirit is not a diminutive member of the Godhead. No, he is fully God. He is the source of Jesus' power (v 18)— his healing power, miracle power, creative power, resurrection power, protective power, delivering power, keeping power. No one was ever so effectual and powerful both in word and deed as he. Consequently, news about him "spread through the whole countryside" (v 37). Luke says, "Everyone praised him" (v 15) and "all spoke well of him and were amazed at the gracious words that came from his lips" (v 22). His teaching stunned people "because his message had authority" (v 32). All this because he went forth in the power of the Spirit.

Rhema: Jesus wants to empower you with the Holy Spirit. After his resurrection he said, "You will receive power but stay in the city until you have been clothed with power from on high" (24:49, Acts 1:8). He wants to give you the same power he had so you can witness and work for him. Jesus demonstrated the power of the Spirit is indispensable for serving God.

ANOINTED WITH THE HOLY SPIRIT

*The **Spirit** of the Lord is on me, because he has anointed me to proclaim good news to the poor. He has sent me to proclaim freedom for the prisoners and recovery of sight for the blind, to set the oppressed free, to proclaim the year of the Lord's favor.* –LUKE 4:18–19

"Anointed" is a fascinating word that means to invest a person with power and authority, a special endowment to fulfill their divine mission. Everything about Jesus—his conception, baptism, temptation, and ministry involves the Holy Spirit. As he begins his public ministry, he turned to Isaiah to read aloud God's plan for his life. "The Spirit of the Lord is on me because he has anointed me." Then addressing those assembled he declared, "This day this Scripture is fulfilled in your hearing" (v 21). Amazing! After centuries of anticipation, the marvelous moment had arrived.

Isaiah gave five reasons the Spirit anointed Jesus. (1) To preach good news to the poor. (2) To proclaim freedom for the prisoners. (3) To provide sight for the blind. (4) To liberate the oppressed. (5) To proclaim the acceptable year of the Lord. The Spirit anointed him so he could free everyone oppressed by Satan and inaugurate the Year of Jubilee. This was wonderful news for anyone who suffered shame, bondage, oppression, and loss because of Satan.

The purpose of anointing Jesus with the Holy Spirit was to help him minister to the whole person—body, soul, and spirit. Without it he would have no powerful word to preach to people who had nothing. No power to release anyone from their bondage and no right to show them the way, the truth, and the life. Jesus came to emancipate the oppressed and introduce them to the extraordinary blessing of God's acceptance and approval.

Rhema: The end-time promises of God's favor have begun. If you are poor, captive, blind, and oppressed, rejoice because your day of blessing has arrived. Jesus has come to liberate you from the oppression and domination of the devil. Celebrate your Jubilee, a time when slaves are set free and debts are cancelled. The Spirit has anointed and empowered him to usher in an unprecedented time of God's goodwill and spiritual blessing. Your days of bondage and disorder are over.

MAY 4 | LUKE 10:1–24

FULL OF JOY THROUGH THE HOLY SPIRIT

*At that time Jesus, full of joy through the **Holy Spirit**, said, "I praise you, Father, Lord of heaven and earth, because you have hidden these things from the wise and learned, and revealed them to little children. Yes, Father, for this is what you were pleased to do.* **–LUKE 10:21**

Can you feel elation and excitement in this story? Notice how many expressions of joy occur. The seventy-two returned with "joy." Jesus said, "Do not rejoice that the spirits submit to you, but rejoice that your names are written in heaven." He himself was "full of joy through the Holy Spirit." Besides, he exclaims, "Blessed" are the eyes that see what you see (v 23). Lastly, the Father is "pleased." The seventy-two, the Father, Son, and Holy Spirit all experienced great delight.

What caused this boundless joy? A simple answer is getting the devil out of people. When our Lord's ambassadors returned from their mission, they were thrilled to report deliverances. Elated, they said, "Even the demons submit to us in your name" (v 17). To which Jesus replied, "I saw Satan fall like lightning from heaven" (v 18). The demise of God's archenemy caused this superabundance of ecstasy.

Satan and his forces are active and responsible for all forms of evil and oppression. Jesus came to set people free from their ravages. For this reason, he sent out these representatives to "heal the sick" and proclaim the kingdom of God (v 9). Before their eyes they saw the realization of God's first ever promise of salvation—they witnessed the offspring of a woman crush the head of the Serpent (Gen 3:14–15). Kings and prophets of old longed to see its fulfillment. Now Jesus and his disciples were delivering a crushing blow to that old snake.

Rhema: We can call Luke's Gospel a gospel of joy. From a babe leaping in his mother's womb for pure delight (1:41) to the close of the book (24:52) joyfulness is prominent. Luke's overarching message is unmistakable: the Holy Spirit fills us with joy whenever we observe God at work saving and delivering people. We are to cheer the ruin of Satan's evil and destructive powers. As Jesus pointed out, however, it is more important to rejoice because our names are in the Lamb's book of life.

MAY 5 | LUKE 11:1–13

ASK FOR THE HOLY SPIRIT

*If you then, though you are evil, know how to give good gifts to your children, how much more will your Father in heaven give the **Holy Spirit** to those who ask him!* –LUKE **11:13**

Do you like gifts? Great gifts? Father God has one very special present for you—just for the asking. Seeking it ought to be a priority. This chapter opens with one of Jesus' disciples asking him to teach them how to ask God for things. After watching him pray, the disciple wanted to learn how Jesus presented his requests. No one is better to instruct us because he not only got his prayers answered but amazing things happened when he prayed.

"Start your request," Jesus said, "by recognizing God is your Father. He is good and wants to bestow excellent gifts on his children. All his gifts are valuable, pleasing, and beneficial." The key to asking God for anything begins with knowing his nature and character. Our Father, he tells them, desires to give his children gifts that increase their well-being. No need to fear—he will never give a bad gift. Nor will he fail to respond to the needs of his children because fatherly neglect will place his hallowed name at risk. Even imperfect earthly fathers "know how to give good gifts" to their children. Our heavenly Father surpasses them because he gives good and greater gifts.

The greatest gift we can ever receive is the Holy Spirit. God gave his Son the Spirit at his baptism and now he wants to do the same for us. Our theology, Jesus intimates, affects how we pray. A weak or erroneous understanding of the Father robs us of confidence and limits our faith. Jesus knows him so well he has no hesitation asking him for anything. God will do no less than our earthly fathers, imperfect as they are. In contrast, he will do a whole lot more because he is perfect and gives the supreme gift.

Rhema: Jesus encourages us to ask God for the gift of the Holy Spirit. Nothing will benefit us more. We can trust his fatherly nature to award us this precious gift. In fact, this is the first time in the Bible we are encouraged to ask for the Holy Spirit; it will not be the last.

May 6 | Luke 12:1–10

BLASPHEMING THE HOLY SPIRIT

And everyone who speaks a word against the Son of Man will be forgiven, but anyone who blasphemes against the **Holy Spirit** *will not be forgiven.* **–LUKE 12:10**

Jesus stunned his disciples when he declared one sin was unpardonable. Of the many iniquities mankind makes, he singled out just one that will not be forgiven. Every heinous wrong against others may be forgiven; every wicked transgression against God and his Son is forgivable. Nevertheless, blasphemy against the Holy Spirit goes far beyond the reach of God's grace.

To understand the nature of this sin, we must look at it in context. With thousands trampling each other to hear him, Jesus warns against duplicity. He says to his followers, "Be on your guard against the yeast of the Pharisees, which is hypocrisy" (v 1). Originally, hypocrisy meant playacting or pretending—saying things on stage or making declarations one knows is not true. On this basis, a hypocrite speaks or acts in direct opposition to what he or she knows to be right. The sin against the Holy Spirit is not about unbelief; it is about hypocrisy.

The Pharisees knew in their hearts Jesus was the Messiah, but they did not want to acknowledge it. As they listened to and observed him, the Holy Spirit provided overwhelming and indisputable evidence he was God's Son. Since he was so full of the Spirit, they realized they were encountering God. In the depths of their being, they knew beyond a doubt his words and deeds had no human equal. No individual could do the miracles or speak the words he did unless God was with him (Jn 3:2).

Blaspheming the Holy Spirit is not from a lack of proof or a wavering of faith. Instead, the sin for which there is no forgiveness is a denial of an intense inner conviction brought about by the Spirit. To despise and reject this witness is hypocritical because if they were true to themselves and true to what they knew, they would acknowledge Jesus is the Son of God.

Rhema: If you value the Spirit's leading, his witness, and his operation, you never need fear you have committed the unpardonable sin. Nevertheless, when the Spirit manifests Christ's presence, care must be taken not to discredit, disparage, or defame him. That's unforgiveable!

MAY 7 | LUKE 12:11–12; ACTS 6:8–15, 7:54–60

TAUGHT BY THE HOLY SPIRIT

When you are brought before synagogues, rulers and authorities, do not worry about how you will defend yourselves or what you will say, for the **Holy Spirit** *will teach you at that time what you should say.*
–LUKE 12:11–12

Expect to defend your faith in Jesus Christ. Jesus was prophetic when he told his disciples they would be brought before various authorities to give an account of the gospel. Although risking their lives was real, they should not be anxious.

The book of Acts gives examples of the Holy Spirit helping the disciples witness. When the authorities dragged them into court, they experienced the Spirit helping them defend their faith. Chapters are filled with the Holy Spirit teaching them what to utter. One example is Stephen. He had been performing "great wonders and miraculous signs among the people" (Acts 6:8). Little did he know when he began healing folk that day enemies would arrest him. Like a common criminal, they hauled him off to explain these mighty miracles.

When the authorities argued with him, they found they were no match because of the words coming out of his mouth. Luke states, "They could not stand up against the wisdom the Spirit gave him as he spoke" (Acts 6:10). Losing the argument, they resorted to underhanded means to stop him. They "secretly persuaded some men" to accuse him of blasphemy. Besides, they "stirred up the people" and "produced false witnesses who testified" against him. Then his opponents seized him and brought him before the Jewish court.

Just as Jesus said, the Spirit taught him what to say. Stephen gave a remarkable account of their history, unlike anything they ever heard. Starting with Abraham and ending with the death of Jesus he told them they "always resist the Holy Spirit" (Acts 6:51). Upon hearing this, "they were furious and gnashed their teeth at him" (Acts 7:54). Livid, the leaders lashed out against him. When they could listen no more, they dragged him out of the city and stoned him (Acts 7:57–58). Stephen, the first martyr, a hero of the faith, slipped peacefully into the presence of God.

Rhema: The Holy Spirit who works in our everyday life will likewise give us the words to speak when under attack.

MAY 8 | JOHN 1:29–34

MARKED BY THE HOLY SPIRIT

*Then John gave this testimony: "I saw the **Spirit** come down from heaven as a dove and remain on him." –JOHN 1:32*

Jesus was a marked man. He bore the mark of the Holy Spirit. God had revealed to John the Baptist that the person on whom he saw the Spirit descend was the Son of God. This was a God-given mark that identified him as the long-awaited Messiah.

In John's Gospel, the Holy Spirit's role is to make the Lord real. Because Jesus was tattooed with the Spirit, the Baptist could speak about him with clarity and confidence. He said, "I have the proof of what I am saying because I saw the Spirit come down from heaven as a dove and remain on him." Giving the Lord this unique trademark enabled his forerunner to become his powerful promoter.

This revelation had a profound effect on John. Seeing the Spirit mark Jesus so transformed him he was never the same again. Immediately, the change was seen in his preaching. Because the Spirit singled Jesus out, John's personal testimony and public proclamations were phenomenal. His knowledge of Christ was not based on speculation or hearsay but on divine disclosure.

After this transforming experience, John preached about Jesus like no one else. Notice his never before articulated awesome announcements. First, he declared Jesus was "the Lamb of God, who takes away the sin of the world" (v 29). Second, he affirmed his preexistence and eternal nature (v 30). Third, Jesus would baptize them with the Holy Spirit (v 33). Fourth, the Baptist declared Christ's deity with absolute certainty. He said, "I have seen and I testify that this is the Son of God" (v 34). Just reflect on those unique declarations! These revelations are mind-blowing. Jesus is the preexistent, eternal Son of God who has come to sacrifice his life for the sin of the world and to baptize believers with the Holy Spirit.

Rhema: Does the Holy Spirit make Jesus stand out for you? His purpose in our lives is to give us this same confidence, clarity, and power to bear witness to Jesus as John. The Spirit of God comes on us for the express purpose of marking us so we can declare Jesus to others.

MAY 9 | JOHN 1:29–34; 15:1–17

A HOME FOR THE HOLY SPIRIT

And I myself did not know him, but the one who sent me to baptize with water told me, 'The man on whom you see the Spirit come down and remain is the one who will baptize with the Holy Spirit." –JOHN 1:33

Where's home for you? The place we call home is special because it depicts our deepest values and offers us comfort and safety. It is where we rest and relax, let our hair down, and take off our shoes. Like a bird who builds a nest, our home is essential to our lives, the place from which we fly off to engage the world and the sanctuary to which we return at close of day.

When John states the Spirit remained on Jesus, he implies the Holy Spirit made his home in the Lord. The word "remain" can mean a place of abode, to stay with, dwell, abide, and live. The Spirit descended to dwell with Jesus. Only John's gospel highlights this feature of our Lord's baptism. In fact, he mentions this twice because dwelling, remaining, and abiding are important to him. The word, "remain," occurs more than forty times in John, making it one of his favorite terms.

The Spirit resides with Jesus in an exceptional way. He is always in residence to help him with his work and to keep him company. He makes his abode in Christ not for a mere season or for a specific task but forever. For this to happen, Jesus had to welcome and want the Holy Spirit in his life. As a result, an inseparable relationship developed between them.

Rhema: It is important for us to make the Holy Spirit feel at home in our lives. If we are to get the most out of this amazing relationship, we must make him feel comfortable. He wants to reside with us now and forever in an intimate bond of fellowship.

When the Spirit descends on you, your body becomes his home. You are his dwelling place. He brings joy and laughter, peace and love. Heaven resides in you. As you interact with him, he brings you incredible resources so you can achieve God's purpose for your life. You are never alone for wherever you are he is.

MAY 10 | JOHN 1:29–34; ACTS 1:1–5

BAPTIZED WITH THE HOLY SPIRIT

And I myself did not know him, but the one who sent me to baptize with water told me, "The man on whom you see the Spirit come down and remain is the one who will baptize with the Holy Spirit." –JOHN 1:33

He will baptize you with the Holy Spirit. This great promise highlighted in all four gospels and Acts is for you. To have rivers of living water well up within you is not incidental to the gospel but its major purpose (4:14). The full impact of God's redemptive act is not realized in your life until you are baptized in the Spirit. To say this in no way minimizes Christ's sacrificial death on the cross for he is the Lamb of God that takes away the sin of the world. God, however, must first deal with sin by his Son's sacrifice before he can inundate us with his Spirit.

Implementing this glorious promise had to wait until Christ rose from the dead. After his resurrection, Jesus instructed his disciples to wait in Jerusalem for the promised gift. He said, "For John baptized with water, but in a few days, you will be baptized with the Holy Spirit" (Acts 1:5). Jesus announced something entirely new—his death and resurrection would make the Spirit available in a way never before possible. The New Covenant in his blood is also the New Covenant of the Spirit.

The purpose of Christ's redemptive mission is more than a matter of justification by faith. The gospel does not end with his resurrection. John summarizes God's saving work in Christ with reference to the Third Person of the Trinity. Jesus received the Spirit from the Father to inaugurate the Age of Fulfillment when he would baptize with the Spirit. Christ came to give the Holy Spirit to everyone who believed in him—to everyone made righteous by his death.

Rhema: God himself coined the phrase, to "baptize with the Holy Spirit." He revealed to John that the one upon whom his Spirit descended would inundate them with the Spirit. The term implies a thorough drenching or soaking. The abundant, lavish deluge of the Spirit resulting from Christ's saving death is for you. It is the central part of the gospel. Jesus came, John says, to baptize with the Spirit.

MAY 11 | JOHN 3:1–5

BORN OF THE SPIRIT

*Then Jesus answered, "Very truly I tell you, no one can enter the kingdom of God unless they are born of water and the **Spirit**." –JOHN 3:5*

Nicodemus, a prominent senator in Israel, recognized God was not working in his life as much as he wanted. He and Jesus operated on different levels. Although supremely religious, he saw no miracles in his life. Even though he fasted, prayed, tithed, and studied God's word, he realized he had a deficiency. God was with Jesus in a way he was not with him. He came to the Lord in the still of night to find out why.

The answer he gave Nicodemus was unexpected. Jesus said to him, "You cannot see what God is doing unless you are born again." We must be born of the Spirit to have any part in what God is doing. Unless we are born from above (v 3), we cannot take part in the kingdom of God. He told Israel's teacher a new kind of birth is necessary if he desires to encounter God. To experience the long-awaited end-time promises of salvation, he needed a spiritual regeneration.

This stunning answer must have been difficult for Nicodemus to embrace. It left him wondering how he could start life over again and have a new beginning. Not only was this physically impossible, but why was it necessary for a man of his gifts and righteousness? Jesus told him he needed a radical renovation before he could enter God's kingdom and experience these mighty things.

His problem centered on a lack of spiritual understanding. Bound by human perception and functioning on a natural, earthly level prevented him from taking part in Christ's activities. Dumfounded he asks, "How can someone be born when they are old?" Without the Spirit to enlighten, he can only think in the natural. He knows it is preposterous to enter a second time into his mother's womb. Jesus picks up on this and says, "Yes, you do need to be born of water," meaning an ordinary birth. Then he adds, "But you also need to be born of the Spirit."

Rhema: To participate in the kingdom of God, we need to be born of the Spirit. The old religious ways of Nicodemus are insufficient to see God at work.

MAY 12 | JOHN 3:1–6

THE SPIRIT GIVES BIRTH TO SPIRIT

*Flesh gives birth to flesh, but the **Spirit** gives birth to spirit.* –JOHN 3:6

Nicodemus needed to be born of the Spirit to gain access to God. Despite his religious achievements, he was still only flesh. Jesus said, "Flesh gives birth to flesh, but the Spirit gives birth to the spirit." Even in a religious individual such as Nicodemus, the flesh is still weak and incapable of relating to God. Only the Spirit can give us a new nature capable of embracing the divine.

Without the Spirit, we are spiritually inept. Human nature in and of itself can never lead to full participation in spiritual things. Flesh does not energize our soul or empower us to live a life pleasing to God. Nor does it prepare us to enter eternity or embrace God's presence. To function in the divine realm is beyond human ability; it must be birthed of God's Spirit. Truly, this makes Christianity different from all religions.

Everything Jesus said to Israel's teacher was news to him. Not for a moment did he realize he needed spiritual regeneration. He thought he could embrace God through religious activities, but they counted for naught. Because he only operated on an earthly plane, his best efforts left him ignorant of heavenly things. He was incapable of making himself fit for the kingdom of God.

A great gulf is fixed between the realms of the flesh and the spirit: man is flesh, God is spirit. Man in his human condition is powerless to save himself. Flesh can only give birth to flesh. Therefore, we need the Spirit if we are to understand spiritual things. Nor can we live the Christian life until the Spirit generates new life within. Then everything changes—our thoughts, desires, deeds, and worship. With the Spirit, we have a different power in our lives, a divine energy to help us live for God. The Spirit transforms us from the natural to the spiritual.

Rhema: The Spirit births new spiritual realities. Bible reading comes alive because the one who inspired Scripture now illuminates it. Prayer changes because the Spirit who communicates with our spirit puts us in direct contact with God. Behavior changes because a power from on high leads us in paths pleasing to God. Indeed, old things pass away, all things become new.

MAY 13 | JOHN 3:5–21

THE SPIRIT IS LIKE THE WIND

The wind blows wherever it pleases. You hear its sound, but you cannot tell where it comes from or where it is going. So it is with everyone born of the Spirit. –JOHN 3:8

Robert Louis Stevenson penned these words in *The Wind*: "I saw you toss the kites on high and blow the birds about the sky; and all around I heard you pass, like ladies' skirts across the grass." Wind, an unseen presence that drives the clouds, rustles the leaves, and creates the waves symbolizes the Spirit.

In comparing the Spirit with wind, Jesus affirms his sovereignty. "The wind blows wherever it pleases." No one can tell the wind what to do; it is its own master. No one can control the wind nor understand its origin or its destination. In the same way, there is no ordering the Spirit, no dictating where he blows. As an invisible stream of power, he has the capability to renew and refresh, to rustle, and rouse. No one sees him create a new life, nevertheless his presence is obvious.

Each person born of the Spirit is like wind. Nicodemus must understand the way of the wind before he can understand the way of the Spirit. At times wind is as gentle as a lullaby refreshing and relaxing the soul. At other times it ignites a fire and fans into flames a passion for the Lord. The heavenly zephyrs move the clouds and animate the fields and forests: they are like the breath of God that brings life to dust. God soars on the "wings of the wind" (II Sam 22:11) and invites us to join in his triumph over his enemies. The heavenly gale breaks the branches of habitual sin (I Jn 3:9). The wind is to a sailboat what the Spirit is to believers: he fills their sails to propel them on the right course (I Jn 2:29). With a power from above they can live above the pressures and temptations below.

Rhema: Profound and mysterious changes take place in our lives when we are under the sway of the Spirit. A new divine dynamism enters to effect change. Ride the wind and let it envelop you with divine power and purpose. Let it fill your sails and steer you in the right direction.

MAY 14 | JOHN 3:22–36

SPIRIT UNLIMITED

For the one whom God has sent speaks the words of God, for God gives the **Spirit** *without limit.* –JOHN 3:34

Jesus had the Spirit without limit. What does that mean? It meant no curbs were placed on what he knew or what he could do. Because Christ has the Spirit *par excellence*, he can communicate God's words with accuracy and authority. His intimate knowledge and understanding of God, heaven, and eternity surpasses everyone. This is why he knows more than Nicodemus, Israel's teacher.

Think of it! Jesus "comes from heaven" and "testifies to what he has seen and heard." When he describes spiritual things, he need not speculate, wonder, or make hypothetical constructs. He knows the truth and has no need of metaphysical presuppositions. Reality beyond human experience and outside the realm of science is perfectly known to him. Unlike the philosopher, scientist, and religious guru limited by their earthly experiences, his words are reliable and true.

Jesus' teachings are superior to even God's anointed prophets. After all, he is the Word (1:1–2) made flesh. "The Son is the radiance of God's glory and the exact representation of his being" (Heb 1:3). Since he has the fullness of the Spirit, no barrier exists between him and the Father. His pronouncements take precedence over Moses, Elijah, and Isaiah (Mt 5:21). In contrast to them, "he comes from above and is above all" (3:31). Everything they said must be measured against his teachings because they have never been to the hereafter; they are of the earth. "A man can only receive what is given him from heaven" (v 27). Jesus bridges the chasm between the earthly and heavenly because he has personal knowledge of God and eternity.

To have the Spirit without measure means his anointing knows no limit. In some ultimate and final way, he possesses the Spirit. The Spirit not only directs and controls him but inspires all his words and makes them true revelations of God. Because he is sent by God with the full measure of the Spirit, he can deliver his words without distortion or dilution.

Rhema: For us it means the more of the Spirit we possess, the better we can know God and make him known. Our anointing is in direct correlation to our apportionment of the Spirit.

MAY 15 | JOHN 4:1–26

THE SPIRIT CREATES A TRUE WORSHIPER

*Yet a time is coming and has now come when the true worshipers will worship the Father in the **Spirit** and in truth, for they are the kind of worshipers the Father seeks. —JOHN 4:23*

What kind of worshiper is God seeking? It might come as a surprise to realize he is not too concerned whether we praise him with hymns or choruses. Nor is he much worried whether the style is contemporary, traditional, or blended. After all, he is eternal. Furthermore, whether we venerate him in a tabernacle, temple, or a tin shack is of little consequence. The Father is looking for "true worshipers."

This new era initiated by Jesus required a new truth—worship must change. He said, "True worshipers will worship the Father in the Spirit and truth." The same Spirit responsible for the new birth makes possible a new genre of worship. Adoration the Father seeks is created by the Holy Spirit, so every person born from above can worship him the way he wants.

In Jesus' encounter with the woman at the well, the question of worship surfaced. Jews and Samaritans had conflicting views on how to honor and glorify God. They argued mostly over sacred time and space, but Jesus told her holy places such as Gerizim and Jerusalem are unimportant. The time has come, he added, for worship to change from externals, such as gender, race, and place to things of the Spirit. Therefore, one who is born of the Spirit and, consequently, a member of his family—one who passes from the earthly realm to God's realm—has direct access to the Father.

God wants Spirit-generated worship. When the Spirit enters our lives everything changes, including our devotion to God. The Spirit transforms how we approach the Father. No longer do we worship him from a distance or through material aids. Nor do we need religious systems, hierarchies, mediators, or a reliance on the "flesh." Rather, God wants us to approach him Spirit to spirit so our worship like a bubbling fountain (v 14) overflows with praise and adoration.

Rhema: The Spirit births a unique veneration of God. When we are born of the Spirit, we are no longer like the Samaritan woman marginalized and alienated from God. Instead, the Spirit ushers us into the Father's immediate presence.

MAY 16 | JOHN 4:19–26; I CORINTHIANS 2:6–16

WORSHIPERS MUST WORSHIP IN THE SPIRIT

*Yet God is spirit, and his worshipers must worship in the **Spirit** and in truth.* –JOHN 4:24

The new birth opens the way for a new worship. Just as God is light and God is love, so also is he spirit. He is free from all limitations of time and space and is present everywhere. As a spiritual being, he is immaterial, invisible, and incomprehensible. Man, by contrast, is material, finite, earthly, and incapable of approaching God until born of the Spirit. We must access the one who is spirit in the power of the Spirit. Since God in essence is spirit, he is unlike anything in the material world. Therefore, he cannot be grasped by our senses. For this reason, we need to be born again to worship him as he desires. Otherwise, coming before him and entering his presence is unattainable.

This is the first time the Bible speaks of worship in these terms. "God is Spirit, and his worshipers must worship in the Spirit and truth." Jesus is offering a new truth because we can only come before God as spirit after we are regenerated by the Spirit. To worship him as he wants requires the presence and activity of the Third Person of the Trinity. When we are born from above, we are given that ability to enjoy God as he is.

Material aspects of worship such as place, time, or rituals are inconsequential. Through the Spirit we have unconditional access to God. Entering his presence by the Spirit is far superior to sensual, material, or rational worship. Nothing pleases the Father more than his children of the Spirit pouring forth their praises like streams of living water (Eph 5:18–20). True adoration wells up within as the Spirit makes Jesus real. Only when we have been regenerated are we able to offer worship pleasing to God and in accordance with his nature.

Rhema: Always guard against worship that is mechanical, material, and Spiritless. The Holy Spirit removes the old barriers between man who is flesh and God who is spirit. When we are born from above, we take part in a new kind of worship that was previously unavailable. To present continuous and living praise to our heavenly Father, we must receive a new power and an inner dynamic.

THE SPIRIT GIVES LIFE

*The **Spirit** gives life; the flesh counts for nothing.* –JOHN 6:63

He had a knack for explaining mind-boggling concepts with the simplest of terms. In one short sentence, he resolves the current hermeneutical crisis and explains why people have trouble understanding Scripture. Many mistakenly believe if they only knew the language, culture, and history of Israel they could comprehend the text. If that were the case, everyone who listened to Jesus would understand what he said. But they didn't. The reason? Without the Spirit, spiritual apprehension is impossible.

We must be born of the Spirit before we can understand the words of Jesus Christ. When he says, "The Spirit gives life; the flesh counts for nothing," he exposes the inadequacy of human effort to figure him out. In this regard, the flesh is of no help whatsoever; it is the direct opposite of the Spirit. Jesus means we cannot get his point if we only use human means and methods. Nicodemus and the woman at the well failed to make sense of what he told them because they were not yet regenerated. What profits is the Spirit in our lives.

Jesus' words belong to the realm of the Spirit. They are the true manna from heaven that gives eternal life. The flesh is powerless to comprehend the spiritual import of his words. All our learning, study, and rational efforts will not open our minds to grasp his teachings. His words are full of divine life borne along by the breath of God. Therefore, they need the Spirit to make them come alive and yield their life-giving significance. Only through the Holy Spirit, the Spirit of truth, can we plumb the full depth of Christ's teachings.

The natural man cannot understand the things of the Spirit. That is why many who heard Jesus explain his incarnation were incapable of understanding him. When he told them they had to eat his flesh if they were to live forever, they said, "This is a hard saying" and asked, "Who can accept it?" Numerous followers became offended and quit (v 66).

Rhema: For Christ's teachings to benefit us, we need the Spirit. The flesh is unable to increase our knowledge of spiritual things. Before reading the Bible, ask the Holy Spirit to breathe upon its pages and bring its words to life.

MAY 18 | JOHN 6:25–42; 5:16–30

WORDS FULL OF THE SPIRIT

*The words I have spoken to you—they are full of the **Spirit** and life.*
–John 6:63

Do you want a great body? Is health a priority? Our growth, development, and health always depend upon eating the right food. The same applies to our Christian lives. To be healthy and growing in our walk with the Lord requires the right diet, eating food that will make us fit. Jesus told of a delicious cuisine that will feed our spirit and nourish our soul.

He refers to himself as the "Living Bread" (v 51). Of course, Jesus is using a metaphor to teach spiritual realities. For him, eating this bread is equivalent to believing in him. Anyone who eats "this bread will live forever" (v 58). By that he means anyone who believes in him has everlasting life (v 47). We nourish our spiritual life by accepting Jesus and ingesting his words.

Jesus said, "The words I have spoken to you—they are full of the Spirit and life." Most who heard him grumbled and complained, refusing to accept his teaching. How is it that people can hear his words and not understand them? The fault is not in the word but in the hearer. Christ's words belong to the realm of the Spirit and only those who possess the Spirit can digest them.

The words of Jesus are the source of our divine life. They will more than help nourish and strengthen us. Everything Jesus spoke is full of the Spirit. Every word is full of life. So when we have faith in his word, appropriate it and make it part of our diet Christ speaks life into us. The life of the Living God enlivens our spirit. His sayings are powerful, the cause of his miracles. At his word, water became wine (2:7), the lame walked (3:8), and Lazarus came forth (11:43). They have the power to save, heal, and deliver.

Rhema: Recognize Jesus has "the words of eternal life" (v 68). Consequently, spiritual health depends upon eating them. Feed your own soul with them. Then you will grow a healthy, spiritually robust body. Similarly, Christ's body needs words full of the Spirit and life and not the mere words of men. Otherwise, it will fail for lack of the bread of heaven.

MAY 19 | JOHN 7:25–44

THE SPIRIT RELEASES
RIVERS OF LIVING WATER

*Whoever believes in me, as Scripture has said, rivers of living water will flow from within them. By this he meant the **Spirit**, whom those who believed in him were later to receive.* **–JOHN 7:38–39**

Are you feeling a little fatigued and dry today? When we are dehydrated, our energy level dips and our brain refuses to work. Are you dwelling in a dry and thirsty land? Does your soul crave satisfaction? It too needs hydrating.

Having the Spirit is like having rivers of living water gushing within. Jesus made this amazing proclamation on the last and greatest day of the Feast of Tabernacles. For seven days, spectacular ceremonies took place commemorating the wilderness wanderings when Moses smote the rock and water gushed out. As a result, the desert dwelling Israelites enjoyed a forty-year supply of the life-giving water. Jesus said he himself is the true rock. When he is smitten, he will give a continuous supply of living water to everyone who believes on him. His living water has far better benefits than the rock in the wilderness.

When Jesus promised these waters, he of course was referring to the Spirit. Everyone believing on him would receive the Holy Spirit. Obtaining this gift is like carrying around a constantly replenished water bottle hooked to a fire hydrant. In life's dry deserts, cool rivers flow from the depths of our being. These quench our yearnings and satisfy our soul's deepest longings. We will never thirst again. The living waters are spiritual rivers designed to sustain, refresh, and invigorate. Jesus is the source of an ever-fresh supply he will pour out on believers after his ascension.

Rhema: Jesus is the fulfillment of the prophetic promise contained in the Jewish feast. Greater than Moses, he offers you life-giving water to refresh and invigorate you. The exalted Lord will pour out upon you an unending supply of the life of God that extinguishes your longings and cravings. These waters will make you flourish and become a fruitful vine. Jesus says, "Let anyone who is thirsty come to me and drink" (v 37). These rivers are abundant, copious, and plentiful. They flow, bubble up, and brim over. Through the Spirit Jesus is your continuous and abundant reservoir of spiritual life, the source of the fullness of the Spirit.

MAY 20 | JOHN 7:1–24; 40–52

WHEN DOES THE SPIRIT
BECOME AVAILABLE?

*Up to that time the **Spirit** had not been given, since Jesus had not yet been glorified.* –JOHN 7:39

Someone said, "Our souls crave intimacy." God will go to great lengths and risk everything to bring you close to himself. He finds you interesting, intriguing, and irresistible. God has yearned for tender union with you. The Bible's story is the unfolding of God's plan to bring you cheek-to-cheek with him because sin had ruptured any hope of intimacy. Jesus came, therefore, to remove the flaming sword that drove Adam and Eve from his presence in Paradise. His sacrificial death on the cross and his pouring out the Spirit opened the way to personally experience God's unbounded love.

The Spirit, however, was not available until after Jesus' death and ascension. Believers must wait to receive God's indwelling presence until the sin problem was resolved. Only after our Lord died in our place and returned to the Father was it possible to receive the Holy Spirit. A new covenant in his blood for the forgiveness of sins must supersede the old (Mt 26:28) before he could release the Spirit.

The spiritual reality to which Jesus referred had to wait until he returned to heaven. Then he poured out the Spirit. One era must end before another begins. To give believers the Spirit, therefore, is different from previous spiritual encounters. What is different in this age is not only the new birth but a new measure of the Holy Spirit's presence. The dispensation of the fullness of the Spirit is unique. Through the Spirit God creates in us a new heart with a powerful impulse to love him and live for him. This does not imply the Holy Spirit was inactive in people's lives before. Rather, it means because we are born of the Spirit we have a distinct, deeper, and fuller experience.

Rhema: To experience the magnitude of God's affection is impossible until you receive the Spirit. Then his divine love will flood your heart by the Holy Spirit (Rms 5:5). Love's rapturous delights will bubble up in your innermost being. Waves of tenderness, waves of fondness will break upon you—more than you can ever comprehend. Call it holy intimacy. By deluging you with his Spirit, he fills your heart with a continuous stream of his immeasurable affection.

MAY 21 | JOHN 14:15–24

THE SPIRIT IS OUR HELPER

*And I will ask the Father, and he will give you another advocate to help you and be with you forever— the **Spirit** of truth. The world cannot accept him, because it neither sees him nor knows him. But you know him, for he lives with you and will be in you* –JOHN **14:16–17**

After living a short time on earth Jesus, the Son of Man, realized life is too harsh to live alone. Therefore, he promised to give his disciples in his absence the one who helped him. "Another advocate to help you and be with you forever" was what he promised them. The term translated "advocate" is *parakletos* in the original, meaning to call alongside. Jesus referred to the Holy Spirit as the one who will be at their side as a helper, comforter, encourager, and an advisor.

This is the first of four times our Lord in his Upper Room Farewell Discourse (14–16) speaks of the Spirit as "the Paraclete." Each of these occurrences expands on what Jesus meant. He is trying to console his distressed disciples after he said he would be with them for "only a little longer" (13:33). Peter speaks up and says he cannot imagine living a day without him. That is when our Lord begins his good-bye chat, saying, "Do not let your hearts be troubled" (v 1).

Jesus says he will ask his heavenly Father to give them someone like himself—another helper. After all, he is trying to comfort his disciples. His replacement will come alongside them just as he did and be their teacher and helper. In fact, the Spirit is equivalent to him and will take on his familiar roles, such as companion, coach, comforter, and consultant. When they are down, the Spirit will lift them up; when they face accusers, he will give them words to say.

Rhema: We need someone in our lives to do for us what Jesus did for his disciples. As their friend, he encouraged, advised, and strengthened them. When he walked among them, he was physically limited to one place but now he is always present with us by the Spirit. Our advocate-comforter-helper is not inferior to or less than our Lord. Instead, the Paraclete, the Holy Spirit, is our helper in every way Jesus helped his disciples.

May 22 | John 14:25–31

THE SPIRIT TEACHES US

But the Advocate, the **Holy Spirit**, *whom the Father will send in my name, will teach you all things and will remind you of everything I have said to you.* –John 14:26

Have you ever tried to imagine how wonderful it was for the disciples to hear Jesus teach? The thing they might have missed most about his departure was those evening fireside chats. They all sat around and listened to him with rapt attention. Peter once declared, "Lord, you have the words of eternal life." Jesus said things that blew them away. When alone with his disciples, he gave insightful explanations pertaining to the mysteries of the kingdom of God.

As good as it was to learn from Jesus, he tells his disciples something even better is coming. "It was for their good," he said, he was going away. What could be better? What could surpass his thrilling teaching? He had in mind none other than "the Advocate, the Holy Spirit, whom the Father will send in my name." The Spirit of truth would come and teach them. His specific role is to impart truth Jesus withheld teaching because of their unreadiness. In addition, he will remind them of everything our Lord said.

Nothing is better this side of heaven. Imagine having our own heavenly teacher present to instruct and remind of what Jesus taught. The Spirit perpetuates our Lord's teaching ministry by keeping his words active and alive. No need to lament his physical absence—his exciting revelations continue once we receive the Spirit of truth. Without the Spirit, we are incapable of understanding or remembering the Master's teaching.

Rhema: In whatever ways Jesus helped his disciples learn the things of God, the Holy Spirit will help you. Because he indwells you, you live in constant intimacy and unity with Christ. You are never alone, never on your own, never without help. The Father sends you the Spirit to come alongside of you to make Jesus' presence and teaching real. Although eternal truths appear as incoherent and illogical absurdities without him, he nevertheless makes Christ's teachings as real today as when he first taught them. The truth to which the Spirit gives you access is Jesus himself who said, "I am the way, and the truth and the life" (v 6).

MAY 23 | JOHN 15:18–27

THE SPIRIT TESTIFIES ABOUT JESUS

When the Advocate comes, whom I will send to you from the Father—the **Spirit** *of truth who goes out from the Father—he will testify about me.* **–JOHN 15:26**

In the courtroom truth is based upon the sworn statement of witnesses. Some of the most important decisions in the world rest on testimony. Witnesses swear to tell the truth, the whole truth and nothing but the truth. One of the Spirit's primary roles is to serve as Jesus' witness before a hostile, unbelieving world. In the court of world opinion, the truth about Jesus Christ is resisted and rejected. God the Father, however, sends the Spirit as the primary witness to attest to Jesus.

The jury must decide the truthfulness of Jesus' claims. Is he the Son of God? The way, the truth, and the life? Since he is in heaven, the Spirit must provide convincing truth about him. His trial did not end while he was on earth but continues after his departure. Everyone must decide who he is. The verdict is important because eternal destinies weigh in the balance. How can we know today the veracity of his words and deeds 2,000 years ago? Likewise, how can Christ sitting at the Father's right hand be known without the Spirit?

Truthfulness is essential for a witness. The Father sends the Holy Spirit to testify as the "Spirit of truth." Everything he says about Jesus is trustworthy; every untruth he challenges. Although Jesus is physically absent, he is personally present in the Spirit. Therefore, the purpose of the Spirit's witness is to help believers stay connected to him and help the undecided believe in him.

Compared to human testimony, the Spirit's is superior—he cannot lie. With men, the risk to skew the truth by perjury, poor memory, or personal interest is always present. Because mankind is prone to stretch the truth, individuals are often required to swear upon the Bible and say, "So help me God." The Holy Spirit is God; he need not swear upon the Bible. What he says is absolute truth. He proceeds from the Father to present relevant and important evidence concerning Christ in our world today.

Rhema: The Spirit's testimony, therefore, is right, reliable, and immediate. Everyone's eternal destiny rests on whether it is believed or not.

MAY 24 | JOHN 16:1–11

THE SPIRIT'S WORK IN THE WORLD

*Unless I go away, the **Advocate** will not come to you; but if I go, I will send him to you. When he comes, he will prove the world to be in the wrong about sin and righteousness and judgment.* –JOHN **16:7–8**

The Holy Spirit has a specific role regarding the world. As an Advocate, a prosecuting attorney, he challenges the world's false conceptions of Christ. He refutes arguments and exposes unbelief. His assignment is to convict mankind of its guilt and prove their rejection of Christ is wrong.

The world is mistaken about Jesus, so the Spirit is sent to prove it wrong. His primary role is always to bear witness to Christ. How does he do that? We are the key for how this takes place. The Spirit does not work in a vacuum; he works through us. In fact, every conversion story in the NT—Pentecost, Judea, Samaria, Paul and his converts results from the Holy Spirit working through believers. Jesus said, "I will send him to you." Christ connects the Spirit in believers with his conviction of the world.

Through our Spirit-transformed lives and witness, heaven's Prosecutor confronts people on three matters: sin, righteousness, and judgment. First, the Spirit challenges unbelievers for not accepting Christ. He led us to believe in Jesus, why haven't they? Every sin is subsumed under unbelief (v 9) because "whoever does not believe stands condemned already" (3:18). On the final day everyone will have to answer this question: "What have you done with Jesus?"

Second, the Spirit challenges the world about its view of right and wrong. God has only one standard: the righteousness of Jesus Christ. God credits the merits of his Son's perfect life to us through faith. In him we not only meet God's moral standard but we live for him in the power of the Spirit. What is their excuse? In the third place, the Holy Spirit convicts the *cosmos* of its mistaken belief about judgment. God has done everything possible to save the world—only judgment remains. Since "the prince of this world now stands condemned," the prosecution has already begun.

Rhema: The most convincing argument to prove the truth of Christ is a believer set on fire by the Holy Spirit, living and witnessing in his power.

MAY 25 | JOHN 16:12–33

THE SPIRIT GUIDES US INTO ALL TRUTH

*But when he, the **Spirit** of truth, comes, he will guide you into all the truth. He will not speak on his own; he will speak only what he hears, and he will tell you what is yet to come.* –JOHN 16:13

With Jesus in heaven, how can we keep growing in him? If he is not present to speak into our lives, will not our love and affection for him grow cold? The Lord understood these spiritual hazards his physical departure would create, so he told his disciples he will send the Spirit to help with their spiritual development and guide them into all truth.

To think of our heavenly guide funneling all truth into us is remarkable. He gives us a profound understanding of Jesus' death, burial, and resurrection. Truth enters our inner parts. Our new leader helps us comprehend spiritual things for he searches "the deep things of God." He even guarantees access to the Father. Jesus says the Spirit will show us the future, the things that are "yet to come." Revealed are things that eye has not seen nor ear heard. He brings to our consciousness unimaginable truth concerning what God has prepared for us who love him (I Cor 2:9). The Spirit of truth continues our knowledge of Christ. He keeps us contemporary so we can adapt to changing circumstances.

Jesus said the Spirit of truth is sent to guide us into all truth. He knows and understands everything in every field, area, and sphere. Knowledge exists because of him. When Adam was created, the breath of God turned dust to consciousness. The focus of the Spirit's revelations, however, is Jesus Christ and making him real. The Spirit "will not speak on his own; he will speak only what he hears." He tells us what we need to know and reports what is trending in heaven.

Rhema: The Spirit ensures we never tire of Jesus; instead, we will always enjoy a vibrant walk with him. Through the Spirit, our Lord continues to communicate with us and stay vitally connected. The Spirit works to mold and shape us, to teach and guide us so we become more and more like Jesus. Any apprehension over knowing him less with the fading of time is truly unfounded.

MAY 26 | I CORINTHIANS 1:18–31

THE SPIRIT MAKES JESUS REAL

*He will glorify me because it is from me that he will receive what he will
make known to you. All that belongs to the Father is mine. That is why
I said the **Spirit** will receive from me what he will make known to you.*
–JOHN 16:14–15

Jesus' disciples knew him better after his ascension than before.
Their knowledge of his earthly life pales compared to what they
learned by the Spirit. He wanted to teach them many things, but they
had to wait until he poured out the Spirit upon them. Then they would
be equipped to know him better.

To understand the gospel, for instance, requires the Holy Spirit.
To unbelievers the good news is just so much foolishness, but to us
"Christ is the power of God and the wisdom of God" (I Cor 1:23).
Paul declares, "The gospel I preached is not of human origin. I did
not receive it from any man, nor was I taught it; rather, I received it by
revelation from Jesus Christ" (Gal 1:11–12). The apostle said he gained
his remarkable insights not by human wisdom but "in words taught by
the Spirit" (I Cor 2:13). This is what Jesus meant when he said, "The
Spirit will receive from me what he will make known to you."

On this basis, the real source of the NT is Jesus. The four gospels
are far more than historical accounts of his life. The epistles are more
than apostolic answers to church problems. Acts is more than a history of the spread of Christianity. Rather, they constitute our Lord's
work and teaching through the Spirit. The last book of the Bible is
specifically called "a revelation of Jesus Christ" (Rev 1:1) because it
not only is about him but comes from him. John said he was "in the
Spirit" (Rev 1:10) when he received it.

*Rhema: Many believers are quick to embrace Jesus but wary of the Holy Spirit.
This should not be. Every word, insight, teaching, or revelation of the Spirit originates from God's Son. When the Spirit speaks, Jesus is speaking. When we receive
a vision, it comes from Christ. When the Spirit gives us directions, the advice is
from the Lord. To belittle the Spirit is to disparage the Lord Jesus Christ.*

JESUS AND THE SPIRIT REVERSE ROLES

*And with that he breathed on them and said, "Receive the **Holy Spirit**."*
–JOHN 20:22

Two things happened after Jesus rose from the dead that pertain to the Spirit. First, he and the Spirit reversed roles. Second, his disciples received the Spirit.

Christ's resurrection marks a turning point in his relationship with the Spirit. Up to then he was led by the Spirit, empowered by the Spirit, and submissive to the Spirit. Now their roles reverse, and the Spirit submits to him. Christ's resurrection and glorification changed him forever. Before, he took orders from the Spirit; now he directs the Spirit.

Because of this role reversal, Jesus can breathe on his disciples and say, "Receive the Holy Spirit." What happened? We are not told but this amazing incident parallels two great events in Scripture. First, in Genesis 2:7, God formed man from the dust of the earth and breathed into him, making him a living soul. Similarly, Jesus breathes on his disciples perhaps to indicate their spiritual rebirth. Second, in Ezekiel 37, "breath," the same word for Spirit, occurs seven times in association with the vision of the valley of dry bones. God says, "I will put breath (Spirit) in you, and you will come to life." At once, "Breath entered them; they came to life and stood up on their feet—a vast army (Ezek 37:10). Based on these parallels, we may assume his disciples were the first to be born of the Spirit.

This post-resurrection experience is not the baptism in the Holy Spirit. Forty days later, for instance, Jesus tells these same disciples they must wait in Jerusalem for the "gift of my Father" (Acts 1:4). Then they will be "baptized in the Holy Spirit" (Acts 1:5). Besides, John's language here (vv 19–31) is not the language of Pentecost but of conversion. In this passage, he records the Great Commission (v 21), speaks of peace three times, forgiveness four times, and believing six times. Further, he mentions Jesus' nail-scarred hands and wounded side three times. His purpose in writing is that we might believe and "have life in his name" (v 31).

Rhema: If we believe in his death, burial, and resurrection, he will breathe on us and make us part of his new creation fashioned after his likeness.

MAY 28 | ACTS 1:1–3; LUKE 24:36–49

INSTRUCTIONS THROUGH THE SPIRIT

*In my former book, Theophilus, I wrote about all that Jesus began to do and to teach until the day he was taken up to heaven, after giving instructions through the **Holy Spirit** to the apostles he had chosen.*
–ACTS 1:1–2

Christianity is unique because its founder is still alive. The same Jesus who spoke to his disciples continues to work and speak to us today. This is the author's point. The Gospel of Luke, his former book, records the beginning of Christ's ministry—what he began to do and teach. His work, however, does not end with the conclusion of his Gospel. In fact, the book of Acts is written to show it continues.

During the forty days between his resurrection and ascension, Jesus gave his disciples instructions through the Holy Spirit. What does this mean? He always spoke under the Spirit's influence, but this suggests something else. Now he communicates by the Spirit. Luke draws attention to our Lord's commands during this time.

These post-resurrection directives focus on continuing Jesus' mission to the world. The world is in a mess, lost, and without God. To reach it with the gospel is the disciples' most urgent task. Just as he was sent by his Father and empowered by the Spirit, so now he sends them. First, he ordered them to wait in Jerusalem until they received power from on high (v 4; Lk 24:49). If they are going to reach the ends of the earth with his message of salvation, they will need the Holy Spirit. The Lord through the Spirit was preparing them for the greatest mission the world has ever seen. Little do they realize they were soon to turn it upside down.

This is the first mention of the Holy Spirit in Acts. The work Jesus began to do with his disciples he now continues through his disciples. But how can a small band of believers in the absence of their leader impact the world? The most amazing answer to that question is found in this book.

Rhema: *Jesus, exalted, ascended, and glorified is present with you through the Spirit. When you have his Spirit you hear his voice, feel his compassion, and work in his power. Jesus is still alive, still active, still speaking—through the Holy Spirit.*

MAY 29 | ACTS 1:1–6

WAITING FOR THE HOLY SPIRIT

*On one occasion, while he was eating with them, he gave them this command: "Do not leave Jerusalem, but wait for the gift my Father promised, which you have heard me speak about. For John baptized with water, but in a few days you will be baptized with the **Holy Spirit**."*
—ACTS 1:4–5

For three years, Jesus spoke of this day. He said, "You have heard me speak about" it. His forerunner predicted it. Christ began and concluded his ministry teaching of a distinctive work of the Holy Spirit. Of course, no one knew what to expect because it had never happened before. Our Lord's entire life, however, pointed to this all-important event. The Father promised the gift. The Son distributes the gift. The Holy Spirit is the gift. With his departure imminent, Jesus wanted them to focus on his promise. His death, burial, and resurrection paved the way for this mighty spiritual eruption.

Jesus gave this command during the forty days between his resurrection and ascension. His order to wait in Jerusalem for the Father's gift was key to God's grand design to advance his work in the end times. The word "command" means to give directives, and is a strong military term occurring several times in Acts (4:18, 16:18, and 17:30). Just think, his disciples have been waiting for this promise since they joined him. God, however, has waited since creation to give it. In a few days, they will experience it. God's amazing gift is made available by Christ's death and resurrection.

What the Spirit did in and through their Lord the disciples are soon to experience for themselves. The Father's promise is soon realized in them. Being inundated with the Spirit will empower them to continue his work. They will have the same power, help, and anointing he had. How amazing to be endowed with the Holy Spirit.

These believers were to encounter a new phase in God's plan of salvation. Jesus' last words connect the kingdom of God (v 3) with Spirit baptism. The long-awaited kingdom would manifest itself on earth through the demonstration of the Spirit. The Father's promised gift was the sign a new, wonderful era had begun.

Rhema: He wants to give the amazing gift of the Holy Spirit to everyone who believes in him.

MAY 30 | ACTS 1:7–14

THE POWER OF THE SPIRIT TO WITNESS

*But you will receive power when the **Holy Spirit** comes on you; and you will be my witnesses in Jerusalem, and in all Judea and Samaria, and to the ends of the earth.* –ACTS 1:8

Stephen Covey said, "The main thing is to keep the main thing the main thing." He realized losing one's focus leads to discouragement, mediocrity, and missed opportunities. Unfortunately, many things can derail us from fulfilling our life's purpose. Since we live in an age of distractions, reaching our objectives may be difficult. If we divert our attention to issues of little importance, we might never flourish or achieve our best.

Jesus recognized that. His disciples would encounter many diversions that could derail the Great Commission. When he wanted to talk about receiving power, for instance, they wanted to talk about the end of the age. They inquired, "Lord, are you at this time going to restore the kingdom to Israel?" That is an interesting question, but it distracts from the main thing. A preoccupation with end-time events is not as important as receiving power to witness for Christ.

The disciples were soon to embark on a mission such as the world had never seen. To accomplish it, Christ promised them a superabundance of spiritual strength. Provided they keep their focus no obstacle will overcome them, neither prison, persecution, nor adversity. After the Holy Spirit comes upon them, they will be equipped to carry on God's work.

It is so easy to get our eyes off our mission and miss the target. We must never switch our attention from spreading the good news to lesser matters. Jerusalem and Judea are our spheres of influence, such as family, friends, and associates. Samaria is where we feel uncomfortable witnessing for Jesus. The uttermost parts of the earth are unfamiliar people and places. It is no easy task sharing Jesus in any of these places, but we can if spiritually empowered.

Rhema: The Spirit supplies the same power he gave the apostles, so we too can tell others what Jesus has done for us. In this way we can share firsthand experiences of his resurrection life in us. Until the consummation of the age, the power from on high is necessary if we are to carry on Christ's work in the world.

MAY 31 | ACTS 1:15–26

THE SPIRIT SPEAKS THROUGH SCRIPTURE

*In those days Peter stood up among the believers (a group numbering about a hundred and twenty) and said, "Brothers and sisters the Scripture had to be fulfilled in which the **Holy Spirit** spoke long ago through David concerning Judas, who served as guide for those who arrested Jesus. He was one of our number and shared in our ministry." –ACTS 1:15–16*

What should we do when we face inexplicable tragedy and are unsure of how to respond? After the ascension of Jesus (v 9), the believers came together and found themselves in the same situation. Judas, one of their leaders, had betrayed them and committed suicide. Faced with this horrible catastrophe, they choose to seek God and study Scripture for an answer.

Stepping forward, Peter guides them by using God's word. He says, "The Scripture had to be fulfilled in which the Holy Spirit spoke long ago through David concerning Judas." Following days of waiting on God, Peter realized the Spirit had predicted the betrayal and replacement of Judas. Then he cites two of David's Psalms (v 20). Moreover, he tells them the Spirit had foreseen this misadventure and its outcome. In as much as the Spirit gave him insight into God's word, he can help them understand this tragedy and respond appropriately.

Peter was a changed man after Jesus breathed the Holy Spirit upon him (Jn 20:22). One obvious difference was his grasp of Scripture. God's word opened up to him so he can apply it to their critical circumstances. Before, Peter stumbled along and seemed spiritually obtuse. His transformation may best be explained by the Holy Spirit illuminating him. With fresh insight into Scripture, the apostle directs his fellow believers to fill a vacancy in the Twelve created by Judas' defection and suicide.

Peter equates David's words with the Holy Spirit's voice and relies on both for guidance. For him the Holy Spirit is as much an authoritative, trustworthy guide as is Scripture. The same Spirit who spoke through David helped him understand and apply God's word.

Rhema: You can learn much from this example. People of the Spirit are also people of the word. Word and Spirit agree and will work together to guide you through tragedy and uncertainty. The Spirit can make God's word come alive and address your contemporary situations.

JUNE 1 | ACTS 2:1–13

EVERYONE WAS FILLED WITH THE HOLY SPIRIT

*All of them were filled with the **Holy Spirit** and began to speak in other tongues as the Spirit enabled them.* –ACTS 2:4

People witnessed the Holy Spirit's arrival. "Suddenly a sound like the blowing of a violent wind came from heaven and filled the whole house where they were sitting" (v 2). Folks heard the tumultuous roar and saw the leaping flames dance on believers' heads. "They saw what seemed to be tongues of fire that separated and came to rest on each of them" (v 3). The Spirit descended to revolutionize a handful of believers to become a world-changing movement. This was the birth of the church, a supernatural event originating in heaven.

Years of waiting for the full realization of the Feast of Pentecost were over. The national holiday occurred fifty days after Passover to celebrate the firstfruits of harvest. For good reason the Spirit's dynamic outpouring coincided with this feast. Believers who received the Spirit's fullness were firstfruits of Christ's sacrifice. Pentecost, therefore, was indispensably related to his death.

Peter along with the Twelve experienced this awesome immersion in the Spirit. "All of them were filled with the Holy Spirit." All one hundred and twenty new believers including Mary, Jesus' mother, and his brothers experienced this fire from heaven. Jesus was alive, exalted at his Father's right hand, pouring out the Spirit. Just as he began his ministry with the life-changing descent of the Spirit, so do his followers. Truly, John the Baptist's prophecy was fulfilled—Jesus was baptizing believers in the Holy Spirit and clothing them "with power from on high" (Lk 24:49).

Rhema: Pentecost is much more than filling a few believers with the Holy Spirit. It entails a tectonic shift from the Old Covenant to the New. This momentous event explains the amazing results detailed in Acts. The birth of the church and its worldwide impact are direct results of the Spirit's outpouring. Pentecost marked the time when Jesus poured out the Spirit on his followers to enable them to live and minister in the same power he enjoyed. The gift of the Spirit is freely available to those who believe in Jesus and repent of their sins. Therefore, the coming of the Spirit is for you and is intended to empower your witness.

JUNE 2 | ACTS 2:1–13

THE SPIRIT ENABLES SPEAKING IN TONGUES

*All of them were filled with the Holy Spirit and began to speak in other tongues as the **Spirit** enabled them.* –ACTS 2:4

The Holy Spirit's action always seems to create a mixed reaction. Luke says the crowd was "utterly amazed." The more they saw and heard the more their astonishment grew. What they experienced "blew their minds away." A few made fun of the believers and said, "They have had too much wine." Jokingly they said, "They are drunk." Never had anyone observed such linguistic prowess by people so untrained. Believers spoke in the visitors' local dialects. Coming face to face with the Spirit's dynamic activity stunned these onlookers.

The Spirit enabled these new believers to speak in other tongues. Coinciding with the Spirit's arrival was this sudden explosive outburst of foreign languages. A crowd rapidly gathered to see what was happening. When they heard praises erupting like a volcano, they became mystified and said, "We hear them declaring the wonders of God in our own tongues!" Multitudes of God-fearing people visiting Jerusalem because of Pentecost experienced this amazing phenomenon. They could not understand how Christ's followers were able to speak languages they had not learned.

The ability to speak in tongues is best explained as a supernatural work of the Holy Spirit. By his miraculous power believers praised God in languages they had not learned and even though uneducated, they were fluent in fifteen or more different dialects.

What should we make of this? The first instance of speaking in tongues relates to making known to the nations God's mighty works. Spirit-filled believers fulfilled Christ's last words—"You will be my witnesses" (1:8). By speaking in tongues, they spoke God's words to representatives of "every nation under heaven" (v 5). Receiving the Spirit immediately resulted in a supernatural ability to speak for God.

Rhema: A new end-time reality began on the day of Pentecost. It marked the giving of the Holy Spirit with power to those who believed in Jesus. The first expression of that power was speaking in tongues. The Spirit helped them to overcome language barriers and proclaim God's mighty deeds "to the ends of the earth." Being able to proclaim with divine power God's great accomplishments in Christ's recent death and resurrection marked a further advancement in his plan of salvation.

JUNE 3 | ACTS 2:14–24

GOD POURS OUT HIS SPIRIT ON ALL PEOPLE

In the last days, God says, I will pour out my Spirit on all people. Your sons and daughters will prophesy, your young men will see visions, your old men will dream dreams. —ACTS 2:17

God's wonderful gift reserved for the last days was poured out on the day of Pentecost, the birthday of the church. Until then, no one ever received the Holy Spirit in that way. The Father's promise came with force and sent everyone reeling. No they were not drunk, Peter explained, but filled with the Spirit. Everyone babbled in unlearned tongues to proclaim God's new, unparalleled day.

Peter declared they were witnessing the fulfillment of Scripture. His powerful explanation of these unusual events began by quoting Joel's end-time prophecy (Joel 2:28–32). God said he would pour out his Spirit upon all people. These extraordinary phenomena, signs, and wonders occurred that day to show God's intervention in human affairs. The Holy Spirit descended to empower believers irrespective of age, sex, or social standing. Old men will dream dreams; young men will see visions. Sons and daughters will prophesy. An anointing once limited to kings, priests, and prophets is now given freely to every believer. In this new eon brought about by Christ's death and resurrection, God was doing something new.

The fulfillment of Joel's prophesy is significant. It means the OT prophecies of the universal bestowal of the Spirit are taking place. This outpouring is a glorious sign we are living in the last days, equipped to take part in God's end-time plan. The book of Acts reveals Spirit-filled believers casting out demons, raising the dead, healing the sick, and preaching with power. As God unleashes the powers of the age to come, he makes this wonderful provision available "for all whom the Lord our God will call" (v 39).

Rhema: *This amazing event is not just for the one hundred and twenty, but also for you. Pray it for your sons and daughters. Pray it for your mother and father. Pray it for your spiritual leaders. Pray it for yourself. God wants every believer to experience the outpouring of his Spirit. This event begins the age of the Spirit, the last epoch of human history before the Lord returns. So receive his blessing and live in his fullness.*

JUNE 4 | ACTS 2:14–24

PROPHETIC EMPOWERMENT BY THE SPIRIT

*Even on my servants, both men and women, I will pour out my **Spirit** in those days, and they will prophesy.* –ACTS 2:18

Pouring out of God's Spirit is an end-time phenomenon empowering us to prophesy. When we are immersed in the Spirit we become servants of God, men and women who can speak for him. Since the Spirit reveals the things of God, we can share these revelations with others and proclaim these spiritual insights in the power of the Spirit. Everyone can prophesy! (vv 17–18; I Cor 14:31). By spiritual transformation, believers become God's mouthpieces.

To prophesy is a divine enablement to trumpet the truth of God in a timely and relevant manner. These are the last days when God anoints us to announce his revelations. In fact, the entire Spirit-filled community is to speak for God with supernatural power.

The Holy Spirit manifested himself in the OT through prophecy. He communicated the mind and will of God to prophets through dreams and visions. Often, they heard an audible voice or a word from the Lord. Then they took these divine discoveries and delivered them. The prophet, Zechariah, said people should listen to God's prophets because they speak his words through the Spirit (Zech 7:12).

Prophetic activity immediately increased with the outpouring of the Spirit. Peter's message on the day of Pentecost is a good example of NT prophecy. Set in motion by the power from on high, he addressed the multitude and proclaimed God's timely and relevant truth—"This is that" (v 16). Like Elijah of old, he called people to repentance (vv 21, 38, 40). His sermon was filled with revelation (vv 22–37). He announced things to come (vv 19–20) and proclaimed the mind and will of God (v 36, 38–39). Look at the stunning results of his empowered proclamation! "Those who accepted his message were baptized, and about three thousand were added to their number that day" (v 41).

Rhema: From Pentecost to our day the Spirit is present, dwelling within us. He gives insight into God's word and an understanding of spiritual things. As part of the new prophetic community, the Spirit empowers us like he did Peter to proclaim God's revelation of himself in Christ and offer his final invitation of salvation to a broken world.

JUNE 5 | ACTS 2:25–36

WHAT DOES IT MEAN TO RECEIVE THE PROMISED SPIRIT?

*Exalted to the right hand of God, he has received from the Father the promised **Holy Spirit** and has poured out what you now see and hear.*
–ACTS 2:33

Do you want proof of God's desire to bless you beyond your wildest dream? There is proof! What they saw and heard is evidence. The tongues of fire. The sound of a rushing mighty wind. Speaking in tongues. The outpouring of the Spirit. These miraculous phenomena demonstrated a new era had begun after Christ completed his work and was exalted to heaven. These amazing events confirmed a heavenly transaction had occurred. Upon his exaltation, Jesus "received from the Father the promised Holy Spirit." By pouring out the Spirit, Christ enacts in believers the fullness of his redemptive work. Believing the gospel culminates in a distinctive blessing—heaven opens upon us.

What did Jesus do first in his exalted position? He took the promised Holy Spirit and poured him out upon believers. It could not have happened until he was glorified and his atoning sacrifice accepted. The gift of the Spirit is not only a promise fulfilled but also a pledge made that heaven's favors and blessings are ours. Christ's first executive act was to baptize people with the Holy Spirit and transform them into God's dwelling place.

People wanted to know what Pentecost and its phenomena meant (v 12). Peter, empowered by the Spirit, stood up before the crowd and proclaimed its marvelous meaning. It means Jesus fulfilled Joel's prophecy by pouring out his Spirit in the last days. It means Jesus is the Messiah who has provided pardon, eternal salvation, and victory over the powers of darkness. It means believers take part in God's end-time mission of proclaiming salvation to the world. It means Jesus is now at his Father's right hand distributing and directing the Holy Spirit. It means a new historical era has begun characterized by the impartation of the Holy Spirit. It also means the Father works with his Son to pour out heaven's blessings.

Rhema: Therefore, we must not neglect Pentecost's significance or limit the Holy Spirit's work and activity. Not in us and not in the church. Everyone who believes in Jesus can enjoy the Father's favor, power, and presence through the Holy Spirit (Gal 3:14).

JUNE 6 | ACTS 2:37–47

THE GIFT OF THE SPIRIT AND SALVATION

Peter replied, "Repent and be baptized, every one of you, in the name of Jesus Christ for the forgiveness of your sins. And you will receive the gift of the **Holy Spirit***. The promise is for you and your children and for all who are far off—for all whom the Lord our God will call." –ACTS 2:38*

What an extraordinary verse! Nowhere else in the Bible are so many aspects of salvation connected with receiving the Spirit—repentance, water baptism, name of Jesus, forgiveness of sins, and election. Every feature is a prerequisite to receiving the Father's gift. Like Elijah, the prophet of fire, Peter's powerful, prophetic message cuts to the heart, convicts his audience, and awakens their consciences. People asked him what they should do.

The apostle told them to experience salvation, they must repent and be baptized. A new possibility to get right with God now existed because of Christ's death and resurrection. He preached repentance (Lk 24:27). The word means to change one's mind and do an about-face. Because of its two-directional nature, he urged them to turn away from their past behavior so offensive to God and accept his Son. They needed to accept, adore, and acknowledge Jesus as their Lord. After they repented they must be baptized in his name for the forgiveness of sins.

The Father would then give them the Spirit as a gift. What the 120 had just experienced was available to them. Peter makes the reception of the Spirit distinct from water baptism and the remission of sins. He declares, "And you will receive the gift of the Holy Spirit." Although the gift is distinct from salvation, it is an essential facet. Three thousand acted on his message, identified themselves with Jesus through water baptism, and received the Father's promise.

Rhema: This promise of a personal experience of the Holy Spirit extends to all future generations. The Lord wants to pour out his Spirit upon each one of us so we too can experience the fulfillment of Joel's prophecy. God offers us what Peter and the 120 received—an essential part of our salvation. He said, "The promise is for you and your children and for all who are far off." What they experienced on the day of Pentecost is for you today.

JUNE 7 | ACTS 4:1–22

EMBOLDEN BY THE SPIRIT

*Then Peter, filled with the **Holy Spirit**, said to them: "Rulers and elders of the people!"* –ACTS 4:8

What were they going to do? Jewish authorities had arrested Peter and John for healing a man and preaching about it. For the first time they must face hostility without Jesus present. Luke names their antagonists. Annas. Caiaphas. John. Alexander. Members of the High Priest's family. Besides these there were elders, Sadducees, teachers of the Law, and the captain of the temple guard. Wow! Talk about stacking the deck. Powerful, moneyed elite arrayed themselves against these two fishermen from Galilee.

Peter and John posed a threat to the establishment. The nation's leaders got rid of Jesus but now they must deal with his followers. Most disturbing to them was teaching Jesus was alive from the dead. Were the apostles going to become tongue-tied thoroughly overcome by trepidation? At that crucial moment, subsequent to their filling at Pentecost, the Holy Spirit came to their aid with a special enabling. The Spirit had not leaked out of them like air from a balloon but because they faced a new need, he gave them a fresh infilling. Instead of being controlled by fear, they were emboldened to rise above it and empowered to witness.

The Spirit gave Peter boldness to respond to his accusers. Inspired, he declared, "It is by the name of Jesus Christ of Nazareth, whom you crucified but whom God raised from the dead, that this man stands before you healed" (v 10). Jesus had said to take no thought when you stand before authorities and must give an account. The Holy Spirit will give you what to say. Peter and John's boldness caught the attention of their adversaries who were astonished anyone so unschooled could speak with such confidence.

Rhema: The world thinks it can stop the Holy Spirit by threats, intimidation, and power. Little does it know no power can defeat him. The rulers had no answer when Peter, filled with the Spirit, spoke. He seized the moment to witness to these power brokers regarding Jesus. God had raised the Jesus they crucified, he told them. So when your emotions threaten to dominate and control you and you feel intimidated by the world, you can ask God for a fresh filling of his Spirit.

THE RELATIONSHIP AMONG SAINTS, SCRIPTURE, AND THE SPIRIT

You spoke by the **Holy Spirit** *through the mouth of your servant, our father David: "Why do the nations rage and the peoples plot in vain? The kings of the earth rise up and the rulers band together against the Lord and against his anointed one."* **–ACTS 4:25**

Have you ever prayed the Scriptures when struggling with life's problems? That is what the early believers did when persecutors turned their venom on them. Faced with threats and suffering persecution, they turned to God's word. Because they had received the Spirit, they developed a special relationship with Scripture. Before they had trouble understanding it, but now the Spirit illuminated it and showed them things they had not previously realized.

On this occasion the Spirit lit up the Second Psalm and revealed how it applied to both Christ and themselves. His death and their persecution were predicted in Scripture. This realization, therefore, was a prophetic experience brought about through a dynamic relationship among these saints, the Scriptures, and the Spirit. The Spirit in them was the same as in the word. This explains why the word of God, spoken by the Spirit through David, took on a new vitality. God spoke personally to them and addressed their suffering with a living word. When they heard the Spirit speaking to them through Scripture, they heard God himself speak.

With this spiritual insight, the believers prayed a powerful, earth-shaking prayer (v 31). By incorporating God's word into their plea, they were able to talk to God in his very own words. Informed by the Spirit, they knew how to pray so as not to ask amiss—they understood their suffering was God's will. Like a coach the Spirit called in the plays. They did not ask to be spared persecution. By divine illumination they realized the rulers were only doing "what [God's] power and will had decided beforehand should happen" (v 28). Encouraged and enlightened by Scripture and the Spirit, they asked God for boldness and even more miracles (vv 29–30).

Rhema: The Spirit desires to speak to you through Scripture. In doing so he continues Christ's work of helping you understand the word (Lk 24:27). God's written word is not static, a mere object to be studied, but alive and active (Heb 4:12).

A FRESH FILLING OF THE HOLY SPIRIT

After they prayed, the place where they were meeting was shaken. And they were all filled with the **Holy Spirit** *and spoke the word of God boldly.* —ACTS 4:31

Someone said, "Every good story needs conflict." Well, God's story is not fiction but it is filled with conflict—good over evil, light banishing darkness, Christ conquering Satan. Conflict is essentially a power struggle between opposing forces. This explains why the nations rage; the peoples plot in vain; the kings of the earth take their stand and the rulers gather against the Lord (vv 25–26). God's enemies come against his Anointed One. Because his followers belong to the Lord, they get caught up in the great cosmic combat.

What were Peter and John and fellow believers to do? Authorities had threatened them to no longer speak or teach in the name of Jesus. They must choose between two equally undesirable alternatives: obey man and disobey God or obey God and disobey man. Talk about conflict! Faced with a terrible dilemma, they raised their voices together and cried out to God.

Confronted with a difficult and dangerous quandary, they reminded themselves that God, their Creator, was still on the throne. In faith they exclaimed, "Sovereign Lord, you made the heavens and the earth and the sea, and everything in them" (v 24). They realized these antagonists were little league compared to God's sovereignty. The early church prayed, "Now, Lord, consider their threats and enable your servants to speak your word with great boldness" (v 29).

Because they were in a bind, they made this special request. Feeling their adversaries breathing fury down their necks made them beg for more power and boldness (vv 29–30). God answered: he shook the place where they were meeting and he filled them with the Spirit. Consequently, "With great power the apostles continued to testify to the resurrection of the Lord Jesus" (v 33).

Rhema: Let this be an encouragement whenever you face spiritual opposition. We do not lose the Spirit's fullness like a tire with a slow leak that needs pumping up again. No, God gives a fresh infilling of his Spirit to help us confront forces of darkness opposing his work. He wants to shake up these power structures and fill us to proclaim his word.

JUNE 10 | ACTS 4:32–5:6

LYING TO THE HOLY SPIRIT

*Then Peter said, "Ananias, how is it that Satan has so filled your heart that you have lied to the **Holy Spirit** and have kept for yourself some of the money you received for the land?"* —ACTS 5:3

What does it mean to lie to the Holy Spirit? He is a most important person, coequal with the Father and the Son. He can be wronged, offended, and lied to. Peter declared to Ananias, "You have not lied just to human beings but to God" (v 4). Lying to the Spirit implies Ananias perpetuated a falsehood, snubbed the Holy Spirit, and tried to deceive the Spirit of truth. By doing so he made a "covenant with death" (Is 28:15). To think he could deceive the Spirit-filled community not only opposed, offended, and disrespected the Spirit but demanded severe discipline. He more resembled Satan, a liar from the beginning, than God who cannot lie.

Peter asks Ananias, "Why have you lied to the Holy Spirit?" He allowed Satan to fill his heart with deception, a wicked ploy of the enemy designed to undermine the infant church's integrity. Satan desired to drive a wedge into its pure and beautiful fellowship. Luke says, "All the believers were one in heart and mind. No one claimed any of their possessions was their own, but they shared everything they had" (4:32). Everyone enjoyed equality; none was poor. Nobody said, "This is mine" for they held all things in common. Societal barriers disappeared, and friendships flourished because the Spirit lived in them.

This is the first time the term "church" occurs in Acts (v 11). Since the day of Pentecost, the Holy Spirit had been molding, shaping, and filling believers. He made them a new creation, different from the world. Together they shared life and were open and transparent with one another. The Spirit empowered them to live like Jesus. Who then would dream of damaging the Spirit's handiwork?

Rhema: Dishonesty, deception, and duplicity are Satan's works of darkness and, if allowed to go undetected, they would destroy the church's integrity and disrupt its accord. Since lies belong to Satan, the Spirit rose up to protect the infant church from the powers of darkness. Ananias incurred God's wrath and died suddenly because he covenanted with death when he lied to the Holy Spirit.

June 11 | Acts 5:7–11; Joshua 7:1–13

Testing the Spirit of the Lord

*Peter said to her, "How could you conspire to test the **Spirit** of the Lord? Listen! The feet of the men who buried your husband are at the door, and they will carry you out also." —Acts 5:9*

Did Sapphira suppose she could put one over on the Holy Spirit? Did she not realize he knows everything? She and her husband erred believing he who was so active in the church would allow their deception to go undetected. To ask the Holy Spirit to overlook their dishonesty was too much.

The church is a Spirit-filled community, God's dwelling place. When Ananias and Sapphira conspired to deceive believers by pretending to be more generous than they were, they provoked the Spirit. To their demise they discovered how much dishonesty he would tolerate before acting. Instead of honoring the Spirit, Ananias and Sapphira allowed Satan to fill their hearts with worldly desires. The love of money and the praise of men meant more to them than truthfulness. Their flagrant carnality tested the Spirit's resolve.

Why does Peter refer to him as the "Spirit of the Lord"? Perhaps he remembers our Lord's words to Satan: "Do not put the Lord your God to the test" (Mt 4:7). Clearly we are to understand the Holy Spirit is as much God as is the Father and the Son. Therefore, he is not to be treated less than they for he too can be tested and lied to. In addition, Peter is saying the same Spirit who was in Jesus is in the church. Therefore, do not vex the Holy One (Ps 78:41).

Rhema: Ananias and Sapphira's tragic story teaches us many things about the Holy Spirit. Since he always knows what is going on in our hearts and the church, we cannot hide anything from him. Deception and dishonesty among God's people are diseases that if left untreated weaken Christ's body and render it powerless before the enemy (Josh 7:12). Whatever threatens the church's integrity and forward movement provokes him. Not only does Christ send his Spirit to protect his church but also to make it like him. That is why authenticity and integrity were the early church's secret to power. After they died, Luke reports, "The apostles performed many signs and wonders among the people" (v 12).

JUNE 12 | ACTS 5:17–42

THE HOLY SPIRIT IS A WITNESS
OF THESE THINGS

We are witnesses of these things, and so is the **Holy Spirit**, *whom God has given to those who obey him.* **–ACTS 5:32**

The key witness was there. Not only did he observe the most important event in human history, but he also took part in it. Inside the sealed sepulcher, in the cold darkness he hovered over the freshly wrapped body. In a flash as quick as a twinkling of an eye, the Spirit of life conquered death. No one was present to witness Christ's resurrection besides the Third Person of the Trinity. Therefore, he can give the ultimate testimony of that earth-shattering moment.

How does the Spirit bear witness that Jesus is alive? Jesus said the Spirit "will testify of me" (Jn 15:26). Simply, he reveals Jesus. In his resurrected state Christ makes himself known to us through the Spirit. We know about Christ through teaching and preaching but the Spirit makes Jesus known to us personally. That is how his sheep hear his voice. The resurrected Christ comes to us in the Spirit and he says, "Here I am! I stand at the door and knock. If anyone hears my voice and opens the door, I will come in and eat with that person, and they with me" (Rev 3:20). We know beyond any doubt he is alive because we are in living communion with him. No scientific evidence is needed. No one needs to roll back history to his resurrection because he is present in us today by the Spirit.

The Spirit testified in other ways too. Certainly, the vast crowds coming to faith in Christ count as evidence. Because the Spirit worked to convict and convince, "more and more men and women believed in the Lord and were added to their number" (v 14). Then again through many powerful miracles, signs, and wonders he proved Jesus was alive (v 12). Even jail could not contain Peter and John (v 25). The Spirit's presence and activity in believers offered further proof Jesus had risen from the dead. Disciples transformed from wimpy cowards to powerful preachers demonstrated the reality of his resurrection.

Rhema: The point is through the Spirit we personally experience Jesus. He is alive. Hear his voice! Open the door! Sup with him today!

JUNE 13 | ACTS 6:1–4

CHOOSE LEADERS FULL OF THE SPIRIT AND WISDOM

Brothers and sisters, choose seven men from among you who are known to be full of the Spirit and wisdom. We will turn this responsibility over to them and will give our attention to prayer and the ministry of the word. –ACTS 6:3–4

Someone said success creates its own problems. This was true of the young church experiencing explosive growth. First, Jewish authorities filled with jealousy (5:17) persecuted and threatened their leaders. Then Ananias and Sapphira lied to the Holy Spirit and deceived believers. But who foresaw the next source of trouble? The number of disciples increased faster than organizational structures could handle. As a result the apostles spread themselves too thin, and the church overlooked many needs of its members.

The Jerusalem congregation was multicultural. A split along racial lines loomed large if the crisis was not handled well. Those who spoke Greek complained their widows were treated poorly compared to the Aramaic-speaking women. Wisdom was needed to handle any perceived racial discrimination. The apostles established criteria for selecting the seven overseers: they must be sensible and operate from a spiritual base. Look for individuals, they said, who have distinguished themselves as people of the Spirit. They must be wise, so they can fathom the crisis and execute a plan.

Unless handled with care, success can breed failure. Recognizing this, the apostles provided a solution. For the health of the church, they themselves must unload and delegate secondary tasks they had assumed. The Twelve had the spiritual savvy to know God's people will suffer if they abandoned their primary responsibilities. Proposing seven believers full of the Spirit and wisdom to help them was ingenuous. It would reduce rancor among the membership and would free the apostles to concentrate on their important ministry. To create organizational structures in keeping with the church's rapid growth and complexity proved prudent.

Rhema: Two important leadership principles develop from this account. When we select ministry leaders, choose individuals full of the Holy Spirit and wisdom. This decision ensured the new flock's continued growth (v 7). In addition, we must prioritize ministries. Every service rendered to God and his people is important but none more so than prayer and the ministry of the word. Complex situations require both know-how and the Spirit, apostolic ministry and table ministry.

CHOOSE LEADERS FULL OF THE
SPIRIT AND FAITH

*This proposal pleased the whole group. They chose Stephen, a man full of faith and of the **Holy Spirit**; also Philip, Procorus, Nicanor, Timon, Parmenas, and Nicolas from Antioch, a convert to Judaism.* –ACTS 6:5

Have you ever longed for more of God, more faith, more answers to prayer? Stephen, one of the seven chosen to distribute food to Greek widows, was such a person. He was overflowing with faith and impregnated with the Spirit. Luke portrays him as "a man full of God's grace," full of "power," "full of faith," and full of "the Holy Spirit."

Luke says Stephen "performed great wonders and signs among the people" (v 8). To do these miracles, he needed to be abounding with confidence in God. Even when we are loaded with spiritual gifts and are bursting with the grace of God, we still need to exercise faith. Perhaps you wonder how you can have more faith, faith that can believe God and see incredible answers to prayer. Faith comes from God as we hear his word (Rms 10:17). By looking at Stephen's message in Chapter 7, the longest sermon in Acts, it is obvious he saturated himself with Scripture. Faith also comes from the Holy Spirit as a spiritual gift (I Cor 12:9). Because faith "comes," we can always ask God for more.

Before moving on, the author sums up the church's remarkable advances. He has made it abundantly evident the early church's success was a direct result of the Spirit's activity. Here are just a few amazing outcomes attributed to the Holy Spirit. Extraordinary miracles. Averted threats. A ready supply of leaders full of faith. Outstanding individuals full of the Holy Spirit. Most telling of all, is this summary: "So the word of God spread. The number of disciples in Jerusalem increased rapidly, and a large number of priests became obedient to the faith" (v 7).

Rhema: Since the day of Pentecost thousands upon thousands of Jerusalem's residents believed on Jesus. The city that had killed our Lord experienced a mighty move of God. When the church insisted on upholding the right spiritual order, the gospel made impressive headway. In those momentous times God needed individuals, such as Stephen, to be teeming with faith and awash in the Spirit. The same is true today.

THE SPIRIT HELPS US STAY CALM

*But they could not stand up against the wisdom the **Spirit** gave him as he spoke.* **–ACTS 6:10**

A real test of strength is the ability to remain calm under pressure. Whether playing in a championship game or facing our critics, staying composed is a great accomplishment. The Holy Spirit helped believers stay unruffled under fierce attack and say the right words at the right time. When "a great persecution broke out against the church in Jerusalem" (8:1), the disciples stayed strong. A case in point is Stephen, one of the Seven whose arrest and defense opened the floodgates of wrath.

Success made him a lightning rod for the persecutors who tried to squelch him. Because he was a Spirit-filled follower of Christ full of God's grace, he did many wonders and miracles among the people. The impact of his ministry precipitated opposition from Greek-speaking Jews from the provinces. Every argument put forward against Stephen was unsuccessful. Even their brightest minds and strongest persuaders were no match for "they could not stand up against the wisdom the Spirit gave him." Time and again they tried to shut him down, but they failed for the Spirit made him powerful in word and deed.

Consumed with venomous hatred, his attackers bullied people into making false accusations against him. They also stirred up the people, the elders, and teachers of the Law. Eventually, his opponents had Stephen arrested and brought before the Jewish Court. If we want to see what cool looks like, look at him! Unnerved and unfazed, his face was like the face of an angel (v 15).

How did he manage his emotions under such duress and continue being calm and courageous? The attackers charged him with the most serious offenses imaginable. Blasphemy against God, Moses, the Temple, and the Law. With reddening faces and gnashing teeth, the council tore into Stephen. However, he showed no sign of panic even in the face of a bloodthirsty throng intent on stoning him to death.

Rhema: Stephen was not alone; he had a friend standing by his side advising him. Realize the wonderful Holy Spirit, the Advocate Jesus promised, is your friend who will be with you as he was with the disciples. Your divine companion will comfort, encourage, and help you act wisely when stressed or attacked.

JUNE 16 | ACTS 7:1–3; 37–53

ALWAYS RESISTING THE HOLY SPIRIT

*You stiff-necked people! Your hearts and ears are still uncircumcised. You are just like your ancestors: You always resist the **Holy Spirit**!*
–ACTS 7:51

This is Stephen's summary statement. Powerful. Cutting. Incisive. From the beginning of their national history, the verdict is the same: "You always resist the Holy Spirit." Uncircumcised in heart. Stiff-necked in resolve. Spiritually incorrigible. "Was there ever a prophet your ancestors did not persecute?" he asks. Their hatred and hostility climaxed in killing "the Prophet," "the Righteous One," Jesus the Messiah. And now they are bent on stoning Stephen.

In resisting him, the nation treated the Spirit as their enemy, as one to war against, pounce on, and disarm. To resist means a hostile and violent opposition to someone. Stephen reviews how their forefathers treated Spirit-filled persons such as Joseph (v 9; Gen 41:38)) and Moses (vv 35–43; Num 11:17)) and it was not good. Joseph's brothers, the founders of the nation, pounced on him and wanted to kill him because of his prophetic dreams. Instead, they sold their own flesh and blood into slavery. Moses fared no better. "They rejected" him both before and after the Exodus. Their forefathers "refused to obey" him and turned their hearts back to Egypt.

The way their ancestors treated Joseph and Moses was the way the Jewish leaders were treating Stephen. He too brimmed with the Holy Spirit but in rejecting him they were vigorously opposing the Holy Spirit. They had no concern for spiritual things or any desire to move in God, nor did they have any interest in listening to the Spirit. By refusing to attend to the apostles' preaching and Stephen's defense, the leaders continued to act as their fathers did before them. The pattern of refusing the Holy Spirit continued. First, they did not heed God's prophets. Then Jesus and his apostles. And now Stephen—even though all were full of the Holy Spirit and spoke for God.

Rhema: Stephen made an interesting deduction. People who reject God's prophets are in fact rejecting the Holy Spirit. God is looking for men and women with ears to hear what the Spirit is saying. He seeks individuals with open, receptive hearts that believe and obey him. When they do they live in harmony with God's purposes.

JUNE 17 | ACTS 7:54–8:3

THE FIRST SPIRIT FILLED MARTYR

*But Stephen, full of the **Holy Spirit**, looked up to heaven and saw the glory of God, and Jesus standing at the right hand of God.* –ACTS 7:55

Hell rages, heaven beams. Here we contemplate the stark contrast between men inflamed by hell and a man set on fire by heaven. When the Jewish Court heard Stephen's accusations, "they were furious and gnashed their teeth at him." He is so full of the Holy Spirit it seems as if he already has one foot in heaven. With his face shining like an angel (6:15) he says, "I see heaven open and the Son of Man standing at the right hand of God" (v 56). Powerful in word and deed, he is faithful to the end. Jesus is so pleased with him he stands to his feet to welcome his heroic witness home.

When working or suffering for Christ is hard, remember we have divine help. Being full of the Spirit will ease our difficulties just it did for Stephen. Twice we are told he overflows with the Spirit. The first time takes place when he was selected to work alongside the apostles distributing food to the widows. This time, he endures persecution and becomes the church's first martyr. Because he was empowered from above, he could look past his troubles and turmoil and view Jesus in all his glory.

How does the Holy Spirit assist us with difficult and trying situations? In Stephen's case the Spirit gave him a glimpse of heaven and the glory of God. At that moment he was one with the Spirit, dwelling in the eternal while the things of earth fell away. The Spirit opened his eyes to the reality above where he saw Jesus, coequal with the Father, rise to receive him. He was so full of God he was oblivious of the insanity surrounding him. As his persecutors pummeled his body with rocks, Stephen dropped to his knees and prayed for their forgiveness. One fatal blow and he fell asleep in the arms of his Lord.

Rhema: There was no cursing or damning on his part nor any grieving or lament. Instead, the Spirit directed him heavenwards to Jesus whom he was about to join. Happiness abounds there; all pain ceases. He was full of the Holy Spirit.

JUNE 18 | ACTS 8:4–15

PRAY TO RECEIVE THE HOLY SPIRIT

*When they arrived, they prayed for the new believers there that they might receive the **Holy Spirit**. –*ACTS 8:15

Believers fleeing persecution brought Pentecost's fire to Samaria. Philip evangelized the entire region and saw many come to Christ. As he declared God's word he performed miraculous signs, healed the sick, and cast out demons. Many Samaritans believed as "he proclaimed the good news of the kingdom of God and the name of Jesus Christ" (v 12).

How was it possible for Samaritans to be saved? was a question on the minds of many Jewish believers. Jews did not associate with them (Jn 4:9). So to accept them into the fold was a huge stretch. That is why the author of Acts makes two things clear: their salvation is genuine, and they receive the Holy Spirit. Then Jewish believers would be more inclined to embrace them as full members of the church.

Luke first shows the Samaritans were saved. "They believed Philip as he preached the good news." To confirm their faith in Christ, they were baptized in water. Even Simon, a sorcerer, "believed and was baptized." News of their amazing conversion found its way back to leaders in the mother church. "When the apostles in Jerusalem heard that Samaria had accepted the word of God, they sent Peter and John to Samaria" (v 14).

After establishing their salvation, Luke then shows the Samaritans received the Holy Spirit. Weeks or months later, Peter and John came down from Jerusalem to meet with them. The apostles "prayed for the new believers there that they might receive the Holy Spirit." Although they came to faith and were baptized, they had not received the promise of the Spirit (Ac 2:38–39). God had delayed his gift until the apostles were present. As they prayed and laid hands on them, the Samaritan believers received the Holy Spirit (v 17).

Acts associates receiving the Holy Spirit with prayer. After all, Jesus himself received the Spirit "as he was praying" (Lk 3:21–22). The descent of the Spirit at Pentecost occurred as the believers (1:15) "all joined together constantly in prayer" (1:14). This pattern continued as Peter and John prayed for these new converts.

Rhema: Likewise, if you have not received the Holy Spirit since you believed, specifically ask God for his magnificent gift.

JUNE 19 | LUKE 9:51–56; JOHN 4:4–9, 39–42

THE DELAY OF THE SPIRIT

When they arrived, they prayed for the new believers there that they might receive the Holy Spirit, because the **Holy Spirit** *had not yet come on any of them; they had simply been baptized in the name of the Lord Jesus.* –ACTS 8:15–16

God is always stretching us and expanding our horizons. He wants us to understand his ways are greater than ours. We tend to put him in a box and limit him to what we think he should do. Since he is God he does as he pleases, often surprising us with his grace and shattering our misconceptions. Up to this point the gospel message only went to Jews, even though Jesus told his disciples they would be his witnesses to the ends of the earth. Now was Samaria's time of visitation.

Peter and John prayed for the Samaritans to receive the Holy Spirit because the Spirit "had not yet come on any of them." Why the delay? Although they believed and were baptized, none received the Spirit. Peter and John felt no necessity to preach to them for they accepted the genuineness of their salvation. Nor did they baptize any Samaritans as no need existed. The delay did not result from any oversight or shortcoming in Phillip's ministry: any postponement was God's sovereign act.

Why did God defer sending the Spirit to the Samaritans? This puzzle was not like Pentecost where believers must wait ten days—they waited from the ascension of Jesus to the pouring out of the Spirit. They must wait until the day of Pentecost "had fully come." With the Samaritans, however, the Spirit is stayed because of unusual circumstances. Since the Jews refused to associate with Samaritans, God delayed their Pentecost until the apostles could witness it firsthand. If questions arose or others resisted accepting non-Jewish believers as full-fledged church members, the apostles can point to God's sovereignty.

Rhema: Experience has a way of shaping our theology, challenging our presuppositions and stretching our faith. God no longer distinguished between Jews and Samaritans. He poured out his Spirit on both because in Christ there is no difference. The Samaritan believers were as much a part of the church as the Jewish. In one marvelous day, the Spirit swept away centuries of deep prejudice and hatred.

JUNE 20 | GENESIS 48:1–22

LAYING ON OF HANDS TO
RECEIVE THE HOLY SPIRIT

Then Peter and John placed their hands on them, and they received the
Holy Spirit. –ACTS 8:17

Through touch we communicate a range of emotions: joy, love, gratitude, and sympathy. To touch another we must be close. Touching is a way to bond. A connectivity. Laying on of hands entails all that and more. Who would deny Jacob's powerful emotions when he placed his hands on Joseph's sons? In this touching moment, grandsons he never thought of seeing received his blessing (Gen 48:14). Jacob not only communicated his emotions to his grandchildren but also his spiritual blessing. Laying on of hands occurs throughout Scripture as a means to confer God's blessings.

When Peter and John laid hands on the Samaritans, God used them to bestow his gift of the Holy Spirit. This is not the only way to receive the Spirit, for it happened in a different way at Pentecost and with the house of Cornelius (10:44–46). With the Samaritans, however, it signified solidarity with believers in Jerusalem. Peter and John came as an official delegation. Their gesture communicated acceptance, respect, joy, and love for a despised and unwanted group. They became family. To have the church's most prominent leaders lay their hands on them meant they were special.

Concern for unity was paramount. Jerusalem sent two apostles to prevent God's work from fragmenting along racial lines. The Spirit came to create a new unity among his people without the old divisions and prejudices. In the Age of the Spirit, God removes antiquated distinctions and hostilities that made Jews superior to others. What matters is "a new creation." No inequities should exist between Jews and Samaritans, for the Spirit unites them into one new people of God. Their unification ends the old dualities and creates a new way of living. A pristine freedom where there was no longer subordination or hierarchies or where one group was superior to others was ushered in by the Spirit.

Rhema: Three times in this story laying on of hands is associated with receiving the Holy Spirit (vv 17, 18, 19). To have the Spirit is a wonderful blessing. The practice may not be necessary, but it serves as a pattern to follow when praying for others to receive the great blessing of the Holy Spirit.

THE WORKS OF THE SPIRIT
DIFFER FROM MAGIC

When Simon saw that the **Spirit** *was given at the laying on of the apostles' hands, he offered them money and said, "Give me also this ability so that everyone on whom I lay my hands may receive the Holy Spirit."*
–ACTS 8:18–19

How do we differentiate between the works of the Spirit and the works of darkness? We must never confuse the two or mix Christianity with pagan or occult practices. Residual effects from rituals, charms, spells, fortunetelling, and black magic are deceptive tricks, works of the devil. Simon, a local magician, "had practiced sorcery in the city and amazed all the people of Samaria" (v 9). Through his magic arts, he gained an illustrious reputation and earned an income by exploitation. Some claimed he was divine, the Great Power (v 10).

The Samaritan's reception of the Spirit was awesome. Something amazing happened as soon as Peter and John laid their hands on these new believers. We are not told what transpired but Simon was awestruck and craved that power so much he offered to purchase it. His offer challenged their faith because they now had to decide between the power of the gospel or the power of sorcery.

To distribute the Holy Spirit through laying on of hands would be an amazing addition to Simon's black bag of tricks. He failed, however, to distinguish his own deceptive works of darkness from the Spirit's life-giving ministry. To him it was a great business investment to advance his own interests and gain further notoriety.

Rhema: Several differences between sorcery and the Spirit surface in this story. For instance, how each is acquired is dissimilar. The gifts and power of God are not for sale. They are not bought, learned, or earned. Spiritual abilities are free and undeserved. God gives them to whomever he desires. Our reason for wanting these gifts is not to make ourselves rich or great but to bless others and to glorify God. Simon did not understand this. Another disparity pertains to their origin. One is of God, the other of Satan. The latter involves the devil's subtle plan to turn people away from the living God. Without money, our heavenly Father, by contrast, gives the Holy Spirit to do inestimable good and counter the works of darkness.

June 22 | II Kings 5:1–27

Repent for Trying to Buy the Spirit

*Give me also this ability so that everyone on whom I lay my hands may receive the **Holy Spirit**. –Acts 8:19*

Enabled by the Spirit, Peter exposes what is behind Simon's request. Unless the conniver takes drastic action, reversing course, he is damned. Peter rebukes him. "May your money perish with you, because you thought you could buy the gift of God with money!" (v 20). He must repent "of his wickedness" and pray for forgiveness. To assume he can buy the Holy Spirit and manipulate him for his personal gain is a gross misunderstanding of God's grace and power.

How wicked to conceive of the Spirit's activity as just another form of sorcery. Someone said, "Trying to buy heaven's gift with the mammon of man is scandalous." The deceiver wants to hustle the Holy Spirit for his own financial gain. How dare he offer the proceeds of sorcery for the pure and holy treasure of heaven?

Simon is not serious with God nor is his heart right. Instead of embracing the fullness of the Spirit with all his heart, he seeks to acquire it for monetary advantage. Therefore, he never asks Peter and John to lay their hands on him. The occultist wants their power, not their blessing. To avoid utter spiritual ruin he must repent otherwise his ambitious, scheming heart will destroy him.

Peter discerns that bitterness is behind the sorcerer's request. After confronting him the apostle says, "For I see that you are full of bitterness and captive to sin" (v 23). Is he envious of Philip and the apostles? After all, a new power has entered his turf where many considered him as the "Great One, the power of God." Because he is still a prisoner of sin, his old thought patterns hold him captive. To be free from the stronghold, Simon needs to turn from his perverse ways.

Rhema: Wanting God's gifts to make ourselves rich or look great is always wrong. We never see Peter, John, or Philip exalting or enriching themselves. If we want more of the power of God in our lives, we must ensure our heart and motivation are right. Lest the gifts of God ruin us, we need to ask ourselves, "Can God trust us with his power?"

TRUSTING THE LEADING OF THE SPIRIT

The **Spirit** *told Philip, "Go to that chariot and stay near it."*
—ACTS 8:29

Has the Spirit ever asked you to do something that at the time did not make sense? That is what happened to Phillip. An angel told him to leave the exciting revival erupting in Samaria. Although he was ministering to throngs of people, he was directed to get out of town. A powerful move of God swept through Samaria. Countless numbers were coming to faith, being baptized in water and receiving the Holy Spirit. Even Jesus did not have such remarkable results. To our natural way of thinking, to drop what he is doing and leave it all behind is just so much foolishness. And what is even more unusual is God instructed him to go to a dusty, deserted desert road. To his credit, Philip did not object but trusted and obeyed.

When we follow the leading of the Spirit, we will see unusual blessing and God's higher purposes. If God involves himself in something, our expectancy should rise because good things are about to happen. As Phillip begins pounding the dust, he has a most extraordinary encounter. He meets an important official responsible for the treasury of Ethiopia's queen. Suddenly, the Holy Spirit speaks to the evangelist and gives him a personal, timely directive. He says, "Glue yourself to that chariot." The official was returning from Jerusalem where he had gone to worship. Philip found him reading out loud a passage of Scripture.

Approaching the chariot, Phillip asked if he understood what he was reading. The official replied he could not unless someone explained it to him. He had been examining Isaiah 53: "He was led like a sheep to the slaughter, and as a lamb before its shearer is silent, so he did not open his mouth." What an awesome God moment! To his surprise, Phillip found this high-level seeker open to God. Starting from that Scripture, Phillip told him all about Jesus. As they traveled further down the road, the officer saw water and requested Philip to baptize him.

Rhema: When we are led by the Spirit, we will see God work in ways never thought imaginable. Good things happen. We must learn to trust and obey because nothing is an accident when the Spirit leads us.

THE SPIRIT ORCHESTRATES
THE CHURCH'S GROWTH

*When they came up out of the water, the **Spirit** of the Lord suddenly took Philip away, and the eunuch did not see him again, but went on his way rejoicing. –ACTS 8:39*

Day after day the Spirit orchestrated the spread of the gospel: to the north, the south, and to the west. As a conductor he chose the score, set the tempo, guided the musicians, and kept everyone in time. He gave Phillip a leading part in Samaria and then directed him to an Ethiopian eunuch from North Africa.

The author gives a snapshot of the astounding things taking place in Phillip's Spirit-led ministry. In just two events he demonstrated the Holy Spirit's role in taking the gospel across racial boundaries. The despised Samaritans had a wonderful move of God. Philip healed many paralytics and cripples. Demons came out shrieking. A variety of miracles occurred. The place was vibrating with God's presence. Great joy filled the city. Any time powers of darkness rose up, they were quashed. Amidst everything, an angel appeared to Philip instructing him to leave and go south. Straightway he has an amazing encounter with an Ethiopian eunuch who believed and was baptized. In a flash, the Spirit whisked Philip away in rapturelike fashion, leaving the official to go on his way singing. Seven times Luke mentions the Holy Spirit in connection with the Samaritan revival and the Ethiopian's conversion.

Let there be no doubt: it was heaven on earth. Joy. Rejoicing. Miracles. An angel. Extraordinary miracles. Salvations. Baptisms in the Holy Spirit. The routing of evil. What is the Spirit saying in all these things? Reading between the lines, the message is clear. It pleases God when the gospel crosses cultural barriers. As we can see, he puts his seal of approval on it.

Rhema: How interesting—the Twelve are not directing the church's affairs, nor are they responsible for this marvelous advancement. The divine conductor is assigning parts to every member and directing them. What is happening is far greater than any human leader can devise. Phillip is a powerful example on how to respond to to the orchestra leader. You must not be afraid to follow the Spirit's leading. If he gives you unusual directives or parts to play, come in on cue and obey.

JUNE 25 | ACTS 9:1–19

SAUL'S CONVERSION AND INFILLING OF THE SPIRIT

Then Ananias went to the house and entered it. Placing his hands on Saul, he said, "Brother Saul, the Lord—Jesus, who appeared to you on the road as you were coming here—has sent me so that you may see again and be filled with the **Holy Spirit.**" –ACTS 9:17

The conversion of Saul of Tarsus, the early church's arch persecutor, is a defining moment in the history of Christianity. Luke will tell the story of his conversion three times to show its significance. At one moment, Saul is doing everything in his power to curtail the spread of "the Way." The next Jesus meets him, and everything changes.

A blinding "light from heaven" flashes around him. He hears a voice saying, "Saul, Saul, why do you persecute me?" When he asks, "Who are you, Lord," the answer stuns him: "I am Jesus, whom you are persecuting." A thunderbolt of lightning explodes in his heart. In that instant, he knows Stephen and the apostles were right—Jesus is alive. Saul's encounter with Jesus is the most profound conversion in the NT.

Saul, a new believer, at once obeys the Lord and enters the city. Once in Damascus he spends three days in fasting and prayer. During this time, he receives a vision of a man, named Ananias, coming to lay hands on him to restore his sight. We further learn of Saul's unique calling to the Gentiles, rulers, and Israel. When Ananias comes and lays hands on "Brother Saul," two amazing things happen: he recovers his sight and he is filled with the Holy Spirit.

After believing on the Lord, Saul is filled with the Spirit to empower him for his mission. In this moment, Jesus anoints and equips him as his "chosen instrument" (v 15). The immediate impact of his experience with Christ and infilling of the Spirit is awesome. "At once he began to preach in the synagogues that Jesus is the Son of God" (v 20). Flesh and blood did not instruct him; he received this by divine revelation (Gal 1:11–12).

Rhema: Next to Jesus, Saul became the most effective person in the kingdom of God. Similarly, the Lord desires to fill us with his Spirit after our conversion so we too can be effectual for him.

JUNE 26 | ACTS 9:19–31

ENCOURAGED BY THE HOLY SPIRIT

*Then the church throughout Judea, Galilee and Samaria enjoyed a time of peace and was strengthened. Living in the fear of the Lord and encouraged by the **Holy Spirit**, it increased in numbers.* –ACTS 9:31

Do you have someone to help you reach your goals and shape your life? I mean someone who offers you consistent encouragement and support to steady you on your life's journey? How fortunate to have a friend who not only celebrates your success but also infuses you with courage, so you can keep moving forward. What is needed most when fighting fears and facing obstacles is an ally who personally cares for your well-being.

In reality, you have a helper who cares heaps for you. Believers "throughout Judea, Galilee and Samaria enjoyed a time of peace and [were] strengthened," by the Spirit. Luke describes the Spirit's pivotal role in helping God's battle-scarred, wounded people recover from years of persecution and turmoil. To say they were strengthened means the Spirit built them up as a carpenter builds a house. Interestingly, the Greek word for strengthened is used to describe how the Lord God *made* a woman from Adam's rib (Gen 2:22 LXX). The Spirit is in the process of making the bride of Christ—she is under construction.

Responsibility for the church's health and growth is in part attributed to the Holy Spirit. As the *paraclete*, he came alongside to supply just what the beleaguered believers needed: encouragement. His gentle touch and kind words helped them mend from their days of believer bashing. Through prophetic utterances, his gracious exhortations were like "a honeycomb, sweet to the soul and healing to the bones" (Prov 16:24). Energy spent on surviving is now directed to thriving. Under the Spirit's favorable influence and consolation, the church grew not only in numbers but in word and ministry.

Rhema: Remember, the Holy Spirit is not some distant power for good. He is a person; a friend and helper sent by Jesus to support and strengthen you. In addition, he helps you stay focused on life's goal. You need not journey alone during difficult and turbulent times, because he is a companion who speaks and guides. He is the one who gives you power "to walk in the fear of the Lord."

JUNE 27 | ACTS 10:1–23

THE SPIRIT PREPARES US FOR NEW THINGS

While Peter was still thinking about the vision, the **Spirit** *said to him, "Simon, three men are looking for you. So get up and go downstairs. Do not hesitate to go with them, for I have sent them." –*ACTS **10:19–20**

When God desires to do something new, he prepares us by his Spirit. Our difficult attitudinal and cultural views often stand in the way of his eternal purposes, so the Holy Spirit must act. That is why Luke mentions the Spirit eight times in this story. To ensure believers took the gospel to the Gentiles required some prep work. Because the church was mostly Jewish, she was unprepared to reach out to non-Jews.

None of the believers, not even the apostles, understood the full extent of what Jesus meant when he said, "You shall be my witnesses…unto the ends of the earth" (1:8). Accepting Gentiles into God's fold was not on their radar. No one in their wildest dreams ever imagined God's plan included "unclean" Gentiles as equals.

The drama begins with two men, Peter and Cornelius. Both receive visions independent of each other while praying. Visions belong to the Age of the Spirit—"Your young men will see visions" (2:17). Cornelius, a Roman centurion stationed in Caesarea, is a devout, God-fearing Gentile. In his vision, he hears an angel tell him to get Peter who is residing in Joppa, thirty or so miles away.

Peter's unusual vision, on the other hand, prepares him for what is about to happen. Three times he sees heaven open and a sheet unfurl with all kinds of unclean animals, prohibited for Jews to eat. The apostle is instructed to kill and eat these forbidden animals but being a good Jew, objects. When he protests, a heavenly voice says to him, "Do not call anything impure that God has made clean" (v 15). While he is pondering what all this means, the Spirit tells him to meet three men standing outside. The Spirit says, "Do not hesitate to go with them, for I have sent them."

Rhema: God wants you to grow in him. Although growth is sometimes difficult, he wants to expand your narrow views that hinder his plans. When you allow the Holy Spirit to operate in your life without reservation, he will present unimagined possibilities.

JUNE 28 | ACTS 10:24–38

ANOINTED WITH THE SPIRIT TO DO GOOD

*You know what has happened throughout the province of Judea, begin-
ning in Galilee after the baptism that John preached— how God anointed
Jesus of Nazareth with the **Holy Spirit** and power, and how he went
around doing good and healing all who were under the power of the devil,
because God was with him.* **–ACTS 10:37–38**

God anointed Jesus with the Holy Spirit and power to do good.
The remarkable life and ministry of God's Son is a direct result
of being empowered with the Holy Spirit. The gospel Peter preached
to Cornelius was a full gospel, not some watered-down drivel stripped
of its essential features. Doing good by crushing the devil's works in
the power of the Holy Spirit is a vital part of his gospel. He told them
God empowered Jesus with the Spirit so he can reverse the effects of
evil, take on the oppressor, and overcome his destructive works.

Healing and deliverance are also part of Peter's gospel proclamation. Jesus came in the Spirit's power to set people free from every
wicked work of the destroyer. He delivers people from curses, suffering, sickness, strongholds, and demons. Every disease, every infirmity,
every illness besides disabilities and epilepsy Jesus cured because
he was anointed. Everyone the devil had variously oppressed the
Anointed One freed. That is good news! No one else could overturn
the enemy's strangleholds.

In addition, Peter's preaching encompassed Christ's entire life,
from his birth to his death and resurrection. He even told of his role
as "judge of the living and the dead." The gospel is "the good news
of peace through Jesus Christ" (v 36). Everyone who believes in him,
Peter proclaimed, receives forgiveness of sins (v 43). At that point,
Cornelius and his household received the Spirit.

*Rhema: Peter's announcement concerning Jesus is the fullest gospel account by
any apostle. Although summarized by the author, in no way is any facet of the
good news minimized. Its central message is clear. God is for you and he has sent
his Son in the Spirit's power to deliver you and to set you free from the devil's death
grip. God's wonder working activity present in Jesus' ministry through the Spirit
is available for you today. You should not overlook, dismiss, or ignore any feature
of this good news.*

JUNE 29 | ACTS 10:34–44

A SURPRISING RECEPTION OF THE SPIRIT

While Peter was still speaking these words, the **Holy Spirit** *came on all who heard the message.* –ACTS **10:44**

Favoritism is toxic. Giving one person special favors or benefits while discounting others creates a hostile environment. That sums up the ancient rivalries between Jews and Gentiles. When God interrupted Peter with an earthshaking, pressing, unpredictable blessing, he ended the divisiveness. Before Peter finished speaking, the Holy Spirit fell on the Gentiles as he did upon the Jews at Pentecost. In an instant, the Father threw his arms around them. He embraced each one with his deepest love. Before any were baptized in water or had hands laid on them, the Spirit unexpectedly fell on them. This extraordinary occurrence meant Cornelius and his household received the Holy Spirit as Jewish believers did but without having to become Jews first.

In telling this story, Luke wants his readers to know the Gentiles responded to the gospel that day and believed on Jesus. As Peter spoke of faith and forgiveness of sins, the Holy Spirit came on them. When they accepted the gospel, also called the word of God (11:1), God saw their believing hearts and reciprocated by sending the Spirit.

As a Gentile, Cornelius had gone as far in God as possible. He was devout, God-fearing, and a man of prayer who overflowed with generosity. God expected all Gentiles to live like this. All that remained in his spiritual journey was to receive salvation in the NT sense—believe on Jesus Christ and receive the Holy Spirit. Cornelius and everyone under his roof who listened to Peter's salvation message were cleansed (10:15) through faith and accepted by God (15:7–8). At that precise moment, "the Holy Spirit came on all who heard the message."

The Spirit had brought together Peter and Cornelius for this special moment where the good news was extended to the Gentiles. It marks the crossing of the cultural barrier from Jew to Gentile. In short, this remarkable incident fulfills Peter's opening words to Cornelius: "I now realize how true it is that God does not show favoritism but accepts from every nation the one who fears him and does what is right" (vv 34–35).

Rhema: God is no respecter of persons but gives the Spirit to all who commit themselves to Christ.

JUNE 30 | ACTS 10:44–45; 11:15–18

ASTONISHED BY THE GIFT
OF THE HOLY SPIRIT

*The circumcised believers who had come with Peter were astonished that the gift of the **Holy Spirit** had been poured out even on Gentiles. For they heard them speaking in tongues and praising God.* –ACTS 10:45–46

How could this be? What, even Gentiles receive the gift of the Holy Spirit! It was just not Cornelius who needed converting that day. The six circumcised believers who accompanied Peter also needed a radical change of heart. They were astonished at what they saw and heard. The word "astonished" means to stand outside of one-self, to come unglued. God blew their norms out of the water! To see "unclean" Gentiles receive the Spirit and speak in tongues exploded their racial prejudices and disjointed theological attitudes.

It took a miracle to convince them to accept Gentiles as equal heirs of salvation. Peter expressed this attitude when he said, "You are well aware that it is against our law for a Jew to associate with or visit a Gentile" (v 28). They did not even eat together or come into each other's homes. Jews saw themselves as God's people and, therefore, special, circumcised, privileged, favored. In their eyes, other nations were common, unclean, uncircumcised, cursed. Like an old wooden ship heaving up and down sighing and creaking as it rubs against the pilings, the Jewish contingent struggled with their laden loads of prejudice and incredulity.

God demonstrated that these Gentile believers were as accepted as any Jewish believer. They were saved and filled with the Spirit just as were Peter, James, and John. The Spirit is the great equalizer, removing racial distinctions between a Jewish apostle and a Roman centurion. What took place in the Upper Room with the 120 occurred with this Gentile household. They all spoke in tongues and praised God. In the natural a great gulf existed between them, but in the Spirit they are made equal.

Rhema: Many today still find the Holy Spirit makes them uncomfortable. Prejudice, unbelief, false teaching, and traditions have contributed to misguided views of the Spirit. When God is doing a new thing, he must shatter these old views. Theological mindsets can hinder God's work in our lives. Therefore, we must not put him in a box and tell him what he can or cannot do.

JULY 1 | ACTS 10:44–48

GENTILES RECEIVE THE SPIRIT

*Then Peter said, "Surely no one can stand in the way of their being baptized with water. They have received the **Holy Spirit** just as we have."*
–ACTS 10:46–47

Can you imagine how it shocked these six circumcised believers? This epochal event turned their prejudices upside down. Gentiles speaking in tongues and praising God to the top of their lungs was too much. What unfolded before their eyes reminded them of their own reception of the Spirit on the day of Pentecost ten years earlier. Peter asked if they had any objections to baptizing these Gentile believers. None protested. The evidence God accepted them was overwhelming—they had received the Spirit. Therefore, they were baptized "in the name of Jesus Christ" and welcomed into the church.

The Gentile believers met the essential requirements for water baptism. They believed on the Lord and repented of their sins, otherwise they would not have received the Holy Spirit. This meant the "unclean" were now clean and the unacceptable were acceptable. A point often overlooked is experience not doctrine determined whether they were true believers. For non-Jews to receive the Spirit without adhering to the OT Law was a theological breakthrough that would rock the church. Later, when Peter reported what happened, he was careful to mention their faith and repentance. The reason he preached to Cornelius in the first place was to bring them a salvation message. An angel had told Cornelius to get Peter because "he will bring you a message through which you and all your household will be saved" (11:14).

A huge hurdle had to be overcome before they could baptize these Gentiles. Peter's accomplices needed a compelling confirmation they were doing the right thing. So God must first show his acceptance of the Gentiles by giving them the gift of the Holy Spirit. Only then did the Jewish believers baptize them and accept them as full-fledged believers.

Rhema: Sometimes we become upset when God does something different from our expectations. It requires humility to admit our beliefs might need to change. After all, perfect knowledge must wait until we get to heaven. What we must never do, however, is oppose God or limit his gracious gift of salvation. Peter had to admit, "Who was I to think that I could stand in God's way" (11:17).

JULY 2 | ACTS 11:1–14

OBEYING THE SPIRIT

The Spirit told me to have no hesitation about going with them. These six brothers also went with me, and we entered the man's house. –ACTS 11:12

It did not take long for word of what happened to the Gentiles to find its way back home. News of the momentous event traveled far and wide. Mouths wagged. Indignities flared. "Circumcised believers" critical of Peter were waiting for him. They could not believe he "went into the house of uncircumcised men and ate with them" (v 3). Since he was at the center of this heated controversy, he must defend his actions. His critics did not rejoice in the Gentiles' amazing salvation. Instead, the sourpusses only found fault. In their minds the only way for Gentiles to eat and fellowship with a Jew was first to become one.

Peter is careful to explain how he came to visit Cornelius. He revealed to them his visions and the voice that said *kill and eat* these unclean animals. When he protested, a voice from heaven said, "Do not call anything impure that God has made clean" (v 9). At that precise moment, he told them, a delegation from Cornelius appeared outside his house. That is when, the apostle said, "The Spirit told me to have no hesitation about going with them."

The Spirit ordered him not to discriminate. So he did not wave the flag of Jewish superiority and look down upon these Gentiles. Even though the Spirit required behavior contrary to his ethnic and religious value system, he still went with them. The old ceremonial law given by God was no longer in effect. What the Spirit said challenged and changed Peter's inadequate and outmoded theological beliefs. To respect and obey the Spirit was not easy. To disobey Scripture and submit to the Spirit no doubt filled him with angst, impelling him to go in *fear and trembling*.

Rhema: How can the Spirit lead us if we disobey him? Some think ignoring him does not matter. To defy the Spirit, however, is to defy God. Nothing is more "substantial" than the Spirit; he is, after all, God. Nothing is greater. Following the Spirit's leading, admittedly, is sometimes difficult, especially when he challenges traditions, councils, presuppositions, theologies, interpretations, and social structures. Peter is to be commended for his courage and obedience.

JULY 3 | ACTS 11:15–18

THE SPIRIT COMES UPON THE GENTILES

*As I began to speak, the **Holy Spirit** came on them as he had come on us at the beginning.* **—ACTS 11:15**

Have you ever wondered who's in and who's out, who's a real child of God? Jews who criticized Peter for fellowshipping with a Gentile thought they knew but they didn't. Old distinctions no longer applied after Christ came and poured out his Spirit. Since then one thing defines and identifies the people of God: have they received the Spirit? Peter declared, "The Holy Spirit came on them as he had come on us at the beginning." Without coaxing or any action on Peter's part, the Spirit fell. What happened in Jerusalem reoccurred in Cornelius' home.

It is worth noting Peter considers the Spirit's descent at Pentecost "the beginning." In his mind, something new began then. What was it? The promises of both John the Baptist and Jesus became a reality. They said, "You will be baptized with the Holy Spirit." This phenomenal spiritual outpouring demonstrated a new era had arrived. Pentecost marked the beginning of the end times; it also marked the church's birthday. In Christ, God makes no distinction between Jewish and Gentile believers as both share the full blessings of the new era.

The Spirit, therefore, makes believers the true people of God. Whatever the apostles and the 120 became at Pentecost, the Gentiles became. Gentiles with the Spirit are just as much members of Christ's church as is Peter and the rest in Jerusalem, Judea, and Samaria. The Spirit has come upon Jew and Gentile alike to cleanse them, so he can birth them into the church. Peter tells his antagonists that God gave the Gentiles "the same gift as he gave us" (v 17). Once these Gentiles "believed in the Lord Jesus Christ," the Spirit came on them.

Rhema: The Spirit's descent upon Cornelius and his household was a dramatic, watershed moment. Swiftly and suddenly, he fell upon them and saturated them with the water of life. As abrupt as the Spirit's reception was, it was also irresistible, unstoppable, unleashed. One minute they are listening to Peter's words, the next they are awash in the Holy Spirit. In an instant they started speaking in tongues and praising God, but more importantly, they were integrated into the family of God.

DAY 185

EVEN GENTILES ARE BAPTIZED
WITH THE SPIRIT

*Then I remembered what the Lord had said: "John baptized with water,
but you will be baptized with the **Holy Spirit**." –ACTS 11:16*

What part of "no" don't you understand? That was Peter's tacit
question when he explained God's no exclusion provision—the
people of God include Gentiles. When he saw the Spirit come upon
Cornelius, he remembered Jesus had said, "John baptized with water,
but you will be baptized with the Holy Spirit" (1:5). At that time, he
never imagined this prophetic declaration included Gentiles. Not until
Jesus baptized these Gentiles with the Holy Spirit did he change his
shortsighted view. Having come to this new revelation, Peter asks,
"Who was I to withhold water baptism from them?"

Luke uses various terms to describe this momentous event.
For the eighth time he mentions the Holy Spirit in connection with
Cornelius. In fact, Acts pays more attention to the Spirit's outpouring
upon Gentiles than the initial outpouring at Pentecost. No doubt the
reason is to silence critics and bring them to realize God has granted
"even the Gentiles repentance unto life" (v 18). Once Jewish believers
understood God saved and filled Cornelius, the way was clear to take
the gospel to the ends of the earth.

It might be helpful to single out the different expressions the
author utilized to chronicle this pivotal event. Far too many people
misunderstand its importance and meaning, and consequently miss
out on one of the most essential Jesus-experiences in their lives. This
glorious experience intended for every believer is described in the
following italicized terms. The Holy Spirit *came on* all who heard the
message (10:44). The gift of the Holy Spirit had been *poured out* even
on Gentiles (10:45). They have *received* the Holy Spirit just as we have
(10:47). The Holy Spirit *came on* them as he had *come on* us at the
beginning (11:15). You will be *baptized* with the Holy Spirit (11:16).
He accepted them by *giving* the Holy Spirit to them, just as he did to
us (15:8).

*Rhema: For Gentile believers to receive the Holy Spirit was of utmost impor-
tance because it was a straightforward sign they were children of God and equal
members in the church. The same is true of us today.*

A Good Man Full of the Holy Spirit

*He was a good man, full of the **Holy Spirit** and faith, and a great number of people were brought to the Lord.* –Acts **11:24**

What kind of person do you send to investigate and help a new outreach? You send "a good man, full of the Holy Spirit and faith." Such an individual will not be afraid or censorious of something strange and suspicious. Because he is generous in spirit, he will rejoice in and bless new successes. You would send a risk-taker like Barnabas. Without hesitation he welcomed into the fold Saul, the converted persecutor. He is so bighearted others try to emulate him. You know if God is doing something new and unprecedented he is the person to send.

The church in Jerusalem sent Barnabas to Antioch where a unique people group encountered the gospel. These individuals were not Jews, nor partial Jews like the Samaritans, nor even Gentile God-fearers such as Cornelius. No, they were Greeks—pagans with no apparent inclination for God. Believers scattered by Stephen's martyrdom came and witnessed to the Greeks, "telling them the good news about the Lord Jesus."

Upon his arrival in Antioch, Barnabas jubilated at seeing so many pagan Gentiles come to faith in Jesus Christ. With his own eyes, he "saw what the grace of God had done." "A great number of people believed and turned to the Lord." We can be sure he did not find fault or criticize this marvelous move of God. Instead, "he was glad and encouraged them all to remain true to the Lord with all their hearts." The man bursting with faith even found Saul to help him tutor them in the word of God.

Rhema: Barnabas had such a positive attitude because he was brimming with the Holy Spirit. Likewise, the Spirit can fill us with Christian graces and fruit. He will help us become love personified (I Cor 13:4–5): patient, kind, does not envy, does not boast, and is not self-seeking. As the Spirit has his way in our lives, we become encouragers (4:36) and exude the fruit of the Spirit (Gal 5:22–23). Therefore, we will overflow with love, joy, peace, patience, kindness, goodness, faithfulness, gentleness, and self-control. Under his influence, our lives will impact unbelievers like they did in Antioch (v 26).

JULY 6 | ACTS 11:27–29; GENESIS 41:28–40

PREDICTIONS THROUGH THE SPIRIT

One of them, named Agabus, stood up and through the Spirit predicted that a severe famine would spread over the entire Roman world.
–ACTS 11:28

This is the first mention in Acts of a NT prophet. Agabus came to Antioch with several other prophets to establish the new believers and help build a remarkable church. Like his OT counterparts, Agabus made a prediction through the Spirit.

Believers took his prophecy of a severe, worldwide famine seriously. Acting on it, they sent financial support to the Jewish disciples in Jerusalem who had suffered loss through persecution. The famine would hit them the hardest. Agabus' prophecy allowed the church to take preemptive action to stave off the full impact of the crisis. In this way, he was like Joseph in the OT whose prophetic abilities helped save lives and avoid much suffering. The Spirit spoke so believers could respond with appropriate social action.

Sometimes people are critical of prophetic predictions and are suspicious of prophets. For this reason, they are reluctant to put any trust in them or their forecasting, but not so the church in Antioch. This extraordinary body of believers esteemed its prophets and realized their invaluable contribution to the church's growth and development. Prophets are immensely valuable because they are Christ's gifts to his church. Their purpose is "to prepare God's people for works of service, so that the body of Christ may be built up" (Eph 4:12). In fact, they are foundational in establishing the church (Eph 2:20). Antioch which does not seem to have any apostles in direct association with it relies instead upon its prophets and teachers to lead it (13:1).

We are not told how Agabus received his revelation about the famine. How prophets came by their knowledge is not always clear but somehow the Spirit showed them future events. Furthermore, we should expect the Spirit to speak to us, to show us the things of Christ, and to reveal things to come (Jn 16:13–14). This spiritual ability, however, is more developed in prophets.

Rhema: Know the Spirit speaks. Sometimes he may give you a direct word or a vision. Other times he may reveal something less definite, such as an impression, deduction, or awareness. Regardless, whatever the Spirit brings into your consciousness he intends for it to be profitable.

JULY 7 | ACTS 13:1–3; 11:29; 12:25

A SPIRIT-DRIVEN CHURCH

*While they were worshiping the Lord and fasting, the **Holy Spirit** said, "Set apart for me Barnabas and Saul for the work to which I have called them."* –ACTS **13:2**

What should drive the church? Some recommend purpose others vision. Sometimes it's money or reputation. In the NT, however, the foremost driving force is the Holy Spirit. The early church was propelled by the Third Person of the Trinity!

After an extended time of prayer, fasting and waiting on God, the Spirit gave the church in Antioch a powerful directive. He spoke and instructed them to set apart Barnabas and Saul for the work to which he had called them. Realize he selected the work as well as the workers. In uttering this command, the Spirit took the initiative to make these believers even more outward focused even though they had already been reaching and discipling Greeks.

From its beginning, the church in Antioch developed unique characteristics. Remember, this is where believers were first called Christians and intentionally reached out to Greeks. Further, they functioned with a different leadership structure, one centered on its prophets and teachers. In addition, Antioch had a tremendous hunger and thirst for God. Equally far-reaching was their willingness to step out in faith and follow the Spirit's leading. What a template for God's work today.

When the Spirit ordered them to set apart Barnabas and Saul, he selected two of the most gifted individuals in the assembly. He picked the church's best to advance the gospel. Antioch, no doubt, would experience the loss of its most eminent workers.

As a commanding officer, the Spirit expressed himself when he wanted the gospel to go in a new direction. This was the third time in Acts the "Spirit spoke." The first incident occurred when he directed Philip to speak to the Ethiopian eunuch (8:29). The second transpired when he told Peter to go to the house of Cornelius (10:19). On this occasion, his directive resulted in the historic missionary journeys of Paul and his partners as they took the gospel worldwide.

Rhema: The Spirit's involvement helps explain the early church's phenomenal success. Likewise, God wants us to allow his Spirit to be the primary driving force of his church today. To not only direct its focus but also appoint its workers.

July 8 | Acts 13:4–5; Matthew 10:1–16

SENT OUT BY THE SPIRIT

The two of them, sent on their way by the Holy Spirit, went down to Seleucia and sailed from there to Cyprus. –ACTS 13:4

They were sent on their way by the Holy Spirit. Where would Christianity be without his active involvement? The church in Antioch became the NT's great missions center because it sought the will of God and allowed the Spirit to direct it. The Divine Director of Mission gave an order to separate Barnabas and Saul for the purposes of God. He yearned for them to take the gospel to the ends of the earth. The Spirit in the final analysis called them, commissioned them, and accompanied them.

Is this a pattern for us today? What might happen in our churches if more people waited on the Lord to speak and relied on the Spirit to guide them? In Antioch, they responded to the Spirit's command with more fasting and prayer (v 3) before laying their hands on Barnabas and Saul and sending them on the road. Although believers took part in the missionary enterprise, the initiative was not theirs but the Spirit's. The church can recognize, confirm, and release members chosen by the Spirit but ultimately he sends them.

The impetus for reaching new people originated with the Spirit. After all, he spoke to the church with a fresh directive. To expand its mission to other regions was not the result of a committee or task force but of a special time seeking God. The Spirit spoke and guided them in response to their intense enquiring of God's will.

As Jesus sent the Twelve, so the Holy Spirit sent Barnabas and Saul. The Spirit is a person who acts as Jesus did when he called and commissioned his disciples. Similarly, he propelled them into parts of the world where the good news had never gone. As their mission unfolded, he blessed them with amazing results. As we will see, he opened doors, protected them, and confirmed their message with signs and wonders.

Rhema: Given opportunity, the Spirit will embed Christ's DNA within the church. That is how it will maintain its integrity and loyalty to the Great Commission. Allowing the Holy Spirit to expand the church's mission by raising up and sending out new workers is of vital importance.

JULY 9 | ACTS 13:6–12

THE SPIRIT AND SPIRITUAL WARFARE

*But Saul, who was also known as Paul, filled with the **Holy Spirit**, fixed his gaze on him, and said, "You who are full of all deceit and fraud, you son of the devil, you enemy of all righteousness, will you not cease to make crooked the straight ways of the Lord?" –ACTS 13:9*

The gospel's entrance into pagan regions led to an inevitable battle with the evil works of darkness. No sooner had Paul and Barnabas set foot on the island of Cyprus when they were opposed by a false prophet called Elymas. By the Spirit Paul exposed the prevaricator of the truth. Acting in the fullness of the Spirit, the apostle engaged in a power encounter with him. As a semiautomatic, Paul rifled off five piercing bullets. He told the charlatan he was full of deceit, a fraud, the son of the devil, the enemy of righteousness, and a distorter of the straight ways of the Lord. The Spirit exposed the sorcerer as none other than a villainous deceiver who was behaving like the devil and making himself God's enemy.

Paul, filled with the Holy Spirit, discerned the deception taking place in the palace. Elymas tried to hinder the proconsul from accepting the gospel. The governing ruler of Cyprus, Sergius Paulus, had sought out Paul and Barnabas because he heard about their ministry. When they began proclaiming God's word, Elymas opposed "them, seeking to turn the proconsul away from the faith." The false prophet practiced magic to influence the governor. Through him the adversary sought to hold the island in darkness, but the Holy Spirit tore off the mask.

Brimming with the Spirit, Paul pronounced a supernatural judgment upon the devil's henchman. At once Elymas became blind, incurring God's wrath because he was hindering people from coming to faith in Jesus Christ. Hence Paul's declaration, "Now, behold, the hand of the Lord is upon you, and you will be blind and not see the sun for a time." The apostle no doubt remembered his own blindness when he tried to stop Christians from preaching about Jesus.

Rhema: Discerning of spirits is one of the most powerful weapons in our arsenal against the enemy. It lets us identify the powers of darkness hindering God's work, so we can come against them in the Spirit.

JULY 10 | ACTS 13:13–52

CONTINUALLY FILLED WITH JOY
AND THE SPIRIT

*And the disciples were continually filled with joy and with the **Holy
Spirit**.* –ACTS 13:52

Can you imagine wave after wave of irrepressible joy? Intense,
ecstatic happiness welling up in your heart like playful dolphins
splashing about in the surf? This is what these new believers experienced when Paul and Barnabas took the gospel to Pisidian Antioch.
The most intense pleasure they ever experienced flooded every vacu-
ous part of their being. They were continually filled with joy and with
the Holy Spirit.

When the Holy Spirit is at work, joy bubbles to the surface.
Exhilaration wells up. Ecstasy fills the soul. The one from heaven
expands our capacity for elation. He kept on filling these new believers and pouring out on them the oil of gladness. Even when Paul
and Barnabas moved on to the next place, the disciples remained in a
heightened state of spiritual bliss. The work of the Spirit made church
a fun place to be.

Amazing things happened as the Spirit drove the church's irresistible worldwide expansion. Sent by the Spirit, Paul and Barnabas
went to the synagogue and announced the "good news" (v 32). They
proclaimed grace, not law; liberty not legalism. Jesus provided what
the law could never do. In him, there was total, complete forgiveness
of sins and God's declaration of righteousness. They trumpeted that
everyone who accepts Christ is set free from the requirements of the
law of Moses (vv 38–39).

Those who heard Paul and Barnabas were so excited by the message
of grace they told everyone about it. One week later, "almost the whole
city gathered to hear the word of the Lord" (v 44). When Jews saw
throngs of people interested in God, they became jealous and rejected
the message of "eternal life." At this juncture, the apostles declared,
"We now turn to the Gentiles" (v 46). The new believers, however,
rejoiced and thanked God as the Spirit set another city ablaze with joy.

*Rhema: Although the good news messengers were driven from the city, the Holy
Spirit remained filling new believers with the joy of heaven. Likewise, God wants
to give you the same bliss (Rom 14:17) by keeping you full of the Spirit. He wants
you to experience complete joy brimming up and running over every day.*

JULY 11 | ACTS 15:1–21

HAVING THE SPIRIT IS PROOF ENOUGH

God, who knows the heart, showed that he accepted them by giving the **Holy Spirit** *to them, just as he did to us.* –ACTS **15:8**

Everyone likes success. Right? Apparently not. To some, the rapid increase of Gentile believers created distress. Perhaps, they feared a loss of their identity and control because of the ever-increasing progress of the Gentile mission. Through Paul and Barnabas' ministry so many turned to the Lord that Gentile believers outnumbered Jewish. As a result, many heated debates erupted. A few Jewish believers who were Pharisees came down to Antioch where they clashed with Barnabas and Paul. They were legalists who insisted, "Unless you are circumcised, according to the custom taught by Moses, you cannot be saved" (v 1).

Believers at Antioch referred this controversy to the apostles and elders in Jerusalem. It was a major theological issue centering on one question: on what basis can Gentiles be admitted to the church? The division ran deep. When all interested parties had gathered, those raising these concerns spoke first. They argued believers in Christ must be circumcised and adhere to the law of Moses. In other words, to be saved Gentiles had to become Jews first.

Peter, Paul, Barnabas, and finally James, the main overseer of the Jerusalem church, challenged this claim. The thrust of Peter's argument was to recount his experience with Cornelius. God gave the Spirit to them, he said, without requiring circumcision or adherence to the law of Moses. His argument was simple: the Lord himself determines whom he admits to the church. Peter, in effect, was saying, *We know God accepted us because we received his Spirit. He gave the Gentiles the Holy Spirit in the same way. Therefore, he must have accepted them. So should we and not put him to the test!*

Rhema: It is interesting to see how the apostles resorted to experience to settle their theological debates. Proof one is a Christian and belongs to God is having the Holy Spirit. Salvation is by grace through faith in the sufficiency of Christ's death. No amount of human effort or any "work of the flesh" will be more efficacious. Only God knows the heart's state and decides whom he will accept. Unarguable, indisputable proof of his acceptance is not doctrine but possession of the Holy Spirit.

July 12 | Acts 15:22–35

It Seemed Good to the Holy Spirit

*It seemed good to the **Holy Spirit** and to us not to burden you with anything beyond the following requirements.* —Acts 15:28

Differences of opinion will happen. Strong disagreements will likely occur whenever two or more people get together even if they are family, friends, or foreigners. A major controversy threatened the early church's unity. In fact, emotions were so charged the dispute was referred to a resolution council comprising the apostles and elders of the mother church. To describe this tense scene, Luke uses words such as "sharp dispute," "much discussion," and "debate." Individuals at both ends of the spectrum stood their ground.

Eventually, they came to an amiable resolution whereupon Luke adds, "It seemed good to the Holy Spirit." What does that mean? It shows the Holy Spirit had an important role in their decision. After all, he not only worked miracles among the Gentiles and dwelt in them, but he also guided the council in its decision. In other words, he provided them with an inner witness to substantiate his external verification of God's acceptance of the Gentiles. In this way, the church experienced the Spirit's assistance in resolving their differences; everyone present at the meeting recognized it.

We must not overlook what Jesus said the Spirit would do in his absence—lead us into all truth. For this reason, they refused to make regulations for the Gentiles where the Spirit made none. Believers declined to act only on their own authority but sought to work in harmony with God's Spirit. Somehow, they allowed him to guide and influence their spiritual and ethical judgments. Because cultural diversity always presents challenges, peace and fellowship were sometimes difficult to maintain in the early church, but the Spirit helped hold believers together.

Rhema: As oil poured on troubled waters, the Spirit ensures unity in the face of agitation, harmony amidst discord. The Counselor helped avert a disastrous dichotomy in which Jewish and Gentile believers might go their separate ways. Instead, with his help they came to a resolution allowing them to extend the right hand of fellowship to each other. Therefore, when you are facing contentious matters and trying to resolve difficult controversies, you need to know God's Spirit is available to help and guide you. He wants to help you make God-honoring decisions.

JULY 13 | ACTS 15:36–16:6

FORBIDDEN BY THE HOLY SPIRIT

*Paul and his companions traveled throughout the region of Phrygia and Galatia, having been kept by the **Holy Spirit** from preaching the word in the province of Asia.* –ACTS 16:6

Have you ever fought God and resisted his leading? To do so is not good. The apostle found himself in that position. The Holy Spirit forbade him to minister in the province of Asia. For an unknown reason, he prevented his efforts to enter this region (modern Turkey). As an air traffic controller, the Spirit would not let him land there. Paul wanted to head south, but the Spirit put a stop to that because he had in mind another plan.

This verse shows the apostle did not have a detailed road map when he began his second missionary journey. He felt, however, he and Barnabas should visit the churches they had established earlier and make them aware of the Jerusalem Council's decision. As it turned out, the two of them parted company. Barnabas took John Mark to Cyprus and Paul went with Silas to the mainland where Timothy joined them. After completing his visit to the churches of Phrygia and Galatia, Paul needed new marching orders to know what to do next.

Usually the Spirit empowers believers for witness and helps them in positive ways, but here he thwarts the gospel team. He opposed every plan Paul entertained, blocking his path. We can sense his frustration with the Spirit's urgency and forthrightness. The Divine Director of Mission needs Paul to fall into line. If he does not follow the Spirit's leading, he will be out of God's will. In fact, the only time in the NT the Holy Spirit places roadblocks in someone's ministry is here.

Rhema: When our plans do not coincide with God's, the Spirit is distraught. Our natural inclinations and well-thought-out designs will only take us so far. The apostle aimed to go to Asia, but God had something else in store. He meant for the gospel to enter Europe instead. If Paul had his way, the mighty works in Philippi, Thessalonica, and Corinth may not have occurred. This one act of the Holy Spirit of keeping Paul out of Asia changed world history. If you follow the Spirit, you too will be at the right place at the right time.

JULY 14 | ACTS 16:6–15

THE SPIRIT OF JESUS CLOSES THE DOOR

*When they came to the border of Mysia, they tried to enter Bithynia, but the **Spirit** of Jesus would not allow them to.* –ACTS 16:7

We dislike closed doors. They are frustrating and sometimes disappointing. When things do not work out, we are often discombobulated. When God shuts a door, however, he is only telling us what we are not to do. Until he opens a new one, we live with uncertainty about a way forward. Living between God's no and the unrevealed future is difficult and tense. During such times, nevertheless, we must learn to trust him. Little do we know if a door of undreamed opportunity is about to swing open.

Forbidden by the Holy Spirit to enter Asia, the apostle attempted to go north into Bithynia. The Spirit of Jesus closed that door too and made it impossible for him to go there. What is Luke suggesting by the unique expression, "the Spirit of Jesus"? Was Paul so bent on following his own plans he needed reminding that Jesus was directing him? After all, he is the Executive Director of the Holy Spirit and following the Spirit is obeying the Lord. Exalted to the Father's right hand is the place from which our Lord presides over the spread of the gospel. The Spirit, therefore, does not act independently of our risen Lord but in submission to his will.

Hemmed in on every side by the Spirit they continued west until they came to Troas on the coast of the Aegean Sea. God finally gave Paul and his team the direction for which they were waiting. That night, "Paul had a vision of a man of Macedonia standing and begging him, 'Come over to Macedonia and help us'" (v 7). Paul welcomed the fresh vision. Through the Spirit Jesus was quarterbacking them into the region of Alexander the Great, the Greek world. It is here that Luke, the author of Acts, joins the team (v 10). Together, Paul, Silas, Timothy, and Luke embark on a fantastic mission to the Greeks.

Rhema: A closed door does not mean God is finished with you. Just the opposite. Because he cares so much, he does not want you to make a grave mistake and miss the wonderful opportunity he has planned for you.

JULY 15 | ACTS 18:24–19:5

THE JOURNEY OF FAITH AND
THE RECEPTION OF THE SPIRIT

There he found some disciples and asked them, "Did you receive the **Holy Spirit** *when you believed?"* –ACTS 19:2

Why did Paul ask these disciples if they had received the Holy Spirit when they believed? Did he detect a shortcoming or deficiency in their faith? As it turned out, the reason they did not receive the Spirit was their limited understanding of Jesus. Their experience shows one's faith journey has several stages of development. Paul detected these disciples needed more instruction if they were to make progress and receive the Spirit.

These "disciples" were like Apollos. Even though he knew the Scriptures and "had been instructed in the way of the Lord," his beliefs were incomplete. Luke says he "taught about Jesus accurately, though he knew only the baptism of John" (18:25). Something lacked in his experience compared to Paul's disciples. When Priscilla and Aquila heard him, they recognized his deficiency. So they invited him to their home where they "explained to him the way of God more adequately" (18:26). Apollos needed someone to fill him in on what it meant to be a follower of Christ.

At times, the growth and expansion of the gospel was messy. Even teachers such as Apollos lacked full understanding of salvation and the Spirit. Obviously, not everyone comprehended what walking with the Lord entailed. The reason may lie in the fact that those far removed from Jerusalem, the birth and center of Christianity, would not be exposed to teachers of the Way. A few like Apollos could preach about Jesus but apparently were never informed of how his death, resurrection, and the pouring out of the Spirit applied to their lives.

Rhema: Everyone is at a different stage in their spiritual journey. Therefore, it is important to ask ourselves if we have all that God has for us. Have we received the Holy Spirit since we believed? These disciples represent people without a full knowledge of Jesus; they are without the Spirit. Another key point is these disciples did not resist the reception of the Spirit; they were unaware of it. Fortunately, no one taught them against it. Paul and the early church expected everyone who put their trust in Jesus Christ to receive the gift of the Spirit.

JULY 16 | ACTS 19:1–5; MARK 1:1–8

THE SPIRIT AND FULL SALVATION

*They answered, "No, we have not even heard that there is a **Holy Spirit**." –ACTS 19:2*

When Paul asked if they had received the Holy Spirit, they said no. How interesting. He must have identified deficiencies in their faith as well as their experience. It mattered to him these Gentiles reach the same benchmark experience as the Jewish believers at Pentecost. He considered it normal for every believer to receive the Father's gift. For one thing, the Spirit's transformational power in believers' lives is what makes them holy and acceptable to God. These disciples had not received the Spirit; they knew nothing of the experience. Because they did not have the Spirit, they did not enjoy the full blessing of salvation. With that in mind, Paul did not ask these men what they believed. Instead, he asked them if the Holy Spirit was in their lives.

These twelve men, at the least, were disciples of John the Baptist. At the most, undeveloped followers of Christ. They said, "We have not even heard that there is a Holy Spirit." The apostle realized how important it was for these Gentile believers to receive the Holy Spirit. Possession of the Spirit entitled them to membership and fellowship in the church. Apparently, no one ever taught them even though this was the distinguishing characteristic of accepting Christ.

Realizing they knew little about the Spirit, Paul asked them what baptism they had received. They said, "John's." His, however, was preparatory, a baptism of repentance made obsolete by Jesus' death and resurrection. In contrast to John's, Jesus came to baptize them in the Holy Spirit. After Paul told them about Christ, they were first baptized in water then he laid his hands on them whereupon the Holy Spirit came on them. As at Pentecost, they all spoke in tongues and prophesied.

Rhema: The importance of the Holy Spirit in our salvation experience must not be underestimated. Just as we cannot live without breath, we cannot live without him. To experience God's fullest blessing, we need the Spirit. From this interesting account, we see a continuum of related but distinct spiritual experiences. Believing on Jesus, conversion, water baptism, and the gift of the Holy Spirit are part of God's provision but are separate experiences. So be sure to have them all.

July 17 | Acts 19:1–6

Balancing Doctrine with the Spirit

*When Paul placed his hands on them, the **Holy Spirit** came on them, and they spoke in tongues and prophesied.* **–Acts 19:6**

What is more important in our Christian lives, doctrine or experience? Paul had detected that both their beliefs and experience had deficiencies. He did not criticize them because of their limited doctrinal position. Nor did he chastise them for not possessing the Spirit. Both our doctrine and our experience are critical; we must keep them in balance. The apostle did not overemphasize the one over the other. To receive the Holy Spirit with speaking in tongues was just as significant as their faith. Nor did he promulgate wild spiritual experiences at the expense of a correct theology. As can be seen, he did not divorce Christian teaching from a personal encounter with the Holy Spirit.

Paul, however, delayed placing his hands on these disciples until their teaching was adequate. He made sure their faith reflected the new reality in Christ before praying for them to receive the Holy Spirit. They needed to move from being followers of John the Baptist to Christ. Starting where they were, he proceeded to teach them about Jesus and the the Spirit. Only when he was sure of their beliefs did Paul pray for them.

When he brought them to a place of faith in Jesus, they were "baptized into the name of the Lord" (v 5). This is the only place in Acts where those baptized under John's baptism were later rebaptized into Jesus. It is hard to know what to call these disciples before Paul introduced them to Christ. Were they pre-Christians, partial believers, or semi-Christians? In any event they more closely resembled OT believers than followers of Christ. To complete and validate John the Baptist's ministry, they needed to believe in Christ and receive the Holy Spirit.

The Spirit came on them with a miraculous manifestation after Paul laid his hands on them. People realized they received the Spirit because they spoke in tongues and prophesied just as in Acts 2. The accompanying spiritual phenomena indicated their admissibility into the church.

Rhema: It is important to realize they represent a new advancement of the gospel—if our doctrine needs updating or our experience is lacking, we can bring both into line through proper teaching and prayer.

JULY 18 | ACTS 20:13–22

COMPELLED BY THE SPIRIT

*And now, compelled by the **Spirit**, I am going to Jerusalem, not knowing what will happen to me there.* —ACTS 20:22

What does it mean to be compelled by the Spirit? Paul purposed to follow the Spirit's leading by placing himself under his authority. As a wife was bound to obey her husband, so he was bound to the Spirit. Cords of love and submission wrapped them together for one singular purpose. In this way, he complied with God's will. Because the Spirit chose his missionary exploits, he could say, "Not my will but thine be done." Binding himself to the Spirit meant he restricted his life to doing God's business.

This binding was not sudden but the ongoing controlling directive for his life. From the time of his conversion and call, he realized he was not his own. The Spirit set him apart for a specific work (13:2) and sent on his way (13:4). Ever since that dramatic day he has been doing the Holy Spirit's will, never his own. It does not matter what happens to him, whether imprisonment, persecution, or hardships: the Spirit chose his way. Whatever limitations confronted him mattered not because of his inner constriction. Perhaps no person was as tied to the Spirit as Paul.

Many voices cry out to us but like Paul, we can tune them out. The apostle does not listen to the allure of the world or the cries of his own body for ease or safety. He pays no attention to the counsel of good friends who urge him to spare himself the trouble and live another day. Whenever he hears the luring siren of foolish joys, he hits the mute button. The internal voice of his partner quiets all his fears and anxieties.

Rhema: Many things can deter us from God's will. It might be the prospect of danger or trouble. Uncertainty or even the comforts of the present may tempt us to draw back. It is so easy to luxuriate in past success and retreat to the pillowy solaces of home. Paul's future did not look bright. Everywhere he went yellow flashing lights warned him of the dangers ahead. Like Paul we do not know the specifics of what lies ahead, yet we can with full confidence bind ourselves to the Holy Spirit.

JULY 19 | ACTS 20:22–24

THE SPIRIT GUIDES OUR LIFE CHANGES

*I only know that in every city the **Holy Spirit** warns me that prison and hardships are facing me.* –ACTS 20:23

What an incredible individual. Tell him of hardship and imprisonment. Warn him of facing horrific storms and what does he do? He says, "I consider my life worth nothing to me" (v 24). To him, only one thing mattered—completing the task. Wherever Paul went, the Spirit warned him of the trouble he would face in Jerusalem; prophets in every place prophesied suffering awaited him.

No question the Spirit had a powerful influence on him. In fact, a continuous and fascinating interaction existed between them as the Spirit told him of things he must endure. Sometimes it was to give him helpful information. Other times so Paul would know how to prepare himself and pray into these situations. The apostle learned to get through it; he needed to depend completely upon his relationship with the Holy Spirit.

Another reason his divine friend forewarned him was so he could make necessary adjustments to his life. His final meeting with the Ephesian elders, for instance, appears to have occasioned a monumental reset. The apostle must readjust his attitude and activity, for once he is in Jerusalem Paul the missionary will become Paul the prisoner. To ease the emotional ordeal, he sought encouragement from these cherished elders. This was his Gethsemane and he leaned on them for emotional support.

Paul, however, found a wonderful place of peace, regardless of what awaited him. Through many warnings and prophetic utterances, the Spirit helped him develop sufficient resolve to finish the race and stay the course. To help him leave the old and grip the new was the Spirit's faithful and frequent testimony. Life as he knew it was about to change and he needed to make the necessary mental and emotional adjustments.

Rhema: Dealing with unsettling transitions is not easy. What can you do when life throws you a curve ball? You can fight it or embrace it. Although major life changes can shake up your world, the Holy Spirit is present to guide you through them. He not only wants to help you avoid the harrowing anxiety often associated with bringing closure to a major chapter in your life, but also lead you into the next.

JULY 20 | ACTS 20:25–38

THE HOLY SPIRIT SETS LEADERS IN PLACE

*Keep watch over yourselves and all the flock of which the **Holy Spirit** has made you overseers. Be shepherds of the church of God, which he bought with his own blood.* **–ACTS 20:28**

Who owns the church? Ultimately God, since he purchased it with the blood of his own Son. Therefore, the church does not belong to the pastor, board, or members, nor is it someone's pet project or platform. To him, the church is priceless. As a precious treasure, God's people are more important than anything else in the universe.

The Holy Spirit creates the church. He orders, structures, and arranges every part. Everyone who believes in Jesus and is born of the Spirit is placed in a certain position. A few members he appoints and equips to oversee God's people. Just as God set the stars in place (Ps 8:3), the Holy Spirit sets leaders in the church. He gives them the responsibility to ensure its safety, growth, and integrity. They are to feed, lead, and protect God's flock. Consequently, spiritual guardians should be watchmen, people of the Spirit, and gifted for the task.

How does the Holy Spirit make anyone fit for a particular role? For instance, he made Abraham a father of many nations, David king, and Paul an apostle. First, the Spirit makes God's will known. In each of the above examples, God's will was expressed through a promise or a declaration. Paul makes a similar declaration concerning the overseers in Ephesus. Second, the Spirit operates in their lives so they can attain the necessary qualifications. Third, he helps others recognize those God has chosen. Above all, church leadership is a sovereign act of the Holy Spirit.

Believers whom the Spirit appoints to leadership have a unique and special relationship to him. Their chief responsibility, therefore, is to execute the Spirit's will, follow his agenda, and pay close attention to what he is saying to the church. In no way is their authority to contravene the Spirit's.

Rhema: The Holy Spirit not only makes overseers, but he also assigns you a role or function in the body of Christ. This is your spiritual job description. So you can execute his agenda, he empowers and gifts you. He knows what is best for you and the church and works to bring it about.

JULY 21 | ACTS 21:1–6

CONFLICTING MESSAGES
FROM THE HOLY SPIRIT

*We sought out the disciples there and stayed with them seven days. Through the **Spirit** they urged Paul not to go on to Jerusalem.* **–ACTS 21:4**

Does the Spirit ever contradict himself? We read in Acts 20:22 the Spirit compelled Paul to go to Jerusalem but the believers at Tyre urged him "through the Spirit not to go." Obviously, someone or something is amiss. Paul, in fact, proceeds with his planned trip and does not act on this exhortation. One reason things did not go well for him in Jerusalem, some argue, was he disobeyed the Spirit and stepped out of God's will. Acts, incidentally, closes by showing Paul was never free again. Was he wrong to go? Such contradictions make many people skeptical of prophetic words.

To imagine the Spirit of Truth, however, would contradict himself is inconceivable. In every church Paul visited, the Holy Spirit spoke concerning the troubles and imprisonment he would face. Through prophetic utterances believers warned him. In Tyre, despite having the same revelation, they urged him not to go contrary to what Paul understood God's will to be.

How do we resolve this clash? We must wonder if these disciples added a human component to the revelation. When they heard of Paul's predicament, they may have wrongly concluded he should not go. Because revelation may be rightly received but wrongly applied, all prophetic utterances must be "tested" (II Cor 14:29). We must identify if any human distortion or misinterpretation exists. Nothing was wrong with the Spirit's divulgement, but human emotion, understandably, may have tainted the prophetic message.

If we are listening to the Spirit, we should know God's will for our lives better than others. After all, we are responsible for our actions and choices. That was true of Paul. Not once does he ever imagine that by going to Jerusalem he disobeyed God. He understood the Lord chose him to proclaim his name to the Gentiles, their kings, and to the people of Israel (9:15). Up to now, one aspect of his call is unrealized—preaching to Gentile kings. Because he went to Jerusalem, he ended up testifying before several Roman rulers—Felix, Festus, and Agrippa.

Rhema: In conflicting circumstances like this, it is best to respond as Paul did and follow what the Lord had already said to him.

July 22 | Acts 21:7–36

Personal Prophesy Through the Spirit

*Coming over to us, he took Paul's belt, tied his own hands and feet with it and said, "The **Holy Spirit** says, 'In this way the Jewish leaders in Jerusalem will bind the owner of this belt and will hand him over to the Gentiles.'" –Acts 21:11*

One last time the Spirit tells Paul what will happen to him in Jerusalem. The Comforter speaks through the well-known and trusted prophet, Agabus, who seems to have come down from Judea just for this purpose. In dramatic fashion, he declares, "The Holy Spirit says." This declaration parallels the OT's oft-repeated expression, "Thus says the Lord." Like Ezekiel of old, by a prophetic symbolic act he takes Paul's belt and gives him a personal prophecy. The apostle will be bound hand and foot by Jewish leaders and turned over to the Romans.

"Thus says the Holy Spirit" is intentional and forceful, and therefore should be taken as authoritative as any OT prophet's proclamation. Agabus is claiming divine authority for his words. The prophet is not telling Paul anything new but assures him God who knows the future has everything under control. Receiving this personal prophetic word must reassure and strengthen Christ's global ambassador as he makes his final resolve to go to Jerusalem. It confirms Paul's own understanding of God' will. Note Agabus, to his credit, did not tell Paul he should not go even though Luke (c.f. we, v 12) and others around Paul pleaded with him to avoid Jerusalem.

Some teach this personal prophecy is unreliable, faulty, or of a lesser authority than the OT prophets. They base their prejudicial claim on supposed variations between what Agabus said here and in 21:30–36. It seems the Romans bound and arrested Paul, not the Jews. Luke, however, uses two different words to describe the Jews' arrest of Paul (vv 27 and 30). The second word is the same term used of his arrest by the Romans. Paul's own account of what occurred, moreover, disagrees with these critics. In retelling of his arrest in Jerusalem he says, "I was arrested in Jerusalem and handed over to the Romans" (28:17). He uses the same word Agabus did.

Rhema: We should not be quick to dismiss what the Spirit says to us; he is, after all, God and his word is true.

JULY 23 | ACTS 28:11–31; ISAIAH 1:1–13

THE HOLY SPIRIT IS REJECTED AGAIN

*They disagreed among themselves and began to leave after Paul had made this final statement: "The **Holy Spirit** spoke the truth to your ancestors when he said through Isaiah the prophet: 'Go to this people and say, "You will be ever hearing but never understanding; you will be ever seeing but never perceiving."'* **–ACTS 28:25–26**

This is the last Holy Spirit reference in Acts. Tracing his words and activities, hopefully, has been a wonderful journey. Without him the church would not exist nor the book of Acts. In the final analysis, the Spirit created the church. Filled its members. Appointed its leaders. Sent out its workers. Discerned counterfeits. Appointed and empowered for service. Resolved theological differences. Established leaders. And opened and closed doors.

This terminating reference to the Spirit occurs one day when Paul, a prisoner in Rome, met with many Jewish leaders. He was trying to convince them of the truth about Jesus. From morning to evening he reasoned with them from their Scriptures. Although a few came to faith, "others would not believe." Suddenly, everything erupted when they began arguing among themselves. Paul had made a shocking statement regarding the Spirit, and it immediately emptied the room. He told them they were just like their fathers in Isaiah's day who rejected the Holy Spirit.

Acts, after chronicling the Holy Spirit's amazing acts, concludes with a damning condemnation. Certain individuals will resist the Spirit just as they did in the OT. It does not matter what the Spirit says or does; the result is the same. Many will remain obstinate. In their foolish refusal they close their eyes, plug their ears, and harden their hearts. Their defiance and unbelief amount to the same thing—a choice to reject God by ignoring the Holy Spirit's powerful witness.

Rhema: The book's final mention of the Spirit serves as a solemn warning. The terrible sin in the NT era is a resolved rejection of the Spirit. Despite convincing evidence, many still fail to see God at work. When willful neglect and prejudice is directed toward the Spirit, the human heart becomes impenetrable. Indeed, no amount of reason, conviction, or supernatural evidence will change it. To obstinately refuse the Holy Spirit today still results in people missing God and what is best for their lives.

JULY 24 | ROMANS 1:1–17

THE SPIRIT OF HOLINESS

*...and who through the **Spirit** of holiness was appointed the Son of God in power by his resurrection from the dead: Jesus Christ our Lord.*
–ROMANS 1:4

Imagine drawing a line in the sand. Everything we want is on one side—God, life, and freedom; everything we loathe on the other—dread, death, and damnation. What we crave, however, is on the side that is unreachable through our best efforts. Our fallen human existence prevents our crossing the line.

The basic biblical meaning of holiness is separation like a line drawn in the sand. Because God is separate from everything he made, he is on one side, everything else on the other. His separateness or holiness is unique. God is absolute, pure, untarnished, and incorruptible. No one else is like him in majesty, glory, power, wisdom, or love. Only he is without defect or deficiency; he cannot lie or sin and, therefore, is in a class all by himself—the holy.

Our existential conundrum is: how do we cross the line and enter the realm of the holy? Or, are we forever doomed to exist in the finite domain of flesh and wretchedness? How can we, unholy fallen creatures, be made fit for God's presence? In Genesis 3:24, a flaming sword acts as a boundary marker, a horizon separating man from Paradise, the unholy from the holy. By what miraculous power can we cross the horizon of our tragic existence and be transformed to live with a holy God?

Jesus shows the way. When he was resurrected in power, the Spirit "appointed" him as God's Son. The term "appointed" means to draw a boundary line like the horizon separating earth from heaven. Before his resurrection, no one ever passed from death to life. By bringing him back from the grave, the Spirit showed Jesus had crossed the line from death to life because he was the holy Son of God.

Rhema: Romans answers the question of how we cross the line. The Spirit of holiness is the solution because he has the power—the same power used to raise Christ from the dead—to bring us into the holy realm of God. By his incomparable might, the Spirit transforms us from our fallen existence to a glorious reality as children of God.

JULY 25 | ROMANS 2:17–29

THE SPIRIT CIRCUMCISES THE HEART

*No, a person is a Jew who is one inwardly; and circumcision is circumcision of the heart, by the **Spirit**, not by the written code.* –ROMANS 2:29

Circumcision was one of the boundary lines that marked off Jews from Gentiles. As an external symbol of separation, it implied total and complete devotion to God. Many Jews believed because they bore in their flesh the symbol of God's covenant with Abraham (Gen 10:10–11), their hearts did not need inner transformation. Circumcision by itself, they believed, made them right with God. Paul disagreed. He argued only the Holy Spirit can make the heart right in God's sight.

A true Jew undergoes an inward work of the Spirit. NT salvation is not a matter of an external act or even being a descendant of Abraham. Paul says, "A person is not a Jew who is one only outwardly, nor is circumcision merely outward and physical" (v 28). To become a true child of God requires an inner spiritual work. Circumcision with a sinful heart does no good because Jews who break God's law are rendered uncircumcised (v 25).

The Spirit accomplishes what physical acts of devotion cannot—he circumcises the heart by purifying and separating it for God. External acts such as circumcision, baptism, self-denial, and so forth can never bring us into union and fellowship with God. Instead, we need the Spirit to consecrate us before we can find favor with God. Our wholehearted obedience to the leading of the Spirit is what pleases the Father and makes us his children. The real boundary marker separating a child of God from others is living according to the Spirit, not the "written code."

Rhema: Moses captured the essence of circumcision. He said, "The Lord your God will circumcise your hearts and the hearts of your descendants, so that you may love him with all your heart and with all your soul, and live" (Deut 30:6). Inward circumcision implies a total consecration to God made possible through the Holy Spirit. That is the reason Paul declares, "Such a person's praise is not from other people, but from God" (v 29). The term, "Jew," perhaps a derivative of the tribal name Judah, means "praise" (Gen 29:35; 49:8). True Jews, circumcised by the Spirit, bring praise to God.

JULY 26 | ROMANS 5:1–11

THE SPIRIT POURS OUT GOD'S LOVE

*And hope does not put us to shame, because God's love has been poured out into our hearts through the **Holy Spirit**, who has been given to us.*
–Romans 5:5

Love is the most dynamic force in the universe. God's love is the profound motivation for creation and our redemption. Because God is love, he seeks a deep intimate relationship with us by infusing our hearts with his actual love. Through the Spirit we commune together nestled in boundless, infinite love.

The Holy Spirit drenches our hearts with God's affection. When we accept Jesus Christ, the Father is so pleased he can share life with us he pours his affection into us with the force of a gushing river. The arrival of the Spirit in our hearts confirms his abounding love and every day he refreshes it. This is not a vague emotion or a platonic fancy but an actual personal experience. In the depths of our being, we sense how much God cares for us. His love prompted him to shower us with two priceless gifts from heaven. He gave the gift of his one and only Son to take our place on the cross. Then he gave his Spirit to let us experience his overflowing heart.

To "pour out" is the language of salvation and Pentecost. Loving us means more to him than anything else in heaven or on earth. At the cross, Jesus pours out his blood (Mt 26:28). At Pentecost, God pours out the Holy Spirit (Acts 2:33). The Holy Spirit conveys to our hearts the extravagant outpouring of God's gracious passion.

When God pours his love into our hearts, we experience a measure of future glory. We are able "to rejoice in the hope of the glory of God" (vv 2–3). It is no illusion, nor is it a mere doctrine we hold but an ongoing celebration. Our hearts are swept away in rapturous delight when we realize eternity is not long enough for him to tell us, "I love you forever."

Rhema: Every day the delightful scent of heaven fills the inner recesses of your heart. He says to you, "You are on my heart from the first thing in the morning to when you close your eyes at night. I am admiring you with every breath you take."

Serving in the New Way of the Spirit

But now, by dying to what once bound us, we have been released from the law so that we serve in the new way of the Spirit, and not in the old way of the written code. —**Romans 7:6**

Anyone living under the OT law was like a woman married to a demanding husband. He showed no grace. All he did was threaten, command, and forbid. Because he demanded absolute perfection and slavish adherence to minute details, he proved himself unreasonable and impossible to please. Even though he was "holy, righteous, and good," he brought out the worst in her by awakening her sinful passions. After marrying him she behaved badly, doing many horrible things she never imagined. To inform her of her wrong was the most he could do, but he lacked power to transform her. The only way to dissolve her unhappy marriage and free her from his tyranny was for him to die.

After he died, she married a new husband and her life greatly improved. The woman was so happy she thought she had died and gone to heaven. Marriage now was wonderful, so freeing and life-giving. She lived in a new way no longer serving her new husband because of duty but because of love. She lived without condemnation or guilt.

The parable above illustrates how Christ's death frees us from the law and introduces us to a new way to live for God. We have "died to the law through the body of Christ" that we might belong to another. In Christ, we have new life and power, joy and delight, freedom from sin and the law. Because we died in him, we are rescued from an unsatisfactory wedlock; living by the Spirit gives us a free and fruitful life.

Rhema: Being wed to Jesus is a dream unlike anything you can imagine because he loves you and cherishes you. He puts you first in his life, so put him first in yours. Serve him in the Spirit's power. It beats trying to keep the law in your strength because the letter kills, but the Spirit gives life. The new way of loving Christ is fresh and filled with resurrection power. The Spirit who raised him from the dead transforms your heart to love and obey him.

JULY 28 | ROMANS 8:1–4; 7:14–25

THE LAW OF THE SPIRIT

Therefore, there is now no condemnation for those who are in Christ Jesus, because through Christ Jesus the law of the Spirit who gives life has set you free from the law of sin and death. –ROMANS 8:1–2

The law of the Spirit is the first reference to the Holy Spirit in this chapter. In fact, as it relates to the Third Person of the Trinity this chapter supersedes every other passage in the Bible. Romans chapter eight has over twenty references. Like no other, it abounds with a juxtaposition of unusual phrases and overwhelming concepts of the Spirit.

The expression "the law of the Spirit" is one of those memorable phrases that only occurs here. It contrasts with the law of sin and death. These opposing but absolute governing forces represent two ways to live. Until we turn to Christ, we live under sin's universal sway characterized by wretchedness, slavery, imprisonment, and death (7:14–25). We never overcome our sinful tendencies because our flesh has control over our conduct—it is a force making us sin and condemning us to the grave. When we come to Christ, however, we are born of the Spirit. Then a new lawlike authority enters our life more powerful than any life-destroying domination. New life in Christ is governed by the Spirit, freeing us from guilt, condemnation, sin, and death.

Living life under the Spirit's rule and power is terrific. His role in our salvation has far-reaching consequences. One enormous effect is contained in Paul's opening declaration, "Therefore, there is now no condemnation." It takes the entire chapter to explain how our new life in the Spirit governs our behavior. Since on our behalf Jesus has fulfilled all God's requirements contained in the written code, we are no longer condemned for disobeying it. Instead, we live by a new authority, the law of the Spirit, which sets us free from the law of sin and death.

Rhema: Either our sinful nature or God's Spirit governs our behavior. Instead of restraining our evil tendencies by his law, God replaces it with his Spirit. The Spirit operates in us as a law just as real as the law of sin and death but far more powerful. The Spirit gives us life and frees us from condemnation.

JULY 29 | ROMANS 8:1–4; 6:1–14

THE SPIRIT GIVES US POWER OVER SIN

*And so he condemned sin in the flesh, in order that the righteous require-
ment of the law might be fully met in us, who do not live according to the
flesh but according to the Spirit.* –ROMANS 8:3–4

What on earth can make us live right? Punishment? Prison?
Persuasion? Promises? Even God's revealed will with its threats
and rewards didn't produce one sinless person. We have a problem!
Every attempt to make anyone holy fizzled. What God's law was powerless to do, the Spirit does.

The law, however, is good; it is spiritual, reveals God's will, and is
intended to bring life. Although it expresses God's righteous requirements, it is helpless to make us conform to it. To illustrate, consider
what transpires when we experience a power failure in our homes.
Without electricity, our appliances cannot behave as intended. We have
no lights, TV, or coffee. The law is like that. All it can do is prescribe
because it has no power to crush our moral weakness. That is why sin
is said to reign in us and make us slaves to its jurisdiction.

To solve this problem, God sent his Son to do what the law could
not do and free us from the power of sin. The eternal, preexistent
Son of God came in the flesh to handle sin. Although sin ruled and
reigned supreme through the generations because of our fallen human
nature, Jesus triumphed over the flesh. He condemned sin in the flesh,
meaning he paid our debt and bore the full punishment for breaking
God's law.

Christ's death ended the law's authority over us. What now will
ensure we obey God and satisfy his righteous requirements? If we are
"in Christ," the Spirit takes the law's place. He not only writes God's
law on the tablets of our hearts but gives us the power to fulfill it.

*Rhema: When you are born of the Spirit, you are given a wonderful, new
nature. Instead of succumbing to sin and moral weakness, the Spirit becomes the
dominating force in your life. His unlimited power displayed in creation and raising
Christ from the dead works in you, so you can please God. He gives you abundant
power to do what is right and live victorious over sin.*

JULY 30 | ROMANS 8:5–8; 6:15–23

LIVING IN HARMONY WITH THE SPIRIT

Those who live according to the flesh have their minds set on what the flesh desires; but those who live in accordance with the **Spirit** *have their minds set on what the Spirit desires.* –ROMANS 8:5

To live in harmony with the Spirit introduces a new supernatural dimension to our lives. This is the one factor that makes believers true children of God. Living every day under the Spirit's sway complying with his leading and concurring with his urgings transforms us. No longer are we at odds with God because our minds are set on fleshly desires. Instead, allowing his divine presence to supersede and overwhelm the flesh gives our human existence a new dynamic. The one sent from heaven helps actualize God's original purpose for us. Through the Spirit we fulfill our potential and become all that God intended for Adam.

The Holy Spirit's power impacts the way we live. He helps us do things we never thought of doing, things that please God. Old habits, attitudes, and behavior pass away while new ones congruent with the Spirit take their place. We are new creations part of a new order. Therefore, we can love God and others in ways we never imagined. With every passing day the Spirit floods our soul with heaven's joyous atmosphere as he fashions us to look more and more like Jesus.

To orient ourselves around the Spirit brings us in line with God's purposes. It helps us to move from inability to spiritual ability. What our fallen human nature was incapable of doing, the Spirit empowers us to do. We stop trying to do things in our own strength, the way we used to before coming to Christ. To be a Christ follower born of the Spirit means we walk in a power from on high. We are connected to him like a car guided by a GPS. Directions come from a heavenly source, so we can navigate the treacheries of earth. The Holy Spirit guides us so we are always in tune with heaven safe from sin and free from self-destruction.

Rhema: Life is peaceful and fulfilling when we are in sync with the Spirit. No longer do we fight God or argue with him about what is best for us. Instead, our lives chime with his approval.

JULY 31 | ROMANS 8:5–8

MINDING WHAT THE SPIRIT DESIRES

*Those who live according to the flesh have their minds set on what the flesh desires; but those who live in accordance with the Spirit have their minds set on what the **Spirit** desires.* **–ROMANS 8:5**

What kind of person are you? Are you the type who sees the glass half full or the type that sees the glass half empty? We divide people into these categories based on their predispositions. Similarly, people have differing mindsets about the things of God. A mindset is a set of ideas and attitudes that shape the way they think of themselves, the world, and God. Paul contrasts those who mind the things of the Spirit with those who mind the things of the flesh.

Everyone following the Spirit's leading develops a set of attitudes that will predetermine their behavior. That person will do what the Spirit desires. A spiritual predisposition is a set of attitudes and beliefs that orients behavior to what pleases God. Those without the Spirit, on the other hand, will do what the flesh desires, the flesh being their fallen human nature. The mindset of those without the Spirit leads to death, but those centering their thoughts on the Spirit lead to life and peace. Dependence, therefore, either on the Spirit or the flesh will dictate what type of person we are.

These two mindsets oppose each other. We cannot have both at once, for either we focus on matters of importance to the Spirit or not. As believers, we should not flip-flop between the flesh one day and the Spirit the next. Our daily lifestyles—our behavior, attitudes, and outlook on life—are based on our thought processes. That is why Paul says, "Be transformed by the renewing of your mind" (Rms 12:2).

Rhema: The Spirit longs for you to depend upon him and concern yourself with what matters to him. Since he opposes the sinful cravings of the flesh, he wants you to live a life transformed by his power and walk in faith, hope, and love. He yearns for you to possess every spiritual blessing in Christ Jesus, to live in the atmosphere of heaven and to let nothing hinder your access to God. He also desires that you love God with all your heart, mind, and body and your neighbor as yourself.

AUGUST 1 | ROMANS 8:5–8; PHILIPPIANS 4:1–9

THE MIND GOVERNED BY THE SPIRIT

The mind governed by the flesh is death, but the mind governed by the **Spirit** *is life and peace.* –ROMANS 8:6

The indwelling Spirit affects every part of our being, especially our minds. When he governs our mental processes, we develop new attitudes so we can respond to situations in God-honoring ways. The Spirit's influence affects all our emotions, thoughts, and even our wills. It impacts our life purposes, values, and assumptions. Change a person's attitude and their life will change. That is what the Spirit does.

Before we came to Christ, we were "of the flesh" and our minds were governed by our sinful, fallen human nature. Under the control and influence of the flesh, our mental faculties focused on things that displeased God. We developed anti-God, hostile attitudes. Being self-focused, moreover, prevented us from truly loving others. The flesh gave rise to jealousy, envy, and immorality. It alienated us from God and made us unconcerned with the things that matter most to him. Because our minds were dominated by the flesh, we pursued destructive paths filled with anger.

When Paul talks of the "mind," he is referring to the contents of what is going on in our head. The brain must be given something on which to focus (Phil 4:8). Objects of thought vary depending on our spiritual condition. If we set our thoughts on spiritual things, our minds will concern themselves with things that please God. If the mental cargo comes from the flesh, the mind will fixate on things conflicting with God.

Huge consequences result from whether the fallen human nature or the Spirit rule our mental faculties. The contrast cannot be greater than life and death. What does it mean to say the mind governed by the flesh is death? Just look at Adam and Eve! The day they allowed the intentions of their hearts to oppose God's commandment, they died. On the other hand, letting the Spirit control our minds leads to eternal life and peace with God.

Rhema: You can face life's problems two ways: either in the flesh or the Spirit. When the flesh is in control of your mind, your emotions and will react negatively. But when the Spirit dominates your thinking, feelings, and behavior, you will experience the peace and life of God.

AUGUST 2 | ROMANS 8:9–11

LIVING IN THE REALM OF THE SPIRIT

You, however, are not in the realm of the flesh but are in the realm of the **Spirit***, if indeed the Spirit of God lives in you.* –ROMANS 8:9

People can be categorized various ways. They may be wise or foolish, good or bad, male or female, rich or poor. Paul divides humanity into two groups: those with the Spirit and those without. Anyone born of the Spirit lives in the realm of the Spirit. Everyone else lives in the world of the flesh, their fallen human nature. This binary flesh/Spirit division distinguishes those who are Christ's from those who are not.

Paul's amazing declaration builds upon what Jesus said to Nicodemus, "You must be born of the Spirit." When we are born from above, we enter a new world where we see and experience the kingdom of God and live Spirit-controlled lives. We are "in the Spirit" and the Spirit lives in us. No longer are we "in the flesh." Because "the Spirit of God lives" in us, we pass from death to life. Regeneration by the Spirit, moreover, makes us God's children so we can claim him as our Father (vv 15–16).

Those who live their lives "in the flesh" can never please God (v 8). Their sinful and fallen nature so dominates their mind they always break his law. For them to be at peace with the Lord God Almighty is impossible. Without being Spirit-born, they exist in the rebellious realm of the flesh, slaves of sin, no matter their best efforts. Such a precarious condition necessitates a second birth.

Living in the Spirit's domain describes the new reality true of all genuine believers. When we are born of the Spirit, the author of life and the giver of everything good resides in us. This is the true mark of salvation, the commencement of the Christian life. Our intimate connectedness to the Spirit derives from this miraculous personal experience. We belong to God, so we can live in the atmosphere of heaven instead of the world, the flesh, and the devil.

Rhema: Sometimes too much emphasis is placed upon doctrines, creeds, and rituals. Above all, we must never ignore or underestimate salvation's experiential side. Ultimately, the reception of the Spirit of God is what enables us to live in God.

AUGUST 3 | ROMANS 8:9–11; 7:14–25

THE SPIRIT OF GOD
MAKES HIS HOME IN US

*You, however, are not in the realm of the flesh but are in the realm of the Spirit, if indeed the **Spirit** of God lives in you.* **–ROMANS 8:9**

Someone said, "Home is where the heart is." Home is where we experience belongingness, specialness, fondness. Without a familiar dwelling place, we suffer existential fragmentation. We all want a place to call home, even God. Your heart is his home! To say the Spirit of God makes his home in us signifies a deep emotional relationship. When he lives in us we feel safe, loved, and cared for. Care must be taken that we do not intellectualize salvation, making it cerebral instead of personal. God wants intimacy with us so much he found a way through the Spirit to dwell with us forever and ever.

Because God's Spirit lives in us, we live in the same domicile as the Spirit. Imagine that! He makes us his dwelling place. The word "lives" in the original language means to dwell, take up residence, or to make a home. The Spirit of God inhabits us, making us his home. He is no overnight guest but a permanent resident always present. The Third Person of the Trinity is not an impersonal force or an idea but a divine being. We live in a lasting intimate relation with him as household members.

What a stark contrast with what Paul said earlier: "It is sin living in me" (7:20). The same word is used of sin's home as the Spirit's. Nothing good ever came from having sin as a house partner. In fact, just the opposite—"Evil is right there with me" (7:21). Before coming to Christ, sin lodged in us. Our fallen human nature welcomed it home. The terrible result—imprisonment, domination, and death. What a wretched household arrangement (7:21–25). Sin took over the house and made us slaves.

Rhema: Do you fully appreciate and comprehend what it means to declare, "The Spirit of God lives in you"? God who created the starry heavens dwells in your heart. The Shekinah glory that used to dwell between the cherubim in the temple now resides in you. The incomprehensible, omnipotent, all-knowing, all-loving and all-wise God lives in you through his Spirit. Selah.

AUGUST 4 | ROMANS 8:9–11

THE SPIRIT OF CHRIST

*And if anyone does not have the **Spirit** of Christ, they do not belong to Christ.* **–ROMANS 8:9**

Have you ever wished you could know Christ better—learn from him, sit in his presence, or hear his voice? You can! All of that is entailed in the important phrase, "The Spirit of Christ." This is the climax of Paul's teaching concerning the Spirit in chapter eight. When we receive his Spirit, we belong to Christ. Similarly, Paul had said as much to the Galatians, "God sent the Spirit of his Son into our hearts" (Gal 4:6). Believers living in the realm of the Spirit receive Christ's Spirit so they can enjoy him to the fullest.

A close connection exists between the Spirit and Christ. We who have his Spirit dwelling within belong to Christ. The Spirit connects us with him so we become members of his body, united with him and joint heirs. Through the Spirit, we have a personal experience with our risen Savior. This is how he is active and present to us.

Christ's saving work, moreover, materializes through the Holy Spirit. Without the Spirit, no one could believe the good news. No one could come under conviction, be born again, or possess power to live like Jesus. After his ascension, our Lord poured out his Spirit to bring us into a personal relationship with him so we can belong to him. In fact, all our encounters and experiences with him are through the Spirit. Jesus said the Spirit will take the things belonging to him and make them known to us (Jn 16:14). Therefore, the Spirit's work and ministry centers on Jesus.

For anyone uncomfortable with the Spirit, realize he is the Spirit of Christ. He takes on the personality and character of our Savior. To not honor him is to dishonor our Lord. Without him, no personal relationship with Jesus is possible for without his Spirit we "do not belong to Christ."

Rhema: Throughout church history, the Third Person of the Trinity has been neglected, shunned, and feared. It was wrong! Some must think Christ's story ends with his ascension. On the contrary, it continues with Pentecost and the outpouring of his Spirit. To experience the Holy Spirit in our lives is not mysticism or enthusiasm but Christ himself.

AUGUST 5 | ROMANS 5:12–21

THE SPIRIT GIVES LIFE

*But if Christ is in you, then even though your body is subject to death because of sin, the **Spirit** gives life because of righteousness.*
–ROMANS 8:10

What is life? Astrophysicists to zoologists have attempted an answer. Some try without success to reduce it to physics, chemistry, or a binary code. Scientists, philosophers, and theologians cannot define it because life is an indefinable something that is given, derived, and passed on from other living things. In ultimate terms, only God possesses life in himself (Jn 5:26), so that all living things derive their existence from him (Jn 1:4).

Jesus said, "I am the resurrection and the life" (Jn 11:25). If we have Christ, we have the source of life in us. Paul explains this spiritual reality when he says, "Christ is in you." He equates the indwelling of the Spirit with the indwelling of Christ. Therefore, to experience the Spirit is to encounter Christ. His indwelling fills us with divine energy and vitality. Apostle Paul grasped this when he declared, "It is no longer I who lives but Christ lives in me. The life I now live in the body, I live by faith in the Son of God" (Gal 2:20).

When Christ takes up residence in us, we experience an entire new reality. Our biography changes. Eternal life is added to our *curriculum vitae*. Spiritually, we are delivered from the realm of sin and death because the Spirit of Christ transfers us into the realm of everlasting life and righteousness. No longer are we weaklings dead in trespasses and sins, abused and used by Satan. Our bodies are subject to death (7:24) because of disobedience in the Garden (Gen 2:17), but their life is reestablished by Christ's resurrection and life. It matters not if our bodies eventually get sick and die—the Spirit raises the dead. The agent of life and righteousness injects powerful life into our mortal bodies for now and forever.

Rhema: For Christ to live in you through the Spirit has tremendous life-changing benefits. Since he is in you, then the Spirit of life is in you. This means that divine, eternal life is present and active in your mortal body. Although it is destined for death because of sin, the Spirit supernaturally infuses your body with Christ's resurrected, eternal, and holy life.

AUGUST 6 | ROMANS 4:1–25

THE SPIRIT OF HIM WHO RAISED JESUS FROM THE DEAD

*And if the **Spirit** of him who raised Jesus from the dead is living in you, he who raised Christ from the dead will also give life to your mortal bodies because of his Spirit who lives in you.* **–ROMANS 8:11**

To kick a football or hurl it through space requires energy. To propel an automobile and fly a plane takes much more. A continuous supply of food is needed to energize our bodies and keep them healthy. The big question facing our existence is how much energy does it take to reverse death's grip? Sin and death entered the world through Adam's single act of disobedience. "Sin reigned in death," condemning us all (5:12). Paul asks, "Who will rescue me from this body of death?" (7:24) How will the grim reaper's tyranny be overthrown?

To resolve the sin and death problem of human existence requires power. Only one source of irresistible energy exists capable of such a supernatural feat. The power that created the universe *ex nihilo* and hurled it into space at the speed of light can do it. The all-powerful Creator is "the God who gives life to the dead and calls into being things that were not" (4:17).

Whenever the Almighty does anything on earth, he does it through his Spirit. "The Spirit of him who raised Jesus from the dead" refers to the Creator of life. The resurrection of Jesus Christ was God's doing. Only through his Spirit can he enter death's dungeon and bring Jesus back from its lair. Resurrection power comes from God: not anyone else.

Rhema: God's power exercised in raising his Son from the dead now dwells in you. He is the God of the resurrection. Instead of sin making its home in you, the Almighty does. Your body houses his Spirit. Think of it! Omnipotence dwells in a tent of flesh. Miracle might, the muscle of creation, infuses your mortal body. Divine irresistibility is the fuel of the age to come. For God to raise your body from the dead is no more difficult than creating a billion galaxies. His ability to raise Christ from a lifeless grave is the power living in you to triumph over sin, and to give life to your mortal body.

THE SPIRIT GIVES LIFE
TO OUR MORTAL BODIES

And if the Spirit of him who raised Jesus from the dead is living in you, he who raised Christ from the dead will also give life to your mortal bodies because of his Spirit who lives in you. **–ROMANS 8:11**

The body, doomed for death, matters to God. After all, he created it. Should the vehicle for our life's journey, the means of our service to others and God cease to exist as if it were nothing? Does it have a glorious destiny, or does it return to dust from whence it came?

The gospel not only answers these questions but also offers proof of the body's resurrection. Two guarantees are found in this verse! The first is Christ's resurrection. No one can say, "There is no resurrection" (I Cor 15:13). Jesus, killed on the cross and buried in a tomb, rose from the dead proving the dead can rise. The second guarantee is the indwelling Spirit. Since he lives in us, then we have the power of the resurrection within us. The Spirit of him who raised Jesus will give life to our mortal bodies because the eternal Spirit lives in them.

Paul reveals the glorious effects the Spirit has on our bodies. What happened to Jesus' body will happen to ours. His underwent a radical change and was transformed from the earthly to make it suitable for heaven. Likewise, the same Spirit that raised him from the dead lives in us. When we receive the Spirit, a new life begins. This new life is eternal. "To give life" is the language of creation, but it now applies to the body's ultimate destiny. In the resurrection, the consummation of all creation, our new bodies will be different—free from disease, deformity, and death. They will be like his glorious body.

Rhema: *Your body is important to God. He proved this when he raised and glorified the body of Jesus. What sickness, infirmity, disease, or any other weakness has done to yours is reversed. Even in this life, through faith, the Spirit can give life and healing to your body ruined and racked by sin and disease. Praise God! One glorious day the perishable will be raised imperishable. Weakness will become strength. Until then resurrection power dwells in you, thereby guaranteeing your own resurrection.*

OUR OBLIGATION TO THE SPIRIT

For if you live according to the flesh, you will die; but if by the Spirit you put to death the misdeeds of the body, you will live. –ROMANS 8:13

Have you ever felt a moral responsibility to do something? You respond because it is right not because a law requires it. Acts to conserve water, help the poor, and to keep our word, for instance, arise more out of our consciences than legal requirements. In the same way, we are duty-bound to honor and respect someone who has treated us with kindness and helped us out in need. To do otherwise is morally reprehensible.

We have a moral obligation to the Holy Spirit (v 12). Considering what he has done for us, we owe him big time. Like a mother he conceives us, gives us birth, nurses us on the milk of the word, and takes us by the hand. In addition, he gives us a new nature, showers us with the Father's love, and gives life to our mortal bodies. He even allows us to enjoy part of our eternal inheritance now. Since he has done this for us and more, our ethical compunction is to live every day in his awesome power.

Our obligation screams at us to live according to the Spirit rather than according to the flesh. The way we fulfill our indebtedness is by putting to death the misdeeds of the body. We owe the flesh nothing! What has our sinful nature done for us besides alienate us from God? For the Spirit to indwell us is not enough: we must murder the sinful deeds of the body by cooperating with him.

Moral empowerment and victory over the flesh comes from the indwelling Holy Spirit operating in our lives. In our own strength, we are incapable of mortifying the body's evil practices. To yield to the Spirit and surrender to his powerful presence is key to avoid doing anything that displeases God. The Spirit will help us kill every misdeed inspired by our sinful nature. To mind the things of the flesh only leads to death, but concentrating on spiritual things leads to life.

Rhema: Therefore, we are duty-bound to live under the impress, direction, and power of the indwelling Spirit.

AUGUST 9 | EXODUS 6:2–8; 13:21–22

ALL THOSE LED BY THE SPIRIT
ARE CHILDREN OF GOD

*For those who are led by the **Spirit** of God are the children of God.*
–ROMANS 8:14

So much rests on establishing the fatherhood of a child. Once paternity is determined, the child can petition for gifts, privileges, and inheritance. The more prominent the father, the more is at stake. How do we know, therefore, if we are God's offspring? Can we produce a certificate? Show a family resemblance? Conduct a DNA test? Jesus said everyone who believes on him has "the right to become children of God...children born of God" (Jn 1:12–13). The surefire test we are God's is whether we are led by the Spirit.

It should not come as a surprise that immediately after new birth, we show traits and behavior resembling our Father. As we live new lives directed and empowered by the Spirit, our eminent lineage becomes apparent. All those led by the Spirit are God's precious children.

To be led of the Spirit means we act as God's sons and daughters and care about the things important to him. Our new spiritual nature makes us desirous to spend time with our heavenly Father and other members of his family. We mind the things of God, seek first his kingdom, and warm to our Father's heartbeat. As his children, we are careful to do nothing that will cast aspersion upon his name.

Many ask, how does the Spirit lead? To answer this question, we can refer to how God led his people out of Egypt, freeing them from bondage and bringing them into fullness. The Spirit is to us what the cloud by day and pillar of fire at night were to the Israelites. When the cloud moved they moved, and when it stopped they stopped. Similarly, the Spirit moves or rests in us as he enlightens, protects, and directs. Inwardly we know when he is he at peace, agitated, or stirring. Our ever-present guide who is never distant nor silent helps us navigate the tough issues of life.

Rhema: When the Holy Spirit dwells in us, he is there forever speaking into every aspect of our lives. He not only cries within us, "Abba Father" (v 15), but also "testifies with our spirit we are God's children" (v16).

AUGUST 10 | ROMANS 8:13–17; GENESIS 21:1–14

THE SPIRIT DOES NOT MAKE US SLAVES

*The **Spirit** you received does not make you slaves, so that you live in fear again; rather, the Spirit you received brought about your adoption to sonship.* **–ROMANS 8:15**

What an amazing assurance. The Holy Spirit does not make us slaves; rather, he makes us God's children. To live by the Spirit is not exchanging one system of bondage for another. No, we are children of God, not slaves of sin and the fallen human nature. Nor does God treat us as servants but as his own dear children. Slaves may be terrified by their masters, but we who are God's offspring have nothing to fear. All who live according to the Spirit need never fear condemnation or punishment, but instead experience the sheer joy and privilege of being his blessed children.

Life before receiving the Spirit is best described as fearful bondage. We were terrified slaves bossed around by the law of sin and death. Every day we shivered in the terrifying shadow of eternal punishment. Every sin sent shudders of doom through our entire being. When we received the Spirit of God, he freed us from all our anxious fears. To this end he released us from the law that bound us, so we could live above and beyond oppression and heartlessness. Where no law exists, no punishment is possible. No flames of hell threaten our every wayward deed. Instead, assurances of joy, security, and privilege flood our hearts.

To come under the Spirit's tutelage is not burdensome, difficult, or onerous but delightful. He brings us into a beautiful, warm, and intimate relationship with the Father. We live with advantage, opportunity, and exceptional honor in stark contrast to slaves. Before the Spirit entered our lives, we endured abject slavery with no rights or privileges. Afterwards we became children of God, heirs of all things.

Rhema: To enjoy your new favored status requires a different mindset. The life of a slave is sometimes no better than death, which may be preferable. Journeying with the Spirit through life, however, is life itself. To renounce a slave consciousness and develop a favored child mentality is not easy. The one sent from heaven will help transform your mind as he keeps on reminding you of your blessed, privileged position as God's dear child.

AUGUST 11 | LUKE 15:11–32

THE SPIRIT OF SONSHIP

*The Spirit you received does not make you slaves, so that you live in fear again; rather, the **Spirit** you received brought about your adoption to sonship. And by him we cry, "Abba, Father."* **–ROMANS 8:15**

Bring out the party whistles and strike up the band! In effect that is what the Spirit tells us to do. He says, *You are children of God. You have unimaginable rights and privileges. All things are yours! Now celebrate it!* The fascinating work of the Spirit makes us aware of this glorious reality.

From the depths of our being the Spirit moves us to cry out to God as a child would to his dear loving father. The story Jesus told of the Prodigal son sheds light upon how much our heavenly Father loves us. The wayward wasteful waif never understood how much his father treasured him nor did he know how he might be received. Upon his return he only aspired to be treated as one of the servants, but his father had none of it. Before he even arrived home, his father ran to his tattered son, threw his arms around him, and kissed him. To celebrate his lost son's return he threw a party, gave him the best robe in the house, and put a ring on his finger.

The Spirit's inner work causes us to experience this kind of father's love. The Spirit penetrates our innermost self and helps us love our heavenly Father. Possession of the Spirit constitutes proof we are God's children. Our adoption, moreover, is linked to the Holy Spirit. To that end he helps us not only realize our new status but helps us live in a loving relationship with God. By the Spirit we cry, "Abba, Father." Our endearment is like Jewish children of old calling their fathers, "Daddy, Daddy."

Our cry, "Abba, Father," is the same as Jesus' when he addressed his Father in Gethsemane. Feeling overwhelmed with bearing our sin, he called out, "Abba, Father" (Mk 14:36). Intimacy with his Father gave our Savior comfort and strength. With love like that, he could do anything.

Rhema: The Spirit causes us to enjoy the same familial relationship as Jesus had with his Father. The cry of the Spirit, therefore, is a celebratory shout of wonderment that God is our Father.

AUGUST 12 | GALATIANS 4:1–7

THE SPIRIT TESTIFIES WITH OUR SPIRIT

*The **Spirit** himself testifies with our spirit that we are God's children.*
–ROMANS 8:16

No one likes to be rejected, turned down, or turned away. Rejection usually leaves us feeling angry, disappointed, and frustrated. What if God were to turn us away? To assuage these fears and encourage intimacy, the Spirit bears witness with our spirit we are God's children.

Knowing we are his children has huge ramifications for our spiritual journey. When praying, for instance, we never need to worry about being brushed off. We come before him not as slaves or beggars but as beloved and favored children. Confidence is everything in drawing near him. From the depths of our being we come to the great Creator of the universe, crying, "Abba, Father." When the Spirit corroborates with our spirit and confirms our special relationship, we can approach God without any fear he will give us the cold shoulder.

The enemy always attempts to discredit our identity. In fact, he did this with Jesus by calling into question his sonship. The tempter's pernicious tactic began with, "If you are the Son of God." In the hope of weakening our faith and eroding our confidence, Satan tries to make us doubt our relationship with our heavenly Father. God, on the other hand, calls for us to draw near with boldness—we are not slaves but his sons and daughters.

The Spirit's testimony is important because our inheritance rests on our favored status. Our future destiny is based on this factual reality— we are *God's* children. The implications are huge. If we are his offspring, then we are his heirs and coheirs with Christ. To be his children entitles us to all of heaven's blessings. Think of these breathtaking blessings—assurance, authority, and affection to name a few. To realize he has lavished us his children with every spiritual blessing is mind-blowing. All things are ours. The Spirit keeps on telling us of our unlimited privileges.

Rhema: The inner experience of the Spirit is a supernatural dynamic substantiating our lineage. Therefore, Paul does not appeal to theology, doctrine, or ritual to assure us of these realities. Instead, he appeals to a genuine personal experience of the Holy Spirit whose unassailable affidavit cannot be taken from us. It is personal. Profound. Powerful. Permanent.

FIRSTFRUITS OF THE SPIRIT

Not only so, but we ourselves, who have the firstfruits of the Spirit, groan inwardly as we wait eagerly for our adoption to sonship, the redemption of our bodies. **–ROMANS 8:23**

Are you suffering? Feeling pain? Do you ever wonder where God is? Suffering is so much a part of our existence none of us escapes it. Who has not had a tear course down a cheek? A few handle intense pain and agony by becoming philosophical like Friedrich Nietzsche who said, "To live is to suffer, to survive is to find some meaning in the suffering."

To suffer is not limited to us; creation aches with frustration (v 20). God designed this earth to be a happy place free of pain, suffering, and death. The cosmos groans while awaiting our joyous destiny (v 21). Is escape from our existential malaise possible? Do not despair! The good news is "Yes." Our hope comes with a guarantee. God gives us proof the future will indeed be glorious and free of grief. Evidence the created order will experience liberty from decay is already in play.

The indwelling Spirit is proof of our glorious future. He is just beginning to actualize the wonderful things God has prepared for us. To have his Spirit in us is likened unto a harvest. He is the firstfruits. The first swaths of grain or the first pickings of the vine prophesy the realization of the full crop. Our present-day Holy Spirit experiences are proof positive our future glory will be devoid of pain and suffering.

How is the Holy Spirit a hopeful guarantor of our deepest yearnings? He is just the beginning, a mere sample of future magnificence. His indwelling is the initial step towards the full adoption to sonship, the redemption of our bodies. After all, when the Spirit takes up residence in us eternity has broken into time to begin the process.

Rhema: Life in the Spirit fills us "with an inexpressible and glorious joy" (I Pet 1:8). For example, he gives us power over the flesh. Through healing, miracles, and spiritual gifts, our mortal bodies experience resurrection power. Right now in our sorrows and afflictions, the Spirit grants us immediate access to Jesus' wonderful presence. If these are the firstfruits, what must the complete harvest be like?

AUGUST 14 | ECCLESIASTES 1:1–18

THE SPIRIT HELPS OUR WEAKNESS

*In the same way, the **Spirit** helps us in our weakness. We do not know what we ought to pray for, but the Spirit himself intercedes for us through wordless groans.* **–ROMANS 8:26**

Why do I get sick when the Spirit gives life to my mortal body? Why are prayers so hard to get answered when I am a child of God? Why do I suffer when I live for God? We ask these questions because of our weakness. Although we are God's children, we have not obtained our full destiny. Until we experience "the glorious freedom of the children of God" (v 21), we need supernatural help.

The sufferings we are going through now "are not worth comparing with the glory that will be revealed in us" (v 18). Still, we experience limitation. Both our faith and our flesh are weak. We live in a world hampered by the effects of sin and subject to frustration (v 20). Creation is broken. Bodies get sick. Faith wanes. That is why the "preacher" said, "Everything is meaningless" (Eccl 1:2) and a "chasing after the wind" (Eccl 1:14). Although we are God's children, we still struggle, become ill, and die. Our human condition makes life frustrating.

Jesus said, "The flesh is weak." The limitations of human existence, however, do not define us because Christ gives the Spirit to help us. This phrase, "to help," means to come alongside and work together. The Spirit comes alongside to assist us in our many and varied problems. This term occurs in the Mary and Martha story. Martha cumbered with too many cares asks Jesus to tell her sister to help her (Mt 26:41). Additionally, when Moses needed help, the Lord gave him seventy elders to "share the burden of the people"...so he would "not have to carry it alone" (Nu 11:17). Similarly, the Spirit helps us with our struggles.

Rhema: Whatever your burden or responsibility you can count on the Spirit to lend you a hand. Like Jesus, he takes the heavy end of the burden and lightens the load. Let him get a hold of you if you need help to overcome temptation, grow strong in faith, or know how to pray. With his support and cooperation, you can live a life that reflects your future glory.

THE SPIRIT INTERCEDES FOR US

*In the same way, the Spirit helps us in our weakness. We do not know what we ought to pray for, but the **Spirit** himself intercedes for us through wordless groans.* —ROMANS 8:26

Imagine praying perfect powerful prayers! Prayers that hit their mark and score a bull's eye every time. God must be frustrated when we bring petitions to him that are contrary to his will. What is he to do? Because we lack knowledge of his purposes in any given situation, we are apt to pray amiss. Asking him for the wrong things most often occurs when we are suffering and do not understand his end plan. How many of us, for instance, "glory in our sufferings, because we know that suffering produces perseverance; perseverance, character; and character, hope" (Rms 5:3)? For this reason, we need help to pray effective prayers.

To address this inability, the Spirit steps forward to intercede for us. Any weakness on our part because of our human condition is more than made up for by him. He knows the mind and will of Father God because he has a unique interaction and interconnectivity. When we are at our lowest seemingly going through hell not knowing for what to pray, the Great Intercessor articulates the inarticulable.

Our weakness prevents our praying as we should. Inability to understand God's will is a heavy burden that weighs us down and deprives us of confidence and faith. Frustration mounts when we pray incorrectly and do not get our prayers answered. In our impotence, Omnipotence steps up and shoulders the load. The Spirit carries our concerns and struggles to the Father like a ship laden with cargo. He ensures our prayers arrive safely at their destination.

Rhema: The Spirit himself intercedes for you through wordless groans. He comes before God burdened with your weaknesses. The effects of sin have made a mess of things, causing all creation to groan (v 22) and bring tears to your own eyes (v 23). Despite the consequences of the Fall, he prays on your behalf. No language is needed because the Father knows and understands what the Spirit desires. What you cannot express in words he does without words. From the depths of your being, he cries out to God the Father the things for which you need to pray. Therefore, pray in the Spirit!

GOD KNOWS THE MIND OF THE SPIRIT

*And he who searches our hearts knows the mind of the **Spirit**, because the Spirit intercedes for God's people in accordance with the will of God.*
–ROMANS 8:27

One of the biggest problems facing us is uttering prayers that harmonize with God's will. Even in our most enlightened state, we at best "see a poor reflection as in a mirror" (I Cor 13:12). We can only "know in part" (I Cor 13:9). How can we ever pray as we ought when we are so limited? Despite our intelligence, no amount of mental acuity can fathom the ways of the Lord. His judgements are unsearchable and his paths beyond tracing out (11:33).

God who searches our hearts knows perfectly the mind of the Spirit and grasps his inexpressible groanings. What we cannot tell God because of our inability to articulate is not lost nor left unspoken. What matters is God knows and understand the ineffable "groans that words cannot express." It does not matter, therefore, if our minds are dim and cannot grasp God's purposes because he knows for what the Spirit yearns.

Rhema: The Spirit's mindfulness has no limitations and apprehends with perfect perception everything pertaining to you. He never needs teaching, training, or an instruction manual to know you. Nor is he ever confused, shortsighted, or ignorant concerning God's perfect will for your life. He has insight into all your matters and plans accordingly for every exigency. Nothing surprises him nor catches him off guard. You are always on his mind. These loving thoughts filling his mind are always oriented to what is lovely, good, true, noble, and admirable (Phil 4:8) with regards to you. The Spirit has absolute awareness regarding your circumstances and knows your interests. Regardless of your weaknesses, his superintelligence and creative solutions will always benefit you.

God responds to the Spirit's wordless groans concerning you. Like a super search engine, he finds and locates them in the mind of the Spirit. You can rest assured the Spirit who has complete awareness of you and God's will will get things right. For this reason, all things work together for good (v 28). In this remarkable way, the Spirit offsets your incomplete and imperfect condition while you live in weakness awaiting your full redemption as a child of God.

THE SPIRIT INTERCEDES
ACCORDING TO GOD'S WILL

And he who searches our hearts knows the mind of the Spirit, because the **Spirit** *intercedes for God's people in accordance with the will of God.*
*–*ROMANS 8:27

D o you know God's perfect plan for your life? The Spirit does. He always acts on your behalf according to God's will. His intercession, therefore, harmonizes with the "good, pleasing, and perfect" will of God (12:2). Although you may not realize it, he fully knows God's best for you. He prays God's will be done with no distortion, disillusionment, distraction, or dilution.

The Spirit's intercession has powerful results. The things for which he prays work out for your good. When he comes before God to make a request on your behalf, the Father goes to work. In other words, he makes the forces of the universe conspire to bring together what is best for you. "And we know that in all things God works for the good of those who love him, who have been called according to his purpose" (v 28). The "all things" include everything pertaining to you—your jobs, relationships, friendships, churches, opportunities. When you have followed the Spirit, you can look back at your life and see God's goodness and mercy (Ps 23:6).

The Spirit desires to orchestrate your steps at the highest possible levels. To avoid making mistakes, he orders your days and leads you into God's perfect will. More than you realize, he involves himself in the many details that make up your life. When you make decisions, you need to be aware of this. God has wonderful plans for you (Jer 29:11–14), plans full of divine purpose. The Spirit will direct you in them. You are chosen, lovingly selected to have God's perfect agenda fulfilled in you.

Rhema: Sometimes our own intentions need redirection. What we might consider a closed door or a setback, for instance, is none other than God at work. In these situations, rather than fighting them, we must learn to submit to his will and trust him. Although the future will always remain a mystery, we have to learn to lean on the Spirit because he connects us with the throne of God. There he presses our cause so that God's purpose for our lives will overflow with divine favor and blessing.

AUGUST 18 | ROMANS 9:1–29

THE SPIRIT RENEWS THE CONSCIENCE

I speak the truth in Christ—I am not lying, my conscience confirms it through the **Holy Spirit** *–*ROMANS 9:1

Will Rogers said, "People are getting smarter nowadays; they are letting lawyers, instead of their conscience, be their guide." The conscience judges the morality of our own words, attitudes, and deeds. It serves as an internal referee approving or disapproving our thoughts and actions. God implanted in us this moral ability to know what is good and evil, right and wrong when he inscribed his law upon our hearts (2:15). Our conscience, therefore, sits in judgment accusing or excusing our thinking and behavior.

The conscience, however, is not always reliable since sin has weakened its ability to operate as God intended. As part of the fallen human nature, it can be weak, ignorant, and err in its moral adjudication. Moreover, it is unreliable because it functions in the realm of the flesh. Individuals may feel their conscience is clear, but that does not make them innocent (I Cor 4:4). One person's interior censor allows behavior that another's forbids. Therefore, it cannot serve as an absolute infallible guide.

Paul wants his readers to grasp the intense distress he suffers for his unbelieving countrymen. Even though they were his enemies, he still had "great sorrow and unceasing anguish" for them. For years, they made his life miserable and tried to kill him. He was willing to suffer the utmost loss if that would make a difference. Lest they misjudge his sincerity, he affirms what he claims is true by two unusual appeals. The truth he speaks in Christ is confirmed by the joint testimony of his conscience and the Holy Spirit.

Rhema: The conscience needs renewing by the Holy Spirit. When we are born of the Spirit, we gain an infallible referee—the Holy Spirit who enlightens our moral compass. Indeed, he sits in authority over the conscience. Since he indwells, he can testify to the correctness of what we say and do. Because he is a moral umpire who knows our cogitations and conduct, he can help our conscience make good moral decisions. In fact, we must learn to allow him to influence it in a way that never existed before conversion. Now he can guide, correct, and certify our moral judgments either approving or disapproving them.

AUGUST 19 | ROMANS 14:1–23

THE KINGDOM IS IN THE HOLY SPIRIT

*For the kingdom of God is not a matter of eating and drinking, but of righteousness, peace and joy in the **Holy Spirit**.* –ROMANS 14:17

Questions of conscience were robbing the Roman believers of their peace and joy. Heated arguments broke out over what they may eat and drink. Some understood their freedom in Christ permitted them to eat anything. Others believed relinquishing their Jewish customs was wrong. Back and forth they went denouncing and judging each other. What a mess! They could not enjoy a simple meal of Christian fellowship together.

The kingdom of God is not concerned with eating and drinking. Today we could extend this to include contemporary externals such as makeup, clothes, and tattoos. This is not what church is about. The more believers walk in the Spirit, the more they will experience righteousness, peace, and joy. We are to serve Christ "in the new way of the Spirit, and not in the old way of the written code" (7:6). Living according to the Spirit is practical but has nothing to do with "eating and drinking."

The kingdom of God, however, does concern itself with the following three essentials. First, God's kingdom is righteousness in the Holy Spirit. Paul means the manifestation of the kingdom is not expressed through dietary regulations but in behavior induced by the Spirit. When he controls us, we serve Christ with a new morality: our conduct "is pleasing to God and receives human approval" (v 18).

Second, the kingdom of God is peace in the Holy Spirit. Heavenlike harmony settles on us as we walk in the Spirit. If we are Spirit-governed, for instance, we "will make every effort to do what leads to peace" (v 19). Allowing him to have his way with us produces concord (Gal 5:22) because the mind controlled by the Spirit is life and peace (8:6) .

Third, the future rule of God also expresses itself in the present with joy in the Holy Spirit. When we allow the Spirit to be active in our lives and follow his leading, we will experience incredible joy. Indeed, we are God's children anointed with the oil of joy. Heaven indwells our being.

Rhema: Therefore, the blessed future reign of God is actualized in your life whenever the Holy Spirit empowers you to live like Christ.

AUGUST 20 | ROMANS 15:1–13

THE SPIRIT SUPPLIES HOPE IN ABUNDANCE

*May the God of hope fill you with all joy and peace as you trust in him, so that you may overflow with hope by the power of the **Holy Spirit**.*
–ROMANS 15:13

Despair and depression are hard to overcome. Life can become hopeless. When we are down, God does not want us to paste on a hypocritical smiley face. Nor does he ask us to pretend all is well and deny our true feelings. No. God has a different answer. He yearns to flood our souls with hope by the Holy Spirit's power.

The hope God supplies differs from wishful thinking. It is more than wishing our team wins when it doesn't have a hope in heaven. We need something so powerful when things are awful we long to get off the bus. But once we introduce the God of hope into the picture, everything changes. He is the source and foundation of a buoyant anticipation everything will work out for our good (8:28).

The full manifestation and actualization of his promises rests on a guarantee. The proof is the indwelling Holy Spirit. When we experience his presence, we are given a foretaste of our magnificent destiny. The one sent from heaven fills us with Paradise's matchless peace and joy. He brings heaven's atmosphere into the depths of our despair and replaces it with eternal joy.

God thirsts for us to abound in divine, supernatural hope, in the faith-filled anticipation of his promises. We live in a time when people have lost hope in so many matters. Releasing the Holy Spirit in our lives, however, will cause us to overflow with the joyful expectation of his glorious future. His manifest presence provides us with an unparalleled assurance of eternal salvation. In like manner, joy and peace, essential characteristics of the kingdom of God, the Spirit's fruit, fuel our certain anticipation.

Rhema: Many things drag us down, but the God of hope lifts us up by the power of the Spirit. So go to him with the darkest and most depressing part of your life. Don't give up and quit. Instead, begin praising the Lord in the Spirit. Let a superabundance of hope bubble up and wash over your doubts and despair. As you wait, he will whisper in your ear, "With God all things are possible."

AUGUST 21 | ROMANS 15:1–16

MADE HOLY BY THE HOLY SPIRIT

He gave me the priestly duty of proclaiming the gospel of God, so that the Gentiles might become an offering acceptable to God, sanctified by the Holy Spirit. **–ROMANS 15:16**

The ancient Roman Empire was not known for its piety but for its debauchery. Every imaginable perversion known to man pervaded that society. Many believers were once idolaters, swindlers, thieves, drunkards, and fornicators (I Cor 6:9–11). How then could Paul say they were "full of goodness" (v 14)? Since these once-pagan Gentiles came to faith and their behavior changed, they brought praise to God's name (v 9). How was that possible?

The apostle considers Gentiles who accepted his gospel a holy offering to God. This is the God who would not allow anyone other than Moses to approach him on Mt. Sinai. No sick, diseased, or deformed animal was tolerated on his altars. Yet Paul considers these Gentile believers an acceptable sacrifice? How did they become admissible to God's awesome presence?

By what miracle did they become holy and acceptable to God? They did not wake up one morning and decide to live by the holy book. No, the power to transform and fill them with goodness did not originate with them but with the Spirit. As soon as they believed the gospel, they were born of the Spirit. In that instant, a new power from above started working in their lives to sanctify them.

To be sanctified means to be made holy, to belong to God, or be brought into his presence. The Holy Spirit does all this in two ways. First, as the Spirit of holiness he sets believers apart for God—everyone indwelt by him is holy. Second, the Spirit gives them the liberating power to gain victory over the flesh. No longer are they slaves of a fallen human nature unable to do God's will. Instead, they are regenerated by the Spirit, so their moral behavior flows from the divine nature.

Rhema: To believe the gospel is crucial for salvation, but the key to Romans is having the Spirit. Although faith in Christ brings us into a right relationship with God, the Spirit, in fact, makes us righteous. This means no one is so awful, so terrible, or so unholy the Holy Spirit cannot make them holy.

AUGUST 22 | ROMANS 15:17–29

MINISTERING IN THE POWER OF THE SPIRIT

I will not venture to speak of anything except what Christ has accomplished through me in leading the Gentiles to obey God by what I have said and done— by the power of signs and wonders, through the power of the Spirit of God. So from Jerusalem all the way around to Illyricum, I have fully proclaimed the gospel of Christ. **–ROMANS 15:19**

What made Paul so effective? As he looks back over his life, he attributes his success to the Spirit's power. It was not his human abilities that enabled him to enter the great pagan cities of the ancient world, filled with demonic darkness, and emerge with a group of believers transformed by God's power. No, it was the Spirit of God. Power evangelism was the principal reason for the phenomenal spread of the gospel and the displacement of paganism in the Roman Empire.

Christ accomplished great things in Paul's ministry through the Holy Spirit. The Lord gave him remarkable results as he helped many Gentiles come to faith. In word and deed, by powerful preaching and extraordinary miracles, the apostle advanced the kingdom of God. He credits the Holy Spirit for both his powerful preaching and for confirming it with powerful signs and wonders.

Many in the Roman world heard Paul preach. From Jerusalem to the borders of Illyricum (northwest of Macedonia), he proclaimed Christ. In city after city he planted churches, cast out demons, healed the sick, and performed miracles.

From start to finish, signs and wonders accompanied his ministry. His first recorded miracle in Acts occurs on the island of Cyprus, where Paul, "filled with the Holy Spirit," confronted the powers of darkness. Through this power encounter, he led the governor to faith (Acts 13:12). His last miracles were on Malta. After he survived a shipwreck and a viper's venom, he healed the father of the "chief official of the island." Then he healed everyone else on the isle who was sick (Acts 28:1–10).

Rhema: To "fully proclaim" the gospel, message and miracle must go hand in hand. For Paul, the gospel was only fully preached when God authenticated it with a demonstration of the Spirit. The message of salvation was never intended to consist of mere words, but also by powerful miracles wrought by the Spirit.

AUGUST 23 | ROMANS 15:30–33; I CORINTHIANS 13:1–13

THE HOLY SPIRIT LOVES US

*I urge you, brothers and sisters, by our Lord Jesus Christ and by the love of the **Spirit**, to join me in my struggle by praying to God for me.*
–ROMANS 15:30

Paul always wanted to go "in the full measure of the blessing of Christ" (v 29). Should God answer his prayer and allow him to go to Rome, he is confident good will result. The reason is simple: because the Holy Spirit loves them, he will bless the apostle's ministry.

The Spirit anoints, gifts, and equips because he loves us and wants us to bless others. Miracles, for instance, express his mercy and love. Paul knows many good things will happen when he arrives because the Spirit values them highly. This prompts an important question: do we realize how much the Spirit treasures us? He longs for every believer to enjoy and experience the full effects of Christ's death and resurrection.

We often hear of the love of God in Christ Jesus (8:39). Seldom the Spirit's love for us. When we ask God to make us a blessing, we step into a wide and forceful river of divine love. Because the Spirit works for our best interests, we do not have to coerce him to bestow Christ's blessings. Our struggle in prayer is not because of his disinterest or lack of concern. It is because principalities and powers oppose God's will and war against us. Indeed, the trinity of the world, the flesh, and the devil conspire to hijack our blessings. So we must persevere in prayer for one another, remembering the Holy Spirit who cares for us deeply is on our side.

Rhema: How does the Third Person of the Trinity express his great love? One way is he acts as the conduit to our hearts of God's tender affection (5:5). In fact, everything Christ accomplished on the cross the Spirit makes personal and real in our lives. The Spirit justifies us. Regenerates us. Sanctifies us. Glorifies us. Our mortal bodies receive his power. He whispers love messages telling us God is our daddy. With unutterable groaning he intercedes for us. Every Christian grace, every Christlike trait, every spiritual gift comes through the Spirit. He is our source of righteousness, peace, and joy. Now that is love.

AUGUST 24 | I CORINTHIANS 2:1–5

THE DEMONSTRATION OF THE
SPIRIT'S POWER

My message and my preaching were not with wise and persuasive words, but with a demonstration of the **Spirit's** *power, so that your faith might not rest on human wisdom, but on God's power.* –I CORINTHIANS 2:4–5

The Spirit does more in a moment than we can do in a lifetime. How foolish then to rely on human strength to accomplish God's work. Paul's spectacular success rested not on his wise and persuasive words but on what the Spirit did when he preached. Therefore, eloquent messages will achieve little in God's kingdom unless accompanied with divine power.

His readers understood what he meant when he spoke about "the demonstration of the Spirit's power." The term, "demonstration" only occurs here in the NT and means proof, evidence, or to point out. Mighty things happened when Paul proclaimed the gospel proving God was with him. For instance, the worst among them were transformed. Healings happened. Demons were exorcized. Miracles broke out. Consequently, no one doubted God's presence when Paul preached. For this reason, the apostle declared, "The kingdom of God is not a matter of talk but of power" (4:20). Whenever the apostle announced the good news heaven opened, people turned to Christ, and they experienced the miraculous. The Corinthians need look no further than their own experience.

He did not cave in to the Corinthian ideals of public speaking. Nor did he give them the clever words they craved. Instead he came in weakness, fear, and trembling determined to know "nothing except Jesus Christ and him crucified." The important thing to remember is he proclaimed potent messages in the Spirit's power. His discourses may not have been cute, clever, or entertaining but his preaching was supernatural and full of divine life. Paul wanted their faith to rest on God's power not human wisdom.

The apostle connects the proclamation of salvation with the Spirit's miraculous manifestations. His messages were bathed in omnipotence, the dynamic power of the Spirit. He gloried in his weakness so God's mighty works could manifest themselves in his ministry.

Rhema: Whenever you have an opportunity to speak for the Lord, do not rely on your own strength. If you want to see something accomplished for God, depend on his Spirit. Only the Spirit can do the Spirit's work.

AUGUST 25 | I CORINTHIANS 2:6–10; 1:18–31

THE SPIRIT REVEALS THE HIDDEN THINGS

*These are the things God has revealed to us by his **Spirit**.*
–I CORINTHIANS 2:10

How can a poor preacher ever match wits with learned intellectuals? The Corinthians prided themselves in their rich philosophical heritage. They idolized Socrates, Plato, and Aristotle. What new thing could this Jewish missionary of the cross tell them they did not previously know?

Paul, however, is not to be outdone by their philosophical sophistication. He has a far greater wisdom to teach than their philosophers ever dreamed. What he shares with them is not empirical nor is it analytical. No eye has seen it, no ear has heard it, and no mind has conceived it (v 9). Through the Spirit, surprisingly, he has access to the undiscoverable, inaccessible, and impenetrable wisdom of God.

Paul did not come relying on a superior human intellect. Nevertheless, he came with a wisdom greater than all the Greek, Roman, and Jewish wise men put together. Since God's knowledge is superior, he can tell them divine secrets hidden from the foundation of the world.

Paul asks, "Where is the wise person? Where is the teacher of the law? Where is the philosopher of this age? Has not God made foolish the wisdom of the world?" (1:20). In preaching Christ crucified, God reveals his incomparable sagacity. Christ is the power and wisdom of God (1:24). The message of the cross might be foolishness to those perishing but to us who are being saved it is the power of God (1:18).

No philosophy surpasses God's super narrative in Christ. Apart from the Spirit, reason cannot conceive of the things "that God destined for our glory before time began" (v 7). The world's great philosophers, from the peripatetics to the phenomenologists, may speculate what these might be, but the Spirit has revealed them to us. These eternal things are beyond the philosopher's reach. Only those who are born of the Spirit know and understand what God has revealed. To the natural mind, this wisdom is incomprehensible.

Rhema: Like the Corinthians, the world's wisdom may tempt and seduce us to thinking it is superior to God's acumen. Turning away from what is only accessible through the Spirit is foolish. When we have the Spirit we are not speculating about our future—we are already experiencing it.

AUGUST 26 | I CORINTHIANS 2:10–16

THE SPIRIT SEARCHES THE
DEEP THINGS OF GOD

*The **Spirit** searches all things, even the deep things of God.*
–I CORINTHIANS 2:10

One of the great philosophical problems of all times is God's knowability. Because he is so far above us and unlike anything he created, words fail to describe him. In the book of Job, the question is asked, "How great is God?" The answer: "Beyond our understanding" (Job 36:26)! Again, the book asks, "Can you fathom the mysteries of God? Can you probe the limits of the Almighty? They are higher than the heavens above—what can you do? They are deeper than the depths below—what can you know?" (Job 11:7–8).

Does anyone fully know the Almighty? No philosopher. No theologian. No genius. Only the Holy Spirit knows his true essence, fathoms the depths of his nature, and comprehends the intricacies of his mind. His investigative work even extends to God's inaccessible features. The Holy Spirit is well qualified to reveal the profound mysteries of his divine nature. He searches all things, even the deep things of God, things far beyond human inquiry.

We must have the Spirit to understand and know his revelations. When we are born from above, we are taken into a new realm impenetrable to even this age's wisest. He searches the invisible and inaccessible where no human mind has ever gone before. The word translated "searches" has the basic idea of investigating, looking into, or fully examining. Like a bloodhound tracking game, the Holy Spirit continuously investigates every matter. One of those deep matters is the inexhaustible riches of everything God has done for us in Christ Jesus. Without the Spirit, the message of Christ crucified is incomprehensible, just so much foolishness (1:23).

Rhema: When we receive the Spirit, we come face to face with the overwhelming greatness of God. Made known to us are wonderful future blessings no eye has seen, nor ear heard, and no human heart imagined. Through the Spirit's unique relationship to us and God, we experience God who is love, life, and light. Love because God pours out his love into our hearts through the Spirit. Life because our mortal bodies are infused with the eternal breath of heaven. Light because the Spirit illuminates our minds. Since the Spirit knows God, he can reveal him to us.

AUGUST 27 | REVELATION 5:1–14

THE SPIRIT REVEALS THE MIND OF GOD

*For who knows a person's thoughts except their own spirit within them? In the same way no one knows the thoughts of God except the **Spirit** of God.* –I CORINTHIANS 2:11

World famous cosmologist, Stephen Hawking, claimed if we knew the mind of God, we would understand the workings of the universe. By the same token, we would see how it came into being and why. Trying to penetrate the mysteries of life, for instance, always leads to the inexplicable. But this we know: behind everything stands something our minds cannot grasp. God's mind is too vast for our puny intellect to comprehend. In fact, no one knows the thoughts of God except the Spirit. No angel. No demon. No human. His thoughts, therefore, are beyond our reach until the Spirit reveals them to us.

Even at the human level, much mystery surrounds the inner workings of our minds. Perhaps, nothing is more wonderful or complex. Although no one has ever seen the mind, it manages much of our lives. Each of us has secrets unknown to others but only known to our own spirit. Without self-disclosure, these impenetrable secrets are beyond the reach of others. This human ability is like the Spirit's knowledge of God's mind.

If our minds are wonderful and complex, think how magnificent God's is. The Spirit has intimate awareness and personal knowledge of his mind. He knows firsthand the profundities of its hidden and inaccessible depths. In this age, the Holy Spirit is tasked with the responsibility of making known to us the awesome mind of God.

One of those thoughts the Spirit unveils is the wonder, majesty, and glory of God's deep and magnificent purpose in Christ crucified. God's wisdom contained in the cross was hidden from before the creation of the world, but the Spirit makes it known. After all, Paul's knowledge and preaching about Jesus Christ came to him by a special revelation. No man taught him (Gal 1:12).

Rhema: In eternity, "every creature in heaven and on earth and under the earth and on the sea" will comprehend the reason for Christ's death. Upon its full exposé, everyone will break out in celestial praise as they finally realize God's wisdom. The cross is the power of God responsible for our restoration, Satan's defeat, and the full manifestation of the kingdom of God.

AUGUST 28 | PROVERBS 2:1–22

THE SPIRIT HELPS US UNDERSTAND
THE THINGS OF GOD

What we have received is not the spirit of the world, but the Spirit who is from God, so that we may understand what God has freely given us.
–I CORINTHIANS 2:12

Are we in danger of substituting the Spirit for the wisdom of the world? It seems as if the church in Corinth was. They prided themselves in secular insights which they felt were superior to Paul's teaching and methods. Thoughts and ideas, strategies and theories from the brightest brains sounded more alluring than his message and preaching.

Valuing the world's wisdom above God's created divisions and tension within the church. Some thought Paul might achieve better results if he used the strategies of a skilled rhetorician. They wanted him to come "with wise and persuasive words." If he were alive today, they might urge him to solve their behavioral problems with the latest psychological or sociological insights or his congregational complications with current organizational theories.

Paul's answer was not to denigrate intelligence and ability. Instead, he asserted the Spirit who knows the mind of God accomplishes far greater results than any secular means. What comes from God's mind through the Spirit far exceeds anything from man. In reality, displacing the Spirit and operating without him robs believers of their great spiritual benefits. Besides, Paul had no intention of substituting God's wisdom for the ways of the world.

It is impossible for human wisdom, reason, and knowledge to supersede the Spirit's know-how. The reasons are clear. No matter his intelligence and learning, the natural man can never understand the things of God. Saving faith does not come from Socrates. The wisdom of men will never give spiritual life, save a soul, or build faith. For another thing, human effort will never release God's power. Without the Spirit, no one can grasp the things of God.

Rhema: To sum up, we can ask whether churches would be better off if they relied more on the Spirit than adopting secular knowledge and practices. The answer: if we want to see spiritual results and understand what God has done for us, we cannot afford to rely upon the wisdom of the world or our own intelligence. Only the Spirit can make us aware of what God has freely given us.

WORDS TAUGHT BY THE SPIRIT

This is what we speak, not in words taught us by human wisdom but in words taught by the Spirit, explaining spiritual realities with Spirit-taught words. **–I CORINTHIANS 2:13**

Only the Holy Spirit can teach us God's truth—truth obtained not in the fashion of the Greeks but as intimate husbands and wives know each other. Therefore, the operation of the Spirit is indispensable for knowing God the way he wishes to be known. Paul is profound when he contrasts the vaunted Greek way of knowing God with the Spirit's way. God is not an object to be studied and objectified, but a person who wants us to know him through an intimate encounter.

Spiritual realities need Spirit-taught explanations. For example, after we are regenerated, the Divine Teacher helps us understand the will of God and what pleases him. Jesus said, "The Holy Spirit, whom the Father will send in my name, will teach you all things" (Jn 14:26). Not only that, "He will guide you into all truth" (Jn 16:13). Everyone born from above is equipped by the Spirit to receive God's true wisdom. So when we communicate with one another, it should comprise Spirit-taught lessons. Consequently, as Paul says later, "Everyone has a word of instruction or a revelation" (14:26). Because believers have the Spirit, they indeed encounter God. Anyone who is not experiencing God must not have his Spirit.

When Paul says, "This is what we speak," his focus is on a spiritual experience. Recall what Jesus said: "The Spirit gives life; the flesh counts for nothing. The words I have spoken to you—they are full of the Spirit and life" (Jn 6:63). The words the Spirit teaches us are supercharged with life and power. We need more than the rationalistic propositions of educators, theologians, and philosophers. Why settle for Greek wisdom when we can learn of God through an intimate encounter and experience him firsthand?

Rhema: Spiritual understanding does not rest with how smart we are but whether the heavenly Educator dwells within (v 12). Only then can we receive his teachings. Therefore, we are blessed far above the wisest and smartest persons who function without the Spirit. Imagine, we are taught by God (Jn 6:45). The Holy Spirit is essential for knowing God and understanding spiritual realities.

AUGUST 30 | ACTS 17:16–34

WHO CAN RECEIVE THINGS
FROM THE SPIRIT

*The person without the Spirit does not accept the things that come from the **Spirit** of God but considers them foolishness, and cannot understand them because they are discerned only through the Spirit.*
–I CORINTHIANS 2:14

We can learn lessons the easy way or the hard way. When Paul went to Athens, he learned the hard way that teaching the things of God is not like teaching the things of men. Something more is needed besides facts, definitions, and persuasion. He used the wisdom of the world, rhetoric, and argumentation to turn people to Christ. He failed. His attempt at cultural relevance did not work. In the end, he had few results and was laughed out of town.

When he arrived in Corinth, however, he determined not to have a repeat performance (vv 1–5). Logical argumentation, he discovered, is insufficient because becoming a believer is more than following a syllogism. Rather, in fear and trembling, he proclaimed God's revelation in supernatural power. In so doing he shifted from trying to match wits with philosophers to fully depend upon the Spirit.

To communicate truth revealed by the Spirit, we must realize, differs from teaching history or physics. After all, God cannot be put under a microscope or treated as an object. "The things that come from the Spirit" require a personal relationship with him to understand them. When it comes to God, Paul instructs, our knowledge is not like the Greeks—speculative, metaphysical, and ontological. Our knowledge and understanding of him is personal like a husband's knowledge of his wife. In fact, the word to know and understand in these verses is the same word as found in Genesis 4:1 (LXX). Adam is said to have "known" Eve or made love to her. If a husband wants to "know" his wife, he does not need a theologian, scholar, or philosopher to tell him about women. Far superior and more satisfying than the "experts" knowledge is an intimate encounter.

Rhema: Having God's Spirit sets you off from those who don't. This means you do not need to check with a theologian, philosopher, or a learned scholar to know the things of God. Because you have his Spirit dwelling in you means you are already in a loving, personal relationship with him. You know him firsthand.

AUGUST 31 | I CORINTHIANS 3:1–23

YOU ARE THE TEMPLE OF THE HOLY SPIRIT

Don't you know that you yourselves are God's temple and that God's
Spirit *dwells in your midst?* –I CORINTHIANS 3:16

What an incredible privilege—to be the dwelling place of God's manifested presence. He could have chosen to situate himself anywhere in the universe, but he has chosen to dwell in us. Paul uses temple imagery to describe the local church brought into existence by the Spirit's power. When we gather in Jesus' name, God makes his presence known through the Spirit.

The Corinthians put earthly values before their estimation of the church. What swelled their chests was the glories of Greek culture expressed in art, philosophy, rhetoric, and government. This led to differences of opinion and divisions in the church. Such boasting, however, obscured the wonderful realization of who they were in Christ. The idol of earthly pride blinded their eyes to their own importance.

Paul asked them, "Don't you know who you are? You are God's temple." The Spirit among them made them more important than the posh palaces of kings and emperors. Through the Holy Spirit, the one who inhabits eternity resides in the local congregation—a sacred place where God reveals himself. Therefore, no one must desecrate the church by causing division and undermining its foundation.

Cultural idols have no place in our gatherings. Clinging to human wisdom and abilities was robbing them of the glory they had in Christ. To boast in the wisdom of the world and rely on it accomplishes nothing compared to God's Spirit dwelling in their midst. Their false god was powerless and incapable of ever bringing anyone face to face with God. Never would it give them a word from heaven. Never any spiritual benefit.

Rhema: The local church exists as God's dwelling place. It did not come into being by human wisdom or ability but by the power of the Spirit. To admire and appreciate eloquence and worldly wisdom was wrongheaded and infantile (vv 1–4). Imagine such childish arguments over who is the best speaker? Who had the most persuasive arguments? Who excelled in rhetoric? "No more boasting about men," Paul warns. Human ability has nothing to do with God's presence among his people. Ultimately, local congregations exist by the supernatural operation of the Holy Spirit.

SEPTEMBER 1 | I CORINTHIANS 6:1–11

WASHED, SANCTIFIED, AND JUSTIFIED BY THE SPIRIT

And that is what some of you were. But you were washed, you were sanctified, you were justified in the name of the Lord Jesus Christ and by the **Spirit** *of our God.* **–I CORINTHIANS 6:11**

What a difference Jesus makes in our lives. Likewise, the Spirit. Many Corinthian believers were among the worst of sinners—sexually immoral, idolaters, adulterers, male prostitutes, homosexuals, thieves, greedy, drunkards, slanderers, and swindlers to name a few (vv 9–10). The complete work of Jesus combined with the Spirit's transformation made them fit for God's kingdom. Spiritual metamorphosis is just as much the Holy Spirit's work as the Lord's.

In the NT world, the Corinthians achieved notoriety for their sinful lifestyles. Could they ever change and experience a radical spiritual conversion? To expand their understanding of salvation, Paul explains how Jesus together with the Spirit changed them and made them fit for heaven.

Three words express their amazing salvation: washed, sanctified, and justified. Each term refers to what both Jesus and the Spirit did for them. Because of Christ's death and resurrection, three things happened. Their sins were washed away by his precious blood. Further, they were set apart for God and, thirdly, they were declared righteous.

What is not so readily acknowledged is the parallel role of the Holy Spirit. He also washed, sanctified, and justified these unclean, unsanctified, and unjustified Corinthians. The Spirit appropriated Christ's work on the cross and applied to their lives. First, they were saved and cleansed "through the washing of rebirth and renewal by the Holy Spirit" (Tit 3:5–6). Second, the "Spirit of holiness" (Rms 1:4) sanctified them by marking them off as God's. They became an acceptable offering, "sanctified by the Holy Spirit" (Rms 15:16).

What about justification? What Jesus accomplished on the cross the Holy Spirit actualized in their lives. As they lived by the Spirit, they fulfilled the law's righteous requirements (Rms 8:4). The indwelling Spirit gave them power to live lives right in the sight of God. Now dwelling in them to counter the demands of the flesh was the power that raised Jesus from the dead.

Rhema: To sum up, to fully appreciate and understand our salvation we must recognize not only the important work of Christ but also the indispensable work of God's Spirit.

SEPTEMBER 2 | I CORINTHIANS 6:12–20

OUR BODIES ARE TEMPLES
OF THE HOLY SPIRIT

*Do you not know that your bodies are temples of the **Holy Spirit**, who is in you, whom you have received from God? You are not your own; you were bought at a price. Therefore honor God with your bodies.*
–I CORINTHIANS 6:19

Corinth was "sin city" notorious for conjoining sex and worship. With a temple to Aphrodite, the goddess of love, and hundreds of "sacred prostitutes," the city in the name of religion gave itself over to immorality. Its culture, no doubt, affected the mores of Christian believers and explains why the apostle had to remind them "the body is not meant for sexual immorality" (v 13).

Sexual laxity was so prevalent some believers did not recognize its seriousness. Others, "spoiled by philosophy," may have minimized the body's importance. With this in mind, Paul sets forth several arguments to show sexual relations outside of marriage are wrong. The apostle taught the body and its deeds was important to God. One reason is our bodies do not belong to us but to Christ. Since we have been bought with a price, we are to glorify God with them. Therefore, having sex with a prostitute profaned the body and puts it to an unholy use.

Another reason for warning believers against fornication concerns the Holy Spirit. The body is his dwelling place. Flee sexual immorality, Paul warned, because the Spirit inhabits our bodies! Since he possesses us, we are to keep our bodies fit for his indwelling. Every sexual sin committed by our physical frame defiles the Spirit's holy temple, the Holy of Holies.

Our bodies are so important to God he includes them in his gracious saving efforts. It sounds as if the Corinthians believed the material realm was unimportant in contrast to the spiritual. Paul corrects this faulty theology by asserting our bodies have been bought at a price and are not actually ours. In addition, our bodies are a sphere of divine activity because the Spirit of God resides in them.

Rhema: In conclusion, the body belongs to the Lord Jesus because he has paid for it. But it also belongs to the Spirit because he possesses it and dwells in it. So dedicate your body to the Lord and let his Spirit fill it with his Shekinah glory.

The Holy Spirit Guides
When Scripture Is Silent

*In my judgment, she is happier if she stays as she is—and I think that I too have the **Spirit** of God.* –I Corinthians 7:40

How do we resolve difficult and complex issues when Scripture is silent? When the written word does not cover all areas of our lives, we must depend upon God's Spirit to guide us. Even then we don't need a supernatural revelation to handle every life issue. God did not give Paul a revelation for everything. He says, for instance, "This as a concession, not as a command" (v 6). "I have no command from the Lord" (v 25). "In my judgment" (v 40). God's silence on these personal matters is deafening—he leaves the choice to us.

Nothing is more complicated than marital relationships especially when a couple's circumstances change. The Corinthians had asked the apostle about singleness and marriage. Their questions went something like this: should a believer stay in an unhappy marriage? Must one remain single after divorce? Can virgins marry? Another query was whether widows were free to remarry after their husbands died. His answer to the latter: marriage is a lifelong contract but once a husband dies, the widow is free to marry anyone of her choice provided he is a believer.

On this last question, Paul admits the Lord has not given him any directive. Then he adds, she would be happier if she remained single. When Paul says, "I think that I too have the Spirit of God," he is saying he has not only given them wise counsel but also the Spirit has helped him form a nonbinding opinion. He has no word from the Lord because remaining single as a widow or remarrying is neither morally right nor wrong. Therefore, no commandment is necessary.

Rhema: The Spirit helps us to work out an ethic for our lives when neither the OT nor the New give us any specific directives. As people of the Spirit, our choices should balance our liberty in Christ with seeking first the kingdom of God. Extenuating circumstances also factor into our decisions. Often, we need the wisdom of Solomon to carve our way through the modern maze of moral mindfulness. The Spirit is available to help chart that course.

September 4 | I Corinthians 12:1–3

Anyone Speaking by the Spirit Cannot Blaspheme

*Therefore I want you to know that no one who is speaking by the **Spirit** of God says, "Jesus be cursed," and no one can say, "Jesus is Lord," except by the Holy Spirit.* –I Corinthians 12:3

No one speaking under the influence of the Spirit of God will ever blaspheme Jesus. The Spirit would not lead anyone to say, "Jesus be cursed." After all, his purpose is to exonerate Christ. Every derogatory comment against him, to be sure, is not of God's Spirit.

Corinth, a city full of idolatry, had all kinds of spiritual phenomena taking place. Many of these Gentiles had familiarity with evil spirits especially if they were idolaters (v 2). As Paul explained earlier, various powers of darkness attached themselves to idols (10:20–21). Not only had these evil fiends spoken through them, but they were also responsible for other incidents. Under Satan's influence, these Gentiles experienced dreams, visions, prophecies, trances, miracles, and speaking in tongues. With that background, believers worried about what they might say through the Holy Spirit, particularly when they spoke in tongues. Would they curse or blaspheme Jesus? No doubt the question arose over the use and nature of spiritual gifts.

The Spirit's demonstration differs from demonic activity. Paul does not want believers ignorant of God's unique work in their lives. So, beginning in this chapter, he discusses the "things of the Spirit" to mitigate any confusion. The test to determine whether a person speaks by a demon or by the Holy Spirit is straightforward: does the message honor Christ? In both Christianity and paganism, adherents speak under spiritual influences. Ultimately, any spiritual phenomena opposing Christ is not from Christ's Spirit.

Note the apostle does not shut down the Spirit's work for fear evil spirits may be masquerading around. Instead, he tells the believers how to distinguish between the Holy Spirit and evil spirits. That way spiritual gifts can be sought with confidence (14:1). Any genuine manifestation of God's Spirit will never minimize, belittle, ridicule, or blaspheme Christ.

Rhema: God wants us to realize "no one who is speaking by the Spirit of God" will speak contemptuously of Jesus. Instead of fearing the activity of the Holy Spirit, we should welcome it with both arms because the Spirit will only exalt the Lord.

SEPTEMBER 5 | ACTS 2:22–36

THE SPIRIT REVEALS JESUS AS LORD

Therefore I want you to know that no one who is speaking by the Spirit of God says, "Jesus be cursed," and no one can say, "Jesus is Lord," except by the **Holy Spirit**. *–I* CORINTHIANS **12:3**

Anyone can say the words "Jesus is Lord." So why does Paul state that uttering them is impossible except by the Spirit? To say "Jesus is Lord" is different from stating "Caesar is Lord." Paul is not talking about history, he is dealing with revelation. To confess "Jesus is Lord" because the Holy Spirit has pulled back the curtain to show Christ's identity is a prophetic utterance that leads to everlasting life. This powerful Spirit-generated realization and declaration is the absolute foundation of our faith.

To understand these words without an experience of the Holy Spirit is impossible. Although "Jesus is Lord" is a simple confession, it nevertheless packs a universe of meaning—Jesus of Galilee who is fully man and fully God is my personal Savior. To know him by the Spirit differs from only having a historical or theological knowledge of him (II Cor 5:15–16). When we receive the Spirit, we see everything with respect to Jesus in a different light. He shows us our Lord is more than a man who was born in Bethlehem and died on a cross in Jerusalem. Ultimately, he reveals Jesus as none other than the Christ, the Son of the Living God. To confess him as Lord is an act of saving faith. It is not solely the result of a history lesson or doctrinal teaching. Instead, our confession results from a spiritual experience in which the Spirit makes Jesus personally real.

At the outset of his teaching on the gifts of the Spirit, Paul wants everyone to realize he centers them on Christ. To experience Christ after his resurrection requires the Spirit. Through the Spirit we develop a living relationship with him and enjoy daily fellowship. From a realized experience we can say, "Jesus is Lord."

Rhema: As new believers our first prophetic words, words taught us by the Spirit, concern Jesus—he is Lord. These are saving words, living words, words that lead to eternal life. "For it is the Spirit of prophecy who bears testimony to Jesus" (Rev 19:10).

SEPTEMBER 6 | I CORINTHIANS 12:4–6

THE SPIRIT DISTRIBUTES A BOUQUET OF GIFTS

*There are different kinds of gifts, but the same **Spirit** distributes them.*
–I CORINTHIANS 12:4

Spiritual gifts should reflect the unity and diversity found in the Godhead. Paul reminds the Corinthian believers of this because their disruptive divisions and rivalries led to a misunderstanding of the Spirit's gifts. Although there are different categories of gifts, Paul reminds them the same Spirit distributes them.

Spiritual gifts originate in one source: God. The Trinity's work is indispensable for understanding their purpose, power, and distribution. Whether we are referring to revelations, miracles, prophecies, or other tongues, they all originate with our heavenly Father. Regardless of a gift or ministry, God, the Father, accomplishes his work through them. His power energizes everything that happens in his kingdom (v 6).

The gifts of the Spirit, moreover, extend Christ's ministry (v 5). As we use them we serve the Lord and perpetuate his work. Each gift expresses a particular aspect of his life and work. A word of wisdom, for instance, is part of his wisdom. Miracles are his power at work. Equally important is the role of the Third Person of the Trinity—he partitions off the gifts so the Lord can continue his work. As we can see, the Father, Son, and Holy Spirit involve themselves in important ways with these empowerments. In a word, the Spirit distributes, the Son directs, and the Father empowers.

In a healthy, unified church, not everyone has the same spiritual ability but all have the same Spirit. Not everyone has the same ministry, but all have the same Lord. Members do not have the same function, but each has the same heavenly Father. Just as the Father, Son, and Holy Spirit are united among themselves and cooperate to bring about the purposes of God, so should we.

No gift deserves more emphasis than another. Nor should we neglect any, for each furthers God's work. Pride and competition do not belong in the kingdom of God. Although certain gifts such as performing miracles are more spectacular than others, each one results from God.

Rhema: Every spiritual gift serves an important purpose. Without it churches suffer. Let us humble ourselves and realize these extraordinary gifts are not innate abilities. Rather, they are gracious endowments of spiritual activity involving the Spirit, Son, and Father.

THE MANIFESTATION OF THE SPIRIT IS FOR THE COMMON GOOD

Now to each one the manifestation of the Spirit is given for the common good. –I CORINTHIANS 12:7

When the Holy Spirit makes himself known, everyone benefits. Something marvelous happens. The discouraged are encouraged. The sick are healed. Mountains are cast into the sea. The barren become fruitful. The weak strong. In fact, every manifestation of the Spirit contains a wonderful blessing.

The word "manifestation" means to appear, become evident. We can always tell when the Spirit is working because he makes his presence known. We experience something good. Such was the case with Jesus's first miracle when under the Spirit's anointing (Jn 1:32), he turned water into wine. This wondrous sign revealed or "manifest" his glory (Jn 2:11). Look at the good that happened! It saved a bridegroom from a terrible embarrassment. Of course, everyone enjoyed the splendid beverage. In addition, turning water into the fruit of the vine was a prophetic act announcing his ministry's beneficial effects. It even pointed to the Marriage Supper of the Lamb, his own wedding day (Rev 19:7, 9). The greatest good, however, concerned God's kingdom because from that moment, his disciples "put their faith in him."

Spiritual gifts always show the Spirit's presence and activity. Although we cannot see him, we encounter his activity. He is like the invisible wind whose movements we feel. Through spiritual gifts, God's presence becomes evident. Each gift whispers, "God is here." When Spirit-induced phenomena occur, we see, hear, touch, taste, or smell them. Someone is healed, encouraged, or helped. Whenever the Holy Spirit shows up and manifests his presence, wonderful things occur.

Each of us has at least one spiritual gift that makes us useful to other believers. God places us in the body for this purpose. As the Holy Spirit acts through us to do good, others benefit. The Spirit openly shows himself in ways that unify and strengthen the church, not harming or hurting it. Therefore, by encouraging and allowing for a great diversity of spiritual gifts, churches can grow stronger and profit.

Rhema: *If you have the Spirit, you have an important place in God's kingdom no one else can fill. He has selected you and given you a spiritual ability with which you can bless, strengthen, and build up others.*

SEPTEMBER 8 | PROVERBS 1:20–33

THE SPIRIT GIVES A MESSAGE OF WISDOM

*To one there is given through the **Spirit** a message of wisdom*
–I CORINTHIANS 12:8

Have you ever faced a pressing and highly complicated problem? If you have, then you know success or disaster rests with your response. To navigate the complexities and devise a correct course of action requires a mere snippet of God's wisdom. If anyone can help us master the pragmatics of life with its myriad uncertainties, it is his Spirit. He not only knows every fact but also the consequences of every decision.

Someone defined wisdom as "good judgment and advice about difficult but uncertain matters of life." Without notice, thorny issues can surface to ruin us. How do we best handle an errant child? An unwanted illness? A financial setback? A new job opportunity? Wisdom allows us to understand these complicated matters and respond in a fitting way. We need wisdom. Churches need wisdom. Companies and countries need wisdom.

When facing a knotty situation, the Spirit can give you the right advice—a "message of wisdom." His counsel is helpful because he has the smarts or what psychologists call the "cognitive competencies" to handle difficult circumstances. Because he has perfect knowledge and understanding of everything, he can guide you aright. For that matter, he has more insight than the collective intelligence of everyone on this planet. To help you respond to crises, he provides you with Christ's wisdom (Lk 21:15). Indeed, he conveys an answer from the mind of Christ (2:16). His goal is to help you make good decisions and avoid the unintended consequences of bad ones.

Paul placed wisdom first in his list of spiritual gifts. He may have given it prominence because of its ability to most benefit everyone in the church. He had spoken of wisdom earlier (1:17–2:16). To make any headway with this problem-filled church, the apostle needed a word of wisdom himself. To give the right response to their tough questions required more than the sophistication of the world—their conundrums needed the wisdom from above. In fact, we might consider the entire book of I Corinthians an example of this spiritual gift.

Rhema: *The message of wisdom is the supernatural revelation of God's prudence for a particular plight. You can pray and ask him for it.*

SEPTEMBER 9 | PROVERBS 2:1–11

THE SPIRIT GIVES A MESSAGE
OF KNOWLEDGE

*...to another a message of knowledge by means of the same **Spirit**.*
–I CORINTHIANS 12:8

Meet heaven's sniper. With laserlike precision, he directs a single bullet of knowledge at a specific target. With deadly accuracy, the Spirit releases a fact known to God and shows it to us. This is how Peter knew Ananias and Sapphira had lied to the Holy Spirit (Acts 5:1–11). Heaven's sharpshooter is omniscient and in possession of all facts, whether they are in the past, present, or future. The release of one of those projectiles is called the "message of knowledge." This supernatural gift is not the result of study, research, or experience but is a manifestation of the Spirit.

Many examples of the gift abound in the Bible. For instance, the Spirit told Peter three men were outside looking for him (Acts 10:19). Simeon likewise identified baby Jesus as the Savior of Israel (Lk 2:26–27). By revelation, Paul, the prisoner, predicted his ship's destruction (Acts 27:10, 21–24). To the woman at the well Jesus revealed she had five husbands and her current partner was not her husband (Jn 4:18).

Every one of these examples helped to produce good results. Peter could embrace the Gentile believers with confidence. Simeon's revelation encouraged Jesus' parents. Everyone onboard ship with Paul turned to Christ. The Samaritan woman's testimony led to her entire town's salvation. Beautiful, wonderful things happened when the Holy Spirit shared one data point of divine knowledge.

The gift knows no limit. The divine marksman searches the deep things of God, even his thoughts. Its epitome is the ability "to fathom all mysteries and all knowledge" (13:2). Having a word of knowledge does not mean we know everything the Spirit knows, for then we would be omniscient. What we have is a fragment of the divine mind directed to a specific situation.

Rhema: This remarkable gift has many benefits. We use it in prayer counseling to ask the Spirit to reveal the root cause of a person's deep emotional problems. What may take counselors, psychologists, and psychiatrists years of probing to unravel the Spirit can reveal in a heartbeat. He knows everything about us, even our conception, embryonic development, and birth. Whatever he knows he can bring to our consciousness.

SEPTEMBER 10 | MARK 11:20–25; HEBREWS 11:1–12

THE SPIRIT GIVES THE GIFT OF FAITH

...to another faith by the same Spirit. –I CORINTHIANS 12:9

Mountain-moving faith is another supernatural manifestation of the Spirit (13:2). With this gift, all things are possible. Jesus spoke of this kind of faith when he told his disciples to "have faith in God." If anyone does, he said, he can tell a mountain to be cast into the sea and "it will be done for him" (Mt 11:22–23). Supernatural faith is a special endowment of the Spirit to believe God with absolute assurance.

Many examples of this powerful gift are found in the Bible. In Hebrews, for instance, by faith men and women conquered kingdoms. Shut the mouths of lions. Women received their dead back to life (Heb 11:33–35). Further, this gift explains how Peter healed a man crippled from birth. He said, "It is Jesus' name and the faith that comes through him that has completely healed him, as you can all see" (Acts 3:16). The gift occurs when the Spirit imparts to us Christ's own unshakable dependence on God. His pure and powerful faith becomes ours through the Holy Spirit.

When the Spirit gives us the ability to believe, he gives us an unwavering confidence in God and his promises. Without this special anointing, many heroic acts of God's people would not have occurred. Abraham, for instance, would not have believed against all odds he and Sarah would bear a child in their old age. Noah would not have continued for 120 years to build an ark to save the world. Joshua would not have commanded the sun and moon to stop so he could defeat the enemy.

Rhema: Thank God for those in the church who exercise this awesome ability. With it they can do great things for the kingdom. Not everyone, of course, has the gift of faith just as not everyone has the gift of miracles. Nor should they feel guilty if they do not possess it. These manifestations of the Spirit do not happen when we want but when the Spirit wills. The gifts of the Spirit take place "just as he determines" (v 11). Although this may be true, it should not prevent us from asking him for greater manifestations of faith.

SEPTEMBER 11 | LUKE 9:1–6; 10:8–12

THE SAME SPIRIT GIVES GIFTS OF HEALING

... to another gifts of healing by that one **Spirit** *–*I CORINTHIANS 12:9

The gift of healing is the Spirit's work to heal the sick. What Jesus did on earth he now continues through the Spirit. His power to cure injuries, illnesses, and diseases did not cease when he returned to heaven but continues to this day. The Spirit gives multiple "gifts of healings" (original text). This may indicate he gives one person the spiritual ability to heal cancer while he empowers another to heal different diseases. Just as there are many maladies, so there are many gifts to restore health. Christ's remarkable ministry is extended through the Spirit to believers.

The spiritual ability to cure sickness is connected to Christ's resurrection and the kingdom of God. In the resurrection, we will have no ailments, deformities, genetic defects, or disease. At the present time, however, through the Spirit we can experience eruptions of the power of the age to come. Later, the fullness. Christ's healing ministry was one of the most distinctive and powerful evidences God's kingdom had come. Jesus told his disciples to "heal the sick who are there and tell them, 'The kingdom of God has come near to you'" (Lk 10:9). To cure people of their illnesses in Christ's day was a visible manifestation of God's power even as it is now.

Christ's ability to alleviate suffering knew no limits—there never was a sickness or illness he could not cure. He travelled about "healing every disease and sickness among the people" (Mt 4:23). Teaching, preaching, and healing were the main components of his ministry (Mt 9:35). When Jesus sent out his twelve disciples, he "gave them authority to drive out evil spirits and to heal every disease and sickness" (Mt 10:1).

Rhema: How encouraging to realize our Lord continues his healing ministry today through the Spirit. Sickness is part of our human condition resulting from Adam's sin. Miraculous cures, however, reverse the curse's cruel effects. In fact, this grace is a compassionate response of our Creator and Redeemer to our weakness and frailty. Although healing is in the atonement, the Spirit actualizes it in the gifts of healing. He applies the resurrection power of Jesus to our total being to heal the body, soul, and spirit.

THE SPIRIT DISTRIBUTES
THE GIFTS AS HE PLEASES

All these are the work of one and the same Spirit, *and he distributes them to each one, just as he determines.* **–I CORINTHIANS 12:11**

Have you ever seen God at work? Or does he appear remote and absent? Many confess they have never experienced him doing anything even in church! This was never an issue in the NT Church. He was always at work and everyone knew it—Jews, Gentiles, unbelievers. Paul asked his first converts, "Does God give you his Spirit and work miracles among you by the works of the law, or by your believing what you heard?" (Gal 3:5). He told the Corinthians he came to them demonstrating the Spirit's power (2:4–5). In those days before the doctrines of men banished and silenced the Spirit, it was inconceivable to imagine church without his dynamic presence.

When the Holy Spirit is at work, God is at work. "There are different kinds of working, but in all of them and in everyone it is the same God at work" (v 6). All these gifts are the work of the "one and the same Spirit." The Spirit distributes a great diversity of spiritual gifts throughout the church, so every believer has at least one. When they gathered for worship, everyone had something the Spirit had given them—a hymn, a word of instruction, a revelation, a tongue, or an interpretation (14:26). Consequently, they were infused with God's presence and power.

Spiritual gifts produce spiritual results. God is at work when there are words of wisdom, words of knowledge, faith, healings, miracles, prophecies, discernment of spirits, speaking in tongues and their interpretation. These gifts energize the body of Christ.

The Holy Spirit decides who receives what gifts. His will is the determining factor in their dissemination. As expressions of divine activity, he regulates the degree of power for their operation and apportions who receives it. We cannot buy the gifts or do anything to earn them, but we can make ourselves available to the Holy Spirit to use us.

Rhema: All things considered, let us welcome and expect divine activity among us. We can create an open atmosphere for the Spirit's manifestation. He wants to give us spiritual gifts and have us use them, so everyone can experience God at work.

SEPTEMBER 13 | I CORINTHIANS 12:12–20

THE SPIRIT FORMS ONE INCREDIBLE BODY

For we were all baptized by one Spirit so as to form one body—whether Jews or Gentiles, slave or free—and we were all given the one Spirit to drink. **–I CORINTHIANS 12:13**

Our bodies are amazing. Scientists tell us, for example, our stomach acid can dissolve metal. Our eyes distinguish between millions of colors. Our noses, a trillion smells. So many marvelous parts functioning in unison come together to form a body. Similarly, Christ's body is an astounding creation of God. The Spirit melds us together to form one unique, supernatural, mind-boggling body. Its high purpose is to carry out God's eternal plan.

Whether we are Jews or Greeks, slaves or free, we all have the same common, indispensable experience. Everyone who believes on Jesus and is born of the Spirit is immersed into his body. Jesus baptizes us into the Spirit, but the Spirit baptizes us into Christ. Upon our conversion, the Spirit eternally joins us with Christ. This supernatural new creation is made and fashioned by the Spirit after the likeness of God's Son. Therefore, without the all-important work of the Spirit, the body of Christ would not exist.

The new creation enjoys a special enabling to carry on Christ's work in the world. Through an important relationship among believers, the Son and the Holy Spirit, bring into existence Christ's body. Hence, without Christ's work on the cross and the work of the Holy Spirit, his body the church would not exist. The Spirit joins the head and the body so we can participate in Christ's being and enjoy his fullness, work, and glory. No longer are we separated from God's presence because of sin. The Holy Spirit fuses us with Christ so we form one unique miraculous reality. His body, consequently, is far more than a human sociological unit of society: It is a divine creation.

Rhema: How exciting to be a member of Christ's body! Our bodies can perform many staggering feats like play a musical instrument, build a skyscraper, and fly a jet. Similarly, Christ's body is capable of remarkable exploits. Everything Jesus did in his earthly ministry—speak for God, heal the sick, cast out demons—is continued today through members of his body. The Spirit has assigned each of us an important meaningful function in his body.

SEPTEMBER 14 | NUMBERS 20:1–11

WE ARE ALL GIVEN THE
ONE SPIRIT TO DRINK

For we were all baptized by one Spirit so as to form one body—whether Jews or Gentiles, slave or free—and we were all given the one Spirit to drink. –I CORINTHIANS 12:13

If it were not for the Holy Spirit, we would die of thirst. A fierce sun and scorching sand suffice to roast us alive. When rocks are hotter than frying pans we need water, lots of it. The children of Israel made it through their forty-year wilderness journey because they had a continuous supply of water. God led them "through the barren wilderness, through a land of deserts and ravines, a land of drought and utter darkness, a land where no one travels and no one lives" (Jer 2:6). The reason they survived was "they drank from the spiritual rock that accompanied them, and that rock was Christ" (10:4). Similarly, we survive as believers because we are given a steady and bountiful supply of living water.

Even though differences existed among them in Corinth—whether Jews or Gentiles, rich or poor—everyone took part in the same universal experience. Everyone was supernaturally immersed into Christ's body and "given the one Spirit to drink." Regardless of their significant racial and social distinctions, they were sustained the same way. Not only were they vitally united together in Christ, but they also drank the same sparkling water. Even though we come from different backgrounds and may be at the opposites ends of the economic and social order, we have the same spiritual life.

As new plants need irrigating, so the Spirit floods our new lives in Christ. Jesus invited thirsty souls to come to him and drink. He said, "Whoever believes in me, as Scripture has said, rivers of living water will flow from within them. By this he meant the Spirit, whom those who believed in him were later to receive" (Jn 7:38–39). In a word, we are blessed with a river of life that flows within us.

Rhema: If you are feeling dry and thirsty in a barren land, drink from the river of God. Let it moisten your soul! Let it revive you again! Soak in it! Sip it until satisfied! After all, you are part of Christ's body, an organic entity formed and sustained by the Holy Spirit.

EAGERLY DESIRE THE GIFTS OF THE SPIRIT

Follow the way of love and eagerly desire gifts of the Spirit, especially prophecy. –I CORINTHIANS 14:1

Do you have the right attitude about spiritual gifts? The Corinthians didn't, hence Paul wrote to correct it. They did not seem to know the true purpose of the Spirit's manifestation. So by two exhortations he sought to correct their mindset. First, follow the way of love. Second, eagerly desire the gifts of the Spirit. Desiring spiritual gifts, however, is secondary to loving others.

What does it mean to follow the way of love? The primary foundation for seeking spiritual gifts is love. Our thirst for them is to arise out of a personal concern for others. Spiritual manifestations are not about us but the welfare of others. God wants us to strive after them in the interest of furthering his work and blessing others. No matter how great our gifts may be, we are nothing if we do not express them in love. For instance, we can have the gift of faith and move mountains but if we operate out of self-interest, pride or the flesh, we destroy the good we do (13:2). Thus, the fruit of the Spirit triumphs over the gifts of the Spirit.

To eagerly desire spiritual gifts means to value them and to try to obtain them. God wants us to strive after them like an exhausted deer thirsts for the water brooks. Therefore, make every effort to attain them. Admire them! Value them! Burn with zeal to secure them! We need them. Contrary to what some teach, Paul does not think these gifts will soon cease with his passing.

We value Spirit-phenomena because they do so much good. When he is working through us, invaluable things happen. The more the Spirit operates, the more Christ's body benefits. That is the reason we are to be passionate about them. Besides, it seems strange if he were to give us something we do not want. Who wouldn't want to see the sick healed, the bound set free, miracles, faith, wisdom, and knowledge? Who wouldn't want to see the church built up, strengthened, and encouraged? He manifests himself in us to make us a blessing.

Rhema: Use your spiritual gifts in love and make obtaining them your lifelong ambition.

SEPTEMBER 16 | I CORINTHIANS 14:13–39

UTTERING MYSTERIES BY THE SPIRIT

For anyone who speaks in a tongue does not speak to people but to God. Indeed, no one understands them; they utter mysteries by the **Spirit**.
–I CORINTHIANS 14:2

Speaking in tongues mystifies many. Some who are bewildered and somewhat fearful of it tend to stigmatize this amazing gift. Sad to say, people disobey God when they forbid it (v 39). Be that as it may, in the book of Acts speaking in tongues is a regular and extolled phenomenon. It was a powerful indicator a person had received Christ and belonged to the new faith community.

Many in Corinth misunderstood the gift and thought it was the height of spirituality. While they overemphasized this gift, they neglected others. In short, Paul wrote to correct their overuse and elevated estimation of tongues. His answer, however, was not to forbid speaking in tongues but to regulate its use in public worship.

The first thing Paul says about tongues is we are speaking to God with our private, supernatural, and personal praise. The gift offers us powerful and effective ways to pray, praise, intercede, and give thanks to God (vv 13–17). Tongues, moreover, create a new dimension in prayer, so we can commune with our heavenly Father at a more intimate level, spirit to Spirit. This is how we minister to the Lord.

Speaking in tongues consists of uttering mysteries. No one other than God understands the utterances because their meaning is incomprehensible without revelation. Consequently, no one in the corporate setting can benefit. Even though wonderful things are said, other believers are not edified or encouraged. The Corinthians found the experience exhilarating even though only God understood them. Nevertheless, to speak in tongues is important—it originates with the Spirit and is directed to God.

Rhema: Many other wonderful benefits are associated with speaking in tongues. Paul said, "Anyone who speaks in a tongue edifies themselves" (v 4). Therefore, it is one of the most powerful ways to experience spiritual strength and renewal. When you are exercising this miraculous gift, the Spirit is working in your life. He is energizing you for worship, witness, or spiritual work. In this way, you can stay in a state of readiness for ministry. No wonder Paul said, "I would like every one of you to speak in tongues" (v 5).

SEPTEMBER 17 | I CORINTHIANS 14:6–12

EXQUISITE WORSHIP WITH THE GIFTS OF THE SPIRIT

So it is with you. Since you are eager for gifts of the Spirit, try to excel in those that build up the church. –I CORINTHIANS 14:12

Imagine a symphony composed of great musicians with the finest of instruments. The strings, percussionists, and wind instruments are arranged in distinct sections. Rumor had it they could play the most revered music in all the land. The Great Conductor readied them to begin but when he brought his baton down, every instrument played the same note. There was no variation, tune, or movement. No harmony. At first the audience assumed they were just tuning their instruments, but it continued. Then everyone concluded they were crazy and went home mad. That is what Corinth was like.

Many church members had an undue preoccupation with speaking in tongues. Everyone exercised that one gift to the exclusion of any other. Worship was monochromatic: everyone played only one note. That is why Paul asks, "If I come to you and speak in tongues, what good will I be to you, unless I bring you some revelation or knowledge or prophecy or word of instruction?" (v 6). Seek other gifts, he exhorted, especially those that will build up the church! With such a rich variety of spiritual gifts available, worship gatherings have the potential to be exquisite. As the Spirit directs the melodic abilities of each member, beautiful and beneficial arrangements are rendered with a mastery of orchestration and harmonies.

Paul says to covet gifts that strengthen the church. God wants everyone to leave feeling inspired, encouraged, and uplifted. When the Spirit is allowed to move, he creates enriching worship experiences, a symphony of spiritual celebrations.

Rhema: Think of yourself as a precious brass or wind instrument. Let the divine wind blow through you. His breath in you may result in a spiritual song, a joyful hymn, or a wonderful word of instruction (v 26). Imagine the joy should the Holy Spirit raise your faith to believe God for a miracle, a healing, or a great answer to prayer! Your unique and beautiful music breathed upon by the Spirit will have the touch of heaven. As you yield to him, your contribution will bring delight and contentment to your soul and will bless those around you.

PRAISING GOD IN THE SPIRIT

Otherwise when you are praising God in the Spirit, how can someone else, who is now put in the position of an inquirer, say "Amen" to your thanksgiving, since they do not know what you are saying?
–I CORINTHIANS 14:16

Oh, the foolishness of God! It will destroy the wisdom of the wise. It will frustrate the intelligence of the intelligent (1:19). It will save the perishing (1:18). In a culture intoxicated with human wisdom, knowledge, and reason, the Almighty made the wisdom of the world foolish (1:20).

God's foolishness determined he will not be known by pure, raw genius (2:21). In the cross he turned the world's wisdom on its head. Therefore, man's intelligence is now foolishness, but God's foolishness becomes wisdom. Since that fatal decision in the garden (Gen 3:1–7) to disobey and choose knowledge over love and obedience, man's brilliance can never save. The cross is God's judgment on reason's inadequacy to know him.

It should come as no surprise God has chosen to be known through the Spirit. He has given us his Spirit "so that we may understand what God has freely given us" (2:12). "The person without the Spirit does not accept the things that come from the Spirit of God but considers them foolishness, and cannot understand them because they are discerned only through the Spirit" (2:14). Consequently, speaking in tongues is of the Spirit and is just so much folly to those without him.

When we praise God in the Spirit, our minds are unfruitful. Such worship seems absurd! On the contrary, it is deep and profound, non-rational and unintelligible, but thanking him by the Spirit is direct communication with God. Spirit-generated worship bypasses the mind but edifies our innermost being. Praising the Lord in tongues is a glorious spiritual experience in which his Spirit is released in our lives. Yet it does nothing for those listening because the words are unintelligible. They cannot say, "Amen."

Rhema: *"So what shall I do?" Paul asks. Speaking in tongues operates in two primary realms. There is a public as well as a private use of the gift. On the private or personal level, he praises God in tongues more than them all (v 18). In public, however, he will bless God with intelligible words so that others can understand.*

SEPTEMBER 19 | I CORINTHIANS 14:26–39

STAYING IN TUNE WITH THE SPIRIT

*If anyone thinks they are a prophet or otherwise gifted by the **Spirit**, let them acknowledge that what I am writing to you is the Lord's command.*
–I CORINTHIANS 14:37

How do we recognize if a teaching is from God or man? Paul's directives concerning speaking in tongues and prophesy were actual commands of Jesus. Even though they may have caused resentment and resistance, they are nevertheless authoritative and inspired. As is always the case, anyone gifted by the Spirit should recognize this.

Those who are spiritual and have the gift of prophecy will heed the apostle's instructions. The divine presence in them will resonate with the Spirit in Paul. In fact, should they find themselves at odds with the apostle, they are not in tune with the Spirit. By the same token, to reject his orders makes them out of order. How sad to realize for much of church history Paul's decrees have been suppressed. He has reminded us we are not the originators of God's word (v 36) but he and the apostles are.

Paul's inspired words are as true today as when first written. Notice his summary on spiritual gifts. "Therefore, my brothers and sisters, be eager to prophesy, and do not forbid speaking in tongues. But everything should be done in a fitting and orderly way" (vv 39–40). No contorted hermeneutic or contrived doctrine of man must be permitted to explain away these divine commands. Given this realization, everyone should seek to prophesy because it builds up the congregation. No one should censor speaking in tongues because it edifies individual believers. Prophecy is for the public realm and tongues for the private. God wants us to speak to him in tongues. And he also desires to speak to us through prophecy.

Rhema: Although the Corinthians abounded in spiritual gifts (1:7), their understanding of them was both childish (v 20) and insane (v 23). To focus only on themselves by speaking in tongues and neglect the other gifts was not only selfish but infantile. Additionally, Paul pointed out bedlam in their worship services was not orchestrated by the Spirit because "God is not a God of disorder but of peace" (v 33). The apostle gave these commands so they would get in tune with the Spirit and love one another.

THE SPIRIT GUARANTEES OUR SALVATION

*Now it is God who makes both us and you stand firm in Christ. He anointed us, set his seal of ownership on us, and put his **Spirit** in our hearts as a deposit, guaranteeing what is to come.*
–II CORINTHIANS 1:21–22

Have you ever placed an identification mark upon something you treasured? A microchip in your dog or an engraving on a ring? God does the same with us. He places the Holy Spirit in us as his mark of ownership and a guarantee of our future salvation.

Many make promises to us—politicians, friends, businesses, and family members. Too often they break our hearts because they don't keep their word. The Corinthians accused Paul of breaking his promise to visit them. He faced a firestorm when he didn't come. His change of plans gave his distracters cause to claim his yes turned out to be a no.. "We cannot trust him," they bellowed. "He speaks out of both sides of his mouth." To explain what happened, Paul wrote II Corinthians.

What proof do we have that God will keep his promises regarding our final salvation? The cross of Jesus Christ and our reception of the Holy Spirit guarantee his trustworthiness. "For no matter how many promises God has made, they are 'Yes' in Christ" (v 20). He made our free, full, and future salvation available through the cross.

The Spirit in our lives is a threefold guarantee assuring us God will keep his word. First, after believing in Christ, God anoints us with the Holy Spirit. We enjoy the blessing once reserved for the OT prophets, kings, and priests. Like Christ, the Father anoints us with the Holy Spirit. Second, God sets the seal of the Spirit upon us a visible impression identifying us as his own. The Spirit's activity in our lives is the evidence we belong to him. He will not hang us out to dry. Third, he puts his Spirit in our hearts guaranteeing what is to come. Our present experience of the Holy Spirit is proof the future has already begun in us.

Rhema: Your glorious salvation is never in doubt. God's promises are as real as the eternal future already at work in you. Do not fear the Spirit but enjoy him now and throughout eternity.

SEPTEMBER 21 | II CORINTHIANS 2:12–3:3

LETTERS OF REFERENCE
WRITTEN BY THE SPIRIT

*You show that you are a letter from Christ, the result of our ministry, written not with ink but with the **Spirit** of the living God, not on tablets of stone but on tablets of human hearts. –II CORINTHIANS 3:3*

Were you ever asked for a letter of reference? Employers ask for them to assess one's qualifications for a job. Back in Paul's day, traveling ministers such as Apollos provided letters to attest their ministry (Acts 18:27). The Corinthians may have asked Paul for one. He said he did not need any because they themselves authenticate his apostleship and ministry. They were his letters. His credentials. The result of his ministry. His commendations were not written with ink like the other traveling ministries but by the Spirit of the living God.

Someone said, "God makes a way for a person's ministry." Paul possessed no letters of commendation, but he had something more: God's recommendation. The fruitful results of his ministry gave him credentials. No need to commend himself. Their changed lives, read and realized by everyone, was all he needed. Paul says, "If you want a letter then I refer you to yourselves—you are my letters."

There was no question God endorsed Paul. He says, "Just examine my ministry! The Spirit's transforming work authenticates my apostleship." Before he came to them they were lost, without Christ, steeped in sins. When they believed his message, the Holy Spirit began writing on their hearts. The dynamic work of the Spirit in them proved beyond a doubt God was with him. Remarkable changes in each of them provided the convincing proof God sent him.

Rhema: Christ is writing a wonderful story of redemption on your heart with the ink of the Holy Spirit. When people look at you, they are to see what it means to be born and led of the Spirit. Transformed by the power from above makes you an epistle expressing Christ's grandeur, love, and mercy. Christ's narrative in you describes how the Spirit affects every area of your life. His lovely personality—love, joy, peace, longsuffering, kindness, goodness, gentleness, self-control—is to flow from your heart. Instead of a heart of stone, he creates in you a heart alive and sensitive to God's will.

SEPTEMBER 22 | JEREMIAH 31:26–37

COMPETENT MINISTERS OF THE NEW COVENANT OF THE SPIRIT

He has made us competent as ministers of a new covenant—not of the letter but of the Spirit; for the letter kills, but the Spirit gives life.
–II CORINTHIANS 3:6

Inadequacy—not being good enough—plagues us. Feelings of inadequacy can interfere with our relationships, work, and emotional well-being. Some in Corinth had called into question Paul's competence as a minister. They accused him of not having credentials, being a poor public speaker and weak.

Sometimes we wonder how we can be more effective for God. What does it take to serve him better? Will letters of recommendation, schooling or learning from a master help? Paul had posed this question earlier in the letter, asking, "Who is equal to such a task?" (2:16). When eternal destinies hang in the balance, who in their own strength is capable?

To answer these questions, Paul turned away from himself to the Spirit. The Holy Spirit made him competent to serve the Lord. The apostle did not rely on his own abilities or a certificate of ordination. Instead, he relied on the Spirit to work in and through him. Because of the powerful enabling of the Spirit, Paul proved he was a competent minister of the new covenant. He attributed his many outstanding results to the Holy Spirit, not human ability.

The teachers of the Old Covenant who put their confidence in the flesh tangled with Paul. They had letters, recommendations, and authorization to teach and preach the law of Moses. The only problem was all their rules and regulations could never transform the heart or give it power to live for God. Because it was inadequate, God replaced the law with the new covenant of the Spirit.

To do effective ministry in the age of the Spirit requires the Spirit. Otherwise, people will not experience God's life and power. The Holy Spirit makes us competent; he anoints us to make us effective. He can transform the weakest amongst us into a powerhouse for God. Teaching, preaching, counseling, worship or deliverance done through the Spirit will have spiritual results.

Rhema: No longer do you need to feel inadequate, incompetent, or powerless—these belong to the realm of the flesh. "We are not competent in ourselves to claim anything for ourselves. Our competence comes from God" (v 5).

SEPTEMBER 23 | II CORINTHIANS 3:4–6; EXODUS 20:1–17

THE LETTER KILLS BUT THE
SPIRIT GIVES LIFE

He has made us competent as ministers of a new covenant—not of the letter but of the Spirit; for the letter kills, but the **Spirit** *gives life.*
–II CORINTHIANS 3:6

The letter kills but the Spirit gives life. What a contrast! The old covenant produces death but the new gives life. The law never saved anyone, certainly not Moses. Although he received and delivered it, he ended up breaking the sixth commandment. The law that came through Moses was written by the finger of God on tablets of stone, but it lacked the internal force to help anyone live for God. Nor could it transform a heart; it only informed and condemned to death.

The letter that kills refers to the Ten Commandments and the law Moses received on Mt. Sinai. God wrote his moral imperatives upon cold, stone tablets (v 7). It "was intended to bring life" (Rom 7:10) but nothing in the law enabled anyone to uphold it. The law was "holy, righteous and good" even "spiritual," but it "actually brought death." Moses received it amidst great glory, but it proved destructive. The old dispensation of Moses was "the ministry that brought death, which was engraved in letters on stone" (v 7). Why then, Paul argues, would anyone want to be a minister of the old covenant?

The Spirit, however, initiates a new era of life. How does this work? The Spirit who indwells us is, in fact, the "Spirit of the living God," (v 3) the Third Person of the Trinity. To have him is to receive God's eternal life. We were dead but he raises us from the dead, imparting resurrection life. From within, he gives the dynamic and moral power to live a life of obedience. Therefore, death remains for those who refuse to embrace the new aeon of the Spirit.

Rhema: Regardless of our best efforts and intentions, trying to be a follower of Christ without the Holy Spirit is impossible. To walk in righteousness, we do not need the letter of the law but God's Spirit. He not only writes God's will upon our hearts, but he also gives us the power to do it. By his awesome might, we can walk in victory and obedience and enjoy newness of life.

THE GLORIOUS MINISTRY OF THE SPIRIT

*Now if the ministry that brought death, which was engraved in letters on stone, came with glory, so that the Israelites could not look steadily at the face of Moses because of its glory, transitory though it was, will not the ministry of the **Spirit** be even more glorious?* **–II CORINTHIANS 3:8**

What comes to your mind when you think of the word "spectacular"? A July 4th celebration? Disney World's closing ceremonies? A Super Bowl halftime show? None of these can compare to the hair-raising spectacle on Mt. Sinai when God gave Moses the law. The mountain quaked with a magnitude off the Richter scale. Thunder and lightning ripped through the sky. An ear-piercing trumpet blasted away. Smoke and fire billowed up like a towering inferno. Even Moses' face radiated with dazzling beams of the divine presence. The breathtaking giving of the law was a temporal glorious occasion, but for all its magnificence it did absolutely nothing to alleviate our sinful condition; it only made it worse.

Paul contrasts the glory of old covenant with the new covenant of the Spirit. As impressive as the law was, the dispensation of the Spirit is even more so. How is that possible? The end times began with the coming of Christ and the outpouring of the Spirit. Tongues of fire, speaking in foreign languages, and the sound of a rushing mighty wind birthed the new era. Therefore, everyone who believes in Jesus and is born of the Spirit tastes eternal glory.

The ministry of the Spirit supersedes the old because of its superior and stunning results. To magnify the Law of Moses was a fatal step backwards—it was powerless to fit us for God's awesome presence. The new covenant of the Spirit, on the other hand, makes us righteous and gives us life. In fact, the presence and activity of the Spirit within brings us face to face with God. The Spirit removes the veil to allow us to see his glory. Further, as we walk in the newness of life the Spirit transforms us into the glorious image of the Lord. Something the law could not do.

Rhema: The Spirit initiates us into heaven's eternal blessedness and brings the wonderful end times into the present.

THE LORD IS THE SPIRIT

*Now the Lord is the **Spirit**, and where the Spirit of the Lord is, there is freedom.* **–II CORINTHIANS 3:17**

St. Jerome (AD 5th C.) said, "The face is the mirror of the mind, and eyes without speaking confess the secrets of the heart." When someone wears a veil, however, it is hard to see their face and the secrets of their heart. Conversely, people who wear a veil cannot see the face of others. This is what prevents individuals from seeing the face of God: they have a veil over their hearts.

Spiritual blindness is a veil that prevents people from seeing the Lord. Unbelievers, therefore, cannot see the face of God or know his heart. When anyone turns to the Lord, the Spirit lifts the veil and ushers the person into God's glorious presence. God wants us to know him intently, so we can dwell in his presence face to face.

Paul extols the central role of the Spirit in removing the blanket of blindness, so we can encounter God's presence more fully. In reality, whenever we turn to the Lord, we are turning to the Spirit of the living God. "Now the Lord is the Spirit." To be born of the Spirit means Jesus has come to live in our hearts, increasing our awareness of his presence. Since he has come to live in us, we know him better than Moses knew God because our bodies are his eternal dwelling place, his holy temple. Although "the Lord would speak to Moses face to face, as one speaks to a friend" (Ex 33:11), we have the Lord living and speaking in us.

The Spirit is the Lord. He is the one who uncovers our veil so we can with unveiled faces enter the glorious presence of Christ. Because we are in his presence communing with the Lord, we are given access to revelation. We hear his voice and feel his heartbeat. Masks are removed. His word becomes a living word. This glory does not fade away but ever increases. The more the veil is lifted, the more we see God.

Rhema: The greatest OT blessing was to see the face of God (Nu 6:25–26). Through the Spirit, the Lord makes his face shine on you, showering you with his blessings.

SEPTEMBER 26 | GALATIANS 2:1–10

FREEDOM IN THE SPIRIT

*Now the Lord is the Spirit, and where the **Spirit** of the Lord is, there is freedom.* –II CORINTHIANS 3:17

The Exodus is the greatest story of freedom in human history. Under the leadership of Moses, a million or more slaves march out of Egypt liberated by the mighty hand of God. Israel's freedom from Egypt's servitude is the central redemptive act of the OT. After centuries of slavery, the people are free—free from bondage, free from oppression, free to worship God.

Atop Mt. Sinai, Moses enjoys the highest freedom of all—freedom with God. Nothing prevented his entering the Lord's presence and speaking to him face to face. He did not have to overcome any barriers nor perform any rituals but for forty days and forty nights the two of them fellowshipped together. Revelation flowed like water out of a fire hydrant divulging the Ten Commandments, the blueprints for Tabernacle and, perhaps, the Creation story. During these wonderful days so packed with God, he had no need of food or drink. He was free to worship God.

Moses' remarkable experience is a prophetic picture corresponding to the Spirit in our lives. As Moses encountered the Lord, we in a similar way encounter the Spirit. The Lord is the Spirit: who the Lord was to Moses; the Spirit is to us believers. Where the Spirit of the Lord is, there is freedom. The Spirit removes the barriers separating us from God. Everyone who turns to the Lord is free to come before God. We become like Moses—free to speak to God face to face, free to enter his glorious presence. We are free to come before him with confidence and participate in a Moses-like fellowship.

Rhema: The Spirit gives you access to God's presence through the finished work of Christ on the cross. As you turn to the Lord, the Spirit removes the veil, opens your eyes, and brings you face to face with God. The power of the indwelling Spirit has set you free from the power of sin and death. The Spirit of the living God dwells within, negating the need of religious rituals and regulations. In the Spirit, you have access to the same presence and glory of the Lord as Moses did. There are no barriers, restrictions, or obstructions—just freedom to speak with God.

SEPTEMBER 27 | EXODUS 33:12–34:9

THE SPIRIT TRANSFORMS US
INTO THE IMAGE OF CHRIST

And we all, who with unveiled faces contemplate the Lord's glory, are being transformed into his image with ever-increasing glory, which comes from the Lord, who is the Spirit. –II CORINTHIANS 3:18

The Spirit transforms us into Christ's own likeness. How inspiring? People should be able to look at us and see Jesus. We are letters from Christ written not with ink but with the Holy Spirit. We are mirrors that reflect the splendor of the Lord. As the Spirit works in our lives, he changes us into the image of our Lord with ever-increasing wonder. In fact, the whole purpose of redemption is that we exhibit the image of God's Son.

The Holy Spirit operates in our life, allowing us to behold the glory of the Lord now. Many are waiting until they go to heaven to see his face, but he wants us to encounter his magnificence now. Revealing him in all his majesty is the Spirit's job. When Jesus was on earth, his body of flesh veiled his divine grandeur except on those rare occasions the Father gave glimpses of it (Mt 16:17). Without revelation, people did not grasp he was the one and only begotten of the Father. When the Spirit removes the veil, however, we behold his brightness with no impediment. As Moses was transformed by the presence of the Lord, so should we.

The Spirit reveals Christ to us in new and marvelous ways, enabling us to become more Christlike. For example, Paul said, "I want to know Christ—yes, to know the power of his resurrection and participation in his sufferings, becoming like him in his death" (Phil 3:10). As he was facing his own demise, the apostle wanted to experience how Christ handled suffering and the loss of life. Jesus promised the Spirit would reveal to us things about him we might not otherwise consider.

Rhema: As we face new and challenging life situations, the Spirit will give us new revelations of Christ. Therefore, the Spirit is indispensable if we want to live like Christ and reflect the glory of God. In these new and differing circumstances, the Spirit will hold up Christ like a mirror so we can imitate him. "The Lord, who is the Spirit" gives us an ever-increasing revelation of Jesus.

THE SAME SPIRIT OF FAITH

It is written: "I believed; therefore I have spoken." Since we have that same **spirit** *of faith, we also believe and therefore speak, because we know that the one who raised the Lord Jesus from the dead will also raise us with Jesus and present us with you to himself.*
–II CORINTHIANS 4:13–14

How does the man keep going? Troubled on every side, perplexed, persecuted and struck down, yet he rose from the ashes of affliction. He was always living on the edge of death, but he does not despair. Nothing crushed him. Nothing wore him down. Behind his incredible endurance and resilience was a powerful source of strength.

Are you facing disappointment, disaster, danger? Life is so fragile, difficult, and unpredictable you may wonder how you can keep going without succumbing to despair. If you are struggling to keep your head above water, look at Paul. He says, "Since through God's mercy we have this ministry, we do not lose heart" (v 1). In the Spirit, Paul encounters and experiences the splendor and majesty of the Lord with ever-increasing glory, so he knows his own outcome regardless of his present trouble.

Paul remembers King David, the sweet Psalmist of Israel and his troubles. Just as he was facing death and found strength to go on, so also did the apostle. The Psalmist said, "I believed and therefore I have spoken" (Ps 116:10). David praised and thanked the Lord because he was assured of deliverance from death. Paul says with the "same Spirit of faith we also believe and therefore speak." He is saying the Spirit gives the faith needed to carry on. The secret to his amazing fortitude is the same as David's. Whatever happens, the one who raised Jesus from the dead will raise him.

Rhema: When we are going through a rough patch in life, we have access to the same faith Paul and David had. The Spirit operates in us to ever supply that supernatural conviction of life eternal. We are "jars of clay," susceptible to a complete breakup. Like the Psalmist, tears may pour out of our eyes and our feet may stumble but "we do not lose heart. Though outwardly we are wasting away, yet inwardly we are being renewed day by day" (v 16).

SEPTEMBER 29 | II CORINTHIANS 5:1–21

THE SPIRIT IS A DOWN PAYMENT

*Now the one who has fashioned us for this very purpose is God, who has given us the **Spirit** as a deposit, guaranteeing what is to come.*
–II CORINTHIANS 5:5

How can we be sure God will transform our bodies into glorified, resurrected ones like Jesus'? Our bodies beset with pain and disease tell us we are dying. With every fleeting day, we face increasing limitations reminding us we are not what we used to be. Decay and death make us yearn for immortality. God, however, has given us the Holy Spirit as a down payment to assure us our mortal bodies will put on immortality.

When the Father gave the Spirit, he deposited the initial taste of eternity in us. The Spirit is the first installment of our future glorious inheritance. Our eternal life began the day we were born of the Spirit. Even now, the Spirit renews us day by day with ever-increasing glory. Already we behold the Lord's majesty. Already we take part in the powers of the age to come (Heb 6:5). Already he gives life to our mortal bodies (Rom 8:11). In the Spirit we are enjoying the kingdom of God, but it is just the beginning.

Although our eternal life began with the new birth, it will find completion when the Spirit raises our deceased bodies. The Holy Spirit is the pledge our mortality will "be swallowed up in life" (v 4). Because the Spirit who dwells within is eternal, he connects us to eternity in anticipation of raising us from the dead.

God made us for eternal life; he is the "one who has fashioned us for this very purpose." From before creation he wanted to make us in his image, so we can share everlasting life together. God is preparing a place for us eternal in the heavens where we will dwell in happy harmony with him forever. We will exchange these bodies, poor tents in which we now dwell, for a house not made with hands. "Meanwhile we groan, longing to be clothed instead with our heavenly dwelling" (v 2).

Rhema: What we look like now does not matter considering the Spirit is at work in us preparing us for that day when we have glorified bodies. His presence in us guarantees what is to come.

SEPTEMBER 30 | II CORINTHIANS 6:1–13

WE COMMEND OURSELVES IN THE HOLY SPIRIT

Rather, as servants of God we commend ourselves in every way: in great endurance; in troubles, hardships and distresses; in beatings, imprisonments and riots; in hard work, sleepless nights and hunger; in purity, understanding, patience and kindness; in the Holy Spirit and in sincere love; in truthful speech and in the power of God.
—II CORINTHIANS 6:4–7

Students today assemble a "brag sheet" to help them gain acceptance to college. They tell of their experiences, what sets them apart, and what their greatest strength is. Paul is putting together his brag sheet to commend himself to the Corinthians since these things matter so much to them. He says, "You enjoy boasting. Well, here are things about which I can boast." He doesn't parade before them all his successes or famous people he knows. No, he brags about his reliance upon the Holy Spirit and the power of God in his life.

Paul is not seeking the praise of men for his achievements; rather, he prefers to credit the Holy Spirit for helping him remain faithful to God. As a minister of the new covenant of the Spirit, his ministry is God-honoring and authentic. No one can accuse him of being a stumbling block, of leading people astray or peddling the gospel for money. Instead, he has conducted himself with the utmost integrity, absent of any selfish motives.

The mention of the Holy Spirit in his resume of struggles and virtues is no accident. Despite his hardships, he has remained honorable and true to God. Besides, he has walked in purity, patience, and kindness. The apostle commends himself to the church as one who has lived and ministered in the power from on high. To stay positive amidst adversity is heroic, but he praises the Holy Spirit for his accomplishments and endurance.

Rhema: Whenever we feel weak and overwhelmed with difficulties, we can look at Paul's example. In the center of his brag sheet is the reference of the Holy Spirit. The apostle wants us to rely not on our own strength but upon the power of the Spirit. With his help, we can overcome our trials and tribulations. The Spirit's sufficiency enables us to live in grace and victory; he more than offsets our human weaknesses.

THE HOLY SPIRIT IS
ESSENTIAL FOR SALVATION

*For if someone comes to you and preaches a Jesus other than the Jesus we preached, or if you receive a different spirit from the **Spirit** you received, or a different gospel from the one you accepted, you put up with it easily enough.* –II CORINTHIANS 11:4

Another Jesus. A separate Spirit. Intruders came to Corinth and presented a different gospel. It was shocking the Corinthians "put up with it easily enough" because they faced a real and present crisis. As a chaste virgin pledged to be married to Christ, they could lose their virginity to a seducer (v2). Just as the cunning serpent deceived Eve, they were at risk of being led astray (v 3).

From Paul's response, we learn of the interconnectedness of Jesus, the Spirit, and the gospel. To change or alter any one of them changes the others. Authentic Christianity stresses the importance of all three and ties them together with an inseparable bond. For instance, to decrease the distinctive role of the Holy Spirit in our salvation distorts the gospel and weakens the finished work of Christ on the cross.

Just look at what Paul said concerning the Holy Spirit in his first letter! His preaching was not with wise and persuasive words "but with a demonstration of the Spirit's power." He did this so that their faith would not rest on men's wisdom but on God's power (2:4–5). The Spirit washes, sanctifies, and justifies (6:11). No one can confess "Jesus is Lord" except by the Holy Spirit (12:3). They "were all baptized by one Spirit so as to form one body" and "were all given the one Spirit to drink" (12:13).

In II Corinthians he continues. Twice he assures them God has put his Spirit in their hearts "as a deposit guaranteeing what is to come" (2:22; 5:5). The Spirit wrote upon their hearts proving their conversion and Paul's authenticity (3:3). The apostle discusses the supreme ministry of the Spirit who ushers in and administers the new covenant (3:8). The Spirit gives them free access to God (3:17). Repeatedly, Paul delineates the Spirit's wonderful saving work.

Rhema: Therefore, to become a follower of Jesus Christ is far more than acknowledging a set of beliefs; it incorporates a full and glorious experience of the Holy Spirit.

OCTOBER 2 | II CORINTHIANS 12:11–21

WALKING IN THE SAME SPIRIT

I urged Titus to go to you and I sent our brother with him. Titus did not exploit you, did he? Did we not walk in the same footsteps by the same **Spirit?** –II CORINTHIANS **12:18**

Paul got off to a bad start with the Corinthians. They called into question his apostleship and considered him an "inferior apostle." It was over trivial things—a change of plans, lack of training as a rhetorician, and no letters of recommendation. Now they suspect his handling of money.

His accusers outraged the apostle because they had spread a rumor accusing him of skimming money off the offerings. Although he supported himself while ministering in Corinth, his critics still suspected him of dishonesty. To them, sending two associates to collect the offering for the poor in Jerusalem was pure craftiness. In a devious way, they claimed, he was still diverting part of their collection to his pockets.

Paul defends himself by referencing the Holy Spirit. He and Titus whom they trust walk in the same footsteps because the selfsame Spirit is at work in both their lives. To us, Paul's defense may appear lame until we understand how he views the Holy Spirit. When it comes to day-to-day living, the Spirit is neither distant nor absent in their lives. Both he and Titus walk in integrity because the Holy Spirit is the dominant influence controlling them.

They base their ethic not on a moral principle but upon the dynamic influence of the Third Person of the Trinity. The indwelling Spirit directs, empowers, and forms their ethical behavior. Remember the apostle attributes the Spirit and the power of God for his purity, patience and kindness, as well as his truthfulness and sincere love for them (6:6–7). He is claiming both he and Titus conduct themselves in honesty because they are living their lives under the Spirit's control.

Rhema: The indwelling Holy Spirit guides our behavior when we conduct ourselves in accordance with him. Walking in the same Spirit means the Spirit working in Paul and Titus is active in us. He sits above our consciences critiquing and directing our moral decisions. Sensitivity to the Spirit and obedience to his promptings make our talk and walk exemplary. The way to live with moral integrity is by walking in the Spirit.

OCTOBER 3 | II CORINTHIANS 13:1–14

THE FELLOWSHIP OF THE HOLY SPIRIT

May the grace of the Lord Jesus Christ, and the love of God, and the fellowship of the **Holy Spirit** *be with you all.* **–II CORINTHIANS 13:14**

The solution to the problems in the Corinthian church are found in this verse. The Father, Son, and Holy Spirit together express the fullness of God's provisions. Quarreling, jealousy, anger, factions, slander, gossip, immorality, arrogance, and disorder plagued the congregation. They needed a rich supply of grace, love, and fellowship. If the Corinthian believers were to overcome their terrible deficits, they needed God's help.

All three persons of the Godhead involve themselves in the life of the church. The Holy Spirit shares his work equally with the Father and the Son. The grace of the Lord Jesus and the fellowship of the Holy Spirit flow out of God's love. Since God is love, it is not surprising to see the work and ministry of both Christ and the Holy Spirit express it. Christ exhibited it by dying for us on the cross. The Holy Spirit expresses God's love by spreading it abroad in our hearts.

What helps bring wholeness to the congregation is the fellowship of the Holy Spirit. The Spirit creates true fellowship among believers. Divisions and factions are a result of the flesh which can only be overcome by the power of the Spirit. The indwelling Spirit fills them with a power that triumphs over flesh and selfishness. Although they consider themselves spiritual, the Corinthians are carnal, mere babes, and are not living in the Spirit's power (I Cor 3:1).

Fellowship in the church derives from the intimacy existing between the three persons of the Triune God. It is the most magnificent expression of close association in this universe. Three persons—Father, Son, and Holy Spirit—exist in one harmonious communion. When we have the Spirit living in us, he brings the atmosphere of heaven into our relationships. His presence and power transform and unify as he creates a community that resembles the blessed Trinity instead of the chaotic world.

Rhema: When the Spirit brings the reality of the grace of Jesus Christ and the Father's love into our relationships, selfish ambition is crushed. Through the Spirit, the unity and equity of the Trinity pervades community relationships and binds believers together.

OCTOBER 4 | GALATIANS 2:15–3:5

RECEIVING THE SPIRIT BY FAITH

I would like to learn just one thing from you: Did you receive the Spirit by the works of the law, or by believing what you heard? —GALATIANS 3:2

Paul wants to know who bewitched these foolish Galatians. Their lack of spiritual discernment is incomprehensible. Dumbfounded, he wants to understand why they turned aside from the gospel and allowed their minds to become so muddled considering he preached Christ crucified, not salvation by works. Did someone cast a spell on them? What sleight of hand made them miss the centrality of his message? In the sight of God, he told them, they become righteous through faith in Christ.

The Holy Spirit is central to Paul's argument of attaining righteousness by faith. To settle the question of justification by faith, he appeals to their experience. "Just tell me one thing," Paul asks, "Did you receive the Spirit by the works of the law, or by believing what you heard?" Works of righteousness are unnecessary for the reception of God's Spirit: he is a precious gift for accepting the gospel.

The Galatians understood their experience resulted from faith, not religious deeds. The Holy Spirit entered their lives in such a dynamic way Paul can appeal to their experience as proof of salvation. What makes them think it was necessary to add religious acts to their faith? If they did, they are declaring Christ does not save them. This constitutes a "different gospel," which is not one at all. Worst of all it renders Christ's death void (2:21).

How do we become God's people is the apostle's question. Does circumcision, keeping special days, or abstaining from pork make us his children? No. The sole indicator we are God's is the possession of his Spirit. New birth by the Holy Spirit enables us to inherit God's promises. When we receive the Spirit, we have passed from death to life because God's eternal Spirit gives us life and lives in us. The gift of the Holy Spirit is the evidence we are born again. Without him we are not Christ's.

Rhema: *No one ever received God's Spirit by keeping the law. Similarly, all the blessings of heaven come through faith, not religious deeds. We receive answers to prayer, healing, miracles, and the Holy Spirit because we believe, not because of works.*

OCTOBER 5 | GALATIANS 1:11–2:14

BEGINNING THE CHRISTIAN LIFE
IN THE HOLY SPIRIT

*Are you so foolish? After beginning by means of the **Spirit**, are you now trying to finish by means of the flesh?* –GALATIANS 3:3

Paul is explicit about what it means to be a follower of Christ. Too bad so many didn't listen to him and by veering off have muddied the waters and sowed confusion. For him, two defining things occur when individuals came to faith: God justifies them and gives them the Holy Spirit. The rediscovery of the first marked the Protestant Reformation—the just shall live by faith (2:15–16). Failure to embrace the second has distorted Christianity throughout the centuries.

The apostle expected everyone to receive the Holy Spirit when they believed in Jesus Christ (Acts 19:2). Possession of the Spirit proves one is right with God. The Spirit is the one who helps believers live their new lives in Christ. From the moment of their new birth to the end, the Spirit nurtures and sustains their entire life as a disciple of Christ.

A follower of Jesus Christ begins his or her new life in the supernatural power of God. Paul's point is how can we improve upon or complete the new life in the Spirit by recourse to the flesh. No work of the flesh, no religious act, nor adherence to the law can bring us any closer to God than what we have now in the Spirit. Day by day, from glory to glory, the renewing action of the Spirit transforms us into the image of Christ (II Cor 3:18).

Why would anyone think the flesh could make them perfect? The fatal flaw of all religions including false versions of Christianity is to think that man can come closer to God by human effort. The earthly cannot make us heavenly. Can our sinful human nature by some miracle give us holy desires? No possible way exists for the flesh to change our heart, reorient our lives, and give the power to live for God.

Rhema: When we have the Spirit, we are already close to God—he has taken up residence in us! We do not go deeper in God or make spiritual progress by the flesh because it will never complete what the Spirit started. Spiritual transformation is the work of the Spirit not the flesh.

OCTOBER 6 | GALATIANS 3:6–29

THE SPIRIT CONTINUES HIS ACTIVITY

*So again I ask, does God give you his **Spirit** and work miracles among you by the works of the law, or by your believing what you heard?*
—GALATIANS 3:5

The burning hot issue in the book of Galatians is how do we receive God's wonderful blessings (vv 9, 14). On what basis does he give us the gift of his Spirit and work miracles among us? After we come to faith in Christ God's Spirit continues to work among us and aspires to do more than we can imagine. The ongoing and abiding work of the Spirit occurs because of faith.

When Paul and Barnabas first brought the Galatians the gospel, they experienced powerful miracles. The Lord confirmed their message by enabling them to perform signs and wonders (Acts 14:3). At Lystra, for instance, a cripple who had never walked heard Paul preach. When the apostle saw he had faith to be healed he said, "Stand up on your feet!" Right away, the man jumped up and walked (Acts 14:8–10). It seems Paul himself also received a remarkable miracle when a crowd stoned him and left him for dead. After his disciples gathered around him, he sprang up and continued to minister (Acts 14:19–20).

The miracles and reception of the Spirit continued after Paul left. We know they did not stop after his departure because he acknowledged they were still happening (v 5). The believers continued to witness more people come to faith and receive the Spirit. Consequently, they watched the Spirit's ongoing continuous movement. Signs and wonders. Healing and deliverances. Revelations and prophecy. On what grounds were these things happening, he asks? These marvelous displays of God's power and favor were not the result of works of the law but faith.

Rhema: The Spirit works among us according to our faith. We do not get prayers answered because we have done good works: they get answered because God acts with grace in response to our faith. God supplies our needs not because we worked for them but because we believe. We are saved by grace through faith. In the same way, we will experience a steady stream of the Spirit's manifestation. Therefore, it is a fatal mistake to turn from grace to law and from faith to works to secure God's blessings.

OCTOBER 7 | GALATIANS 3:6–14, 26–29

THE BLESSING OF THE HOLY SPIRIT

He redeemed us in order that the blessing given to Abraham might come to the Gentiles through Christ Jesus, so that by faith we might receive the promise of the **Spirit**. **–GALATIANS 3:14**

How do we put an end to the destructive powers ruining our lives and come under the favor and blessing of God? That is the question the apostle answers. A curse inflicts harm and punishment on our lives and dooms us to destruction and death. Everyone without Christ faces disaster because "all who rely on the works of the law are under a curse" (v 10).

Paul contrasts the cursed life with the blessed life of Abraham, the man of faith. God releases supernatural powers in his life so he can enjoy success in every way (Gen 24:1, 35). The list of blessings is long: greatness, significance, meaning, fruitfulness, wealth, and offspring. Compared to those around him, his crops explode, his herds enlarge, and his children excel. God's favor is so extensive and far-reaching he blesses "all the nations" through him (v 9). God kisses his life! Paul tells us how these things apply in our lives.

When we believe in Jesus Christ, God liberates us from the curse of sin and death and gives us the promises made to Abraham. "Those who rely on faith are blessed along with Abraham" (v 9). For Paul, the gift of the Holy Spirit brings into our lives the supernatural blessings promised to Abraham (Gen 12:2–3). Therefore, Paul can equate justification by faith with receiving the Spirit. The gift of the Spirit is the proof we obtained the blessing of Abraham without keeping the law.

Rhema: Why is receiving the promise of the Spirit so wonderful? The Spirit is the ultimate blessing, the personal realization of God's presence. Through faith in Christ we become the offspring of Abraham, and the remarkable powerful benefits of the "man of faith" become ours. If we have faith like Abraham, then we "are the children of Abraham," (v 7) with access to all things (Rom 8:32). Instead of the curse of death, we receive a blessing of everlasting life. We enjoy God's life in us both now and for eternity. For Martin Luther, God's blessing meant we would be free from all evils and obtain all good things.

OCTOBER 8 | GALATIANS 4:1–7

THE SPIRIT OF HIS SON
LIVES IN OUR HEARTS

*Because you are his sons, God sent the Spirit of his Son into our hearts, the Spirit who calls out, "Abba, Father." –*GALATIANS 4:6

This is a true rags-to-riches story of slaves becoming well-to-do heirs. Slaves had few privileges. Working from dawn to dusk for low wages offered them little opportunity to accumulate wealth. Harsh treatment and abuse made their lives difficult. What was most egregious, however, was seeing the freedoms and privileges of the beloved children of their masters.

Who wants to be a slave when one can be a favored child? Someone owned the slave, but a son or daughter lived in freedom, enjoyed favor, and was entitled to the inheritance. A child had special rights and advantages denied the slave. That happened to us when we believed in Jesus Christ. We went from bondage to adult children of the greatest family on earth. Based on our new identity, we became members of God's family. Paul declares, "So in Christ Jesus you are all children of God through faith" (Gal 3:26).

We used to be slaves to the spiritual forces aligned against God (v 3), but once we believed in Christ the Spirit entered our lives. God sent his Son to purchase our freedom from slavery and sent the Spirit of his Son to adopt us into his family. As such, we received the full rights as his children. Trying to earn these privileges by keeping the law would only plunge us back into slavery to be held captive to the principalities and powers of the world. Why do that, Paul warns, when we know we are God's children?

God sent the Spirit of his Son into our hearts because we are his sons and daughters. Since the Spirit makes us conscious of who we are in Christ, we should live as children of God and not as slaves.

Rhema: Every day, utter these wonderful affirmations: I am a child of God. I am an heir of the King of Kings. I am royalty. I enjoy tremendous rights and privileges. Jesus gave me a new identity. He adopted me into his family. He gave me access to his inheritance. I am purchased with a price. I have worth. I have significance. I am blessed.

OCTOBER 9 | GALATIANS 4:8–11

THE SPIRIT CRIES OUT ABBA FATHER

Because you are his sons, God sent the Spirit of his Son into our hearts, the Spirit who calls out, "Abba, Father." –GALATIANS 4:6

What makes us cry? The times when intense emotion overshadows all other concerns. Take childbirth: mothers delivering their children are not too concerned what others may think of them when excruciating pain grips them. The Bible presents another instance where widows and orphans howl in anguish because their landlords threw them out on the streets (Ex 22:23). The Psalmist David cries out to God when his enemies rose against him and he needed deliverance (Ps 3). The most natural time to cry out to God is during seasons of vulnerability and danger.

We do not cry just from sadness or pain but when joyfulness overwhelms us. Joy flooded the soul of Elizabeth and her baby jumped in her womb the day Mary, pregnant with Jesus, greeted her. Thrilled to pieces, Elizabeth cried out in a loud voice and prophesied (Lk 1:41–42f). Likewise, many a parent seeing their little "baby" graduate from college or get married leak tears of joy.

The indwelling Holy Spirit expresses tears of joy, inducing him to cry out, "Abba Father." He is thrilled with our new position in Christ and rejoices over the miraculous change in our circumstances. The one the Father sent into our hearts makes our intimate relationship with him real and personal. Because he is so happy with our glorious fortune as God's children, he must shout it out. How then can we stay silent when he effervesces in our redemption? We are no longer slaves in the Master's house, looking on with envy, but children; no longer beggars but heirs. "Abba Father" pulsates with joy and delight.

However, we must not overlook the fact the Spirit also cries within us what Jesus, the Son of God, cried in his sad hour of need. In Gethsemane he yelled "Abba, Father" to assure himself his Daddy would look after him.

Rhema: Therefore, whenever you are facing fear and the world pressing in, the Spirit of God's Son will assure you your heavenly Father will watch over you. In your darkest hour the Spirit will cuddle you and in a moment of tender intimacy will weep, "All will be well, my child."

BORN BY THE POWER OF THE SPIRIT

At that time the son born according to the flesh persecuted the son born by the power of the Spirit. It is the same now. –GALATIANS 4:29

The Galatians were born again by the power of the Spirit but those born of the flesh were persecuting them. To address the situation, Paul allegorizes the biblical story of Abraham's two sons, Ishmael and Isaac (v 24). Although he fathered both, Ishmael represents those born according to the flesh and Isaac those born by the Spirit. They illustrate two different ways to secure sonship and eternal life.

We either obtain salvation by works and keep the OT law or by faith and receive it as a gift. Those born in the natural way like Ishmael strive to curry God's favor and blessing in their own power. They put confidence in the flesh as a way to secure a favored status with God and gain a "share in the inheritance" (v 30) but they never succeed.

Unusual circumstances accompanied the births of Abraham's two sons. Isaac was a miracle baby because his parents were beyond the age of childbearing. God promised Abraham an heir to his vast fortune but as the years go by without a son, he took matters into his own hands. Because of Sarah's age she gave permission to her husband to father an heir by Hagar, her slave. The slave woman gave birth to Ishmael, but his birth did not fulfil God's promise. So God assured Abraham his wife would bear him an heir. Soon thereafter Sarah gave birth to Isaac—he was a child of promise.

Isaac came into existence because the mighty Holy Spirit fulfilled the promise. His remarkable supernatural birth parallels our new birth experience when we believe the gospel. Just like Isaac we are "children of promise" (v 28). We are the fond and beloved children of God who enjoy a privileged life.

Rhema: When you are born by the power of the Spirit, you need not try to secure God's favor and inheritance by performing the works of the law. That would make you a slave like Ishmael who was turfed out of the house (vv 30–31). Instead, like Isaac you are an heir, born to live in freedom and entitled to your heavenly Father's inheritance.

OCTOBER 11 | GALATIANS 5:1–12

THE SPIRIT KEEPS OUR HOPE ALIVE

*For through the **Spirit** we eagerly await by faith the righteousness for which we hope.* –GALATIANS 5:5

Imagine the faith a trapeze artist must employ when flying through the air. In the moment between letting go of one bar and grabbing another she has nothing to hold on to but faith. She believes another bar will be there just at the right time.

Many in Paul's ministry struggled with letting go of the law and relying upon the Spirit. They asked, "If I do not keep the law will I not crash and lose out with God?" When we relinquish our trust in the law, we hope something better will take its place. That is what Paul is assuring us in this verse.

Paul feared the Galatians were going to change their minds and return to the law. Outsiders had asserted they must be circumcised to be saved because they believed it was a symbolic sign of being right with God. The apostle replied, "You can't do that without suffering dire consequences. Trying to improve upon the Spirit's work by adding a little of this and a little of that is full of risk. Here is what it means to replace reliance on the Spirit with self-effort. You place yourself again under the yoke of slavery (v 1). Christ becomes of no value to you (v 2). You compel yourself to obey the whole law (v 3). You alienate yourself from Christ (v 4). And, you have fallen away from grace (v 4).

Too often people have told us we can't be saved unless we do this or stop that. The righteousness that comes from God, in contrast, is through the Spirit. He takes the effectual accomplishments of Christ on the cross and applies them to our lives. We are children of promise, born of the Spirit. God sends the Spirit of his Son into our hearts to empower us to live righteous lives. One more thing: on the day of our glorification, the Spirit will raise our bodies from the dead and perfect us, making us incapable of sin. That is what we believe, and that is our hope the Holy Spirit keeps alive.

Rhema: *To keep hope alive we must be ever so careful we do not substitute works for faith and the flesh for the Spirit.*

OCTOBER 12 | GALATIANS 5:13–18

WALKING IN THE SPIRIT

So I say, walk by the **Spirit***, and you will not gratify the desires of the flesh.* **–GALATIANS 5:16**

How are we supposed to live for God? Following the regulations in the OT law offers us no hope of ever pleasing him. Such attempts not only place us under a curse (3:10) but burden us with a yoke of slavery (v 1). For these reasons, Christ came to set us free from the law and its harsh requirements. The answer to this crucial question is: "Walk by the Spirit."

To walk by the Spirit means to conduct ourselves in accordance to a new spiritual reality. From the moment we are born from above, the Spirit enters our lives and gives us a new nature with a heart after God. He makes us capable of hearing his voice and empowers us to overcome our sinful natures. The Spirit is the new supervisor of our lives. We hear the voice of God and become prophetic because the Spirit reveals Jesus to us. By the revelation of the Spirit we know Jesus is the Son of God who takes away the sin of the world. We realize we are sinners in need of God's grace. Only by the Spirit can we confess with our mouth Jesus is Lord. In simple terms, walking by the Spirit is continuing to live in the realm of the Spirit and follow his leading.

This does not mean we are free to do anything we want. Although we are free from the law, we are not free from Christ. Instead of the OT law being our moral, ethical, and spiritual compass, the Holy Spirit is. He will not lead us into sin, but he empowers us to live free from sin, something the law could never do. Obeying him means we "will not gratify the desires of the flesh."

Even when we walk in the Spirit, the possibility of sin still exists. Our fallen human nature will rise up, but the Spirit prevents its complete expression. Instead of focusing our lives around self-interest, the Spirit floods our hearts with God's love. Then we can serve one another in love (v 13) and live up to the law's requirement (v 14).

Rhema: *The antidote to a life dominated by the flesh is to walk according to the Spirit.*

THE FLESH DESIRES WHAT IS CONTRARY TO THE SPIRIT

*For the flesh desires what is contrary to the **Spirit**, and the Spirit what is contrary to the flesh. They are in conflict with each other, so that you are not to do whatever you want.* **–GALATIANS 5:17**

Living the Christian life can be compared to a tug-of-war. Two teams line up in opposition to each other along a rope, face to face, to test their respective strengths. Each team pulls with all its might to gain predominance. The battle is constant until one side draws the other over to its side. A tug-of-war is going on inside of us between the flesh and the Spirit.

The flesh does not want us to live according to the Spirit. It is happier, for example, when believers cave into it by biting and devouring each other (v 15). Paul says "The acts of the flesh are obvious: sexual immorality, impurity and debauchery; idolatry and witchcraft; hatred, discord, jealousy, fits of rage, selfish ambition, dissensions, factions and envy; drunkenness, orgies, and the like" (vv 19–21). We can define the flesh as our fallen human nature bent towards wickedness. It teams us with the world and the devil to wage war against God.

When we are born of the Spirit, however, the flesh is not eradicated but remains in opposition to the Spirit. Neither the flesh nor the Spirit is in full possession of us. The flesh is furious because the Spirit has given us a new nature, freed us from its enslaving power, and transformed our behavior and disposition. The battle is on! Whenever we set our hearts on pleasing God, our old carnal nature wars against us. Every time we attempt something good, the flesh tries to end it.

A day does not go by without the flesh resisting and rebelling against the indwelling Holy Spirit. Its desires are contrary to everything the Spirit desires. It fosters hate instead of love. Moral corruption instead of purity. Dissension instead of unity. Selfishness instead of kindness. Occult practices instead of worshiping the one true God.

Rhema: In this spiritual duel, we are the battleground that will determine the winner. If we yield to the desires of our fallen nature God's enemy wins, but if we walk in the Spirit God's team wins.

OCTOBER 14 | PSALM 5:1–12

THE SPIRIT DESIRES WHAT IS CONTRARY TO THE FLESH

*For the flesh desires what is contrary to the Spirit, and the **Spirit** what is contrary to the flesh. They are in conflict with each other, so that you are not to do whatever you want.* –GALATIANS 5:17

Thank God we are not at the mercy of the flesh. It desires to destroy us, ruin our relationships, and make every person a stage upon which evil is performed. God has given a way out, a supernatural power to live without succumbing to the old nature. We have a promise: if we will walk in the Spirit, we will not gratify the desires of the flesh. God has filled us with a power much greater than the flesh, so we can glorify him in every sphere of our lives. The more we give sway to the Holy Spirit, the more we control our carnal natures.

The Spirit wars against our sinful indulgences. It is natural to want to do what the flesh desires, but the Spirit stands up to fight it with force and ferocity. With unrelenting effort he opposes every sinful tendency the carnal nature craves. The Spirit wants us to do the will of our heavenly Father and live free of sin's power.

God's Spirit gives us a new orientation. He provides us with a different way to live because he has regenerated our hearts, renewed our minds, and reformed our disposition. Therefore, we are no longer the powerless pawns of the world, the flesh and the devil. Of course, following the Spirit is not automatic but the result of an intentional determination. As people born of the Spirit and operating under his power, we must no longer tolerate indulging our fallen human nature.

Rhema: Every thought and deed reflects a corresponding desire of either the flesh or the Spirit. We should ask ourselves which one is influencing us. By identifying our motivation, we realize if we are walking in the Spirit or according to our sinful passions. The flesh lusts for our ruination, the destruction of others, and rebellion against God. The Spirit by contrast desires what is best for us, what is a loving response towards others, and what glorifies God. We decide whether we will sow to the flesh or to the Spirit (6:8).

OCTOBER 15 | JEREMIAH 31:31–34

LED BY THE SPIRIT

But if you are led by the Spirit, you are not under the law.
–GALATIANS 5:18

Life is a journey filled with heartache and joy, hardship and celebration. Many challenges along the way test our courage and faith. Sometimes life seems like a war zone laden with landmines. Other times we lie down in green pastures to restore our souls. Regardless of where we are on the journey, we need a capable guide.

The Holy Spirit plays many roles in our lives. For one he is our Sherpa, knowledgeable and experienced, filled with phenomenal energy to guide us through life's challenges. As important as it is to guide us on the journey of life, the Holy Spirit leads us in the far more important pathway of moral management. To be led by the Spirit means we subjugate our will to his and follow his leadership. Moment by moment he directs our lives in the moral obedience of faith.

In the real world of Christian living, only one way has God's full approval. We must allow his Spirit to take us by the hand and guide our thoughts and behavior. Authentic morality for a follower of Christ is dependent upon the Spirit because only he can reshape our inner world. When we attune every ethical and moral decision to his leading, our character and actions will please the Father. We do not need the law of Moses to whip us into shape or restrain us because we have the Spirit as a moral compass.

Orienting our lives to the Spirit makes adherence to the law unnecessary. The aim of the external code was to point us to love God and love our neighbor as ourselves. Who better to help us love one another and to love God than the Spirit? Because he leads us in the way of love, the law is redundant. That old era is finished. To return to it brings a curse and enslavement to the elemental powers of the earth.

Rhema: What a blessing to have the Spirit as our guide and not have to make those tough decisions on our own. He knows the pitfalls, those nasty traps that ensnare and ruin life and rob us of joy. We are not under a curse when we follow him but under heaven's blessing.

OCTOBER 16 | MATTHEW 7:15–20

THE FRUIT OF THE SPIRIT

But the fruit of the **Spirit** *is love, joy, peace, forbearance, kindness, good-ness, faithfulness, gentleness and self-control. Against such things there is no law.* **–GALATIANS 5:22–23**

What happens when we allow the Spirit to lead us? We exhibit the character of Jesus because the Spirit produces in us the moral qualities God desires. Love is at the top of the list because it fulfills the law. All the other virtues flow from it. Instead of bitterness and conflict, we exhibit joy and peace. Instead of fits of rage, forbearance and kindness. Goodness supersedes malice. Faithfulness is exchanged for fickleness. Gentleness prevents divisions and factions. Self-control supplants sexual immorality and drunkenness. A pleasant cluster of Christlike characteristics grows out of a life lived in the Spirit's power.

The fruit of the Spirit is in sharp contrast to the works of the sinful nature. Fruit develops when we allow the Spirit to control us. Each virtue bursts with life because people living in an atmosphere of love, joy, and peace thrive. Shower kindness, goodness, and faithful-ness upon individuals and they blossom. On the other hand, the deeds of the flesh damage and destroy because anger, sexual unfaithfulness, and hatred blow relationships apart. We must watch what we say or do around angry, jealous, and selfish people because anything might set them off. Therefore, the works of the flesh have no part in the kingdom of God (v 21).

What the Spirit creates comes from love in action. Faith, for exam-ple, needs to express itself in love (v 6). To encourage the dear saints to perform the works of the law had only created a toxic environ-ment—they were "biting and devouring each other" (v 15). Legalism chokes the life out of people, families, and organizations. The antidote is not more rules but more of the Holy Spirit flowing through their lives. It is easy to "serve one another in love" (v 13) when the fruit of the Spirit permeates the place.

Rhema: Against such things there is no law (v 23). Each of these Spirit-generated virtues goes above and beyond the law. There is nothing in Scripture that forbids love or kindness. Showing gentleness and self-control never condemned anyone. The law never finds fault with virtue because if everyone had it, a need for law would cease to exist.

OCTOBER 17 | GALATIANS 2:15–21

WE LIVE BY THE SPIRIT

*Since we live by the **Spirit**, let us keep in step with the Spirit.*
—GALATIANS 5:25

Walk in the Spirit. Be led by the Spirit. And now, "Live by the Spirit." Three times in just a few verses we see the indispensable importance of the Holy Spirit for followers of Christ. We are free! To live by the Spirit means we have a fresh start, a new beginning. The driving impulse is neither the flesh nor the law. It is something new, empowering, wonderful. We enjoy a new way to do life. Living by the Spirit is more than a concept—it means to live in harmony with the indwelling presence of God.

We are all controlled by something—a set of rules, societal norms, a palette of principles, or our sinful passions. Being in Christ, however, means he is the one leading us by his Spirit. His passions, desires, will, and nature flow into us as a pure crystal-clear stream. His Spirit lifts us to the highest ethical plane, above laws, rules, and principles. No one ever lived a more God-pleasing and perfect life than Jesus. His extraordinary life finds expression in us through the blessed Spirit. No ethical system is better or higher than the one the Spirit orchestrates for us in Christ. Living by the Spirit is not unbridled "freedom to indulge the sinful nature" (v13). Rather, we soar as an eagle to catch the updrafts of the breath of God.

When you live a Spirit-directed life, you are connected to the eternal. No longer must you rely on your own strength for spiritual growth. You are born of God! The Spirit in you acquaints you with the transforming power of the world to come. The energy to bring about the new creation renews your mind, directs your steps, and floods your heart with the love of God. You have sprung to life. Your heart, mind, body, and soul are in direct contact with endless life because eternity is in you.

Rhema: In the Spirit, we walk, talk, and live in the kingdom of God. Therefore, we can understand spiritual things and behold God himself at work. Our life in the Spirit begins with the new birth and continues without end. So live by the Spirit!

OCTOBER 18 | ACTS 15:1–29

KEEPING IN STEP WITH THE SPIRIT

*Since we live by the Spirit, let us keep in step with the **Spirit**.*
–GALATIANS 5:25

See the army marching, every soldier in step. The commander sets the pace and each soldier adjusts their stride to achieve uniformity with him. Paul may have this in mind when he snaps the order, "Keep in step with the Spirit." He is commanding this disorderly congregation to get in line with the Spirit. To stay in unison requires frequent realignments if they are to harmonize their lives with the Spirit in the absence of the written code. Their moral code is none other than the revealed desires of the Third Person of the Trinity. Therefore, he exhorts them to "toe the line" by placing their toes in line with the Spirit.

God has done so much for us in saving us we may ask if anything is left for us to do. The answer is yes. Life in the Spirit calls for cooperative action between him and ourselves. We are obliged to conform to the standard set by the Spirit. Although he is within us, we need to give evidence of it by a lifestyle guided by him. Our moral imperative by which we regulate our lives is to keep in step with the Spirit.

This means we have a new command. Paul does not say keep the law but line up your life with the Spirit. This is God's rule for regulating our lives in the new era of freedom. When we are born of the Spirit, we receive a plain marching order: "Let your conduct be in harmony with him!"

This simple rule has amazing consequences. For one thing, putting our toes to the line produces uniformity. Following the Spirit leaves no room for arrogance (v 26) because we are not adhering to any person's standard. We do not have to contend with jealousy, self-interest, or divergent points of view when everyone is in step with the Spirit (Acts 15:28). No individual can point to himself or herself as the criterion for judging others because everyone is following the Spirit.

Rhema: Since we are free in the Lord, God forbid the conscience of another should rule us. No doubt Paul means this when he says, "For why is my freedom being judged by another's conscience?" (I Cor 10:29).

OCTOBER 19 | GALATIANS 6:1–6; II SAMUEL 12:1–14

RESTORING BELIEVERS
WITH THE SPIRIT'S HELP

Brothers and sisters, if someone is caught in a sin, you who live by the **Spirit** *should restore that person gently. But watch yourselves, or you also may be tempted.* **–GALATIANS 6:1**

How do we carry out the new moral imperative of staying in step with the Spirit, especially as it relates to moral failure among believers? Toeing the line seems more like walking on a razor's edge than living in freedom from all the dos and don'ts others are so quick to impose upon us. We must not rely on the flesh for moral improvement. But when one succumbs to the fallen nature, rely upon the Holy Spirit to help restore that person.

If a believer sins, we can guarantee he or she was not living in harmony with the Spirit. What do we do? How should we respond if they have lied, cheated, or worse? We could let our old cranky, impatient, unloving, spiteful, fallen human nature retaliate with anger, cruelty, or coldness. But then we are not responding as people of the Spirit. Consequently, the best people to handle sin are those with spiritual gifts especially when their lives express gentleness, the fruit of the Spirit.

How Nathan, the prophet, dealt with King David after he committed adultery and murder is an example of the Spirit's help. The all-knowing Spirit revealed a word of knowledge to Nathan telling him of David's dastardly deeds. With that insight, he did not go and say, "David, you are one despicable louse—you are a terrible sinner." Instead, he approached the king in the Spirit's gentleness and told him a parable—a veritable word of wisdom. After hearing Nathan's outrageous story, David burned with anger not realizing the prophet was describing him. Only then did Nathan say to him, "You are the man." With the supernatural help of the Spirit, he restored David.

Rhema: Powerful and effective results occur when people rely on the Spirit's help in these thorny issues. The Spirit wants to help us restore those who have engaged in acts of the sinful nature (5:19–20). Too many times believers fail to utilize spiritual aid when handling difficult moral failures. Therefore, people with the Spirit who have both spiritual gifts and the spirituality should deal with erring believers.

OCTOBER 20 | GALATIANS 6:7–10

SOWING TO PLEASE THE SPIRIT

*Whoever sows to please their flesh, from the flesh will reap destruction; whoever sows to please the **Spirit**, from the Spirit will reap eternal life.*
–GALATIANS 6:8

We reap what we sow; the law of the harvest (v 7) applies to the flesh as well as the Spirit. Make no mistake sowing to the flesh has serious repercussions. That is why the apostle warns of reaping destruction (v 8). God has so designed the world that the one who scatters wild oats will reap one trouble after another. If we sow to please the Spirit, alternatively, we will reap one blessing after another. The wonderful blessings of God are a direct consequence of pursuing the Spirit.

What does it mean to sow to please the Spirit? Paul has previously told us. Serve one another in love (5:13). Crucify the sinful nature with its passions and desires (5:24). Restore erring believers with the Spirit's gentleness (v 1). Carry each other's burdens (v 2). Take responsibility for one's own life (v 5) and support the ministry with one's finances (v 6). It means to do good to everyone, especially to those who belong to the family of God (v 10). Focusing on the Spirit results in a series of daily choices to please God and benefit others. Just as a farmer plants his seed in the soil, we are to cast spiritual seed into the soil of our relationships. When we do this we reap life, blessing, and joy.

To set our minds on the things of the flesh, by contrast, is destructive. Biting and devouring one another (5:15) sprouts from the sinful nature. As does sexual immorality, rage, discord, selfish ambition, and the like (5:19–21). Indulging the fallen nature (5:13) germinates conceit, frustration, and envy (5:26). Nothing ruins relationships faster than deeds of the carnal nature. These actions have ravaged congregations, destroyed marriages, and devastated friendships.

Rhema: To live our lives by investing in the Spirit is a decision against the flesh and for God. The more we sow to please the Spirit, the more we will harvest good in this life and the next. The Spirit will always lead us to fulfill God's purposes for human existence and glorify God. A lifestyle focused on the things of the Spirit will produce the harvest of eternal life.

OCTOBER 21 | GALATIANS 6:11–18; JOHN 5:24–30

REAPING ETERNAL LIFE FROM THE SPIRIT

Whoever sows to please their flesh, from the flesh will reap destruction;
whoever sows to please the Spirit, from the **Spirit** *will reap eternal life.*
–GALATIANS 6:8

Eternal life does not begin after death; it begins when we are born of the Spirit. Everyone who believes in Jesus Christ "has eternal life" (Jn 3:16, 36). It continues throughout our time on earth and reaches its climax in the resurrection and the coming of Jesus. Our present spiritual experience is the "life of the ages" to come.

Having the Spirit means we already possess the eternal life of God. Jesus declared that we have passed from death unto life (Jn 5:24). Because the Spirit makes us alive, we enjoy many of heaven's blessings. The one sent from heaven infuses our lives with the love, peace, and joy of the kingdom of God. So we drink of the living water that wells up into eternal life. And we eat the manna from heaven. Jesus said, "The Spirit gives life" (Jn 6:63). He gives the life of the "living God." The life of the "I am that I am." And the life of the one who is the resurrection and the life.

Where the Spirit is there is life—abundant life, life surpassing. The kind of life he gives is packed with the blessing and presence of God. "This is eternal life: that they know you, the only true God, and Jesus Christ, whom you have sent" (Jn 17:3). Such is possible only through the Spirit. It transcends all ages and is forevermore, a life without ceasing. Abundant life. Every time we please the Spirit, the seeds we sow germinate and become the harvest fruit of heaven's fullness. It will continue day after day and will never fade. We already are experiencing in measure the reality of heaven.

Rhema: The harvest corresponds to the sowing. What we sow is what we receive. Those who sow to the wind will reap the whirlwind, but those who sow to the Spirit will reap heaven's blessings. The present is an opportunity to plant seeds and prepare for heaven because the more we sow the more we reap. Let us appropriate by faith the unseen yet real realities of eternal life as we live in the power of the Spirit.

OCTOBER 22 | EPHESIANS 1:1–14

BRANDED WITH THE HOLY SPIRIT

When you believed, you were marked in him with a seal, the promised **Holy Spirit**, *who is a deposit guaranteeing our inheritance until the redemption of those who are God's possession—to the praise of his glory.* **–EPHESIANS 1:13–14**

In the American West, cowboys branded their cattle with a red-hot iron to show ownership. More often today's tattoos, tags, or a microchip serve the same purpose. On the open range herds from different owners could mix, but at roundup time there was no misunderstanding about ownership. The term "branding" comes from an ancient word for burning. With the fire of the Holy Spirit, God the Father brands everyone who believes in Jesus. "When you believed, you were marked." God brands us with the fire-heated mark of the Holy Spirit to show we are his.

You bear the proof God owns you and will protect you. When you encounter the devil's schemes and must battle the principalities and powers of the air (6:10–12), you can point to the brand. Then you can say, "Devil, you have no claim on me because having the indwelling Spirit proves I belong to God." On that basis, you can direct the enemy and every demon of hell to God. The hostile forces "in the heavenlies" cannot have you, so be strong in the Lord and stand firm.

With ownership comes privilege. Our heavenly Father "has blessed us in the heavenly realms with every spiritual blessing in Christ" (v 3). The book of Ephesians begins by enumerating them—chosen (v 4), predestined (v 5), redeemed (v 7), and enlightened (v 9). We experience these through the Spirit because we are "in Christ." He appropriates the myriad blessings provided us through the finished work of Christ and lavishes them on us. Anyone without the Spirit is not Christ's and has no eternal inheritance, but the imprint of the Holy Spirit, however, guarantees our final destiny.

Rhema: Branded with the Holy Spirit is a metaphor to sum up your favored position in Christ. It refers to your ongoing dynamic experiences in the Holy Spirit in which he opens your mind to revelation (v 17) and gives you access to the Father (2:18). The Spirit whom God deposited into your heart makes you his and shows that your wonderful future has already begun.

OCTOBER 23 | EPHESIANS 1:15–23

THE SPIRIT OF WISDOM AND REVELATION

*I keep asking that the God of our Lord Jesus Christ, the glorious Father, may give you the **Spirit** of wisdom and revelation, so that you may know him better.* **–EPHESIANS 1:17**

D o you want to know Jesus better? Do you want to grasp the enormous power of God's might available to you? Do you want to understand the riches of his glorious inheritance? Paul's answer may surprise you because it so differs from what many say. He doesn't tell his readers to find themselves a great teacher, prophet, or apostle and sit at their feet. They already had that. He doesn't tell them to read the latest bestseller for they already had his letter. No, he tells them the revelation of these things comes as an answer to prayer for more of the Holy Spirit.

We need to ask God to give us the Spirit of wisdom and revelation so we can know Jesus better. Revelation was not confined to the apostles nor did it cease with them. Otherwise he would not have instructed his readers to pray to receive it through the Spirit. Paul sees spiritual understanding as an ongoing and necessary work of the Spirit. If believers refuse to walk and live in the Spirit, they will not proceed far in their walk with the Lord.

Remember what Jesus said about knowing him better. He said the Spirit is our teacher, the one who will reveal the truth about him (Jn 16:13–15). Paul knows that, and he realizes we will never understand the "unsearchable riches of Christ" (v 3:8) unless the Spirit opens the eyes of our heart. Our growth and maturity as believers depends upon the Spirit. We need him to help us apprehend what God has accomplished for us in Christ Jesus.

Rhema: We can petition God, the Father, for a greater work of the Holy Spirit in our lives. When he works in us, we can know by experience more and more of what God has done for us. The Spirit wants to take us beyond mere head knowledge to a dynamic lived experience. Then he will open our eyes to our hope of the "riches of his glorious inheritance" (v 18) and the "incomparably great power for us who believe" (v 19). Ask him!

OCTOBER 24 | EPHESIANS 2:1–18

ACCESS TO THE FATHER BY THE SPIRIT

For through him we both have access to the Father by one **Spirit**.
—EPHESIANS 2:18

Heaven is not cloud nine. Heaven is the eternal city, the dwelling place of God (Heb 12:22–24). We have access to it because we can approach God through the saving death of Jesus Christ. We do not enter in our own strength, position, or power but our right of admission is because of Christ. The Spirit enables us to come before the Father as a present reality (Heb 12:22–24).

Think about this long and hard—we enjoy real, genuine access to GOD! Everything the Father, Son, and Holy Spirit accomplished in saving us is to bring us to this one glorious end. Access to God is the most important reality in our lives. Death is expulsion from his presence; life is to dwell with him forever. For sure, being with God in eternity is our hope but we can revel in his presence here and now. The certainty of being seated with Christ in heavenly places (v 6) is real. This very moment, in Christ and through the Spirit we sit before his majesty.

Access to God is a magnificent privilege. To illustrate: in political circles, connection to influential people extends to only a few. People covet this favor because they can ask for favors and things happen. The elite and famous of this world grant access to friends, close family members, and a small inner circle. Clearance and background checks are required but, more importantly, their reason for admission must be compelling. Not anyone has the freedom to speak to them, but God grants us direct and intimate access to himself by the Spirit because we are his children.

Rhema: To help you realize your extraordinary right, the Spirit cries within you, "Abba Father." When you draw near to God in the Spirit, you are approaching the Father for family time to speak and listen to him. Great things can happen when you implore him face to face. Understanding. Enlightenment. Revelation. Answers to prayer. Faith. Vision. Like Jesus you can see what the Father is doing (Jn 5:19). By the Spirit glorious things will be revealed to you, things that no eye has seen or ear heard, or mind has ever conceived (I Cor 2:9–10).

OCTOBER 25 | EPHESIANS 2:19–22; HEBREWS 12:18–24

BECOMING GOD'S DWELLING PLACE
BY THE SPIRIT

*And in him you too are being built together to become a dwelling in which God lives by his **Spirit**.* –EPHESIANS 2:22

Can we experience the presence of God day after day? To do so, we need not make a pilgrimage to a holy place or climb a sacred mountain (Jn 4:21–24). Paul is addressing the Gentiles and surprises them by saying, "You are his temple. You are built on the foundation of the apostles and prophets with Jesus as the cornerstone. You are God's dwelling place where you can encounter him through the Spirit." God wants to fellowship with us and reveal his Shekinah glory.

The term "Shekinah" does not occur in the Bible, but Jewish rabbis coined the word to refer to God's manifested presence. They used it to refer to his presence in Eden, Mt. Sinai, the cloud and pillar of fire in the wilderness, and the supernatural fire burning between the cherubim in the tabernacle and temple. In every age God has manifested his presence. In the gospels Jesus was the Shekinah, the eternal word "dwelling" among us. He said, "If you have seen me you have seen the Father." In the church age, however, God's manifested presence, his Shekinah glory, is experienced in the Holy Spirit. Therefore, the Spirit is essential if we are to enter and enjoy God's presence today.

Through the Holy Spirit you can see, hear, and commune with your heavenly Father. Intimacy with your eternal, immortal, and invisible King is now possible. We are his holy temple, a place created for God to inhabit through the Spirit and make himself known. God's OT people had their temple where he dwelt in the holy of holies, but access was restricted to the High Priest once a year. We, however, are God's holy house where he lives by his Spirit.

When we worship God in the Spirit, we are offering sacrifices of praise and thanksgiving. We sing songs of the Spirit to one another and make music in our hearts to the Lord. Since the Spirit displays God's presence, glorious and marvelous things happen (I Cor 12:6). Spiritual gifts operate—faith, revelation, prophecy. Heaven descends and settles among us.

Rhema: *Let us worship him in the Spirit and let his glorious presence fill this place.*

OCTOBER 26 | EPHESIANS 3:1–13

THE SPIRIT REVEALS THE
MYSTERY OF THE CHURCH

*In reading this, then, you will be able to understand my insight into the mystery of Christ, which was not made known to people in other generations as it has now been revealed by the **Spirit** to God's holy apostles and prophets.* **–EPHESIANS 3:4–5**

American novelist Anne Lamott said, "I do not at all understand the mystery of grace— only that it meets us where we are but does not leave us where it found us." She has captured the essence and mystery of the gospel (v 6). The term "mystery" occurs seven times in the book of Ephesians and four in this chapter alone. It refers to a secret God kept to himself from before the foundation of the world. He devised a top-secret plan for his creation so outrageous it would blow the socks off people (vv 9–10). Although hidden to earlier generations, the Spirit revealed it to the apostles and prophets upon the founding of the church.

The Spirit disclosed to them the mystery of God's secret plan for this universe. What could he do with his fallen creatures and his sin-cursed creation? The planet was in rebellion, incited and dominated by his archenemy. Instead of patching up the old creation racked and ruined by sin, he would begin with a complete new creation in Christ.

The first visible result of God's unfolding mystery was the formation of the church composed of Spirit-born Jews and Gentiles. The Spirit did not reveal his secret plan to the OT prophets but to the NT apostles and prophets. His secret was to restore his creation to its original purpose. God brought the church into existence to carry out his powerful eternal plan. Not the devil, not any demon or person can foil God's scheme to bring history to a glorious end in Christ through the church. The reconciliation of Jews and Gentiles to form a new humanity as the body of Christ prophesies God's ultimate triumph over evil.

Rhema: The divine mystery is playing itself out on the world stage and you are part of it. God's eternal purposes inaccessible to human knowledge before the birth of the church was revealed by the Spirit. By his grace, God has called you to join him in remaking the universe.

OCTOBER 27 | EPHESIANS 3:14–21

BECOMING MIGHTY THROUGH THE SPIRIT

*I pray that out of his glorious riches he may strengthen you with power through his **Spirit** in your inner being, so that Christ may dwell in your hearts through faith.* **—EPHESIANS 3:16–17**

God's inexhaustible power is available to you. When you feel weak as a wet noodle, you can be strong. The Lord does not want you living in defeat or too feeble to do something for him. Rather, he longs for you "to be strong in the Lord and in his mighty power" (6:10) and be filled with "all the fullness of God" (v 19).

Many believers have never considered the extent of God's power at their disposal. They never ask for it and possibly never understood it was available. The word "power" means ability to do something, a capability. Paul realized his own apostolic ministry resulted from God's power working through him (v 7). The Spirit must show us God's "incomparably great power" now residing within (1:19). By faith, we can bring his ability to raise the dead (1:19–20) into our current situations. We need to release his dynamic energy and put it to work.

Ask God for his strength to work in you. What will it do? Through the Spirit, the power of God will strengthen you at the center of your inner being. In that way, Christ becomes more powerful in your life. The more you experience the Spirit's might, the more you can live and act like Christ. Then you can replace your fear and trepidation with boldness and confidence. Instead of doubt and discouragement, your inner being will become strong and energized. You can do all things through him who strengthens you (Phil 4:13). His power will help you love the unlovely and comprehend God's amazing love (vv 17–19). You will walk in victory instead of defeat.

Rhema: God does not intend for the enemy to control and dominate you. He provides his Spirit to strengthen you so you can stand firm against the devil (6:10f). Regardless of Satan's schemes, accessing God's infinite power will make you formidable. Jesus is Lord, not the devil. God wants to fill you with himself because he "is able to do immeasurably more than all [you] ask or imagine, according to his power that is at work within [you]" (v 20).

OCTOBER 28 | EPHESIANS 4:1–16

KEEPING THE UNITY OF THE SPIRIT

*Make every effort to keep the unity of the **Spirit** through the bond of peace.* –EPHESIANS 4:3

Why is it so hard to live in peace and harmony? With so many people of different personalities, backgrounds, and social standings, society struggles to stay unified. Countries turn on each other. Couples break up. Even churches split. How then do we stay together? The simple answer is to allow the Holy Spirit to work continuously among us. What destroys the bonds of peace are the deeds of the flesh. Displays of the fallen human nature shatter relationships. Self-interests, personal agendas, and big egos war against the Spirit. Factions, divisions, and pride are cancers eating away at the unity created by the Spirit.

Essential to preserving peace are four spiritual virtues: humility, gentleness, patience, and forbearance (v 2). They are antithetical to the flesh and promote peaceful relationships. Humility is the proper evaluation of oneself in the light of what Christ has done. Who of us can boast when we are saved by grace through faith and not by works? Gentleness is like oil poured on troubled waters. It takes others into consideration and treats them with respect and courtesy. The third virtue is patience. People under the Spirit's influence do not explode like firecrackers. Instead, they deploy a long fuse and make allowances for the shortcomings of others. Forbearance means treating the failures and weaknesses of others with love. All these emanate from the Spirit working in our lives to make us more like Christ.

Spare no effort to keep the unity of the Spirit, Paul implored. God does not ask us to create unity because the Spirit has already done that. Our task is to preserve and protect it. In fact, we are to make it a priority. Why is this imperative so important? God designed the church to bring unity to this world. In Christ, he destroyed longstanding divisions. Unity is the proof the gospel works.

Rhema: We show the unity of the Spirit through the bond of peace. God's Spirit glues us together in one indissoluble bond. When he has his way, we learn to interact well, resolve conflicts peacefully, and make memories together. Therefore, we must commit ourselves to living in harmony with all the members of God's family by walking in the Spirit.

OCTOBER 29 | PSALM 133; JOHN 17:20–26

ONE BODY AND ONE SPIRIT

*There is one body and one **Spirit**, just as you were called to one hope when you were called; one Lord, one faith, one baptism; one God and Father of all, who is over all and through all and in all.* –EPHESIANS 4:4–6

In the world we find little agreement and accord, but in God there is profound unity. The Father, Son, and Holy Spirit, mentioned here, are diverse among themselves yet they remain one. They form the basis of seven foundational realities constituting our unity. One body. One Spirit. One hope. One Lord. One faith. One baptism. One God. In the same way, despite our differences believers are called upon to reflect God's image and unity.

The church is one indivisible body owing its existence and organic unity to the Spirit. God has called the bride to take part in the hope of achieving cosmic unity throughout his creation. Through Christ God reconciled "to himself all things, whether things on earth or things in heaven, by making peace through his blood, shed on the cross" (Col 1:20). Our Lord's death, therefore, provides the basis for bringing all things together in glorious harmony and restore creation to the way it was before sin disrupted it.

In fact, our peace and harmony show the principalities and powers of the air God will ultimately unify all things in Christ. The cross is God's means of destroying the destroyer of peace. That is why we, the church, must "make every effort to keep the unity of the Spirit through the bond of peace" (v 3). In this one climactic event, God began to restore peace and harmony in his creation.

These wonderful unifying factors brought us together to form one body, his church, called to express God's all-encompassing unity. We affirm the supremacy of one God and Father who is over all, through all, and in all. He alone is the universal father of all that exists and the ground for our unanimity.

Rhema: God exists in three persons in perfect harmony. Each member of the Trinity seeks to bring about peace, agreement, and unity in the universe starting first with us. His church is a new reality in Christ where there is neither Jew nor Gentile, male nor female, bond nor free—we are all one in him.

OCTOBER 30 | EPHESIANS 4:17–32

DO NOT GRIEVE THE HOLY SPIRIT

*And do not grieve the **Holy Spirit** of God, with whom you were sealed for the day of redemption.* **–EPHESIANS 4:30**

Someone said the ones closest to us hurt us the most. The people in our lives we love the most can break our hearts. When they let us down or wrong us, it feels like they punched us in the gut. The same is true of the Holy Spirit. Since he himself is a person, he can be stricken with grief whenever believers hurt each other.

The one thing that inflicts the most pain and sorrow upon the Holy Spirit of God is sin that destroys relationships. Wounding God's people and causing discord distresses him to no end. His pain is an extreme emotional experience. Bitterness, slander, and anger towards those he indwells smacks him in the face. The Spirit strives to tie us together in communities of love, not tear us apart. People of the Spirit are expected to display the atmosphere of heaven not the fumes of hell.

Hurting our brothers and sisters is grievous to the Spirit because it gives the devil a foothold (v 27) in the church. This is the reason Paul says, "Watch your words making sure they are not hurtful but wholesome, helpful rather than destructive" (v 29). Additionally he says, "Get rid of all bitterness, rage and anger, brawling and slander, along with every form of malice" (v 31). A divided and bruised church gives Satan an opportunity to establish a stronghold from which he will introduce no end of mischief and evil. Know for sure he is the source of church discord.

We are members of one body (v 25) marked and identified with the Spirit to show we belong to God. If we make him sad, who will make us glad? Who will baptize us with the joy of heaven? The kingdom of God is righteousness, peace, and joy in the Holy Spirit (Rom 14:17). Therefore, when we are "kind and compassionate to one another, forgiving each other, just as in Christ God forgave [us]" (vv 31–32) he is overjoyed.

Rhema: It will go well for us if we do not grieve the Spirit and join him in preserving the unity of the congregation. But if we anger him it will not.

OCTOBER 31 | EPHESIANS 5:1–18

BE FILLED WITH THE SPIRIT

Do not get drunk on wine, which leads to debauchery. Instead, be filled with the Spirit. –EPHESIANS 5:18

In several ways getting drunk on wine and being filled with the Spirit are similar. Both alter our state of consciousness, make us feel confident, free and happy. But the end results are different. Drunkenness leads to debauchery. In other words, alcohol energizes the flesh, loosens inordinate lusts, and leads to sorrow. To live under the influence of the Spirit, conversely, leads to joy, wholeness, and countless blessings. It is far better to be full of the Spirit than inebriated.

Rather than get drunk, the apostle exhorts us to be taken over by the Spirit. He means every day allow the Spirit to control and change our lives. We need not worry about any excess as we can never get too much of him. Be drunk with the Spirit until all our faculties are under his pleasant influence. Using the drinking metaphor, he says, "Let your mind, your heart, your understanding, your inner being, and your behavior be sloshed with heaven's intoxicant. Drink in the Spirit until he inflames your body, soul and spirit with the passions of the holy one."

Some believers have no idea of the degree to which God wants them to enjoy his glorious salvation. A good saint, they believe, is dour and sober. To them the more misery they can heap upon themselves the better. Critics chided Jesus for having too much fun, but he came that we might have life. He saw himself as offering something the world could not—full, glorious, abundant life so our joy might be full. It is true we should not focus on the pleasures of this world but that does not mean avoiding the higher pleasures of God. He offers far more than happy hour.

We can always tell when someone is under the Spirit's influence. Paul lists three telltale signs. They are careful how they live (v 15); just the opposite of debauchery. Their behavior pleases the Lord (v 10) because they understand his will (v 17). They wisely make the most of every opportunity (v 16) because they realize the days are evil.

Rhema: Let us not satisfy ourselves with a sip but a generous supply of the Spirit.

NOVEMBER 1 | PSALM 40:1–3; EXODUS 15:1–21

SONGS FROM THE SPIRIT

*Instead, be filled with the Spirit, speaking to one another with psalms, hymns, and songs from the **Spirit**. Sing and make music from your heart to the Lord, always giving thanks to God the Father for everything, in the name of our Lord Jesus Christ.* –EPHESIANS 5:18–20

When Israel marched out of Egypt, she came out singing. When we come out of the world, the Spirit fills our soul with song. Our joyful celebration derives not from an excess of wine but from the fullness of the Spirit (v 18). He wants us to sing and make music from our hearts to celebrate our deliverance. Whenever the Spirit is moving in might and power, the church responds with new songs of praise.

We are first encouraged to address one another with songs from the Spirit. Worship is two-directional: horizontal and vertical. Someone said, "Worship is for an audience of one," but is this correct? The Spirit involves himself in the church not only so God is praised but further: so believers are instructed. The importance of gathering together is to teach and admonish one another (Col 3:16) with songs originating with the Spirit. Through the full range of expressions—hymns, psalms and odes—the Spirit helps us share the things of God with others.

Spirit-guided worship, moreover, involves the three persons of the Godhead. Because of the Spirit, the worshiping community gives thanks to God the Father in the name of the Lord Jesus Christ. With the powerful inspiration of the Spirit, we direct our hearts' melodies to the Lord. When the Spirit fills us, the core of our being explodes with heartfelt passion for Jesus. Like Moses and the Israelites, we sing new songs to the Lord and extol his greatness for he is a mighty warrior.

The most significant facet of Spirit-breathed worship is the infusion of the atmosphere of heaven. The throne and courts above vibrate with thunderous song (Rev 5:9, 12). Because the one sent from heaven indwells us, he causes our praise to mirror heaven. He escorts us into the awesome presence of God where we join the angels in singing heaven's songs (Heb 12:22–23).

Rhema: The Spirit fills our hearts with the beautiful music of heaven so we too can sing heaven's songs on earth.

NOVEMBER 2 | EPHESIANS 6:10–17

THE SWORD OF THE SPIRIT

*Take the helmet of salvation and the sword of the **Spirit**, which is the word of God.* –EPHESIANS **6:17**

In our defense against the enemy, no weapon is more potent than the word of God. The Spirit conveys to our consciousness a specific word just for our situation. In the original text, the term used for the "word" of God is *rhema*, which means a single spoken unit. Rather than throwing the entire Bible (Gk *logos*) at the devil, the Holy Spirit focuses on a specific Scripture. Like a piercing sword, the *rhema* neutralizes every utterance of Satan—every lie, half-truth, innuendo, and falsehood. The only thing effective against his lies, deceptions, and untruths is the sword of the Spirit.

God's entire word (*logos*) inspired by the Spirit is full of divine power. Hebrews 4:11 declares: "For the word (*logos*) of God is alive and active. Sharper than any double-edged sword, it penetrates even to dividing soul and spirit, joints and marrow; it judges the thoughts and attitudes of the heart." Like a sword it slices through the deceptions, lies, and misrepresentations of our adversary. No devil or fallen angel of hell can stand against this powerful weapon. When we wield God's word, specified by the Spirit, we send the forces of darkness fleeing.

At his temptation, Jesus overcame the seducer with the sword of the Spirit. He spoke just the right Scripture (*rhema*) into each of the devil's temptations. Before swinging the sword at Satan, he said, "It has been written in the past and it still stands true today." For example, when the devil insinuated, "You are going to go hungry," Jesus declared Deuteronomy 8:3, "Man shall not live on bread alone, but on every word (*rhema*) that comes from the mouth of God" (Mt 4:4). Our fiercest foe cannot stand against the Scripture the Spirit puts in our hands. Likewise, in faith we may take up the specific command, directive, prophesy, or promise to which the Spirit directs us and strike the tempter with a crippling blow.

Rhema: In spiritual warfare, the Spirit will give you the right Scripture to use against the foe. Remember the devil is a liar and the father of lies. The Holy Spirit always has a rhema word to cause that serpent to back down without argument.

November 3 | Ephesians 6:18–20; Colossians 4:2–5

Praying in the Spirit

And pray in the Spirit on all occasions with all kinds of prayers and requests. With this in mind, be alert and always keep on praying for all the Lord's people. **–Ephesians 6:18**

Have you heard the saying, "All dressed up and nowhere to go?" It can aptly apply to the person who has put on the full armor of God but does not know what to do with it. The armor is for engaging the enemy in warfare prayer. Praying in the Spirit with the shield of faith in one hand and the sword of the Spirit in the other is the way to stand up to the spiritual forces of darkness. Since our enemy is real, we must put on the full armor of God. Paul says, "For our struggle is not against flesh and blood, but against the rulers, against the authorities, against the powers of this dark world and against the spiritual forces of evil in the heavenly realms" (v 12).

Putting on the armor of God and praying are closely connected. In faith, by prayer, we can consciously put on each piece of divine protection. Pray, "Lord Jesus, I put on the belt of truth to protect my inner most being. I cover my heart with the breastplate of righteousness to stand uncondemned in your presence. Upon my feet, I put on the readiness to proclaim your good news. I take up the shield of faith with which I can extinguish every fiery arrow of the enemy. Lord Jesus, I am covering my head with your helmet of salvation to protect my thought life. And, I take the sword of the Spirit, the word of God, to go after the enemy and to cut through his lies. Amen."

Nothing makes our prayers more powerful and effective than the Holy Spirit. The most effective way to fight the enemy is praying in the Spirit. How to be strong and pray in power against spiritual forces arrayed against is what Paul is addressing. To pray in the Spirit means we invite him to come upon us and energize our prayers so we can pray in faith and power

Rhema: Therefore, let the Spirit breathe life and power into your every request, intercession, confession, and thanksgiving. Then your prayers will have an amazing effect.

NOVEMBER 4 | PHILIPPIANS 1:1–26

THE SPIRIT OF JESUS CHRIST

Yes, and I will continue to rejoice, for I know that through your prayers and God's provision of the **Spirit** *of Jesus Christ what has happened to me will turn out for my deliverance.* –PHILIPPIANS 1:18–19

Someone said, "When we know the gain, we can endure the pain." That helps understand how Paul can remain so joyful when death seems imminent. He is facing a terrible condition and is prevented from fulfilling his calling because he is chained to a prison floor (v 7). To be one of God's most gifted and talented believers confined to a cold, stark jail does not engender nuances of ecstasy. Yet he says, "I will keep on rejoicing because I realize I will get out here." He exudes confidence to carry on with joy because God will answer the prayers of his people.

The primary reason for his undeterred joy is the help he receives from the Spirit of Jesus Christ. Nowhere else does he refer to the Holy Spirit in this way so the phrase intimates something special. It must comfort him to know Jesus is personally indwelling him through the Spirit. The Spirit who helped sustain Jesus through his trials now resides within to help him face his life and death issues. Whether he lives or dies the Spirit has so infused his life with Christ whatever happens to him he wins. He says, "For to me, to live is Christ and to die is gain" (v 21). His trust in Christ is so complete he will never suffer disappointment.

Paul, however, appears to mean more than that. For instance, his attention is drawn to Job who said, "This will turn out for my deliverance" (Job 13:16). Just as God vindicated and delivered Job from his troubles, so the Spirit of Jesus Christ assures him of a similar deliverance. This may explain how he became convinced of seeing the Philippians again (v 25–26). He will not die, although he is prepared to, because God will free him from imprisonment.

Rhema: Amid his adversity, Paul could rejoice because the Spirit supplied him with a personal promise of deliverance. Likewise, if you are going through a tough spot be assured the Spirit of Jesus Christ can lovingly highlight a Scripture to help you through it.

NOVEMBER 5 | PHILIPPIANS 1:27–30

STANDING FIRM IN THE SPIRIT

Whatever happens, conduct yourselves in a manner worthy of the gospel of Christ. Then, whether I come and see you or only hear about you in my absence, I will know that you stand firm in the one Spirit, striving together as one for the faith of the gospel without being frightened in any way by those who oppose you. –PHILIPPIANS 1:27–28

The citizens at Philippi enjoyed a special status as a colony of Rome and knew they had to stand together in their far-off post. Although separated by 800 miles, they lived under the same laws as the capital. Isolated and in the minority, they had to stand together when threatened by enemies. Similarly, citizens of heaven should live the same way.

As citizens of heaven, we are to do two things. First, we are to strive together to advance the gospel and second, we are to stand together in one Spirit. We advance the gospel when we conduct ourselves in a manner worthy of the gospel. Closely connected to that obligation is maintaining the unity of the Spirit. The apostle realizes their accord is vital not only for their spiritual protection but also for the gospel's success. Because the Spirit has made us all one, we should join hands across all barriers to advance the gospel and carry out heaven's purposes. However, when believers tear down one another they weaken their spiritual protection. Disunity and inner wrangling, moreover, hinder the lost from coming to Christ. Who wants to believe in him if the transforming power of the gospel is not evident in his followers?

The local fellowship of believers is a settlement of heaven just as Philippi was of Rome. Therefore, if we are to abide by the laws of heaven we must let grace abound, love rule, and stand immovable in one Spirit. This is a call for believers to live by the power of the gospel.

Rhema: Since one day we will live together in rapturous tranquility in heaven, let us aim for the same unity here. To stand firm in one Spirit gives us the ability to contend as one person against Satanic attacks and not fear opposition. To live together as good citizens of heaven means we live the truth of the transforming power of the gospel.

NOVEMBER 6 | PHILIPPIANS 2:1–18

THE FELLOWSHIP OF THE SPIRIT

*Therefore if you have any encouragement from being united with Christ, if any comfort from his love, if any common sharing in the **Spirit**, if any tenderness and compassion, then make my joy complete by being like-minded, having the same love, being one in spirit and of one mind.*
–PHILIPPIANS 2:1–2

Like todays' sociologists and psychologists, the apostle Paul understood the importance of close friendships. This is especially true when we experience fear and face opposition (1:27–28). Healthy social integration creates many benefits, such as health, happiness, and longevity. Close relationships increase the quality of our lives because they diminish anxiety and ward off depression.

Have you ever considered developing a warm personal relationship with the Holy Spirit? Cultivating a kinship with him will work wonders. Since he lives in you, you are not alone in this world. Within, he cries, "You are a precious child of God." More than that, he makes Jesus real to you and helps you experience the benefits of belonging to him.

The apostle alludes to the "common sharing in the Spirit," a somewhat cumbersome expression. It means as friends share possessions and give gifts between each other, so does the Holy Spirit. He is our friend who distributes wonderful presents called the gifts of the Spirit. Not only that, he shares Christ's life with us, his love, joy, peace, goodness, and so forth. These we call the fruit of the Spirit.

The Holy Spirit likewise brings us into close caring relationships with other believers. The camaraderie we enjoy is the result of his work among us. Within the church, he deposits what theologians call the "inexpressible communion." Through him we enjoy the same eternal fellowship the Father, Son, and Holy Spirit have. This helps explain why believers with little in common in the natural could have an intimate fellowship in Christ.

Rhema: Through the Holy Spirit, you can enjoy the delightful benefits of life in Christ. Much more important than the Spirit's gifts and fruit is knowing him personally. You can talk to him and listen as he speaks with a still, small voice. When you have an intimate relationship with the Spirit, a river of life flowing from the throne of God is released in you. Indeed, he will share the best things of heaven with you.

SERVING GOD BY HIS SPIRIT

*For it is we who are the circumcision, we who serve God by his **Spirit**, who boast in Christ Jesus, and who put no confidence in the flesh.*
–PHILIPPIANS 3:3

The apostle at one point in his life believed he had found true religion. He excelled in it. You could call him "Mr. Righteousness." In his own words, he said he was faultless (v 6). That was until he met Jesus his Lord (v 8) and everything changed. Before, he boasted in his religious position, privilege, and pedigree (vv 4–6); now he considers these things dung (v 7).

Paul contrasts his former flesh-based religious life with his new life in the Spirit. On this basis, he sets forth two models for worshiping God: by the flesh and by the Spirit. Before he came to Christ, he served God by pious acts performed by the fallen human nature; afterwards he served God by the Spirit. Not until he was born from above could he worship as the Father desires. To be acceptable, devotion must originate with the Spirit as Jesus declared: "God is spirit, and his worshipers must worship in the Spirit and in truth" (Jn 4:24).

New birth by the Spirit reoriented Paul's worship from externals to internals. Being in Christ, he discovered no laws or acts, such as circumcision, were required for him to worship and serve God. Therefore he changed and no longer put any confidence in the flesh, for no human activities or rituals would please God. The true and acceptable worship required a new covenant, a new heart, and spiritual transformation.

Our service to the Father must be by the Spirit. Outward forms and ceremonies can never take the place of worshiping God with a new heart created by the Spirit. Because works of the flesh cannot give access to God, they must not be substituted for that which does. Furthermore, possession of the Spirit, not circumcision, a mutilation of the flesh, is the true sign of a genuine relationship with God.

Rhema: Since Christ came, God approves only one way to worship him—in the Spirit. All service to God that does not originate with the Spirit, regardless of ritual or faithful practice, is unacceptable. Since he is sovereign, he sets the terms under which he accepts our service.

NOVEMBER 8 | COLOSSIANS 1:1–8

LOVING OTHERS IN THE SPIRIT

You learned it from Epaphras, our dear fellow servant, who is a faithful minister of Christ on our behalf, and who also told us of your love in the Spirit. –COLOSSIANS 1:7–8

The Spirit's love is the sweetest of loves. It oozes from believers filled with the scent of heaven. The ardor from above is lovelier than the fragrance of a gardenia, more pervasive than the aroma of an orchard, and more soothing than frankincense and myrrh. Affection is like the end of winter when flowers burst into bloom and the season of singing starts. The doves coo and the vines spread their perfume (Song 2:11–13). Rifts and differences dissolve in the atmosphere of love.

Love freely flowed in this congregation and it extended to all the saints (v 4). The Holy Spirit (Rom 5:5) poured divine love into their hearts transforming their affections. In their direct encounters with God, they felt it and expressed it in many tangible ways. That is the way with God-given love. When others were in need, the Spirit aroused the affections of Christ to help the poor. Instead of focusing on themselves they relieved the plight of the disadvantaged and looked at each other with eyes full of trust and respect.

If love deficits cause most emotional and addictive problems, a wealth of love should heal people. The absence of nurturing care often leaves individuals hurt, wounded, or worse—brokenhearted. Love heals. As Martin Luther said, the church is a hospital. Healing flows in churches where believers express the Spirit's love.

Sad to say, churches can be toxic if selfishness, envy, jealousy, pride, boasting, and malice are prevalent. Colosse was extraordinary. There, love flowed. Dispositions changed. Benevolent action gushed. They embraced the unlovable. People cared for others. Affection for one another arose because the Holy Spirit was at work. Theirs was a love from another world. That is why they treated one another with patience and kindness. Each was gentle and self-controlled. They celebrated when others experienced good things—a raise in pay, a great marriage, or successful children. No one harbored bitterness. Sins were readily forgiven. Generosity overflowed. The church grew.

Rhema: Outsiders knew they were followers of Christ by their exceptional regard for each other. Theirs was a supernatural love born of the Spirit.

THE SPIRIT HELPS US UNDERSTAND GOD'S WILL

*We continually ask God to fill you with the knowledge of his will through all the wisdom and understanding that the **Spirit** gives, so that you may live a life worthy of the Lord and please him in every way.*
–COLOSSIANS 1:9–10

Do you ever struggle with knowing God's will? Ignorance of his plans is the root of heartache and woe. Without knowing what pleases him, we run the risk of making unwise decisions, or worse. We might find ourselves fighting him because our plans are at cross purposes with his. To prevent such mistakes, God wants to fill us with the knowledge of his will and make us wise. We can pray for the Spirit to give us spiritual insight, wisdom, and understanding in every situation.

The Spirit gives the ability to comprehend God's mind, including his will for our lives. Anyone born of the Spirit has an advantage over anyone who is incapable of comprehending God's will. One of the first things the Spirit does to help us appreciate the things of God is renew our minds (Rom 12:1–2). When we have the Spirit, we have the mind of Christ (I Cor 2:16). The purpose of imparting these precious gifts of wisdom, knowledge, and understanding is so we can know what to do.

To have insight into God's purpose for our lives is the result of prayer. Paul specifically asked God to fill the Colossians with this knowledge so they would not miss his high and holy calling. How can we ever feel fulfilled if we fail to know what God wants us to do? The way to make our lives count is to spend time and energy doing his pleasure. That's how to live worthy of the Lord.

Rhema: The Spirit not only gives an understanding of God's will but also the power to do it (v 11). That is how you can bear "fruit in every good work" (v 10). If he has chosen something for you to do, he will give the power to accomplish it. Doing the Father's will brings you to a place of spiritual maturity that ensures continual growth. Therefore, take the risk and pray for God's Spirit to fill you with the knowledge of the exciting things he has chosen for you.

NOVEMBER 10 | COLOSSIANS 3:1–20

SONGS FROM THE SPIRIT

*Let the message of Christ dwell among you richly as you teach and admonish one another with all wisdom through psalms, hymns, and songs from the **Spirit**, singing to God with gratitude in your hearts.*
–COLOSSIANS 3:16

Someone said, "The Spirit anoints us to sing our faith." The book of Colossians funnels our attention on Christ as the author exhorts us to "let the message of Christ dwell among [us] richly." When the Spirit makes Jesus real, our hearts fill with gratitude. The priority of our gatherings is Christ-centered teaching and praise. Few Scriptures lift him on high as does this letter (1:15–20). For instance, Paul taught Christ is the image of the invisible God. The creator of all things. The head of the church. The fullness of God. Everything in the universe is reconciled to God because Christ has made peace through his blood. In him are all the treasures of wisdom and knowledge (2:3). Wow!

True worship is extravagant love. Let the word, the public proclamations, and the songs extol Jesus! Give him full rein in the house! The Father sent the Holy Spirit to help us focus on his Son until we become intoxicated with him. The Spirit knows how to bring forth praise and make it sound like choirs of angels. Give God's Spirit a chance—give him something about Jesus with which to work! He creates wonderful, life-transforming worship when the message is about Christ. As at creation, so in worship. The Holy Spirit is hovering over us awaiting to act on the word concerning "the one who is before all things" (v 17). He desires to bring into existence something beautiful and good.

The Holy Spirit does not work in a vacuum; he operates where teaching about Christ abounds. Not making the Lord the heart of our church services is a huge disservice to the Spirit. Too much focus on man and the wisdom of the world robs the Spirit of any possibility of bringing forth praises to Jesus. Spirit-generated adulation has a high correlation to the richness of Christ in our teaching, preaching, testimony, and songs.

Rhema: Christology infused with the Spirit spurs great hymns, psalms, and songs. God does not want lip service or dead orthodoxy but spontaneous praise from adoring hearts set aflame by the Spirit.

THE HOLY SPIRIT COMES
WITH THE GOSPEL

*For we know, brothers and sisters loved by God, that he has chosen you, because our gospel came to you not simply with words but also with power, with the **Holy Spirit** and deep conviction.* **–I THESSALONIANS 1:4–5**

People often ask, "How do you get the Holy Spirit to show up?" For the apostle, the answer is simple: preach Christ. When he proclaimed the good news about Jesus Christ, the Spirit accompanied his message. The idol-worshipping Thessalonians (v 9) experienced the power of God so mightily they turned to the living and true God.

Paul unlike some was not interested in money but in seeing people experience radical life changes. To him the gospel was not just talk but, on the contrary, it came with the power of the Holy Spirit. When people believed the message, they had a divine encounter—hearing the apostle was hearing God. His preaching was more than human words; it was the voice of the Almighty. No wonder pagans turned away from the depths of darkness to serve God.

God sends his Spirit to accompany the gospel because he wants to verify the message. Many obstacles hinder people from accepting the salvation message. Doubts and fears as well as unbelieving hardened hearts make receiving the gospel hard. Many query what it means to leave the world behind and live for Christ. Besides these things, the enemy of the soul does not want to loosen his grip; unbelievers are his prisoners, slaves to his ways.

Christian conversion does not occur apart from the Spirit. Coming to faith is more than putting up a hand or filling out a card. Words and human persuasion are insufficient to bring someone to faith (I Cor 2:4–5). Instead, a deep conviction brought about by the Spirit sufficient to overcome a person's fears and doubts is needed. The Holy Spirit must convince an individual the gospel that comes with words is more than the words of man—it is the word of God. When the gospel is accompanied with the Holy Spirit, the awesome presence and power of God compellingly convinces a person of the truth of the good news.

Rhema: When we think of it conversion is miraculous, and it does not happen without a spiritual fight.

NOVEMBER 12 | I THESSALONIANS 1:6–10; ACTS 16:19–34

THE JOY OF THE HOLY SPIRIT
IN SUFFERING

*You became imitators of us and of the Lord, for you welcomed the message in the midst of severe suffering with the joy given by the **Holy Spirit**.* –I THESSALONIANS 1:6

What a paradox to experience joy while suffering. As soon as these new believers received the gospel, intense persecution deluged them. Townsfolk and friends pressured the Christ followers to give up their faith and return to their old ways. Perhaps they would have if not for the Holy Spirit. Suffering is a normal part of living for Christ and in this regard, they imitated Paul and the Lord Jesus. Amid their unbearable anguish, the Spirit gave them the joy of heaven.

Paul and Silas were brilliant examples of how the Spirit supplied joy while enduring suffering. Just before coming to Thessalonica, they were arrested for performing an outstanding miracle. City officials tore the apostles' clothes off before beating them with rods. Still not satisfied, the authorities threw the duo in jail, put them in lockdown, and chained their feet to the floor. Talk of affliction and trouble. What did God's servants do? Near midnight Paul and Silas prayed and sang to God, rejoicing they were counted worthy to suffer for Christ. That is when an earthquake shook the place and set them free.

Joy and suffering are at the opposite ends of our emotional spectrum. We rarely think they can coexist simultaneously. In the natural, when going through anguish, we are certainly not experiencing joy, nor do we break out into singing. God's indwelling presence, however, is not bound by what we are feeling. The Spirit's joy is not of this world but from above. Regardless of the circumstances, he can flood our hearts with songs of heaven. Life is full of suffering and heartaches but the one sent from heaven blesses us with festal feelings.

Rhema: Receiving the gladness from on high enables you to rejoice during times of intense anguish. Living under the Spirit's influence transforms every facet of your being. Merriment is not only the fruit of the Spirit but also a distinguishing characteristic of the kingdom of God. When others might curse, bless; when others swear, sing. In the most adverse circumstances, the Holy Spirit creates the most amazing joy.

NOVEMBER 13 | I THESSALONIANS 4:1–12

THE SPIRIT'S ROLE IN A
SEXUALLY CHARGED WORLD

*Therefore, anyone who rejects this instruction does not reject a human being but God, the very God who gives you his **Holy Spirit**.*
–I THESSALONIANS 4:8

We live in a sexually charged world. Every day floods us with the appeals and allure of sensual pleasures because sex sells. Its commercialization together with the body's objectification have spawned untold sexual, gender, and social problems. Society's obsession with sex does nothing to help individuals struggling with gender identity, lustful desires, and addictions. Many long for purity but wonder how to stay clean amid a confused and permissive society.

Sexual purity is far more important to God than many realize. He authored sex when he "created mankind in his own image, in the image of God he created them; male and female he created them" (Gen 1:27). Our Creator, however, allows and encourages sexual fulfillment through marital faithfulness (v 6). Aside from that provision, learning how to control our hormones is honorable. The apostle states, "It is God's will that you should be sanctified; that you should avoid sexual immorality" (v 3).

Chastity is so necessary God gives an explicit warning against immorality (v 6); he also gives the Holy Spirit to counter the lusts of the flesh. Possessing the Spirit helps control our sexual desires. His divine power operates in us to counter carnal desires and empower us to live a holy life. God also gave a set of instructions so we will know how to please him with our sexual conduct. These directives (vv 1–8) make it obvious: we are to lead lives free from sin, especially sexual immorality. God wants us to keep the body under control because he did not create it for pornography, fornication, or adultery. Its purpose is to glorify him through purity.

Rhema: We do not take our standard for sexual behavior from societal norms or the contemporary climate but from God. The spirit of the age is the spirit of disobedience that defies God. To live in physical purity requires a dependence upon the indwelling Spirit and because he lives in us, we have the moral strength to live in victory. We are not left to the dictates of our fallen nature but instead the Holy Spirit gives us self-control (Gal 5:22–23).

NOVEMBER 14 | I THESSALONIANS 5:1–28

DO NOT QUENCH THE SPIRIT

Do not quench the **Spirit**. –I THESSALONIANS 5:19

What if the fire of the Holy Spirit were extinguished? The church would die. Shutting down the movement and manifestation of the Spirit damages the church. A congregation without the Spirit is like a body without the soul; it has a form but no life.

The fervor of the Spirit sets people ablaze. Tongues of fire hovered over the believers at Pentecost to show they were filled with the Spirit. Celestial fire birthed the church; fire from above sustains it. God's Spirit bestows all the gifts, inspires all the prayers, opens our understanding of the word. He empowers her ministers, calls forth her servants, and convicts of sin. The fire reveals Jesus, adds new members, and introduces all born of the Spirit to the kingdom of God. By the Spirit the church speaks to God in prayer, and by the Spirit God speaks to the church in prophesy.

Like fiery flames, we can quench the Spirit. Paul warns against consciously suppressing the work of the Holy Spirit. In context, he means do not despise prophesies (v 20). Because the Spirit inspires them for the edification of believers, prophesies are fuel for the fire. Of course, they need testing to ensure they are of the Spirit (v 21) but when they are, we are to welcome and value them as divine utterances.

Quenching the Spirit was even occurring in Paul's churches, so he commands them to stop doing it. There may be a natural tendency to keep the Spirit from working in the church, but it must be crushed. Despite the warning, some continue to teach believers to suppress God's voice. They want to curtail the demonstration of the Spirit and disallow spiritual gifts. However, God's word declares, "Do not dampen the fire of God. Do not stifle the Spirit. Do not silence God's prophetic voice."

Rhema: The apostle warns against discouraging believers from having dynamic experiences in the Spirit. To criticize them for using spiritual gifts will soon smother the flames of Pentecost. A sure way to extinguish spiritual vitality is to retard the Spirit. In no way should anyone hinder, restrict, or suppress what the Spirit wants to do. Therefore, let us not only welcome him but also supply the oxygen so his fire can burn brighter.

NOVEMBER 15 | II THESSALONIANS 2:1–13

THE SANCTIFYING
WORK OF THE SPIRIT

But we ought always to thank God for you, brothers and sisters loved by the Lord, because God chose you as firstfruits to be saved through the sanctifying work of the **Spirit** *and through belief in the truth.*
–II THESSALONIANS 2:13

Two events must come to pass before Jesus returns. First is the great apostasy where immense numbers will abandon their faith. Second, the unveiling of a world figure in league with Satan. Paul declared, "Don't let anyone deceive you in any way, for that day will not come until the rebellion occurs and the man of lawlessness is revealed, the man doomed to destruction" (v 3). It will be the worst of times. Wickedness, evil, lawlessness, and delusion will overspread the earth. Society will unravel at the seams.

The apostle paints a ghastly portrait of the increase of iniquity that reaches its final climax before day of the Lord. Satan continues to work in everyone who rejects the gospel. He controls them because they refuse salvation and delight themselves in wickedness (v 12). Paul describes the end-time expansion of evil as a time of rebellion Jesus will overthrow and destroy at his coming.

God, however, has a solution to Satan's vile work: the sanctifying work of the Holy Spirit. To sanctify means to make holy, to set apart for God. The Spirit's role is to make every believer Christlike and save them from the evil onslaught gripping the world. He sets them apart from the wickedness and consecrates them to God's purposes. As the first fruits of the harvest in the OT were dedicated to God, so these believers were the first ones in their city set apart for God. The Spirit's job is to mark them as God's and make them holy. Only he can rescue them from the lawless and godless influences in the world.

Rhema: We thank God we are saved through the Spirit. By setting us apart and making us Christlike, he delivers us from the wrath to come. Just as the secret power of lawlessness is active in unbelievers, God's Spirit is active in our lives. He works within to purge us of evil and perfect us before God. Our heavenly Father does not want us to only believe; he wants to make us pure, holy, and undefiled.

NOVEMBER 16 | I TIMOTHY 3:14–16; MATTHEW 16:13–20

VINDICATED BY THE SPIRIT

Beyond all question, the mystery from which true godliness springs is great: He appeared in the flesh, was vindicated by the **Spirit***, was seen by angels, was preached among the nations, was believed on in the world, was taken up in glory.* –I TIMOTHY 3:16

How do we know the gospel is true? Salvation, eternity, life after death, forgiveness of sins, and the resurrection rest on a single truth: Jesus is who he says he is. Like a pillar holding up a bridge, everything hangs on proving he is the Son of God.

The proof Jesus was divine rests in part with the Spirit's demonstration. Even though the apostles accompanied Jesus, they needed the Spirit to show them he was the eternal word made flesh (Jn 1:14). Peter declared, "You are the Christ, the Son of the living God." The Father through the agency of the Spirit identified and endorsed Jesus as his Son (Mt 16:17).

The gospel, the great pillar and foundation of the church, is a mystery. Undiscoverable by reason, the Spirit must convince of its truth. God in the person of Jesus Christ became man, entered our world, lived among us a perfect life, died on the cross for our sins, and rose again to make us holy. Understanding and proclaiming this mystery of godliness is the essential message of the church. But it requires vindication by the Spirit. To vindicate Jesus means to prove he was indeed God manifested in the flesh.

How did the Spirit vindicate him? When he preached, the Spirit said, "He is no mere man for he teaches with authority." When Jesus cast out demons, the Spirit said, "He is greater and more powerful than the prince of darkness." When Jesus healed the sick, the Spirit said, "This is *Jehovah-Rophe*, the God who heals you." Every step our Lord took, the Spirit was present to attest his divinity. But the greatest attestation was when men found him guilty and crucified him. Then the Spirit put things right by raising him from the dead.

Rhema: Forget logic, apologetics, and rational demonstration that have their place. If we give ear to the Spirit, he will prove beyond a doubt Jesus is indeed the Christ, the Son of the living God. We call this faith for a reason.

NOVEMBER 17 | I TIMOTHY 4:1–16

THE SPIRIT WARNS OF
LAST DAYS DECEPTION

*The **Spirit** clearly says that in later times some will abandon the faith and follow deceiving spirits and things taught by demons.* –I TIMOTHY 4:1

We must never muzzle the prophetic voice of the Spirit. He dwells among us to warn of imminent dangers and erroneous teachings. To shut down prophesies, words of knowledge, and discerning of spirits is as foolish and dangerous as shutting down the country's missle defense system. Without 24-hour surveillance, the enemy can attack undetected.

The Spirit sees into the future and alerts us to impending trouble. He scrutinizes everything said and done. As the end approaches, deceptive spirits do not stop their nefarious work but increase their efforts (Rev 12:12). So why silence the Spirit when he can alert us to the tactics of the enemy? If we want to safeguard our homes' valuable contents, we do not unplug the security system. Nor should we turn off the Spirit.

Believers have always had to battle deceiving spirits who stand behind falsehood and deception. Any teaching designed to get our eyes off Christ, his death on the cross, or his precious blood is not of the Spirit (I Jn 4:1–3). Since Paul warns some will abandon the faith and embrace error, we should be concerned it does not happen to us. God wants everyone to be saved and come to the knowledge of the truth (2:3). Therefore, the Spirit discerns every doctrine to ensure it is pure and uncontaminated with the demonic.

Paul was dealing with false teachers who were misleading the saints. They told the believers if they wanted to be more acceptable to God they must add practices, rituals, and dietary rules (v 3) to their faith. Such a departure from salvation by grace (Gal 1:6f) was tantamount to deserting Christ. In I Timothy, the apostle faced and condemned another bogus teaching inspired by demons. He denounced as hypocritical liars those who teach believers will become more holy or better saints if they do not marry (v 3).

Rhema: To prevent latching on to demonic or false teaching, we need ears to hear what the Spirit is saying to the church. The phrase, "the Spirit says," indicates his ongoing surveillance to protect us from apostasy and deception. Definitely we must pay attention to the Spirit's prophetic role.

NOVEMBER 18 | II TIMOTHY 1:1-12

THE SPIRIT DOES NOT MAKE US TIMID

*For the **Spirit** God gave us does not make us timid, but gives us power, love and self-discipline.* –II TIMOTHY 1:7

Has a setback ever rocked your emotional and spiritual equilibrium? Harsh blows and traumas can plunge us into a downer and cool our fervor. Such experiences can leave us weak, fretful, and timid. When our emotions are stretched, we become ineffective and held back from our best.

Young Timothy had become cold and withdrawn. Perhaps it was too much time alone during Paul's imprisonment. Regardless, he was struggling with the weighty load of teaching and preaching. As long as Paul was with him he excelled, but found it a stretch to be the lone man on the field. It may be he was fatigued, battle-weary, and shell-shocked so he turtled. Living and working for God in a sinful city fighting the forces of evil and wickedness is never easy.

The Spirit of God, however, did not make him timid. The word translated "timid" means to act like a coward in the heat of battle. Timothy's heart had become faint, and it was affecting his work and witness. He shelved his spiritual gift (v 7) and became ashamed of Paul and the gospel (v8). Timothy's emotional funk sunk him into despair to the extent he struggled with making good decisions. He lost his aggressiveness for Christ.

The Spirit God gave us does not make us timid. On the contrary, he builds us up, makes us courageous, and reinvigorates us. God wants us to engage in his work with all our hearts and use our spiritual gifts. He wants us to spend time with him in prayer so our strength is renewed and we can mount up with wings of an eagle (Isa 40:29–31).

Rhema: Timothy needed three things from the Holy Spirit: power, love, and self-discipline. The Comforter wants to do the same for you. If you feel weak, battle-worn, and weary, he longs to invigorate you with a fresh touch of his presence. If you feel neglected, alone, or unappreciated, the Holy Spirit desires to flood your soul with God's love. If you feel you have the wrong mental attitude, he wishes to renew your mind. He can help you today develop emotional toughness and, like a good soldier (2:3), endure hardship.

NOVEMBER 19 | II TIMOTHY 1:13–2:19

GUARDING THE GOSPEL
WITH THE SPIRIT'S HELP

*Guard the good deposit that was entrusted to you—guard it with the help of the **Holy Spirit** who lives in us.* –II TIMOTHY 1:14

A weighty legal obligation rests with anyone entrusted with the family fortune. That treasure must be guarded against loss or corruption. "The good deposit" God entrusted to the apostles is the gospel. They knew its value and defended it with their lives because it was the power of God to save the world. The apostle realizes he will soon die, so now he entrusts the word of Christ to Timothy. The gospel is a privileged possession, a divine treasure, an awesome responsibility. To guard its safekeeping requires the supernatural help of the Holy Spirit.

We need to guard the gospel and watch over it as watchmen alert to any breach. Its life-transforming message is precious provided no one change the content by addition or subtraction. The word of life requires careful handling to warrant no error creeps in (2:15). False teaching leads to immorality and destroys faith. Consequently, we must guard the Good News at all costs lest people wander away from the truth (2:17–18). Our ultimate and eternal consequences rest upon the gospel's truth and purity.

Paul wants to make sure the gospel's integrity will outlive him. He appeals to Timothy to preserve it to guarantee its continuing success. His son in the faith had the unique privilege of hearing more than anyone the electrifying teaching and preaching of the apostle. "What you heard from me," Paul says, "keep as the pattern of sound teaching" (v 13). In passing it on, nothing must be lost. Change one vital feature and it ceases being the Good News. "Do it no harm!" "Do not change it!" The apostle implores him to guard the good deposit against compromise, corruption, and distortion. Otherwise the gospel loses its amazing power to save, destroy death, bring holiness and immortality (vv 9–10).

Rhema: The great responsibility of preserving something so invaluable requires the Holy Spirit's help. How does he help us preserve its integrity? The Spirit who lives in us tells us when someone is diluting or distorting the Good News. He becomes agitated and begins waving red flags if he detects departure from the apostolic message.

NOVEMBER 20 | TITUS 3:1-11

SAVED BY THE HOLY SPIRIT

*He saved us through the washing of rebirth and renewal by the **Holy Spirit**, whom he poured out on us generously through Jesus Christ our Savior.* –TITUS 3:5–6

Do you know what salvation means? To save is a marvelous term with a magnificent range of meanings. It means to heal or make whole from the effects of disease. To rescue from danger, peril, or disaster. To keep from harm, to preserve. The ultimate deliverance. Interestingly, nuances of these definitions are distilled in the glorious declaration, "He saved us." The apostle explains the reason and means of our salvation.

The answer for why God saved us is straightforward: we needed saving. It was lights out forever unless he responded to our plight with mercy, love, and kindness (v 4). One verse (v 3) describes our desperate condition. We were spiritual dullards, foolish and lost. Rebellion raced through our veins like adrenalin, making us disobedient to God and authority. Our heads were screwed on wrong, so we followed bad advice and ended up going the wrong way. Even worse—we were slaves addicted to our lusts. We lived in malice and hatred and were mean-spirited. Do we need any more descriptors?

How does God save? The Father, Son, and Holy Spirit each has a distinctive role but our focus is on the Spirit's part or the experiential in salvation. In short, soteriology has a strong pneumatological component. God saved us through the Holy Spirit because of Christ's accomplishments on the cross. The Spirit washed away our filth and birthed us anew. Cleansing from sin and regeneration are his essential works. Further, the Spirit created a new life for us, free from the former sinful contaminants. He restored us to a prefallen, made-in-the-image-of-God state. The word "renewal" means genesis, a new beginning. He gave us another start, like Noah had after the Flood. Just as water washed away the antediluvian corruption, so the Spirit cleanses us of sin and ushers us into a new eon.

Rhema: The Spirit who was so active in creation knows how to make all things new in your life. When he created you new in Christ, he saved you and made you part of God's grand end-time scheme to restore everything marred by sin.

NOVEMBER 21 | HEBREWS 2:1–18

CONFIRMED BY THE GIFTS OF THE HOLY SPIRIT

God also testified to it by signs, wonders and various miracles, and by gifts of the Holy Spirit distributed according to his will. –HEBREWS 2:4

In many areas of life, not paying attention has huge consequences. Carelessness in managing money can lead to financial ruin. Distractions while driving can cause fatal accidents. Most marriages end for lack of attentiveness. When couples become bored with the relationship, lose interest in each other, and preoccupied with other matters, seeds of indifference are sown. It will not be long before they forget what brought them together in the first place and they tiptoe away from their once-passionate relationship.

The author of Hebrews wrote to warn believers of the perils of failing to give their relationship with Christ their undivided attention. Other concerns eclipsed and overshadowed their new life in Christ. So the writer says, "Do not neglect your great salvation." Just as an expensive ring can slip off the finger, they were letting God's amazing gift slip away. Neglecting what God has done in Christ Jesus can eventually end the relationship.

Since nothing on earth is more important, God's gracious gift of salvation demands our full attention. In fact, there is no "escape for ignoring such a great salvation" (v 3). To demonstrate its importance, God himself authenticated the gospel with signs, wonders, miracles, and gifts of the Holy Spirit—it is his final revelation. His last revelation, the gospel, expressed in Jesus is supernaturally verified.

In fact, the gospel is all about the miraculous. When we proclaim it, we are asking people to believe the death of Jesus 2,000 years ago can wash away their sin. The gospel asks people to believe they will rise from the dead, they will live forever, and Jesus will return from heaven for them. Miracles authenticate this glorious message of salvation.

By experiencing the miraculous gifts of the Spirit, we taste "the powers of the world to come" (6:4–5). When the gospel is proclaimed, God himself is speaking. That is why supernatural signs accompany the message. Therefore we should expect signs, wonders, and various miracles including the gifts of the Spirit to attest the importance and veracity of God's offer of eternal life.

Rhema: To neglect the greatest display of God's grace will bring the ultimate consequence.

NOVEMBER 22 | HEBREWS 3:1–19

THE HOLY SPIRIT MAKES THE WORD COME ALIVE

*So, as the **Holy Spirit** says: "Today, if you hear his voice, do not harden your hearts as you did in the rebellion."* –HEBREWS 3:7–8

When we hear or read a Scripture, the Spirit can make it a living encounter with God. What he emphasizes can become a prophetic word for us today. He gives Psalm 95, for example, a contemporary application beyond its original message. The Spirit takes David's inspired word and applies it to the "Hebrews" even though 1,000 years separate the two audiences.

The author of Hebrews claims the Spirit gives the biblical text a new meaning different from its original setting. When he writes, "The Holy Spirit says," he informs his readers the Spirit is speaking to them. As at creation, he is hovering over the believers to actualize God's word in them. The Spirit gives the text life and fills it with the power of God for the new audience. With the full authority of God, he says, "Do not harden your hearts. Do not turn away from the living God. Do not be like the people in the wilderness. Today you are coming face to face with God so, purpose in your hearts to continue on with Christ."

Five times the word "today" is mentioned (vv 7–15, 4:7) to show the Holy Spirit is speaking to them in the present. With their interest in spiritual things flagging, they struggled to remain faithful to Christ. So the Spirit speaks and gives them a similar warning corresponding to the one in Psalm 95. He also gives them a fresh living promise, saying, "Today if you will receive it from God, there remains a wonderful promise. You will enter God's Sabbath rest (4:9) provided you persevere in faith and not harden your hearts."

Rhema: Similarly, the Spirit speaks to us as he breathes life into Scriptures and applies them to us. He says, "This Scripture, this warning, this promise applies to you." The ancient word of God becomes a fresh, powerful, and living word in the hands of the Spirit. The author concludes, "For the word of God is alive and active. Sharper than any double-edged sword, it penetrates even to dividing soul and spirit, joints and marrow; it judges the thoughts and attitudes of the heart" (4:12).

NOVEMBER 23 | HEBREWS 6:1–12

GREAT HOLY SPIRIT EXPERIENCES

*It is impossible for those who have once been enlightened, who have tasted the heavenly gift, who have shared in the **Holy Spirit**, who have tasted the goodness of the word of God and the powers of the coming age and who have fallen away, to be brought back to repentance.*
–HEBREWS 6:4–6

God wants us to grow as followers of Christ. He expects us to mature and move beyond baby steps and milk (5:12). Since he has given us an enormous inheritance (v 12), why live on a few pennies? Growing in God and delighting in his provisions will lead to many gratifying experiences (v 9).

If the virus of spiritual lethargy infects us and stunts our development, we risk great loss. To illustrate, the author gives the example of the Israelites delivered out of Egyptian bondage. They proved themselves unfaithful to the Lord. Although gloriously saved, they hardened their hearts, rebelled, and fell in the desert (3:16–19). Do not be like them, he warns, because they had a sinful, unbelieving heart that turned away from the living God (3:12). They saw awesome miracles, ate manna from heaven, and drank living water from the Rock (I Cor 1–5), but "their bodies were scattered in the wilderness."

Like the Israelites we are graced with many great salvation experiences, but ours are in the Holy Spirit. First, we have been enlightened. The Holy Spirit opens our understanding and gives us knowledge of the truth. Second, after coming to faith we tasted the heavenly gift, the promised Holy Spirit whom the Father sent to our hearts. Third, we benefited from acquiring the Holy Spirit because he indwells us. We are companions eternally connected with the Comforter who guides, advises, and directs.

Fourth, we have tasted the goodness of the word of God. Nothing is as sweet as Scripture brought to life by the Spirit when he gives us a personal *rhema* word. Fifth, we enjoy the powers of the age to come. These are the signs, wonders, miracles, and gifts of the Spirit he distributes among us.

Rhema: Drawing a parallel to the Israelites, the author warns of the dangers of complacency and spiritual stagnation but hopes for a better outcome (v 9). By remaining unreservedly faithful to the Lord, we will by faith inherit God's promises.

NOVEMBER 24 | HEBREWS 9:1–10

THE HOLY SPIRIT INTERPRETS SCRIPTURE

*The **Holy Spirit** was showing by this that the way into the Most Holy Place had not yet been disclosed as long as the first tabernacle was still functioning.* **–HEBREWS 9:8**

Do you long to understand God's word and see its truth come to life? Well, ask God's Spirit to show you spiritual realities. He is the great interpreter of Scripture who can open its spiritual significance. Since he inspired these writings, he alone can unveil what he intended. In hermeneutics, much attention focuses on authorial intent, exegesis, historical setting, and grammar but not enough on the Spirit. Only he can remove the veil and give its divine meaning.

Take, for instance, one of the most prominent accounts in the OT: the sacrificial worship system. Pages, chapters, and books of the OT describe it in minute detail, but what does it signify? Its true significance was obscure until Christ came. Until then it was just so many types and shadows (8:5), a copy of the heavenly, a mere parable (v 9). Because Israel's worship system was temporary, on earth and concerned with external regulations, something superior was needed.

The Holy Spirit reveals the first tabernacle provided incomplete access to God's presence. One major problem with its sacrificial provisions was it did not "clear the conscience of the worshiper" (v 9). Therefore, it needed replacing. Worshipers needed to come into the presence of the Almighty another way. Not until Christ came and poured out the Spirit could anyone enter the sanctuary in heaven. They must be born of the Spirit first; only then can they enjoy face-to-face communion with God. The new era of the Spirit provides the way into the holy presence of Almighty God. Before we enter the Most Holy Place of God's presence, the Holy Spirit must make us holy. What was impossible in the past the Spirit makes possible in the present.

Rhema: You can ask the Spirit to help you understand the Scriptures. He wants to open the eyes of your understanding so you can see biblical truth. Jesus said the one he sends will teach you all things (Jn 16:12–14). He will help you grasp the new reality brought into existence by the sacrifice of Jesus Christ. To receive the Spirit implies you have immediate and full access to God.

NOVEMBER 25 | HEBREWS 9:11–28

THE ETERNAL SPIRIT

How much more, then, will the blood of Christ, who through the eternal **Spirit** *offered himself unblemished to God, cleanse our consciences from acts that lead to death, so that we may serve the living God!*
–HEBREWS 9:14

Why does the author refer to the Holy Spirit as the eternal Spirit? Since this expression occurs only here in the Bible, the writer must consider it important. Of course, he knows the Third Person of the Trinity, the Holy Spirit, is eternal just as is the Father and the Son. Ultimately, he wants to show the eternal Spirit makes Christ's high priesthood (v 11) and sacrifice superior to their counterparts in the OT Levitical system.

God founds our great salvation on something better than the "blood of goats and bulls" (v 13). It rests on Christ our high priest who offered himself and his blood through the eternal Spirit. His offering occurred in heaven a much superior place, in contrast with "an earthly sanctuary" (v 1). The tabernacle and temple were inferior because they were materialistic and man-made (v11). Because their offerings were temporal they needed repeating; Christ's is eternal (vv 23–28) and has everlasting results.

The author, incidentally, reveals the relationship between Christ and the Holy Spirit in a new way. The Spirit conceived, empowered, and raised our Lord from the dead. Now, the Spirit working in the eternal and heavenly realm makes Christ's death efficacious—he empowers the cross. Through the eternal Spirit, Jesus offers himself up as a perfect sacrifice to effect everlasting salvation. In contrast to the blood of bulls and goats, Christ's sacrifice perfects our conscience (v 8) and cleanses it forever. In this way, he removes our guilt and washes away the stain of our sin permanently. No animal sacrifice could ever achieve that.

The Spirit made great things happen when Christ, our high priest, offered himself up to God. What the Spirit did with his blood in heaven makes it possible for us to live the Christian life. Because his blood is sacrificed in the eternal Spirit, it completely removes every hindrance between us and God. Therefore, we can "serve the living God."

Rhema: Having been so mightily cleansed and transformed, you can approach the throne of grace with full confidence and receive your promised eternal inheritance (v 15).

NOVEMBER 26 | HEBREWS 10:1–18

THE HOLY SPIRIT TESTIFIES TO US

*The **Holy Spirit** also testifies to us about this. First he says: "This is the covenant I will make with them after that time, says the Lord. I will put my laws in their hearts, and I will write them on their minds."*
—HEBREWS 10:15–16

Read these words slowly and carefully: "The Holy Spirit also tes- tifies…." It is so easy to lose sight of the important work of the Spirit because the ministry of Christ, our high priest, overshadows it. In Hebrews, the Holy Spirit does important work too: he speaks, reveals, and testifies.

The voice of the Holy Spirit is prominent among the people of the new covenant. This should not come as a surprise. What is surpris- ing is the equivalency between the Lord's voice the prophets heard and the Spirit's voice we hear. God through the agency of the Spirit spoke to the OT prophets and inspired their writings. Just as the apostle Paul asserted, "The Spirit is the Lord," so also the writer to the Hebrews implies something similar. "The Lord" in Jeremiah's prophecy (Jer 31:31–34) quoted here is the Spirit who writes the laws of God on their hearts.

The new covenant made possible by Christ's death (9:15) is not of the letter but of the Spirit (II Cor 3:16). He puts God's laws in our hearts and writes them on our minds (v 16). Under the new covenant, we have been made holy (v 10) and our sins taken away (v 11). Since we have been cleansed once for all time and no longer guilty (v 2), we can draw near to God. The indwelling Spirit tells us what God requires and enables us to "know the Lord" by personal experience (8:11).

Rhema: When we listen to the Scriptures, the Spirit speaks to us in two ways. First, he speaks to us through the written word he inspired. Second, since we are people he indwells he addresses us directly. He bears witness in our hearts and says, "This Scripture is for you. What I declared in the past I am declaring to you today. I have written my law in your inner parts. You are my people and I am your God." In this way, he refocuses the biblical text from the past to make it relevant in the present.

November 27 | Hebrews 10:19–39

Insulting the Spirit of Grace

*How much more severely do you think someone deserves to be punished who has trampled the Son of God underfoot, who has treated as an unholy thing the blood of the covenant that sanctified them, and who has insulted the **Spirit** of grace?* —Hebrews 10:29

Do you hear the musical lilt in the phrase "the Spirit of grace"? It speaks of beauty and sweetness. Grace refers to extravagant generosity and undeserved favor—a free cheerful bestowal of gifts. It is the grandest of kindnesses to the most unworthy, the essence of the gospel.

Conjoin grace with the Spirit and we realize how God showers his goodness, favor, and blessings on us. Without the Spirit we could not experience heaven's kindest blessings resulting from Christ's death. For the Spirit opens our understanding to the truth of God, then floods our hearts with his love. He makes us holy, illuminates the Scriptures, and applies the blood of Christ. Besides empowering us to live for God, he distributes amazing spiritual gifts and manifests God's presence.

Why then would anyone insult the Spirit of grace when he has done so much for them? To insult him means to act in some offensive and outrageous way. This word, "insult," only occurs here in the NT to show the intensity of the hurt inflicted on the Spirit.

What might provoke such intense outrage? The one thing that makes the Holy Spirit so furious is a person's willful abandonment of faith—especially after so much kindness and goodwill was shown them. Giving up on Christ involves three fatal mistakes. First, to trample the Son of God underfoot is to slap the Spirit in the face. After all, he is the Spirit of Christ. Second, to treat the precious blood of Christ as nothing special, the blood the eternal Spirit presented to God, is an affront to the Spirit. Third, to spurn and walk away from the Spirit who is convicting them of the error of their ways is a horrendous injury.

Rhema: To insult the Spirit who extends God's grace is tantamount to committing the unpardonable sin. The language of the author is strong and severe. Forgiveness is not possible because "no sacrifice for sins is left" (v 26). What remains is the "fearful expectation of judgment and of raging fire" (v 27).

NOVEMBER 28 | I PETER 1:1–9; EXODUS 24:1–11

THE SPIRIT MAKES US HOLY

Peter, an apostle of Jesus Christ, To God's elect, exiles scattered through-out the provinces of Pontus, Galatia, Cappadocia, Asia and Bithynia, who have been chosen according to the foreknowledge of God the Father, through the sanctifying work of the **Spirit**, *to be obedient to Jesus Christ and sprinkled with his blood: Grace and peace be yours in abundance.*
–I PETER 1:1–2

Living in moral purity in an impure world is a huge problem, both for us and God. How can a holy God admit unholy people into his presence? God says, "Be holy in all you do" (v 15) "because I am holy" (v 16). If God is to restore us to himself, he must make us holy by removing our sinfulness. How easy is that?

Before the world began, God the Father found a way to make us pure even knowing we would fail and fall into every imaginable evil. Based on his foreknowledge, he chose us to be holy through the new birth (v 3) by creating a new life that cannot sin (I Jn 3:9). Once we are born of God, his indwelling Spirit begins the powerful task of making us in his image. The apostle Peter refers to this transformation as the sanctifying work of the Spirit.

Just how does the Spirit help us live in obedience to God? He infuses us with divine power, something we never had before. When the Spirit enters, all his purity and holiness indwell us. We take part in his divine nature (II Pet 1:4) and undergo continuous spiritual metamorphosis. The Holy Spirit comes into our lives with "his divine power" (II Pet 1:3) to offset the enticements of the world and the desires of our flesh. This is why in part he is called the HOLY SPIRIT: He works to make us holy.

The Spirit does one other thing to fit us for God's presence. Because we fall short of perfection, he takes the blood of Jesus and sprinkles it on us. What Moses did in the old covenant (Ex 24:8) the Spirit does in the new.

Rhema: Despite daily shortcomings, we are ever clean and able to fellowship with God. Our responsibility, therefore, is to live more and more in the power of the Spirit instead of the desires of the flesh.

NOVEMBER 29 | I PETER 1:10–25

THE SPIRIT OF CHRIST IN THE PROPHETS

*Concerning this salvation, the prophets, who spoke of the grace that was to come to you, searched intently and with the greatest care, trying to find out the time and circumstances to which the **Spirit** of Christ in them was pointing when he predicted the sufferings of the Messiah and the glories that would follow.* **–I PETER 1:10–11**

For only the second time in the Bible, the Spirit is referred to as the Spirit of Christ (see Rom 8:9). What does it mean? The Spirit and Christ have such an intimate relationship that seeing and hearing the one is to see and hear the other. Jesus said the Holy Spirit will remind us of everything he said (Jn 14:26). His primary task is to testify about Christ (Jn 15:26) and bring glory to him by taking what is his and making it known to us (Jn 16:14).

In NT times the Spirit's role was to exalt Christ, but he had the same task among the OT prophets. The Spirit in them also exalted Christ. He inspired them to discuss Christ's sufferings and his glories, his death and resurrection. They prophesied both of his weaknesses and his return in the clouds of glory. So the Spirit's assignment whether in OT times, the NT, or the Church Age is to bear witness to Christ.

Hence, viewing the Scriptures Christologically is of utmost importance. Their true spiritual interpretation entails looking at them in relation to Christ. The writers were not just serving themselves or speaking to their own generation but to us (v 12). Just as the Spirit guided them to reveal Christ in their writings, he also is the voice of Christ speaking to us through Scripture.

After his resurrection, Jesus met two grieving disciples on their way to Emmaus. He said to them, "How foolish you are, and how slow to believe all that the prophets have spoken! Did not the Messiah have to suffer these things and then enter his glory?" What Jesus did next is what the Spirit does for us. "And beginning with Moses and all the Prophets, he explained to them what was said in all the Scriptures concerning himself" (Lk 24:25–27).

Rhema: Therefore, when the Spirit "explains" these Scripture to us we are encountering Christ.

NOVEMBER 30 | ACTS 2:14–41

PREACHING BY THE SPIRIT

*It was revealed to them that they were not serving themselves but you, when they spoke of the things that have now been told you by those who have preached the gospel to you by the **Holy Spirit** sent from heaven. Even angels long to look into these things.* —I PETER 1:12

What would happen if every sermon was preached in the power of the Holy Spirit? God wants his saving message proclaimed with the same dynamic force as it was in Peter's day. To carry out his purposes, we must preach God's message in the power of the Spirit. NT preaching won souls, brought glory to God, and transformed entire cities.

The salvation of souls is important to God (v 9). For that reason, he took great care to inspire the OT prophets to foretell our salvation (v 10–11). Then when the fullness of time came, he anointed Christ and his apostles to preach it. The same Spirit in the prophets worked in them. The Spirit, for instance, made the preaching of Jesus powerful. He said, "The Spirit of the Lord is on me, because he has anointed me to preach good news" (Lk 4:18).

Preaching the gospel by the Holy Spirit means that God is present in the proclamation. Through the foolishness of preaching, the Spirit makes the truth of the gospel real. The anointed message has a divine ability to penetrate hearts and bring hearers face to face with God. The gospel is ineffective without the Spirit. Preaching without divine energy will not convert sinners nor transform lives. That is why Jesus made sure the apostles had spiritual clout before they went forth to preach. He commanded them to wait in Jerusalem until power from on high flooded their being (Lk 24:45–49). Examples of their Spirit-anointed preaching fill the book of Acts.

God wants his message delivered with a supernatural anointing and proclaimed by the Spirit's power. He must infuse messages with himself and elevate them beyond mere human discourse, otherwise they are only the musings of men. Peter experienced this divine reality when thousands responded to his preaching saying, "What shall we do?" (Acts 2:36).

Rhema: God desires to fill our land once again with Spirit-empowered preaching because he wants people to know he is present to save.

DECEMBER 1 | I PETER 3:8–22

MADE ALIVE IN THE SPIRIT

For Christ also suffered once for sins, the righteous for the unrighteous, to bring you to God. He was put to death in the body but made alive in the Spirit. –I PETER 3:18

Are you having a dreadful day? Suffering for doing good like Peter's readers? To comfort the maligned believers (vv 14–16), the apostle urges them to look at the example of Christ who was not exempt from suffering.

The apostle saw with his own eyes the abuse and injustice the Lord endured, especially during his crucifixion. Jesus suffered for their sins, the righteous for the unrighteous that he may bring them to God. Although he was put to death in the body, he was made alive in the Spirit. After three days in a tomb, the Spirit raised him from the dead.

Peter wants to show that our spiritual life parallels the Lord's. What happened to Christ has profound consequences for us. Notably, when the Spirit raised him from the dead his life changed. Because he was given life in the Spirit, he was able to enter heaven and sit at his Father's right hand. Instead of suffering defeat at the hands of his enemies, Jesus experienced unparalleled victory. Now angels, authorities, and powers are subject to him (v 22). This is so important for us to understand. We also are made alive in the Spirit and participate in his triumph over death. Ultimately, we are set free from the powers of evil and death.

The purpose of Christ's death was to bring us to God. We are no longer mere mortals trapped within the constraints of the flesh but new creations brought into existence by the Spirit. We are freed from the evil forces determined to destroy us. In his journey from the grave back to heaven, Christ visited the spirits in prison. Many believe they are evil spirits who wreaked havoc in the days of Noah. In his resurrected glorified state, Christ announced to these demons they will never again have power over anyone the Spirit makes alive.

Rhema: In the Spirit, Jesus experienced a complete triumph over evil. The announcement he made to the imprisoned demons is good news for us. Because we are alive in the Spirit, we too can live in victory shielded from the destructive powers of the enemy.

DECEMBER 2 | I PETER 4:1–19

THE SPIRIT OF GLORY RESTS ON YOU

If you are insulted because of the name of Christ, you are blessed, for the **Spirit** *of glory and of God rests on you.* **–I PETER 4:14**

Following Christ is not easy especially when people insult, malign, mock, curse, ridicule, and make fun of you. How do you become Teflonlike so their cruel barbs do not stick? To be blessed for your faith in Christ when people hurl insults at you seems paradoxical. When they do, "Rejoice and leap for joy" (Lk 6:23). In other words, turn the negative things people say about you into something positive.

You may be going through fiery trials but focus instead upon what it means for the Spirit of glory to rest on you. One way to turn negatives into positives is to rejoice. Celebrate! If you join Christ in his sufferings, you will also share in his glory. You may suffer for him now but in the future, you will take part in his unimaginable splendor (v 13). Then the Father will honor you beyond your wildest dreams.

But what of the present? Right now, you feel pain and bewilderment. Realize amid your suffering the Spirit of glory rests on you. Think of it this way: the Spirit who raised Christ from the dead and glorified him dwells in you. As you suffer you possess the glorious Spirit, the giver of heaven's splendorous joy.

Think of the Spirit of glory as the OT pillar of fire and the cloud of God's presence (Num 14:14). The glorious majesty of God's company hovers over you as you walk through the wilderness of your life. Let's explain it one more way. You are the temple of the Holy Spirit and the cloud of his visible radiance rests on you as it did on the OT tabernacle. "Then the cloud covered the tent of meeting, and the glory of the Lord filled the tabernacle. Moses could not enter the tent of meeting because the cloud had settled on it, and the glory of the Lord filled the tabernacle" (Ex 40:34–35).

Rhema: The rich and the famous have glory because of their possessions and positions. You have something greater—you have importance, dignity, fame, and honor. You have the Shekinah glory, God's own presence dwelling in you. Rejoice! Leap for joy!

DECEMBER 3 | II PETER 1:1–21

THE SPIRIT AND INSPIRATION (PART I)

*For prophecy never had its origin in the human will, but prophets, though human, spoke from God as they were carried along by the **Holy Spirit**.*
–II PETER 1:21

Scriptures is unlike any other literature. It is not the result of human imagination, creativity, or poetic genius although it expresses the personality and talents of each author. Instead, it is God's word through human writers. OT prophecy is unique because its ultimate origin was not located in the human will but in God. The prophets spoke from God as aided by the Holy Spirit. Moses, David, Isaiah, and the others never sat down and said, "I want to write a book about my interesting adventures and ideas." Instead, the driving force of their writing was God.

Peter says the prophets "were carried along" by the Holy Spirit. The Greek word used to describe the Spirit's activity is the same as in Acts 2:2 for the "blowing" of the violent wind from heaven. OT writers were like ships with unfurled sails filled with the blowing wind of heaven. As God's breath propelled them, they wrote in human words his amazing revelations. The Holy Spirit took charge and guided them so they could speak a true word from God.

To realize the Holy Spirit controlled the OT prophets is of utmost significance. It means their prophetic writings are "completely reliable" regardless of their outlandish claims (v 19). They are not the mere utterances of man but declarations of the eternal one. Since Scripture originates with God, it is not fiction. The prophetic word is not cleverly invented stories designed to exploit and take advantage of people (2:3). Nor is it wishful thinking when the Bible tells of the power and coming of the Lord Jesus Christ (v 16). Scripture is God's word. Period.

The Spirit has an integral role in the creation of Scripture. He not only revealed God's word to the prophets, but he also preserved it from human error. God's eternal word entered time and human history through the Holy Spirit to give the world words of life, light and salvation. No other literature can compare.

Rhema: Therefore we can never undo, change, or annul God's indestructible word. Because it comes through the Spirit, it demands our full attention and obedience (v 19).

DECEMBER 4 | II PETER 2:1–3; 3:14–18

THE SPIRIT AND INTERPRETATION (PART II)

Above all, you must understand that no prophecy of Scripture came about by the prophet's own interpretation of things. For prophecy never had its origin in the human will, but prophets, though human, spoke from God as they were carried along by the **Holy Spirit**. *–II* PETER 1:20–21

The Spirit not only inspired Scripture, he helps interpret it. We need his help to understand God's word just as much as the prophets needed his assistance to receive it. "To interpret" means to loose, to untie a knot, or explain a difficulty. Without the Spirit's help, Scripture's ultimate meaning is concealed. No one, for instance, could understand Jesus' parables until he "explained" their meaning (Mk 4:34). In this age, the Spirit assumes Christ's interpretive role in helping us properly understand God's word.

No one should give their own private interpretation of Scripture because only the Spirit can construe what he inspired. Peter, for instance, just filled with the Spirit "interpreted" the phenomena of the day of Pentecost. He declared, "This is what was spoken by the prophet Joel" (Acts 2:15). Conjecture, rules of hermeneutics or human reasoning were incapable of explaining the event. The full meaning of Joel's prophecy remained locked up until the Spirit came upon Peter and gave him the explanation. Then he could interpret OT prophecies (Acts 2:25–28; 34–35; 4:25–26).

We need to be careful whenever we try to interpret Scripture without the Spirit's help. Peter writes this letter because false teachers (2:1–3) were misinterpreting it. This grievous error has continued to this day. Obviously, they have not followed the leading of the Spirit. Instead, they have introduced destructive heresies of their own making. Because they operated without the Spirit, they mangled OT prophecies, Paul's writings, and other Scripture (3:16).

To safeguard against the vagaries of human subjectivity in handling God's word necessitates dependence upon the Holy Spirit. Listening to him must take precedence over imposing our ideas, convictions, and theological persuasions. As we humble ourselves and lay aside our presuppositions, we can ask the Inspirer of Scripture to interpret it.

Rhema: To rely upon God's Spirit does not do away with studying Scripture nor decrease its importance. Just the opposite: he releases its true significance. Our private interpretation is not what counts but the Spirit's.

DECEMBER 5 | I JOHN 3:1–24

THE SPIRIT DISSOLVES OUR DOUBTS

The one who keeps God's commands lives in him, and he in them. And this is how we know that he lives in us: We know it by the Spirit he gave us. –I JOHN 3:24

Have you ever doubted your salvation? Many of us encounter a crisis of faith and go through times of spiritual upheaval. John writes this letter so we can know how to "set our hearts at rest in his presence" (v 19) and dissolve these doubts.

The theme of the epistle is abiding in Christ. How can we be sure Jesus dwells in us and we in him? The irrefutable proof is the Holy Spirit. John says, "We know it by the Spirit he gave us." The word "know" used here means knowledge derived from experience. How we come by this knowledge is very special. Often the term refers to personal intimacies, such as Adam's marital "knowledge" of Eve (Gen 4:1). Therefore, what destroys our doubts is the memorable experience of receiving the Spirit. We are convinced Jesus has made his home in our hearts because of our intimate and immediate knowledge of the Spirit.

To have Christ is to have the Spirit. The grounds of our assurance rests on the clear manifestation of divine life in us. God's Spirit verifies Christ lives in by helping us obey his commands. We are "to believe in the name of his Son, Jesus Christ, and to love one another as he commanded us" (v 23). As we become aware of the inner working of the Spirit who helps us obey God, our faith increases and our doubts dissipate.

Another assurance by which the Spirit proves Christ indwells us is by helping us love one another. When the Spirit indwells us, Christ's love saturates our hearts. Thus, this profound love for fellow believers is a manifestation of Christ in us. Anyone with the Spirit will sense it. "Those who obey his commands live in him and he in them" (v 24).

Rhema: The practice of love, the possession of the Spirit, and the profession of faith are irrefutable assurances God lives in you and you in him. To experience him living in you sets your heart at rest. You simply cannot doubt when God is present in you through the Holy Spirit.

DECEMBER 6 | I JOHN 4:1–3; 2:18–27

HOW TO RECOGNIZE THE SPIRIT OF GOD

*This is how you can recognize the **Spirit** of God: Every spirit that acknowledges that Jesus Christ has come in the flesh is from God, but every spirit that does not acknowledge Jesus is not from God.*
–I JOHN 4:2–3

It is a good thing we have the anointing of Christ's Spirit to help us sift through the plethora of ideas and claims today. We are barraged with content from TV, the internet, and media that is decisively not Christian. Truth does not seem to matter anymore. News is often fake. Our world is filled with false teachings, false doctrines, and false religions. The truth of God in Christ Jesus is challenged. How then do we distinguish between truth and error and determine what is of God from what is of the evil one?

Fortunately, we are able to recognize what spirit animates these prevaricators of truth. Behind every educator, prophet, author, politician or preacher stands a spirit. Either the Spirit of God or a demon from hell animates them. Followers of Christ are frequently threatened by demonic powers who particularly try to distort the truth about Jesus. Many claim to have the truth but God gives us a test to know who is telling it and who isn't.

To have the Spirit means you have the spiritual ability to distinguish between truth and error. Because of the anointing, the apostle declared, "All of you know the truth" (2:20). Jesus said, "The Spirit of truth 'will teach you all things'" (Jn 14:26). Since you are anointed you can tell who speaks by the Spirit of God.

We are not to believe every spirit but to check and ascertain if they are from God (v 1). The word "test" is a term used for detecting impure ingredients in a coin. To test means to critically examine before approving something or someone. John furnishes us with a simple test to assay whether someone is of God or not: what does the person say about Jesus? Does the individual acknowledge and confess Jesus came in the flesh? The spirit of antichrist (v 3) denies the true humanity of Christ because without it salvation is impossible.

Rhema: In a word, the Spirit helps us detect delusions and differentiate them from divine truth.

DECEMBER 7 | I JOHN 4:4–12

THE SPIRIT OF TRUTH AND
THE SPIRIT OF FALSEHOOD

*We are from God, and whoever knows God listens to us; but whoever is not from God does not listen to us. This is how we recognize the **Spirit** of truth and the spirit of falsehood.* **–I JOHN 4:6**

Jesus warned false prophets will come in sheep's clothing but inwardly are ravenous wolves. Their toxic teachings pose a serious threat to God's people and can wreak havoc in his flock. If they are not identified and rejected, calamitous harm will result. No teacher is so dangerous as one who deceives and causes people to abandon their faith. Their teachings are like counterfeit life jackets: they look like the real thing until needed. Then anyone trusting them in a shipwreck would drown. The same is true with deceitful teachings that distort the truth of God in Christ Jesus.

God gives us a second test for exposing the spirit of falsehood. We have a way of discriminating between error and truth. Many claim to speak for Christ or to speak by the Spirit but do not. The criterion for discerning the authentic voice of the Spirit is simple: observe people's response to apostolic teaching. John, speaking for all the apostles, declares, "We are from God." Jesus said, "He who belongs to God hears what God says" (Jn 8:47). True prophecy is in accord with the fundamental teachings of the apostles.

Unless a teacher, prophet, writer, or preacher is born of the Spirit, he or she is still in the world and will function from a worldly perspective (v 5). Their words will not save. The spirit of the world opposes Christ (v 4) and is therefore antichristian. A clear line of demarcation exists between true authentic Christian teaching and a false teaching. The litmus test for the authentic voice of the Spirit is adherence to the NT. All who love God hear his voice and will devote themselves "to the apostles' teaching" (Acts 2:42). Rigorous adherence to it is what differentiates the Spirit of truth from the spirit of falsehood.

Rhema: Those born of God must adhere to this test and watch out for those who stray from the NT message by distortion, addition or subtraction. The spirit of falsehood is still at work, savagely attacking God's revelation in Christ.

DECEMBER 8 | I JOHN 4:13–21

THE SPIRIT PROVES WE ARE
TRUE BELIEVERS

This is how we know that we live in him and he in us: He has given us of his Spirit. –I JOHN 4:13

How do we know we are true believers? John was big on tests. In this verse, he offers a test to show if we have been born again. His test is: does God live in our lives? Is he at work in us? If he is dwelling in us, we should see ongoing evidence of his presence. In this way, the Spirit guarantees the genuineness of our salvation.

We understand we are God's because he has given us his Spirit. In two ways, the indwelling Spirit proves he is living in us and we in him. The first is when we love one another (v 12). Because his Spirit endows us with God's nature, his love is made complete in us. We perceive God is working in our lives when we express his unconditional love to others. We realize we are of God because only the Spirit can produce this kind of love. "God is love. Whoever lives in love lives in God, and God in them" (v 16).

Another way his Spirit demonstrates we are genuine believers relates to truth. How do we come to know beyond a doubt "the Father has sent his Son to be the Savior of the world" (v 14)? When our heavenly Father gives us his Spirit, we receive the Spirit of truth and he reveals Jesus to us. His revelation of Christ is so evident and real we can never doubt it. Our salvation rests on confessing this fundamental truth: "If anyone acknowledges that Jesus is the Son of God, God lives in them and they in God" (v 15). To acknowledge means "to agree with" or "to say the same thing." Therefore, to confess this truth is no mere intellectual assent but acceptance of the inner witness of the Spirit.

Rhema: In two ways, the Spirit proves we are true believers. First, we can observe the Spirit operating in our lives because he fills us with God's love for others. Second, as the Spirit of truth he makes Jesus real to us; we know beyond a doubt Jesus is the Son of God, the Savior of the world.

DECEMBER 9 | I JOHN 5:1–12

THE SPIRIT TESTIFIES THAT JESUS IS THE CHRIST

*This is the one who came by water and blood—Jesus Christ. He did not come by water only, but by water and blood. And it is the **Spirit** who testifies, because the Spirit is the truth. –I JOHN 5:6*

To correct any misunderstanding concerning Jesus' human nature, John declared Christ came by water and blood. We take these enigmatic terms as shorthand for Jesus' baptism and crucifixion. Like bookends they bracket the beginning and end of his earthly ministry. The apostle is dealing with false teachers who denied Christ's humanity. If Jesus were not a man, a serious heresy, then he cannot be the second Adam, our representative who died in our place.

Many diverse opinions of Jesus have circulated since he launched his public ministry. He asked his disciples, for instance, whom people thought he was (Mt 16:13–17). Elijah, one of the prophets, or John the Baptist come back from the dead, they replied. But these beliefs were wrong. Peter on the other hand, believed Jesus was the Christ, a belief that came to him by revelation. The churches in John's day, a half century later, still struggled with the humanity of Jesus.

Jesus was an enigma because true knowledge of him transcends history, reason, and experience. Unlike anyone in history, he was fully human and fully God. To deny his humanity was as heretical as a denial of his deity. At the end of the first century AD, heretics bent this truth to fit their philosophy. For them flesh was evil but the spirit was good. Christ was so holy, they taught, he could have nothing to do with the material world. To maintain their view, they must deny his human existence and, consequently, negate the gospel.

Rhema: How do we come to believe the historical Jesus of Nazareth is also the Christ, the Son of God (v 1)? This truth is not derived from reason or sensual perception but by the Spirit. To understand it, we must experience the power of the Holy Spirit to reveal truth. God's truth comes to us as revelation not as objective or subjective truth. Divine truth is different. It requires the Spirit of truth to show us the earthly Jesus is none other than the glorious Son of God.

DECEMBER 10 | I JOHN 5:13–21

THE SPIRIT IS THE TRUTH

And it is the Spirit who testifies, because the Spirit is the truth.
–I JOHN 5:6

The Spirit is not the enemy of biblical or theological truth but the foundation. The apostle asserts, "The Spirit is the truth." How strange then some will trust their doctrines more than they will God's Spirit. Perhaps they fail to realize his witness is prior to and superior to their theological assertions. Christian teaching must always align itself with the Spirit's testimony because truth has been entrusted to him. John emphasizes the Spirit's important role in helping us know divine truth. That is why he elevates the Third Person of the Trinity above our faith assertions. The Spirit's testimony (v 9) is never wrong!

A personal relationship with the Spirit comes before formulating spiritual truth. It was so with the prophets and the apostles. Prior to their writings, they had an encounter with him. That is how we received the Bible. The Spirit is a most wonderful, amazing person. When we are born again, we experience a new reality in which he is always present to address us person to person. He brings to our attention things we have overlooked, verifies what is true, and objects to whatever is false. As the Supreme Person, the Spirit of God is superior to and greater than any theological idea.

The Spirit is sent to testify about Jesus. In the OT he spoke of him through the prophets. In the NT he bore witness to Christ throughout his earthly life. Later, through the apostles. He speaks truth through their records. However, our heavenly Father sent us the Spirit of truth to verify directly that Jesus is the Christ the Son of God. Although this truth is fiercely contested, the Spirit cannot lie. We must, therefore, learn to trust the Spirit because he is the truth.

Rhema: The Spirit who indwells us keeps on testifying to the truth of Jesus Christ. In fact, his ongoing activity in us is greater than the false spirits in the world. They are antichrists who do not speak the truth because they operate under the influence of the spirit of falsehood and deceit. Believing the truth gives us victory over the world and equips us to deal with everything that raises itself up to oppose God (vv 4–5).

DECEMBER 11 | JOHN 1:1–34

THE TESTIMONY OF THE SPIRIT

For there are three that testify: the **Spirit***, the water and the blood; and the three are in agreement.* **–I JOHN 5:7–8**

How can anyone refuse to accept Christianity's most significant claim? To believe Jesus is the Christ the Son of God is fundamental and consequential for salvation. It determines life and death, heaven and hell. God asks no one to put their faith in Christ without supporting evidence. Therefore, he provides overwhelming corroborative confirmation to influence our decision regarding his Son. So anyone investigating the truth about Jesus Christ can examine the evidence for themselves.

In our courts, we accept the testimony of man (v 9). In the apostle's day, many struggled with the humanity of Jesus because they didn't understand how God could take on flesh and blood. To help them overcome this obstacle, the apostle who was present with Jesus offered his own eyewitness account. That is why he says, "We proclaim to you what we have heard and seen" (1:3). He heard Jesus with his own ears, touched him with his own hands, and saw him with his own eyes.

If we accept man's testimony for important decisions, how much more credible is God's? He gives us three witnesses to prove Jesus is indeed his Son who came in the flesh. All three, the Spirit, the water, and the blood, concur.

By water the author most likely meant Christ's baptism. During this extraordinary historical event of our Savior's fleshly existence, the Holy Spirit came upon him. While standing in the water, his Father declared, "This is my Son." Similarly, the blood refers to his crucifixion where he shed his blood and died as a man. The Spirit was prominent in his death in so far as he raised him to life again. So, at both his baptism and death, the Spirit, the water, and the blood converge to offer awesome evidence of Christ's humanity. Since the Holy Spirit was present at these actual events, he is the primary eyewitness to the truth about Jesus. His testimony is the testimony of God.

Rhema: The most wonderful proof of all, however, is the internal testimony of the Spirit. Anyone who believes Jesus is the Son of God "has this testimony in himself" (v 10). Throughout our life, the Spirit continues to testify about Christ.

DECEMBER 12 | JUDE 1:1–19

PEOPLE WITHOUT THE SPIRIT

*These are the people who divide you, who follow mere natural instincts and do not have the **Spirit**.* –JUDE 19

We must contend for the faith (v 3). As believers, our duty is to fight those desiring to disrupt the church. In the last days, scoffers will arise bent on dividing God's people. Jude says to these mockers, "You want to divide the church. Well, let me give you a division. God separates us into two groups: those without the Spirit and those with the Spirit." In his short letter, the author describes individuals without the Spirit.

To be devoid of the Spirit means to be without God and left to one's own fallen human nature. Jude calls such persons soulish (Gr *psychikoi*), because they live by natural instincts instead of spiritual. They subsist on the human plane bereft of the Spirit's holy influences. Instead of his lifting, redeeming, and empowering presence, they follow mere natural impulses. Unable to rise above their human condition, the unregenerate align themselves against God. Therefore, they sneer and despise anything to do with spiritual things. Like Cain (v 11), they have no use for the things of God. They have crept into the church to destroy and distort the grace of God.

Jude has many descriptions for these persons who only operate on the human level. Scoffers. Mockers. Blasphemers. Abusers. Slanderers. Gamblers. Faultfinders. Boasters. Flatterers. Dividers. That is not all. They are waterless clouds. Wild waves. Straying stars. Selfish shepherds. Unfruitful trees. Godless people. Of course! Because their minds are not renewed their ethics, values, and attitudes are worldly. Spiritless people mind the things of men and orient their lives around egregious egos instead of Christ. To them the sensual, mental, and psychological is more important than a life touched and transformed by the Spirit

From God's perspective, the worst thing to say about individuals is they do not have the Spirit. Such personalities might be intelligent, creative, industrious, and lauded for many worthwhile accomplishments. But if they do not have the Spirit living in them, they can rise no higher than their natural instincts.

Rhema: People without the Spirit are lost, imprisoned to the weakness of human nature and in eternal danger. If they want to sort people into groups, they must remember they exist in the one without the Spirit.

DECEMBER 13 | JUDE 20–25

PRAYING IN THE HOLY SPIRIT

But you, dear friends, by building yourselves up in your most holy faith and praying in the **Holy Spirit**, *keep yourselves in God's love as you wait for the mercy of our Lord Jesus Christ to bring you to eternal life.*
–JUDE 20–21

Hostile attacks on our most holy faith are a call to war. The writer rouses us to engage in spiritual warfare. In this verse, he gives three commands ordering us how to confront false teaching. Neutrality and neglect are not options. If we are to survive, we are to fight aggressively.

First, we must build ourselves up in the faith. The reason for this brief letter was to urge believers to defend themselves against false teaching by adhering to the essential truths of the gospel (v 3). The unadulterated teaching of the apostles must never be corrupted, diluted, or changed. Rather, we are to grow in the sacred revealed truth passed down to us through the apostles. Nothing exposes error more.

The second charge is to pray in the Holy Spirit. Two things separate us from false teachers: apostolic teaching and the Holy Spirit. Together, these become a powerful weapon called the sword of the Spirit (Eph 6:17). The word and the Spirit help strengthen our spiritual immune system. Praying the word of God in the power of the Spirit is the way to wage war against the enemy. We must learn how to wait upon the Spirit. As we commune with him, we will hear his voice, discover his promptings, and feel his anointing. In the heat of battle engaged in spiritual warfare, we can pray all kinds of prayers in the Holy Spirit (Eph 6:18). He will bring to our consciousness the word of the Lord we are to pray. Then we will cut through enemy lies, demolish their arguments, and take every false thought into captivity (II Cor 10:4–5).

The third command is to keep ourselves in the love of God. We must always remember we are "loved by God the Father" (v 1) more than we realize (v 2).

Rhema: To engage in spiritual warfare we must take responsibility for our own spiritual growth by building ourselves up in God's word, praying in the Holy Spirit and living in the atmosphere of love.

DECEMBER 14 | REVELATION 1:1–8

THE SPIRIT IN ALL HIS PERFECTIONS

John, To the seven churches in the province of Asia: Grace and peace to you from him who is, and who was, and who is to come, and from the **seven spirits** *before his throne.* –REVELATION 1:4

When terrible things happen we question God's whereabouts, especially if hell is breaking loose. In times like that, we need divine assurance the I AM THAT I AM is on the throne and our enemies will be vanquished. Our God "who is" with us now and "who was" with us in the past will be with us when he sets everything right. Despite what is occurring, he is in control.

The book of Revelation prophesies a tsunami of trouble ready to crash upon the earth. Life as we know it is swept away as the future of God materializes. Believers inherit paradise; unbelievers, a terrible judgment. In the original text, Revelation is called an "apocalypse of Jesus Christ" (v 1) because it is a "prophecy" revealing end-time events. The verb in verse one translated "to show" means to make known by signs. Most modern translations miss this clue but the NASV captures it in the footnote. So "the things which must soon take place" are "signified" in symbols.

This is how we interpret the number seven. The seven spirits before God's throne signify the complete and perfect work of the Holy Spirit. In the OT, the number seven is significant because it speaks of completion or perfection. God finished his creation in seven days. The number is prominent in Revelation—seven stars, seals, horns, trumpets, plagues, etc. The seven churches are literal but may symbolize the Church in its totality from its beginning to its consummation.

Images are helpful when trying to describe heaven and the throne of God. In this way, the author "pictures" the Spirit in all his perfections. The seven spirits (see Isa 11:2) before God's throne connect with these seven churches. In every age and locale churches are charged "to hear what the Spirit says to the churches." Each church's destiny rests with its response to the Holy Spirit.

Rhema: We see God's Spirit before the throne ready to bring redemption to completion. He acts in subordination to the Father and the Son to do their bidding and supply every church its needs.

DECEMBER 15 | REVELATION 1:9–20

TAKEN TO HEAVEN IN THE SPIRIT

*On the Lord's Day I was in the **Spirit**, and I heard behind me a loud voice like a trumpet, which said: "Write on a scroll what you see and send it to the seven churches: to Ephesus, Smyrna, Pergamum, Thyatira, Sardis, Philadelphia and Laodicea." –REVELATION 1:10–11*

Do you ever feel banished, isolated, or cut off from friends and family? John was living in exile on a desolate, deserted isle, the abode of convicts. He was sent there as punishment for testifying about the Lord and preaching the word (v 9). While suffering for his faith, the Spirit of God transformed his worst nightmare into a heavenly experience.

They could bind his hands and feet but could not chain his soul. On Patmos he was secluded but, in the Spirit, he rose to keep company with angels. Circumstances prevented his celebrating the resurrection of Jesus with fellow believers, but the Spirit transported him to the courts of heaven. There the faithful apostle experienced a day like no other when he saw Jesus in all his regal glory (vv 12–18).

What is it to be "in the Spirit?" It means the Spirit brings us into another state of being where the things of heaven become real. He transports us into realms of truth otherwise inaccessible. The Comforter reveals what eye has not seen, nor ear heard, nor mind has conceived (I Cor 2:9–10). John beholds the end of the world as we know it and the dawning of a new day, the Day of the Lord with Jesus upon the throne. Heaven explodes with color, sound, and awesome scenes.

John is not having an out-of-body experience for he hears, sees, feels, weeps, turns around, and falls at the feet of Jesus. Rather, the Spirit brings him into a heightened dimension of prophetic revelation. A great voice, the voice of the infinite, commands him to write what he sees. By the Spirit he expresses the inexpressible as the awesome future of God unfolds before his eyes. What he witnesses becomes the content of the book, the revelation of Jesus Christ (v 1).

Rhema: Today you might be suffering on your own isle of Patmos but be encouraged. In the Spirit, your worst place may become a gateway to the glories of heaven.

DECEMBER 16 | REVELATION 2:1–7

HEAR WHAT THE SPIRIT SAYS
TO THE CHURCH AT EPHESUS

Whoever has ears, let them hear what the Spirit says to the churches. To the one who is victorious, I will give the right to eat from the tree of life, which is in the paradise of God. **–REVELATION 2:7**

The grandest church in the NT found herself in difficulty and her existence endangered. Once the center of a fiery revival that shook the province of Asia, now she has chilled. Most would have noticed nothing amiss, but Jesus detected one fatal flaw. Doctrine was right. Ministry was right. Everything was right except the heart. The congregation had left its first love.

What is a church without love? It is more important than good works, correct doctrine, and enduring hardship. At Ephesus, her worship and preaching were good. But she had walked away from an intimate, passionate devotion to Christ. Fervency was gone. Had her affections and adoration found another? The first sign of spiritual decline is a cold and unresponsive heart.

Ephesus is the first of seven churches Jesus addresses. What he says to her he says to all the churches in every era. He communicates his observations, encouragements, promises, and warnings through the Holy Spirit. If we will heed the Spirit's message to the churches, it will lead to victory below and heaven above.

Be attentive to the prophetic role of the Spirit because his voice is the Lord's. Christ speaks to us today by his Spirit with the same force and authority as he did during his ministry on earth. Therefore, the words of the Spirit are of absolute importance. They are life-giving. "Do not quench the Spirit. Do not treat prophecies with contempt but test them all" (I Thess 5:19–20). The book of Revelation is one huge prophecy (1:3).

To heed the words of the Spirit results in victory and victory leads to paradise. Letting the Spirit inflame us with first-love passion for Jesus gives us the right to eat of the tree of life. Adam and Eve failed in the garden because they left their tender love for their Creator when they disobeyed his word. Christ came to restore paradise, but we must love him with all our hearts to regain it.

Rhema: Hear what the Spirit says and let him reignite your passion for Jesus.

DECEMBER 17 | REVELATION 2:8–11

THE SPIRIT SPEAKS TO THE CHURCH AT SMYRNA

Whoever has ears, let them hear what the Spirit says to the churches. The one who is victorious will not be hurt at all by the second death.
–REVELATION 2:11

Blood from the church's martyrs flows as a river coursing down through the centuries. Perhaps you suffer persecution in its subtler forms. Were you passed over for a promotion or a raise because of your faith in Christ? Harassed? Bullied? Ostracized? You may be placing your life at risk for even meeting in his name. If so, the Spirit of God has a word for you.

The church at Smyrna represents believers in every age who suffered for their faith. Mistreatment may take many forms as it did in this city. Affliction. Poverty. Slander. Persecution. Imprisonment. Martyrdom. Various trials and hardships crushed these Christ followers and made their lives miserable. Many had their goods stolen, their properties confiscated, and their jobs taken away. Others paid the ultimate price.

To encourage you, the Spirit says, "Remember Jesus in his affliction. Although he died he was faithful even to the end. Everything you are going through he has experienced. So he understands your anguish and the mean things people say. I know behind your troubles is an evil foe but consider Jesus who has the first and last word. When down, he came to life again!"

The Spirit has a living word for everyone facing the crushing pressures of persecution. He says, "The one who is victorious will not be hurt at all by the second death." The term "second death" only occurs in the book of Revelation. It refers to eternal death. Anyone rejecting Christ faces a final fatal removal from God's presence after they die. The second death and hell are cast into the lake of fire (20:14). However, they have no power over anyone who puts their trust in Christ and remains faithful unto death.

Rhema: The Spirit says to everyone suffering loss in this life, "You are rich" (v 9). The eternal far outweighs the temporal; the spiritual the material. Do not fear! Do not defect! You may lose your life in this world, but you will receive the crown of life in the next. For overcoming, the glorious victor's crown of eternal life is yours."

DECEMBER 18 | REVELATION 2:12–17

THE SPIRIT SPEAKS TO THE CHURCH AT PERGAMUM

Whoever has ears, let them hear what the Spirit says to the churches. The one who is victorious I will give some of the hidden manna. I will also give that person a white stone with a new name written on it, known only to the one who receives it. **–REVELATION 2:17**

Being a believer in Pergamum was difficult because Satan lived there and set up his throne (v 13). For this reason, popular culture was more aligned with darkness than with God. Several church members succumbed to the lure of the world while others tolerated false teaching and embraced pagan practices (vv 14–15). What does the Spirit say to believers feeling pressure to compromise with the world? He warns them not to accommodate a fallen society.

Many believers remained true to Jesus. The unfaithful, by contrast, believed they could party with the devil and take part in sinful pleasures. The Lord will oppose them with a sharp double-edged sword (1:16, 2:12). Jesus said, "Do not act like Balaam and betray me for fame and fortune. Do not wed yourselves to a wicked society, regardless of the material rewards. Do not sell out to an ungodly culture; otherwise, I will fight against you."

The Spirit says if we are victorious over the world, we will receive two amazing blessings. The first is hidden manna. God's people ate the bread of heaven while sojourning in the wilderness. In symbolic language, he tells us not to worry about forgoing the pleasures of the world; Jesus will give us far greater satisfaction. We get to "experience the joys of life and the exquisite pleasures of [God's] own eternal presence" (Ps 16:11 TLB). The second promise is a white stone with a new name. God gave Jacob the new name, Israel, when he overcame the angel (Gen 32:28) and became a prince with God. Our victory will reveal our true character, personality, and perfect actualization in eternity.

Rhema: Everything Jesus spoke to this church regarding deviating from the faith and compromising with the world the Spirit says to us. Our Lord is mindful of the spiritual climate in which we live. Many of us reside in cities where Satan is strong and the culture opposes God. Even if Satan dominates culture, we must stay true to Christ.

DECEMBER 19 | REVELATION 2:18–29

THE SPIRIT SPEAKS TO THE CHURCH AT THYATIRA

To the one who is victorious and does my will to the end, I will give author-ity over the nations— that one 'will rule them with an iron scepter and will dash them to pieces like pottery'—just as I have received authority from my Father. I will also give that one the morning star. Whoever has ears, let them hear what the Spirit says to the churches.
—REVELATION 2:26–29

Thyatira represents the good, the bad, and the ugly in churches. The good refers to believers who are growing in love, faith, ser-vice, and perseverance (v 19). The bad are those who tolerate Jezebel's teachings that corrupt true worship (v 20). She is the most notorious woman in the Bible and symbolizes the introduction of immorality and false religion into Christianity. The ugly relates to members who adopt her teaching and take part in Satan's deep secrets (v 24). Consequently, the church plunges to new lows.

Christ is alarmed with the direction his church is going so he reveals himself as the Son of God and Judge. His eyes are like blazing fire to show he sees into the secret places of people's hearts and minds (v 23). His feet are burnished bronze (v 18) because he will stomp on those who worship another.

What is the Spirit's message? He says, "Jesus, the Son of God (v 18), is the only one we are to worship." Nothing must take precedence. No doctrine, no teaching, no prophet, no prophetess, and no church official must ever take his place. To do so is idolatry and spiritual adul-tery. Because Jezebel introduced abominable practices into Israel's worship, she typifies the vilest distortions of Christianity.

Rhema: The Spirit says if we keep our doctrine and worship pure, Jesus will give us two rewards. For honoring him and rejecting the lust for worldly power, Christ will give us authority over the nations and the morning star. In the end, we will reign with him forever (Ps 2:8). No government or power will ever threaten, persecute, or destroy us again. He also gives us the morning star which is Christ himself (22:16). He is our ultimate reward—we will share in his authority, inheritance, and glory. When Jesus returns, we will be part of the dawning of a new day.

DECEMBER 20 | REVELATION 3:1–6

THE ONE WHO HOLDS THE
SEVEN SPIRITS OF GOD

*To the angel of the church in Sardis write: These are the words of him who holds the **seven spirits** of God and the seven stars. I know your deeds; you have a reputation of being alive, but you are dead.* –REVELATION 3:1

The opening description of Jesus in each message to the seven churches corresponds to their condition. This church is dead, and she needs the seven spirits of God that Jesus holds in his hands. This is code language to say Jesus has the resources needed to revitalize his dying church.

The seven spirits of God symbolize the fullness of the Spirit. The perfect and complete work of the Holy Spirit is at Jesus' disposal. He can supply the life-giving Spirit to any church suffering spiritual decline. He is ready to impart every vital force to cause them to flourish again. The Spirit, always subordinate to Christ, is his to bestow.

Reliance on past accomplishments may tempt a church to think of herself as more alive than warranted. Over time, however, she may become complacent. A congregation might become like Samson who fell asleep in the lap of the enemy and could not rouse himself as before. His negligence led to a loss of power. Churches must not neglect the Spirit's work. They need up-to-date experiences, not good reputations. The full and complete activity of God's Spirit will revitalize every particle of their being.

What is true of churches is true of us. To lose our spiritual vitality is disastrous. Many signs show when fervor is waning. For instance, we may go through the motions of a follower of Christ even as our light flickers. Our walk with the Lord is more routine than romance. We do things in our own strength rather than in his might. When spiritual things seem stale or boring, we are in the throes of death. Gone is the joy, anticipation, and excitement of his presence. We need the Holy Spirit if we want a vibrant relation with Christ.

Rhema: Like his churches, Jesus desires to direct the richness and power of the Holy Spirit towards us. He wants to reinvigorate our walk, empower our service, and set our hearts ablaze once again. To keep vibrant, we must invite the Spirit to operate fully in our lives.

DECEMBER 21 | REVELATION 3:1–6

THE SPIRIT SPEAKS TO THE CHURCH AT SARDIS

The one who is victorious will, like them, be dressed in white. I will never blot out the name of that person from the book of life, but will acknowledge that name before my Father and his angels. Whoever has ears, let them hear what the Spirit says to the churches. **–REVELATION 3:5–6**

How do we keep revival fires burning? Over time, if we are not vigilant we will lose our spiritual vitality. Although the church in Sardis had a great reputation, it was dead. Jesus detected its lifelessness and acknowledged it had the forms of Christianity, but the underlying reality was absent (v 1). Coasting on past glory, smug in her wealth and size did not compensate for the lack of God's Spirit. Even though it was the place to be on Sunday, little of the Holy Spirit was there.

That is why Jesus reveals himself to this congregation as the one who holds in his hand the seven spirits of God, a symbol for the complete work of the Spirit. More than anything, the church needed a fresh infusion of power from on high. This applies to every church in every age. Jesus wants to give each congregation the fullness of the Spirit to ensure their spiritual health remains vibrant. All the gifts, graces, fruit, and activity of the Spirit, everything a church needs to flourish, is available from Christ.

As with churches so with us. We may wonder why so many believers struggle to enjoy a vivacious walk with God if his Spirit is so freely available. The answer is simple: life in the Spirit is not automatic but comes at a price. Responsibility for our spiritual condition rests with us. Jesus commanded the believers in Sardis, "Wake up!" They had gone to sleep, lost their vigilance, and became too comfortable. To strengthen "what remains and is about to die" (v 2) is our responsibility. We must watch over our souls to prevent our names being erased from the book of life.

Rhema: The Spirit says great rewards await us when we overcome spiritual lethargy. Therefore, abound in the Spirit's fullness. Pay attention to prayer, Bible reading, witnessing, and fellowship. Covet the Spirit's presence and power. Walk in the Spirit. Repent of apathy. We need what Jesus holds in his hand.

DECEMBER 22 | REVELATION 3:7–13

THE SPIRIT SPEAKS TO THE CHURCH AT PHILADELPHIA

*The one who is victorious I will make a pillar in the temple of my God. Never again will they leave it. I will write on them the name of my God and the name of the city of my God, the new Jerusalem, which is coming down out of heaven from my God; and I will also write on them my new name. Whoever has ears, let them hear what the **Spirit** says to the churches.* **–REVELATION 3:12–13**

You do not have to be big to be great. The believers in Philadelphia were few but they impressed the Lord. They only had "a little strength," but Christ was so enthralled by their faithfulness he set before them an open door and gave them multiple blessings. Sometimes church people boast in their massive buildings or jaw-dropping programs, but Jesus is not much impressed by those things.

Two things, however, delight the Lord: keeping his word and not denying his name. Our exalted Savior reveals himself to this church as "holy and true." In essence, he says, "I am the Holy One, Almighty God, the one who is set apart from everything else, the one with absolute authority to speak, order and command. Every word I speak is true and every promise I make I will keep." Jesus is thrilled when believers value his word and walk in obedience to it. By keeping his word, they lived in a way that honored his name. Such faithfulness is a measure of true spiritual greatness.

These believers, consequently, received unique promises for remaining true to the Lord and keeping his word. He promised to keep them from the hour of persecution coming on the world. Not only that, the Lord set an open door before them which only he can open or shut. With the key of David, he opened God's eternal palace and the resources of heaven. Faithfulness, therefore, led to unlimited opportunity and incalculable blessing. In addition, he rewards overcomers—those who keep his word and do not deny his name—with a crown and a place of honor in the city of God.

Rhema: The Spirit says, "Do not be taken up with the things by which men judge greatness but pay attention to what thrills the Lord: preach, teach and keep his word."

DECEMBER 23 | REVELATION 3:14–22

HEAR WHAT THE SPIRIT SAYS
TO THE CHURCH AT LAODICEA

*To the one who is victorious, I will give the right to sit with me on my throne, just as I was victorious and sat down with my Father on his throne. Whoever has ears, let them hear what the **Spirit** says to the churches.* –REVELATION 3:21–22

We cannot live the Christian life without a red-hot passion for Christ. His words to the seventh church sting. Jesus says, "Because you are lukewarm—neither hot nor cold—I am about to spit you out of my mouth" (v 16). This indictment should propel believers to examine their relationship with Jesus. To lose our first love is one thing, but to leave Christ out of our everyday lives is another.

Imagine a church that shuts out Jesus! He is standing outside the door knocking, looking for an invitation to enter (v 20). He craves their fellowship and wants to reenter their lives to sit and sup with them. The church says, "I am rich; I have acquired wealth and do not need a thing" (v 17). She has adopted the sinful values of the surrounding culture and mistakenly believes the world offers her everything. Operating under a false sense of security and blinded by pride, Laodicea entertains a dangerous delusion foolishly thinking she can exist without him.

When Jesus looked at these sickening believers, he declared, "But you do not realize that you are wretched, pitiful, poor, blind and naked" (v 17). They had just enough of Christ to lull them but not enough to make them zealous followers. Jesus counsels them to come to him and purchase the goods they need. He implores, "Buy my gold refined in the fire because I am a treasure above the material things of earth. Buy white raiment because my righteousness will cover your shameful nakedness. Buy eye salve and cure your spiritual blindness."

Rhema: The Spirit's message is we need to know how odious and abominable a lukewarm heart is to the Lord. Without him we can do nothing; without him we are nothing. To be victorious we must overcome spiritual indifference and invite the Spirit to give us a fresh vision of Jesus, so our passion for him will begin to sizzle. For overcoming lukewarmness, we are promised heaven's great reward of reigning with Christ.

DECEMBER 24 | REVELATION 4:1–6

TAKEN INTO THE PRESENCE OF
GOD BY THE SPIRIT

*At once I was in the **Spirit**, and there before me was a throne in heaven with someone sitting on it.* –REVELATION 4:2

Have you ever wished you could escape all your troubles? Travel advertisements ply on this inner longing. A brief respite, the excitement of a new discovery, a time to relax lure tons of travelers to exotic places every year. No doubt John experienced this same pining before the Spirit whisked him off to a more magnificent place.

For him to "witness" the faults and imperfections of these seven churches was grievous. They struggled with persecution, false teachers, and worldly enticements. If they overcame these obstacles, however, they would enjoy the things of heaven John sees. Life on earth is messy even in church—problems, suffering, failures, struggles. Happily, the scene changes and John experiences the dazzling wonder of the divine presence.

After viewing the seven churches (v 1), the Spirit permitted him to see "what must take place after." God's Spirit took the writer from the present to the future. In the Spirit, he crossed the threshold between the troubles on earth to the joys of heaven. Upon that golden shore, he saw the indescribable One sitting on the throne. This is the authentic center of power where decisions affecting earth are made. Not Rome, not the Empire nor powerful worldly centers but this throne decides everything.

The Spirit immersed John into heaven's inspiring atmosphere where he was mesmerized watching multitudes worship the one on the throne. All creation represented by the four living creatures uttered uninterrupted praise. "Day and night they never stop saying: 'Holy, holy, holy is the Lord God Almighty,' who was, and is, and is to come" (v 8). Continuous "glory, honor and thanks" is given to his Majesty. Saints, typified by the twenty-four elders, fell down and cast their crowns before the throne. They said, "You are worthy, our Lord and God, to receive glory and honor and power" (v 11).

Rhema: What a contrast between worship in the churches and the wondrous wonder in heaven. In the Spirit, we can close the gap by leaving our troubling distractions behind and entering the glorious presence of God knowing the Mighty One on the throne has everything under control.

DECEMBER 25 | REVELATION 4:6–11

THE SPIRIT COMPLETES HIS GLORIOUS WORK

From the throne came flashes of lightning, rumblings and peals of thunder. In front of the throne, seven lamps were blazing. These are the **seven spirits** *of God.* –REVELATION 4:5

"Glory to God in the highest" angel hosts exclaimed when Christ was born (Lk 2:14). Come join John this Christmas Day as the Spirit transfers him from the grind of Patmos to the grandeur of paradise. That which is perfect has come. All the great themes of the Bible, all its covenants, all God's purposes converge in this jaw-dropping heavenly scene.

From the throne come rumblings, flashes of lightning, and peals of thunder reminiscent of Mt. Sinai and the Old Covenant (Ex 19:4–9, 16–19). A magnificent rainbow resembling an emerald encircles the throne depicting the "everlasting covenant" made with Noah (Gen 9:12–17). Seven blazing lamps associated with the Abrahamic Covenant (Gen 15:17–21) burn before the throne. These are the seven spirits of God, code language for the perfect and complete work of the Holy Spirit.

See the Holy Spirit situated in front of the throne. He proceeds from the Father and the Son to bring about their will. The celestial fire has brought God's work in creation and redemption to completion. The Spirit of glory brings us, the people of God (the 24 elders) to our final state—seated with Christ, clothed in white, crowned with glory and honor. He helped us overcome. And now we surround the throne of God for eternity, beholding his face, and forever enjoying his presence.

Our personal journey with the Spirit began when he convicted us of sin, brought us to faith, and gave us a new birth. He indwelt us, groaned within us, led us, and assured us we are God's children. The Spirit transformed us from glory to glory, remaking us in the image of Christ. At last he has made us perfect and seated us with Christ in heavenly places. He ushers us into the unclouded joy and resplendent magnificence of heaven. Seven blazing torches symbolize his entire comprehensive activity.

Rhema: The Spirit has completed his work in creation and redemption. He has made us like Christ, perfect, holy, and righteous so we can partake in God's glory. Glorification is the eternal climax of our spiritual journey and the reason for our Savior's birth.

DECEMBER 26 | REVELATION 5:1–14

PERFECT WISDOM OF THE SPIRIT

Then I saw a Lamb, looking as if it had been slain, standing at the center of the throne, encircled by the four living creatures and the elders. The Lamb had seven horns and seven eyes, which are the **seven spirits of God** *sent out into all the earth.* **–REVELATION 5:6**

Mark Twain wrote in *The Prince and the Pauper*, "Now the air was heavy with the hush of suspense and expectancy." This describes the scene in heaven. The introduction of the scroll stops the celebratory singing and causes the apostle to burst into tears. A crisis exists in heaven because no one was found worthy to open its seals and consummate history.

Heaven was frozen in animated suspense until an elder declared, "The Lion of the tribe of Judah has triumphed and can open the seals." Instead of a Lion, we see a Lamb with a sacrificial knife wound on its neck standing at the center of heaven's throne. Only he can unlock the sealed future and complete God's plan for his creation.

The authorization to open the seven-sealed scroll (v 1, 7) is transferred from the Indescribable One who sits on the throne to the Lamb. Symbolized as an ancient Roman legal document, the sealed scroll is God's last will and testament giving us the right to "reign on the earth" (v 10). All creation has suffered and groaned awaiting this moment (Rom 8:18–22), so its importance cannot be overstated.

Besides his sacrificial death, the Lamb is uniquely qualified to regain our eternal inheritance. The first qualification is omnipotence. He has seven horns signifying his perfect power to conquer Satan who usurped man's authority over the earth that Adam had forfeited when he sinned.

The Lamb's second qualifying attribute is omniscience. He has seven eyes that are the seven spirits of God sent out into all the earth. At his disposal is the Spirit's full and complete wisdom and knowledge. Through him, the Lamb knows what is going on throughout the created realm. He knows what the lying, scheming, deceitful enemy is up and how to defeat him.

Rhema: It does not matter nations rage and their people plot against the Lord (Ps 2:1–2). He is now coming against them perfect in power and knowledge to execute the contents of the scroll.

DECEMBER 27 | REVELATION 14:1–20

THE SPIRIT SAYS YES

*Then I heard a voice from heaven say, "Write this: Blessed are the dead who die in the Lord from now on." "Yes," says the Spirit, "they will rest from their labor, for their deeds will follow them." –*REVELATION **14:13**

What is so remarkable about these unfolding events the Holy Spirit exclaim, "Yes?" A voice out of glory instructs John to write, "Blessed are the dead who die in the Lord from now on." To this declaration, the Spirit adds his amen. A turning point has arrived. During the Great Tribulation's darkest hour and final throes, a marvelous promise is made. The Third Person of the Trinity joins in bestowing a special blessing upon those who die for Christ instead of bowing to Satan. "Yeah!" says the Spirit.

The good news of the "eternal gospel" (v 6) proclaims God's hour of judgment has arrived. "Babylon is fallen" (v8). This wonderful news announces the end of Satan, Antichrist, and the Beast. God eradicates evil from his creation and terminates the devil's domination. What a relief! "The fury of God's wrath" (vv 9–11) the wicked experience is far worse than suffering for Christ during the tribulation. To come out of Babylon and follow the Lamb meant inescapable death followed by eternal life. Without the mark of the Beast, faithful followers of Christ could not buy or sell. This hardship made death preferable to a life of unbearable persecution.

We may wonder about the trouble Satan inflicts on us today and question whether loyalty to Christ is worth it. Wouldn't it be easier to just go along with the world and submit to the enemy? Believers in every age face this decision, not just the tribulation martyrs. Hear what the Spirit says to the churches! Serving Christ far outweighs anything we suffer for him. Heaven is for real. We are freed from life's burdens; we will rest from our labors and enter the joy of the Lord. There is no Monday in heaven, only Sunday, a Sabbath Rest of eternal bliss.

Rhema: What we do for Christ is never in vain, never forgotten, never lost. We are like a ship arriving in port with all its cargo intact. The Spirit of truth says, "Yes, these great promises are true." His yes is greater than Satan's no.

DECEMBER 28 | REVELATION 17:1–18

THE SPIRIT REVEALS THE END OF
FALSE WORSHIP

*Then the angel carried me away in the **Spirit** into a wilderness. There I saw a woman sitting on a scarlet beast that was covered with blasphemous names and had seven heads and ten horns.* –REVELATION 17:3

Have you ever wondered why so many false religions exist? The Spirit explains this mystery (v 5) as he carries John away to see their end. For this revelation, he takes the apostle into a wilderness to depict the chaotic conditions they have caused. Then by shocking symbols, the Spirit makes him understand their damnable role and demise.

If this interpretation is correct, then everything from astrology to Zoroastrianism is portrayed as a "great prostitute" (v 2). "The woman sitting on a scarlet beast" depicts every false religious expression. God judges her because she is unfaithful to him. She either misrepresents him or replaces him with something else. Idolatry, false worship, and corruption of the true are equated with a Great Harlot. She controls the scarlet beast. This is code language (seven heads and ten horns) for Gentile rule from beginning to end. False religion depicted as a dazzling prostitute has influenced and seduced every nation. It reaches its worst during the reign of Antichrist.

Throughout Scripture adultery, fornication, prostitution, and abomination serve as metaphors for unfaithfulness to God. Since God reserves our hearts for himself, he regards worshipping another as spiritual prostitution. Turning away from him is betrayal. False worship is like a woman of the streets with her calling card plastered on her forehead. She is "Babylon the great the mother of prostitutes and the abominations of the earth" (v 5).

This interpretation connects false religion to Babylon, the first city founded after Noah's flood. At Babel, the people sought to build a city with a monument to their own accomplishments. They did so to defy God and rebel against his command to spread throughout the earth. Since Babylon (Babel, Gen 11:1–9) was built for religious purposes in opposition to God, she is the originator of spiritual harlotry. So when God confused the languages at the Tower of Babel, the people scattered the seeds of their defiance everywhere.

Rhema: Rebellion against God is at the heart of witchcraft, occultism, astrology, and false religion. In the end, he destroys them (v 1).

DECEMBER 29 | REVELATION 19:1–10

THE SPIRIT OF PROPHECY

At this I fell at his feet to worship him. But he said to me, "Don't do that! I am a fellow servant with you and with your brothers and sisters who hold to the testimony of Jesus. Worship God! For it is the Spirit of prophecy who bears testimony to Jesus." —REVELATION 19:10

What does it mean to say the Spirit of prophecy bears testimony to Jesus? Before answering, keep in mind John sees the glorious future explode like Roman candles. Rapid bursts of revelation are punctuated by Hallelujahs (vv 1, 3, 4, 6). Completely overwhelmed, he must be stopped from worshipping an angel (v 9).

Prophecy is flowing so fast and furious John is blown away. Heaven breaks out into intense, powerful praise. The Harlot is condemned and judged. The Great King reigns unopposed. The Wedding of the Lamb has come. The radiant Bride enters in white. So, flabbergasted seeing history's dramatic conclusion, he falls prostrate before an angel.

The heavenly messenger chastises John by reminding him of the true nature of prophecy. The ultimate design and purpose of prophetic revelation is to bear witness to Jesus. For that reason he says, "Don't worship me! When it comes to our message we are on the same level and our content is identical. Our revelations bear witness to Jesus Christ. He is the focus, not us. Therefore, Worship God!" In effect, he says everything in Revelation is one glorious prophecy about Jesus (1:3) regardless of who delivers it. This is true of all prophecy; all Scripture testifies of him (Jn 5:39).

The book of Revelation, however, is more than a prophecy about Jesus; it is a divine revelation from him (1:1). He is its source as well as its content. It records everything God showed him that "must soon take place." Nothing is more reliable and true than these disclosed future events.

"The Spirit of prophecy" refers to the effect the Spirit has on God's messengers. He produces their prophecy. Since the Spirit testifies about Jesus, then prophetic utterances will concern Christ (I Pet 1:10–11). Prophesies, therefore, point to Jesus Christ (Jn 5:39) and are ultimately fulfilled in him.

Rhema: From start to finish Christ is the central theme of Scripture, especially this breathtaking finale where all things in heaven and earth are consummated in him (Eph 1:10).

DECEMBER 30 | REVELATION 21:1–27

THE SPIRIT REVEALS THE HOLY CITY

*And he carried me away in the **Spirit** to a mountain great and high, and showed me the Holy City, Jerusalem, coming down out of heaven from God.* –REVELATION 21:10

For the final time, the Spirit heightens John's ability to witness the end of all things. He sees a new heaven and a new earth, for the first heaven and the first earth had passed away (v 1). The same angel who carried him away in the Spirit to see the Great Harlot (17:3) transports him to behold the Lamb's wife. The bride is radiant, her beauty magnificent. Attired in God's glory she is the joy of the earth and perfect in her ways. Symbolized as the Holy City, the New Jerusalem, she comes down out of heaven from God.

The great cities of men are drab compared to the indescribable radiance of the Holy City. Nebuchadnezzar's Babylon and the Imperial City of Rome, wonders of the ancient world, sit in ruins. They are of the earth, earthly, but the New Jerusalem is of heaven, heavenly. She is the glorious city Abraham sought which has foundations and whose architect and builder is God (Heb 11:10). This wondrous, incomparable city pictures how God ends and consummates history.

The Spirit takes John to an exceedingly high mountain because the Holy City towers over the great cities of this world. Prepared in heaven for her public manifestation, the bride of Christ, the church, descends to rule and reign with him. The world loathed and reproached her, but to Christ she is his pure and beloved wife. The Spirit enables John to see the Holy City resplendent with the light of God bouncing off her golden streets and pearly gates. The bride in her final condition is magnificent, more beautiful and dazzling than the riches of earth.

Rhema: The Spirit wants us to understand our future as Christ's bride. To comfort us in a fallen, broken world he shows us our final blessed state. Although ungodly, world powers driven by the demonic forces may despise us now, we will triumph. Our history unlike theirs does not end in tragedy but in rapturous triumph. All heaven is present for the great celebration where we are united for eternity with the bridegroom. Forever and forever we will enjoy his love, companionship, and glory.

DECEMBER 31 | REVELATION 22:1–21

THE SPIRIT AND THE BRIDE SAY COME

*The **Spirit** and the bride say, "Come!" And let the one who hears say, "Come!" Let the one who is thirsty come; and let the one who wishes take the free gift of the water of life.* –REVELATION 22:17

"Come!" A single word contains so much. God's eternal purposes. Every divine promise. All our prayers. The Spirit calls for the completion of God's plan. Distilled in this one utterance is our faith, hope, and love. Come and wipe away every tear. Come and defeat death and the devil. Come so the Holy City can descend. Come so the wedding supper of the Lamb can proceed. Come so creation can reach its glorious completion.

Three times in this chapter Jesus says, "I am coming soon." Come is a request for the full realization of his glory. The plea, ever widening and deepening, is like the river of life flowing from God's throne. It begins first with the Holy Spirit, the fountainhead of the prophetic. From the beginning, he has desired to see God's plan of salvation come to fruition. With one unceasing call, the Spirit has yearned for Christ's excellence, splendor and magnificence to be unveiled.

The Spirit has embedded this desire in the bride. She echoes him and says, "Come!" The bride is the church, whose destiny is to share life with the bridegroom. She longs for his appearance and her presentation. With her lamps filled with oil, she awaits the cry, "Here's the bridegroom! Come out to meet him" (Mt 25:6).

When the Spirit speaks, the bride says, "Come!" In the power of the Spirit she invites anyone who is thirsty to come to Christ and take the free gift of the water of life. The bride and the Spirit work together, summoning all who will come to receive Christ. They do so until he returns in the clouds of glory and we see him face to face.

Rhema: Here ends our study of the Spirit. From the beginning of creation to its culmination the Holy Spirit has actualized God's plan, the time for its fulfillment has come (v 10). For that reason, live in the power of the Spirit, as if each moment is the last, and declare, "Come Lord Jesus" (v 20). Amen.

EPILOGUE

After five years of exegeting Scripture, researching the literature, and praying over every Biblical reference to the Spirit, I am left with a question: what does this mean? On the day of Pentecost (Ac 2:12), a bewildered crowd posed the same query. The Holy Spirit's unprecedented, end-time outpouring left people thunderstruck, and so it should. Mystery always surrounds divine manifestations. We should expect incomprehensible, mysterious, and unfathomable incidents whenever we finite creatures encounter the infinite.

The Third Person of the Trinity, like the Father and the Son, cannot be forced into a theological or philosophical box. The Spirit cannot be treated as an object to be studied and defined. No one, including this author, has the last word on these matters. Our approach to spiritual things mandates humility and a willingness to hold preconceived notions in abeyance until that which is perfect comes (I Cor 13:10).

General

With "fear and trembling," I offer a few observations and concluding comments. To find so many Spirit-references—one for each day of the year—surprised me. This sheer preponderance means that despite his primary role of being witness to Jesus, the Holy Spirit is of utmost importance in understanding God's eternal design. He is not only present and active in the first and last chapters of Scripture but involved throughout.

I notice, however, the book of Jeremiah is an exception: the Spirit's absence is conspicuous—not once does he appear. The reason: Israel's relentless rejection of the Spirit led to their darkest days. Because he withdrew his presence, they had no one to comfort them; their enemy prevailed (Lam 1:16). As a corollary, we might say the Spirit's absence led to their lamentation. By stunning contrast, no book of Lamentations occurs in the NT. Instead, where the Spirit is present and prominent, overwhelming joy floods hearts and lives. For instance, Luke speaks of the Spirit in Acts and his Gospel over ninety times—no wonder joy fills these pages.

Another surprise was the diverse responsibilities assigned the Holy Spirit. In Genesis, he is the agent of creation; in Revelation, the one who joins the Bride in calling for its consummation. Between these bookends he not only fills people with God's presence but equips them for divine service. Upon some he bestows artistic skills, special strengths, or leadership abilities. In the NT, he baptizes believers with supernatural power so they can proclaim the gospel to the ends of the earth. His various names or titles—Comforter, Spirit of God, Spirit of Wisdom, Spirit of Power, Spirit of Truth, Spirit of Prophecy, Spirit of Christ, Spirit of Jesus and Spirit of God's Son—express his unique functions. These are awesome roles to fill.

Christology

One of the Spirit's leading roles relates to Christ, not just during his life on earth but also before his Incarnation and after his ascension. Prior to the Incarnation he manifested himself in Israel's OT prophets, enabling them to foretell of Christ's sufferings and subsequent glory (I Pet 1:10–11). In other words, the Spirit in them spoke or testified about Christ. Jesus declared that all Scripture beginning with Moses through the Prophets pointed to him (Lk 24:27). This awareness should impact and guide our interpretation of OT Scripture. For instance, any discussion of creation, man's fall, the Exodus, or the tabernacle and its priesthood without reference to Christ is deficient. Ultimately, God's word that came to these divine spokespersons by the Spirit applies to Jesus (Rev 19:10).

What stood out the most was the extent to which Christ's earthly life was entwined with and dependent on the Holy Spirit. From his conception to his resurrection, Jesus lived by the Spirit's power. That is to say, without him, Jesus would not have been conceived, nor have risen from the dead. Moreover, at his baptism, the Spirit descends from heaven to install and legitimize him as the Messiah. His illustrious ministry results from the Spirit resting upon him and anointing him to proclaim good news.

From the momentous moment of his baptism, he goes forth full of the Holy Spirit to teach, preach, and heal. No doubt, his receiving the Spirit must be associated with calling him "The Christ." The root meaning of Christ (Gr *Christos*) describes one of his unique characteristics or attributes—he is the anointed one or the one with the Spirit. *Christos* occurs over 525 times in the NT, thereby cementing Jesus and the Spirit. Jesus was empowered to fulfill God's plan and, consequently, became known as "the Christ" because he possessed the Spirit.

Interestingly, the Spirit's relationship with Christ extends beyond his earthly life but not without a change. For instance, after he returns to his Father and sits enthroned at his right hand, Jesus no longer submits to him. Instead, the Spirit accedes to our exalted Lord, ever ready to do his will. He was involved in Christ's birth, life, death, resurrection, exaltation, and glorification. Now Jesus, in regal glory, directs and dispenses the one who empowered him—he baptizes believers with the Spirit.

Another key point is that in his exalted state, Jesus makes his personal presence known to his followers through the Spirit. Therefore, to experience the Spirit is to encounter our resurrected, glorified Lord. Likewise, to experience Christ is to encounter the Spirit. Because he interconnects with Christ so intimately, he is called the "Spirit of Christ." As I was reflecting on this, I wondered how anyone who resists, restricts, or refuses the Spirit cannot see how they hurt the Lord.

Soteriology

I suppose after this study I could reevaluate every doctrine from a pneumatological perspective, but that is not my goal. Soteriology, the doctrine of salvation, however, deserves special attention because of the Spirit's integral involvement. He must make us acceptable to God. Theologians often go to great lengths to extol Christ's redemptive role in redemption but not so much for the Father or the Spirit: each member of the triune God has an equally important responsibility. The Son is not greater than the Father or the Spirit: each is coequal. Unfortunately, some seem to imply an individual only needs Christ's work on the cross to be saved. Nothing could be further from the truth—salvation is a joint effort of the Father, Son, and Holy Spirit. *Celestial Fire* highlights the Spirit's unique part.

Although God's saving activity is complex, we can delineate its various components. In fact, from start to finish, salvation forms one long continuum: conviction, repentance, faith, confession, justification, reconciliation, conversion, baptism in the Spirit, adoption, sanctification, assurance, and glorification. As we have shown throughout the devotional, the Holy Spirit involves himself in every one of these major facets. After Jesus died and rose again, the Third Person of the Trinity still had much work to do if believers were to be made holy.

Christ's death as it relates to pneumatology needs a comment. Because our Savior's assignment is so amazing, many often fail to connect it with the Spirit's work and might erroneously conclude the job of the Third Person of the Trinity is unimportant or unnecessary. Indeed, what God has wrought in Christ Jesus is the glorious gospel, yet we must not forget the Spirit's (often uncelebrated) contribution. Take, for instance, Christ's precious blood—to make it efficacious, the eternal Spirit must offer it up to God (Heb 9:14). For God to justify us, the Spirit needs to raise Christ from the dead. The Spirit then glorifies him, gives him a resurrection body, and exalts him to the Father's right hand. Therefore, what the Spirit does is not secondary or inconsequential but essential. In other words, we cannot be saved unless both fulfill their vital roles.

Furthermore, the Spirit has a requisite role in the proclamation of the good news. He answers this question: why extend the gift of eternal life if no one will accept it? We receive God's gracious offer of salvation through faith. In this regard, the Spirit has two all-important tasks. First, he empowers believers so they can proclaim the gospel in power. Preaching in the Spirit's might makes the messenger a coworker with God and hearing the message a divine encounter. Faith then does not rest on man's ability or wisdom but on the Spirit's power.

Second, the Holy Spirit helps people say yes to the gospel. No one believes without divine intervention. Thus, the time between Christ's first appearance and his second coming is a time of grace. God in his patience gives an opportunity for man's faith response that he cannot do without the Spirit. To bring people to repentance, he convicts and convinces them, which includes confirming the message with signs, wonders, and miracles (Heb 2:4). When the Spirit manifests himself both in word and deed, message and miracle, then the gospel is "fully proclaimed" (Rom 15:19).

Holy Spirit Baptism

Perhaps, nothing in the contemporary church has garnered more controversy than Spirit baptism. After examining every Biblical reference to the Spirit, I observed several things of importance concerning this matter. First, the expression "the baptism in the Holy Spirit" does not occur in Scripture. What occurs are six references to John the Baptist's prophecy about Jesus—he will "baptize you with the Holy Spirit." In fact, this expression only occurs once in each Gospel and twice in Acts. Although Luke employs many other terms to describe this experience in Acts, he mentions it twice: in association with the day of Pentecost (Ac 1:5) and the outpouring of the Spirit upon Cornelius (Ac 11:16).

Second, being filled with the Spirit is not the baptism of the Spirit; although they may take place simultaneously, they are different. Baptism in the Spirit is exclusively a NT phenomenon that did not occur until after Christ's death, burial, and resurrection. How could it? This remarkable Spirit-experience linked to the gospel had to wait until Jesus was glorified (Jn 7:39). This is borne out during one of Jesus' resurrection appearances. While dining with his disciples, he said to them,

"In a few days you will be baptized with the Holy Spirit" (Ac 1:5). His prophecy was actualized on the day of Pentecost (Ac 11:15–17).

Being filled with the Spirit, on the other hand, occurs before, during, and after Pentecost. The first person God fills with the Spirit was Bezalel, so he could build the tabernacle. Also, before Pentecost, John the Baptist as well as his mother and father were filled. Obviously, these are not examples of the baptism of the Spirit but of a special anointing to accomplish God's work. On the day of Pentecost, however, "all of them were filled with the Holy Spirit" (Ac 2:4). Some believers were filled again on another occasion to help them rise to new challenges (Ac 4:31). Although believers can be filled multiple times, no instance occurs of anyone being baptized in the Spirit more than once.

A third observation is that NT authors and Jesus attach great significance to Spirit-baptism. Matthew, Mark, Luke, and John begin their gospel accounts by announcing it as the underlying reason for Christ's coming. Four times in total they declare, "He will baptize you with the Holy Spirit." This is the primary promise of their respective gospels. Similarly, Acts begins with Jesus, after his resurrection, reminding his disciples the baptism in the Spirit still awaits them a few days hence (Ac 1:5). This means that whatever Christ came to do in his life and death pertains to something that could not happen until he completed his work on the cross. Jesus came and died so he can baptize his followers in the Spirit.

Fourth, Spirit-baptism is reliant upon the cross. Without forgiveness of sins, immediate access to God is impossible. Therefore, when people believe in Christ their sins are forgiven, and God declares them right in his sight. Consequently, they are eligible to receive the Father's great promise of the heavenly gift. Spirit-baptism was an emersion experience unavailable until the end times when God poured out his Spirit. This is as much a part of the good news as is the forgiveness of sins.

Fifth, to express the magnitude and magnificence of Spirit-baptism, many terms are used. This is the single most important Jesus-experience in a believer's life. Jesus is the baptizer, the one who pours out the heavenly gift. Notice the abundance of terms Luke employs to narrate the overwhelming event in Acts 2. He says things such as they were filled with the Spirit. God pours out his Spirit. Jesus has received from the Father the promised Holy Spirit and pours out what they heard and saw. They received the gift of the Holy Spirit. Furthermore, in Cornelius' case, Luke says the Holy Spirit came upon his household, the gift of the Holy Spirit had been poured out upon them, they have received the Spirit, they will be baptised with the Holy Spirit, and God accepted them by giving them the Spirit. One indication they had received the Spirit was they prophesied and spoke in tongues just as the original believers had done on the day of Pentecost.

Sixth, to be baptized in the Spirit is not a salvation add-on but the primary experience. In the book of Acts, once people believed the gospel they received the Holy Spirit. In every instance they first believed then received. To have the Spirit is to participate in God's end-time promise and become a participant in his kingdom. Therefore, one must be born of the Spirit to see and hear God, to become prophetic, and to take part in the miraculous (Jn 3:3, 5). New birth is not optional but essential if one is to be a follower of Christ.

Seventh, the outpouring of the Spirit begins a new era in which believers interact with God on an entirely different basis. Instead of relating to him through the Jewish Law and the Levitical system of sacrifices, they interact with him, face-to-face, through the Spirit (II Cor 3:16–18). This new relationship with God is called the New Covenant of the Spirit (II Cor 3:6). Because we have his Spirit, we are his sons and daughters, born again members of his family and partakers of his nature. His Spirit indwells us and writes God's law on our hearts. Isaiah, Jeremiah, Ezekiel, and Joel all prophesied this glorious day. They foretold a time when God would make a new covenant with his people and put his Spirit in them. In the OT and prior to Pentecost, the Spirit was "with" people but after Pentecost God's Spirit is "in" them (Jn 14:17).

Eighth, to be baptized with the Spirit is much more than conversion or empowerment for service. Some have tried to make this amazing end-time experience either one or the other. My observation is that being baptized in the Spirit cannot be reduced to either. Conversion is only the beginning of the Spirit's activity in a believer. When one is born of the Spirit, Jesus immerses that person in a mighty river of spiritual life flowing from the throne of God. The river is so wide, the deluge is so overwhelming any attempt to limit it to any one single experience misses the mark. The cross and Pentecost created a tectonic change that when personally experienced alters a believer's fundamental relationship with God. Now Jesus, by the Spirit, indwells believers, flooding them with eternal life and power—power to witness, serve God, counter the flesh, pray, and prophesy. Even the gifts and fruit of the Spirit can be seen as Christ expressing his power and life in the believer through his Spirit.

The Christian Life

This brings me to my final observation: without the Spirit, living for Christ is impossible. In fact, I notice almost every aspect of the believer's life is attributable to the Spirit. We begin our new life in Christ the moment we receive the Spirit; he will also complete it (Gal 3:3). To understand Christian life, we need to view it in relation to the Holy Spirit. Christ's reliance upon him is the model and pattern for his followers. He lived and died in the power of the Spirit. Because he was a Spirit-empowered man, he was able to please God in everything he said and did. To this end, he demonstrated only a person with the Spirit can live for God.

The most singular part about being a Christ follower is the Spirit recreates his life in believers. The parallel between the Spirit in Jesus and in ourselves is significant. For example, he was conceived by the Spirit; we must be born of the Spirit. By living in the Spirit's power, he overcame temptation. Believers need him to help them live and walk in God-pleasing ways. Christ died; we must crucify the sinful human nature by relying on the Spirit's power. God's Spirit raised Christ from the dead, so we can live new lives infused with resurrection power. From start to finish, a believer's life is a Spirit-lived life.

The Spirit accomplishes what religious systems cannot do: empower people to walk in God's ways. Not since Eden has God been able to stroll with his creatures, but with sin's removal, he can dwell with his people once again. Believers with the Spirit live in his awesome presence because they not only are born again but also take part in his divine nature. God's children walk in the Spirit, live in the Spirit, and are led of the Spirit. They are the temple of the Living God, his dwelling place.

One awesome attribute of the Third Person of the Trinity is his ability to transform fallen human nature. Rules can't. The Law can't. Warnings and threats can't. Punishment can't. Because he is the "Holy" Spirit and embodies God's own righteousness, he alone can effect a change in morality. When he is in charge, no rules are required. God's high standard of right and wrong is expressed in believers who are led by the Spirit. To live in accordance with the Spirit means to allow the Holy One to renew their minds and influence their attitudes. Indeed, no one belongs to Jesus without his Spirit working in their lives controlling their conduct (Rom 8:9).

Conclusion

Without the Holy Spirit's vital involvement, creation, continuation, and consummation are impossible. Likewise, Christ would not be conceived, empowered, or exalted. The same is true of God's new creation, the church. No one would ever be born of the Spirit, filled or live in the power of the Spirit. The Third Person of the Trinity is an absolute necessity in all God's works—he is essential for actualizing his plan. Considering these things, we conclude with Paul's commands to the Ephesians: "Do not grieve the Holy Spirit of God" (Eph 4:30) and "Be filled with the Spirit" (Eph 5:18). These two overarching themes run throughout Scripture and apply today.